Agesilaus and the Failure
of Spartan Hegemony

Also by Charles D. Hamilton

Sparta's Bitter Victories:
  Politics and Diplomacy in the Corinthian War

Agesilaus and the Failure of Spartan Hegemony

Charles D. Hamilton

Cornell University Press

ITHACA AND LONDON

First published 1991 by Cornell University Press.

International Standard Book Number 0-8014-2540-9
Library of Congress Catalog Card Number 90-55738
Printed in the United States of America
Librarians: Library of Congress cataloging information appears on the last page of the book.

♾ The paper in this book meets the minimum requirements of the American National Standard for Information Sciences—Permanence of Paper for Printed Library Materials, ANSI Z39.48-1984.

For Lynda,
Whom I Cherish Above All

Contents

Maps

Preface

The surrender of Athens in 404 at the conclusion of the Peloponne-sian War marked the end of an epoch. Gone were the tension and polarity between Athens and Sparta which had characterized the second half of the fifth century. Now Sparta dominated the affairs of Greece and exercised hegemony for over thirty years. Interest in the general problems of Greek history in the period after 404 led me to an earlier investigation and analysis (*Sparta's Bitter Victories*, Cornell University Press, 1979), which was not intended to be a full study of the Spartan Hegemony. The research for that book, however, sparked my interest in the further question of developments in Sparta in the early fourth century; hence the present book. It is written in the hope that it may be of interest not only to specialists in Greek history but also to students and an interested public. Thus, I have not included quotations in Greek, but I have cited the ancient sources quite fully, discussed them at length, and provided references to modern scholarship to aid those who would read further on their own. All translations of the ancient sources are my own, unless otherwise noted, and all dates are B.C.

This book makes three primary contributions. First, it argues that the policies of King Agesilaus II, in domestic politics and foreign affairs, shaped the position of Sparta in the Greek world and contributed sub-stantially to the failure of its hegemony. Second, it devotes considerable attention to the sources, analyzing and evaluating their information on the questions under discussion. Third, it sets Agesilaus' reign in the context of a psychohistorical study. In these three respects, it differs from other recent studies of the topic.

In attempting to assess the question of why Sparta failed to maintain hegemony in the Greek world, other scholars have emphasized military or socioeconomic causes, but I believe that a political and diplomatic explanation is more convincing. I realized that the single most important individual in the period was King Agesilaus, who dominated his state, and that his policies led to Sparta's failure. The first aim of the book is to tell his story as fully as possible. Chapter 1 is an analysis of Agesilaus as a man; that is, a study of his character and personality, as far as they can be understood. The sources are very limited, to be sure, but we have more contemporary material than is available for the study of, say, Themistocles or Pericles, largely in the works of Xenophon, a friend and admirer of Agesilaus. Xenophon wrote an encomium of the king in addition to his general treatment of Greek history from ca. 410 to 362, known as the *Hellenica*. Then there is Plutarch, who also wrote a life of Agesilaus and collected many of his sayings, and whose interest in character led him to preserve important information about Agesilaus from lost writers and to make many significant observations about the king's personality. In addition to these two important sources, there are numerous references in other late writers, some of whom, like Diodorus, derive from fourth-century sources, such as Ephorus of Cumae. But this evidence must be treated with care; it is often contradictory and frequently biased. I have analyzed the sources, therefore, and tried to indicate the reasons for preferring one to another on particular occasions. The evidence is as good as that for almost any figure from ancient Greece—in some sense, better than that for Alexander the Great. If historians can write about Alexander's personality, why not about Agesilaus'?

The topic is twofold: Agesilaus and Sparta. I have asked what sort of king Agesilaus was and what sort of state he ruled over. In chapter 2, I analyze the evidence on the two most important aspects of kingship in Sparta: the political and military roles of the king. I offer a general assessment of his reign, which spanned forty-one years, in order to suggest an overall judgment of his kingship. Chapter 3 is devoted to an examination of Spartan society in the early fourth century, to set the stage for a consideration of the ability of Sparta to meet the challenges it faced in the ensuing period. This portrait of the king, abstracted from the entire history of his reign, and taken together with a picture of Spartan society, can then be used as background to study the events of Spartan history in the years during which Agesilaus clearly played the preponderant role. The remaining chapters of the book treat, in narrative fashion, the years from 397, just after Agesilaus' accession to the throne, to the Second Battle of Mantineia, in 362. It was in this period that the Spartan Hegemony failed.

CHARLES D. HAMILTON

San Diego, California

Acknowledgments

In the course of preparing this work, I have incurred many debts, personal and institutional, which I acknowledge here. First, the scholarship of Donald Kagan, my former mentor at Cornell University, has always inspired me. Although his major efforts, resulting in a masterful four-volume history of the Peloponnesian War, fall outside the period with which my book is primarily concerned, his approach has illuminated the subject and helped to shape my thinking about Greek history. I owe special thanks to three colleagues with whom I have often discussed Greek history, and whose friendship and encouragement over the years have meant much to me: W. Lindsay Adams, Eugene N. Borza, and Lawrence A. Tritle. Among others whose research on fourth-century Greece has contributed much to my understanding of this subject, I especially note John Buckler, Jack Cargill, Paul Cartledge, George Cawkwell, Ephraim David, Stephen Hodkinson, Derek Mosley, and Shalom Perlman. I do not agree with all their opinions, but this book owes a great deal to their work. Finally, I thank the anonymous readers for Cornell University Press, whose close and careful attention to my manuscript saved me from errors and helped me to focus my thinking and to reduce a lengthy work to more manageable proportions.

The American Council of Learned Societies, with support from the National Endowment for the Humanities, granted me a year's fellowship to supplement a sabbatical leave, and San Diego State University also granted me a Summer Faculty Fellowship and several semesters of reduced teaching from a heavy instructional program in order to facilitate my research. The staff of the Interlibrary Loan Department of Love Library, in particular Kelley Martin, expedited my requests for materials not available at San Diego State University. Edmond Frezouls, dean of the Faculty of Humanities at the University of Strasbourg, generously accorded me hospitality for a semester of research during my sabbatical.

I thank the editor of the *Ancient World*, Al. N. Oikonomides, for permission to reprint portions of two articles from that journal, "Agesilaus and the Failure of Spartan Hegemony," *Ancient World* 5 (1982): 67–78; and "The Generalship of King Agesilaus of Sparta," *Ancient World* 8 (1983): 119–27, which appear in modified form in chapters 1, 2, and 4; Mark H. Munn for permission to use his maps from "Agesilaos' Boiotian Campaigns and the Theban Stockade of 378–377 B.C." (*Classical Antiquity* 6 [1987]: 106–38), as the basis for figures 4 and 5, and Anne Brook for drawing all the figures in the book. Kathy Peck typed an early version of the manuscript, before the advent of my computer literacy. Janet Hamann prepared the index. To all, I express sincere thanks.

The most important debt, however, I owe to my wife, Lynda, for years of encouragement, support, patience, and devotion; without her, this book would never have been written.

C. D. H.

San Diego, California

Abbreviations and Short Titles

Modern Works

AHB	*Ancient History Bulletin*
AJAH	*American Journal of Ancient History*
AJP	*American Journal of Philology*
Anderson, *Military Theory*	J. K. Anderson, *Military Theory and Practice in the Age of Xenophon.* Berkeley and Los Angeles, 1970.
Anderson, *Xenophon*	J. K. Anderson, *Xenophon.* New York, 1974.
BCH	*Bulletin de Correspondance Hellénique*
Bruce, *Historical Commentary*	I. A. F. Bruce, *An Historical Commentary on the "Hellenica Oxyrhynchia."* Cambridge, 1967.
Buckler, *Theban Hegemony*	J. Buckler, *The Theban Hegemony.* Cambridge, Mass., 1980.
CA	*Classical Antiquity*
Cargill, *SAL*	J. Cargill, *The Second Athenian League: Empire or Free Alliance?* Berkeley and Los Angeles, 1981.
Cartledge, *Agesilaos*	P. Cartledge, *Agesilaos and the Crisis of Sparta.* Baltimore, 1987.
Cartledge, *Sparta*	P. Cartledge, *Sparta and Lakonia: A Regional History c. 1300–362 B.C.* Boston, 1979.
CP	*Classical Philology*
CQ	*Classical Quarterly*
CSCA	*California Studies in Classical Antiquity*
David, *Sparta*	E. David, *Sparta between Empire and Revolution: 404–243 B.C.: Internal Problems and Their Impact in Contemporary Greek Consciousness.* New York, 1981.
EMC/CV	*Echos du Monde Classique/Classical Views*
GRBS	*Greek, Roman, and Byzantine Studies*
Hamilton, *SBV*	C. D. Hamilton, *Sparta's Bitter Victories: Politics and Diplomacy in the Corinthian War.* Ithaca, N.Y., 1979.
Higgins, *Xenophon*	W. E. Higgins, *Xenophon the Athenian.* Albany, N.Y., 1977.

Hooker, *Ancient Spartans*	J. T. Hooker, *The Ancient Spartans*. London, 1980.
JHS	*Journal of Hellenic Studies*
Lazenby, *Spartan Army*	J. F. Lazenby, *The Spartan Army*. Chicago, 1985.
LCM	*Liverpool Classical Monthly*
Michell, *Sparta*	H. Michell, *Sparta*. Cambridge, 1952.
PCPS	*Proceedings of the Cambridge Philological Society*
Pritchett, *GSaW*	W. K. Pritchett, *The Greek State at War*. 4 vols. Berkeley and Los Angeles, 1971–87.
REG	*Revue des Etudes Grecques*
RSA	*Rivista di Storia dell'Antichità*
Ryder, *Koine Eirene*	T. T. B. Ryder, *Koine Eirene: General Peace and Local Independence in Ancient Greece*. Oxford, 1965.
TAPA	*Transactions of the American Philological Association*
Tod, *GHI*	M. N. Tod, *A Selection of Greek Historical Inscriptions*. Vol. 2. Oxford, 1948.

Ancient Sources

Aesch.	Aeschines, *Orations*
Andoc.	Andocides, *Orations*
Arist.	Aristotle, *Politics*
Dem.	Demosthenes, *Orations*
Diod.	Diodorus Siculus, *Historical Library*
Herod.	Herodotus, *History of the Persian Wars*
Isoc.	Isocrates, *Orations*
Nepos	Cornelius Nepos, *Lives*, as follows:
Ages.	Agesilaus
Tim.	Timotheus
Paus.	Pausanias, *Description of Greece*
Plat.	Plato, *Politicus*
Plut.	Plutarch, *Lives* and *Moralia*, as follows:
Ages.	Agesilaus
Alcib.	Alcibiades
Artax.	Artaxerxes
Lyc.	Lycurgus
Lys.	Lysander
Mor.	Moralia
Pelop.	Pelopidas
Thuc.	Thucydides, *History of the Peloponnesian War*.
Xen.	Xenophon. References of the type Xen. 3.1.1 are to Xenophon, *Hellenica* 3.1.1. Other works as follows:
Ages.	Agesilaus
Anab.	Anabasis
Lac. Pol.	Constitution of the Lacedaemonians

Chronology of the

Life of Agesilaus

370	Revival of Mantineia
	Agesilaus' invasion of Arcadia
	First Theban invasion of Peloponnesus
	Agesilaus' defense of Sparta; uprisings quelled
	Liberation of Messenia
	Alliance between Sparta and Athens
369	Second Theban invasion of Peloponnesus
368	Philiscus' negotiations at Delphi
	Archidamus' Tearless Victory in Arcadia
367	Peace Conference at Sardis; Epaminondas' success
	Third Theban invasion of Peloponnesus
	Agesilaus' mercenary service with Ariobarzanes
366	Corinth and Phlius make peace with Thebes
365	Theban decision to launch a fleet
364	Pelopidas' death
363	Strife between Elis and Arcadia over Olympia
	Agesilaus' return to Sparta (?)
362	Fourth Theban invasion of Peloponnesus
	Second Battle of Mantineia; Epaminondas' death
	Peace Conference; isolation of Sparta
361	Agesilaus' mercenary service in Egypt
359/8	Agesilaus' death on return voyage to Sparta

All dates in the book are B.C. I give the Julian date where possible (371) or the archon year (387/6) when a more precise date cannot be determined. Because the Athenian archon year began in late June or early July in the Julian calendar, and ended in summer of the following year, it is usually expressed in this way: (387/6). For discussion of the dating problems associated with the reign of Agesilaus, see my "Etude chronologique sur le règne d'Agésilas," *Ktema* 7 (1982):281–96.

Agesilaus and the Failure
of Spartan Hegemony

Introduction

At the end of the Peloponnesian War, Sparta dominated the Greek world, and its shadow lay across Greece for the next three decades. The period from the defeat of Athens in 404 until the Battle of Leuctra in 371 is known as that of the Spartan Hegemony. This period also corresponded, in the main, with the reign of King Agesilaus II, who was known as "the greatest and most famous man of his day," as the Greek historian Theopompus of Chios put it. Agesilaus reigned for some forty-one years and, as Plutarch tells us, died at the advanced age of eighty-four, in 359/8. Thus, his reign overlapped all but the first few years of the Spartan Hegemony, and one cannot help asking to what extent his policies and dominance of his state may have shaped the ultimate failure of that hegemony. The focus of this book is twofold, therefore; it is a study of Agesilaus, as a man and as an influential public figure, and of the state he headed, during the period of its domination of much of the Greek world. The book shows the interrelationship between Agesilaus and Sparta, and its central theme is the nature and course of the Spartan Hegemony.

It was Sparta, largely influenced by its powerful and popular admiral, Lysander, who dictated the settlement of the Greek world upon the surrender of Athens. The Athenian Empire, effectively destroyed in the wake of Lysander's great victory over the Athenian fleet at Aegospotami in 405, was officially ended by the peace in spring 404. Over the strenuous objections of several of its allies in the war, most notably the Thebans and Corinthians, Sparta decided not to mete out to Athens the fate that it itself had decreed for Melos, Scione, Torone, and other states

I

that had been destroyed by savage and deliberate act, but rather to spare the city "that had done so much good for Greece in the struggle against the barbarian."[1] It was not out of sentimentality that the Spartans chose to reward Athens for its past services during the Persian Wars by sparing it. Sparta's erstwhile allies, particularly the Thebans, were becoming troublesome, and Sparta had no wish to aggrandize their power in central Greece by destroying Athens. Thus, the decision was a calculated move to leave a much weakened Athens as a counterweight to potential Corinthian or Boeotian ambitions.

The Spartans also dictated the fate of the former members of the Athenian Empire, and Lysander shaped it. He established pro-Spartan oligarchies, composed of his partisans, in the cities, and in time garrisons and military commanders were installed and tribute was imposed. Therefore, at the end of the war, Sparta moved into the power vacuum that the fall of the Athenian Empire had created. The situation of the numerous Greek cities on the west coast of Asia Minor was even more complicated. Sparta's treaty with Darius, the Great King of Persia, had provided for assistance in establishing a fleet to defeat Athens at sea, but the quid pro quo was Spartan recognition of the king's claims to rule the Greek cities in Asia Minor. The Greeks of Ionia and Asia Minor were duly surrendered at the end of the conflict, but rivalry between the satrap Tissaphernes and the Persian prince, Cyrus the Younger, soon boiled over into open warfare, and the Greek cities were torn between the two. When Cyrus marched into the interior of the Persian Empire at the head of a polyglot army, including some thirteen thousand Greek mercenaries, the Spartans sent him support. Then, after his death in battle, they challenged the right of Tissaphernes to reassert control of these Greek cities. Warfare between Sparta, at the head of its empire, and Persia soon ensued and continued from 400 until the so-called King's Peace of 387/6.

Meanwhile, Sparta's high-handed actions in Greece alienated more and more of the states there, and in 395 a coalition, consisting of Thebes at the head of the Boeotian Confederacy, Corinth, Athens, and Sparta's inveterate enemy, Argos, was formed with Persian financial backing to challenge Sparta's domination of the Greek world. The Corinthian War was the first overt attempt to force Sparta to modify its behavior, but the conflict failed to produce the results the allies had wanted. Spartan naval superiority was lost, however, at the Battle of Cnidus in 394, where a Persian fleet, partially manned by Greeks and commanded by

[1] Xen. 2.2.20.

the exiled Athenian admiral, Conon, destroyed the Spartan fleet. As the fortunes of war continued to shift, Sparta was unable to conduct the war effectively both on land and on sea, in Greece and in Asia Minor, hence, Sparta's commander, King Agesilaus, was recalled from Asia Minor in 394. In the end, Sparta again agreed to renounce the cause of the Greeks of Asia Minor in return for an end to Persian support for its enemies in Greece. In the treaty called either the King's Peace or the Peace of Antalcidas (after the Spartan diplomat who had negotiated it), the principle of autonomy was asserted for all poleis, great and small, although those of Asia Minor were surrendered to Persian control. The Greek coalition was unable to continue the struggle against Sparta, and Sparta thus reasserted its predominance in Greece, this time under the guise of the principle of autonomy.

In the implementation of this concept, the Spartans, guided by their king, Agesilaus, dissolved the Boeotian Confederacy, the union of Corinth and Argos which had been formed in the 390s, and the recent attempts by Athens to resuscitate its old fifth-century maritime empire. But the Spartans went beyond these acts and chastised several states during the 380s for offenses, real or imagined, against Sparta. The Spartans intervened within the Peloponnesus in the affairs of Mantineia, which was forced to separate into several constituent villages, and of Phlius, which became a pro-Spartan oligarchy. Olynthus, in northern Greece, in the process of expanding its power through domination of the Chalcidian Confederacy, had to face a Spartan-led Peloponnesian army. After several campaigning seasons, Olynthus surrendered and the confederacy was dissolved, again ostensibly on the grounds that it violated the autonomy of states forced to become members. Finally, a Spartan commander, in collusion with some of the leading men of Thebes, seized the Cadmeia by force and arrested prominent anti-Spartan politicians. Although this act of force, committed in peacetime and without obvious provocation, was almost universally condemned, the Spartans chose to maintain their occupation of Thebes. Furthermore, they put Ismenias and other Thebans on trial and executed them for treason. The incidents involving Mantineia, Phlius, Thebes, and Olynthus brought Sparta to the peak of its power after the King's Peace. In 379 it stood triumphant in the Greek world, apparently even more secure in its hegemony than it had been in the aftermath of the surrender of Athens in 404.

The sequel to the seizure of Thebes, however, proved just how unstable Sparta's position was. Theban exiles crossed the Athenian-Boeotian border at the end of 379 and liberated their city from Spartan control. They had received aid, unofficial though it was, from Athens. When the Spartans retaliated by invading Boeotia, relations rapidly deteriorated. An abortive attempt by a Spartan garrison commander to seize the Peiraeus, Athens' port, on a night march into Attica, led to war between Sparta and Athens. Throughout the 370s, Sparta was frequently at war with Athens and Thebes, although attempts were made to reestablish peace, on the basis of the principle of autonomy, in 375 and 371. Even worse for Sparta was the Athenian establishment of a Second Athenian League in 378/7. This organization, whose charter document has been preserved, was dedicated to maintaining the autonomy of all Greek states and to forcing the Spartans to leave their neighbors in peace. Scores of states eventually joined the Second Athenian League, and Sparta's power shrank as some members of its military alliance, the so-called Peloponnesian League, deserted it to join Athens. When the Peace Conference of 371 failed to produce a settlement satisfactory to all parties, the Spartans prepared to invade Boeotia once again.

Under the leadership of their two great generals, Pelopidas and Epaminondas, the Thebans had reconstituted the Boeotian Confederacy during the 370s. They insisted on signing the peace treaty of 371 in the name of their allies in Boeotia, but King Agesilaus refused to allow this. As a result, a Spartan army commanded by the other Spartan king, Cleombrotus, invaded Boeotia in summer 371 and met signal defeat at the Battle of Leuctra. The Spartan manpower losses at Leuctra were significant, but of even greater significance was the psychological impact that their defeat had throughout Greece. Additional allies of Sparta fell away, and when Epaminondas invaded the Peloponnesus in 370 Sparta had to fight for survival. When Epaminondas marched into Messenia and freed the helots there, thus establishing a new polis, the blow to Spartan morale, as well as the economic hardship, was grave. For the next eight years, the Spartans strove to recover Messenia and to maintain their position of leadership, which continued to erode, within the Peloponnesus. But more and more of their allies deserted them, as the Thebans returned again and again to invade southern Greece. The growth of Theban power alarmed Athens, and it became allied to Sparta after 370. A final invasion of the Peloponnesus culminated in the Second Battle of Mantineia in 362. Most of the major Greek states were involved, but the battle was a stalemate. The Thebans triumphed on the field, but their general Epaminondas was mortally wounded. In the wake of the battle, yet another conference was held to reestablish a Common Peace treaty on the basis of the principle of autonomy, but the

Spartans remained aloof, refusing to acknowledge the loss of Messenia. Their isolation was almost complete at this time, and their hegemony was a thing of the past by 362.

These, in brief, are the public facts of the Spartan Hegemony and the decade that followed it. But history is far more than the public record; it reflects the actions and reactions of those who live it, and it is appropriate for the historian to ask a series of questions of the record. In this case, a central concern is to ask why the Spartan Hegemony failed. And, because the period under consideration is virtually coterminous with the reign of one of Sparta's most famous and powerful kings, Agesilaus, who was instrumental in most of the significant military, political, and diplomatic events of the period, it is natural to ask what role he may have played in them. But because the central focus of this book is the explanation of Sparta's failure to maintain its dominant position in Greece, it must be recognized that a satisfactory explanation must consider who Agesilaus was—as individual, as king, and as general and politician—and must also consider the nature of the state over which he ruled. Thus, this book begins with the premise that the public record of Sparta during the period of its hegemony can be understood only in the light of the nature of Spartan society and of the man who dominated his age, Agesilaus.

It is always difficult to attempt to understand the personality of a public figure. Indeed, studies in the fields of psychology, psychiatry, and psychohistory suggest that individuals themselves may often be ignorant of why they act in particular ways. And if this is true of the study of prominent personalities in comtemporary society, how much more difficult must it be to attempt such a study for a figure from antiquity? Nonetheless, the attempt is worth the effort, and we possess in the case of Agesilaus rather more information than we do for most figures from classical history.

There are several works by the Athenian Xenophon, his friend and admirer. Xenophon wrote a general history of Greece which covered the period in question. Although his *Hellenica* reveals bias, partiality, short-sightedness, and astounding omissions, it remains the only extant, major account of the Spartan Hegemony written by a contemporary. Therefore, despite all its faults, it must be accorded pride of place in this book. Xenophon also produced an encomium of Agesilaus, shortly after his death, which bears his name: the *Agesilaus*. Finally, a number of lesser works from Xenophon's pen, in particular the *Constitution of the Lacedaemonians*, reveal more about Sparta in the early fourth century. The writings of Plutarch, though much later than the period in question, are invaluable. Plutarch had a great interest in questions of character and personality and read widely in the now nonextant literature of classical antiquity. His *Life* of Agesilaus, as well as his *Lives* of Lysander, Pelopidas, and Artaxerxes, the Great King of Persia, furnishes rich material for this work. In addition, Plutarch collected quotations ascribed to famous people, and the sayings of Agesilaus that he preserves reveal much about the king. The historian Diodorus of Sicily, who compiled his *Universal History* in the time of Augustus, relied on contemporary fourth-century sources, such as Ephorus of Cumae, which are now lost, and his books are valuable. They must be approached with caution, however, because Diodorus was often careless in his method, and his chronology in particular creates problems for the modern scholar. Other late sources, such as the traveler Pausanias and the collector of military stratagems Polyaenus, also often furnish valuable bits of information not preserved elsewhere. If we turn from the realm of Agesilaus and Sparta to that of Greek history more generally in the fourth century, there is a particularly rich epigraphical record that illuminates Athenian affairs, and the works of the Athenian orators, especially Isocrates, occasionally shed light on our concerns. Nonetheless, the task of the modern scholar who investigates this period remains largely one of careful assessment of the rather meager surviving sources. There is legitimate difference of opinion among scholars over the relative value of the sources that have survived from antiquity, and not everyone will agree with each interpretation I offer. I have tried, though, to cite the ancient sources liberally so that the interested reader may easily determine the basis for my judgments and, occasionally, reconstructions of the past and also delve further into the subject. Similarly, I have tried to indicate the most valuable or influential modern works in the Notes, both as an explanation of my views and as an aid to further study.

This book, then, attempts to achieve several ends. For all that, it is not a biography, for such is not possible with the limited material at our disposal. Nor is it merely an analysis of military and political events, although these loom large. Finally, it is not primarily a historiographical exercise, though historiographical questions arise often and help to shape the ultimate outcome. It is a book about a man, Agesilaus, and his state, Sparta, during a time of great opportunity, change, and challenge, and about those in antiquity who found Agesilaus and Sparta fascinating and wrote about them.

CHAPTER ONE

The Character and Personality of Agesilaus

The record of Agesilaus' public career, from his accession to the throne in his mid-forties until his death after four decades of rule at eighty-four, reveals a complex and intriguing personality. At times the king appears disarmingly simple in his tastes, his attitudes, and his dealings with others; at other times he manifests indications of deep-seated and powerful emotions—especially hatred, resentment, and un-bridled ambition—which often surfaced in unexpected, sometimes puzzling, and occasionally deleterious acts, at least in regard to the interests of state.[1] On the one hand, Agesilaus often appeared the ideal Spartan citizen: he was brave in combat, frugal and abstemious in his personal habits, modest in dress and demeanor to such an extent that those who met him for the first time found it difficult to believe that he was king of Sparta; he was also loyal and devoted to his friends and associates, often to a fault.[2] His friend Xenophon lavishly praised such qualities and others, including his piety, incorruptibility, and patrio-tism.[3] On the other hand, Agesilaus was capable of turning suddenly and irrevocably on an old friend, or of nursing a political grudge for more than a quarter-century: witness his treatment of Lysander and his attitude toward Thebes. Such behavior hints at a certain instability of

---

[1]Recent studies of Agesilaus have failed to consider adequately the question of his character. Even P. Cartledge's *Agesilaos and the Crisis of Sparta* (Baltimore, 1987), in other respects excellent, does not give sufficient attention to his question. I hope to show that this aspect is crucial to any proper understanding of Agesilaus and his reign.

[2]Xen. *Ages.* 6.1–3; 5.1–7. Cf. 9.3–5; Plut. *Ages.* 36.4–5; 5.1.

[3]Xen. *Ages.* 3.2–5; 4.1–6. Cf. 8.6–8; 7.1–7.

character, or at least at a personality often rendered inflexible when in the grip of strong emotions. These two developments illustrate very well the pathological dimension of Agesilaus' character and, as such, shall be analyzed more fully later. Let us merely review the salient points here.

Agesilaus owed Lysander a great deal. As a youth, he had been selected by Lysander as his *eromenos* (beloved). The relationship of *erastes-eromenos* (lover-beloved) was crucially important in the development of Spartan youth, and it usually forged a lifelong bond between the two partners, one an adolescent and the other a mature male.[4] On the death of King Agis, the half-brother of Agesilaus, Lysander sponsored his claim to the throne against Agis' son, Leotychidas, and it was largely due to Lysander's influence that Leotychidas was declared a bastard and Agesilaus was chosen king.[5] Several years later, when news of Persian preparations reached Sparta, Lysander proposed that Agesilaus lead a military expedition to Asia Minor, and it was through Lysander's influence that the expedition was authorized and Agesilaus was given the command.[6] Thus there were compelling reasons for Agesilaus to feel indebted to his powerful patron. Yet, when the expedition reached Asia Minor, Agesilaus quickly noted that the local Greeks tended to ignore him and to turn to Lysander with their various problems and requests. Agesilaus responded not by confronting Lysander directly with his displeasure and commanding him to cease acting beyond his station, as a king might to his subordinate, or even by trying to negotiate an understanding, as two good friends might have been presumed to do. Instead, he undercut Lysander's influence by indirect means and finally humiliated him by assigning him a servile function to perform, that of meat carver.[7] The response of Agesilaus to a situation admittedly rather demeaning for him seems nonetheless extreme and hardly justified by the circumstances. He appears to have been willing to sacrifice a longstanding relationship in order to satisfy his own sense

[4]Plut. *Ages.* 2.1, *Lys.* 22.3. On the nature of this relationship, see Xen. *Lac. Pol.* 2.13 and *Lyc.* 17.1, 18.4; H. Michell, *Sparta* (Cambridge, 1952), pp. 194–96; and J. T. Hooker, *The Ancient Spartans* (London, 1980), pp. 135–36.

[5]Xen. 3.3.1–4; Plut. *Ages.* 3.3–5; *Lys.* 22.3–6; *Alcib.* 23.7–8; Nepos, *Ages.* 1.2–5; Paus. 3.8.7–10. In his *Agesilaus*, Xenophon omits any reference to Lysander's role in bringing Agesilaus to the throne.

[6]Xen. 3.4.1–3; Plut. *Ages.* 6.1–3; *Lys.* 23.1–2. In the *Agesilaus*, Xenophon chooses to ignore Lysander's influence in the planning of the expedition. These two omissions seem to argue for the prior composition of the *Hellenica*.

[7]Xen. 3.4.7–10; Plut. *Ages.* 7.1–8.4; *Lys.* 23.2–24.2.

of self-importance through his excessively high-handed treatment of
Lysander, which left no room for a rapprochement between the two.
Such radical behavior demands more explanation than the sources pro-
vide.

Agesilaus manifested an implacable hatred and an inflexible attitude
toward Thebes throughout almost his entire career. After the Theban
victory over Sparta at Leuctra, and the subsequent Theban invasions of
the Peloponnesus, which resulted in the liberation of Messenia and the
overturning of centuries-old Spartan domination there, such hatred was
understandable. But Agesilaus' animosity dated from two incidents at
the beginning of his career. The insult he sustained at the hands of the
Boeotarchs when he was attempting to sacrifice at Aulis before sailing
to Asia Minor, and the responsibility of Thebes for starting the Corinthian War, which caused the Spartan authorities to recall Agesilaus
prematurely from Asia Minor, had a profound and lasting effect upon
the king.[8] Throughout the Corinthian War, at the signing of the King's
Peace in 387/6, at the treacherous seizure of the Theban Cadmeia by the
Spartan Phoebidas in 382, in the campaigns in Boeotia following the
liberation of Thebes in 379/8, and, finally, in the Peace Conference of
371, Agesilaus was unwavering in his hostility toward Thebes.[9] He
wished to humble it, to reduce its power, and, if possible, to make it
subject to Spartan domination. He was aware that his policies were
hardly popular everywhere in Sparta, and his opponent Antalcidas
directly criticized him for improving the fighting skills of the Thebans
by campaigning against them so often, in contravention of Lycurgus'
advice on the matter.[10] Moreover, the Battle of Leuctra was the culmi-
nation of a quarter-century of hostility between the two states, for
which Agesilaus was largely responsible on the Spartan side. What lay
behind this much-remarked, almost compulsive desire to humble
Thebes? Other enemies of Sparta, notably Athens and Argos, escaped
the hostile attention of Agesilaus. Here again, a pattern of behavior
demands analysis and explanation that the ancient sources do not adequately afford.

It is important to note that both the rupture with Lysander and the
vendetta against Thebes date to the early years of Agesilaus' reign.

[8]Xen. 3.4.3–4; 3.5.3–7; 4.2.1–5; Plut. *Ages.* 6.4–7, 15.2–6. Once again, Xenophon
has omitted these incidents from his *Agesilaus.*

[9]Xen. 4.3.15–21; 4.5.3–10; 5.1.32–33; 5.2.32; 5.4.13; 5.4.35–37; 5.4.47–55; and
6.3.18–20.

[10]Plut. *Ages.* 26.2–3; *Pelop.* 15.2; *Lyc.* 13.5–6.

Because Agesilaus was in his mid-forties when he came to the throne, it is clear that we are dealing here with the actions of a fully mature man; Agesilaus' character and personality must have already been formed long before this time. In order to attempt to understand these actions, and the personality that was behind them, we must investigate the development of that personality in Agesilaus' childhood and youth. Unfortunately, such a task is not easy, and I shall be able only to suggest certain salient aspects of this development which the sources allow us to glimpse. Nonetheless, the sketch that emerges will help to explain Agesilaus' later actions and behavior.

It is a great pity that Xenophon deliberately declined to record anything about the king's life before his accession to the throne. At the beginning of his encomium of Agesilaus, he suggests that he knew and could write much about his early achievements, but he chose not to do so.[11] Xenophon met the king upon his arrival in Asia Minor in 396 and remained his friend and great admirer throughout Agesilaus' life; within a very few years of his death, in the mid-350s, he wrote an encomium of the king.[12] Xenophon devotes a large part of this treatise to a depiction of the king's virtues, but he does so in static fashion, without providing any explanation of how or why Agesilaus came to be the way he appeared as an adult. Xenophon unquestionably knew the relevant facts of Agesilaus' early life; for some reason, it seemed to him unimportant to introduce this material into his account of the reign of Agesilaus, if his encomium can even be considered to be that. Furthermore, Xenophon omits much that is unfavorable to his hero in an obvious attempt to whitewash Agesilaus. The numerous allusions to criticisms of the king, as well as their implicit refutation, strongly suggest that Xenophon wrote this unusual treatise, patently apologetic in nature, specifically to counter an unfavorable account of Agesilaus and his reign which placed much of the blame for Sparta's failures on the king.[13] A striking aspect of the *Agesilaus* is its omissions (quite apart from the fact that virtually everything before the accession has been omitted).

The overall impression of the *Agesilaus,* carefully and deliberately

---

[11]Xen. *Ages.* 1.5.
[12]See J. K. Anderson, *Xenophon* (New York, 1974), p. 152, and W. E. Higgins, *Xenophon the Athenian: The Problem of the Individual and the Society of the Polis* (Albany, N.Y., 1977), pp. 77–82.
[13]See C. D. Hamilton, "Agesilaus and the Failure of Spartan Hegemony," *Ancient World* 5 (1982)·68n.10, and 70 for discussion of this point. Xen. *Ages.* 2.21, 4.3, 5.6, and 8.7 contain passages that seem to be responses to hostile criticisms; see also Plut. *Ages.* 10.5–6, 30.1, and 34.1 for direct criticisms, perhaps drawn from earlier writers.

designed, is that of a king devoted to the service of his state, to self-control, justice, piety, the support of his friends, and the idea of Pan-hellenism. Lysander is not mentioned in the treatise, and there is hardly a word about a theme known to Xenophon and alluded to in the *Hellenica:* Agesilaus' bitter animosity toward Thebes and his pursuit of an unwavering anti-Theban policy, from the outbreak of the Corinthian War until the Second Battle of Mantineia. It is worth asking why Xenophon ignored this part of Agesilaus' record, and how he justified his approach. Possibly the answer lies with the influence of Isocrates.

The orator Isocrates had developed principles that allowed the shaping of historical material according to the purpose of the writer and that certainly did not always bind him to reveal the whole truth about his subject.[14] Isocrates had advised that encomia should not be overly apologetic in tone, and he followed his own advice. In his *Evagoras,* the earliest extant example of a prose encomium we possess, he described the monarch's "happy old age" and suppressed any reference to his assassination.[15] Xenophon may have found his inspiration here for the approach he adopted in the *Agesilaus.* Xenophon clearly believed Agesilaus was a man of courage and vision, and he portrayed him as the first Greek to conceptualize and attempt to carry out an attack upon the perennial enemy, Persia.[16] The account that resulted from this approach, however, was both partial and incomplete.

For a more balanced assessment of the king's personality, as well as for some significant details about his origins and early life, particularly the formative years of his childhood and youth, we must turn to Plutarch's account of his life. The value of Plutarch's information, of course, depends to a great extent upon the sources that he used in compiling his work.[17] It is quite clear that Plutarch had read and used Xenophon's works for his *Agesilaus;* this is proved not only by several direct citations of Xenophon by name but also by a comparison be-

[14]See C. D. Hamilton, "Greek Rhetoric and History: The Case of Isocrates," in *Arktouros: Hellenic Studies Presented to Bernard M. W. Knox,* ed. W. Burkert et al. (New York, 1979), pp. 290–98, for discussion of this point.

[15]Isoc. 9.71, cf. 10.14. See S. Halliwell, "Traditional Conceptions of Character," in *Characterization and Individuality in Greek Literature,* ed. C. Pelling (Oxford, 1990), pp. 42–56, for a discussion of Isocrates' *Evagoras.*

[16]Xen. *Ages.* 1.7–8; 1.35–36; 7.7.

[17]For modern studies of Plutarch and the value of his work, see C. P. Jones, *Plutarch and Rome* (Oxford, 1971); and A. Wardman, *Plutarch's Lives* (Berkeley and Los Angeles, 1974). Frank Frost, "Plutarch and Clio," in *Panhellenica: Essays in Ancient History and Historiography in Honor of Truesdell S. Brown,* ed. S. M. Burstein and L. Okin (Lawrence, Kans., 1980), pp. 155–70, is also valuable on this point.

tween numerous passages of the two authors.[18] But Plutarch had also read and utilized several other sources in his *Agesilaus,* most notably the fourth-century writers Ephorus and Theopompus.[19] Both of these authors were in a position to gain access to reliable information about Agesilaus, whom Theopompus considered "the greatest and most famous man of his time," and there is no reason to doubt the biographical details that Plutarch furnishes about him, even if their precise attribution cannot be fixed. A number of modern studies of Plutarch, moreover, have demonstrated his great interest in the "moral character" of his subjects.[20] Plutarch himself clearly stated that his object in the *Lives* was not to write history, but rather to delineate the character, including virtues and vices, of the great military and political figures of the past who interested him.[21] Although Plutarch obviously did not have the same view of the development of character and personality which has been advanced by twentieth-century psychologists and psychiatrists,[22] the material he collected may well serve as the raw data for a modern attempt at an assessment of Agesilaus' personality. After examining his personality, we shall be able to consider Agesilaus' break with Lysander and his enmity toward Thebes in better perspective.

Agesilaus' Early Life

What does Plutarch say about Agesilaus' early life? Agesilaus' origins were inauspicious. He was the son of King Archidamus by a second, unpopular marriage. Because his elder half-brother, Agis, was the heir

[18]Plutarch mentions Xenophon at *Agesilaus* 4.1, 18.1, 19.5, and 34.4.

[19]Theopompus is mentioned at *Agesilaus* 10.5, 31.3, and 32.8; Ephorus is not cited in the *Agesilaus,* but he is mentioned in the *Lysander,* at 17.2, 20.6, 25.3, and 30.3 (cf. *Ages.* 20.2–3). It is clear, then, that Plutarch had used Ephorus for those lives that fall in the early fourth century, even if he did not cite Ephorus in the *Agesilaus.*

[20]See, in addition to the works cited in n. 17 above, P. A. Stadter, *Plutarch's Historical Methods: An Analysis of the "Mulierum Virtutes"* (Cambridge, Mass., 1965); R. H. Barrow, *Plutarch and His Times* (London, 1967); and D. A. Russell, *Plutarch* (London, 1973).

[21]Plut. *Alex.* 1, *Pericles* 1.4–5, 2.2–3, and *Mor.* 172.C–E.

[22]On modern attempts to treat historical individuals from a psychoanalytic point of view, see B. Wolman, ed., *The Psychoanalytic Interpretation of History* (New York, 1971); and B. Mazlish, ed., *Psychoanalysis and History* (New York, 1971). For a more recent discussion of the thinkers whose work has shaped and underlies contemporary theories of psychohistory, see P. Pomper, *The Structure of Mind in History* (New York, 1985). On the distinction between character and personality in classical literature, see C. Gill, "The Character-Personality Distinction," in *Characterization and Individuality in Greek Literature,* ed. Pelling, pp. 1–31.

presumptive to the throne, Agesilaus was never expected to reign in Sparta and was given the education of an ordinary citizen. Furthermore, he was born with a birth defect, a deformed leg, which caused him to limp permanently.[23] Despite these beginnings, he won the affection of his fellow citizens, secured the throne on Agis' death, and reigned during one of the most important periods of Spartan history. How was he affected by the circumstances of his birth and the events of his youth, and what sort of person did he become?

According to Plutarch, the ephors opposed Archidamus' decision to marry Eupolia, his second wife, who was to be the mother of Agesilaus, and they fined the king when he persisted despite their opposition. The grounds alleged for their opposition are not convincing: because Eupolia was small of stature, they claimed that she would "bear them a race of kinglets."[24] This explanation is contradicted by Plutarch's own evidence to the effect that Agis, the lawful heir to the throne, was expected to, and did, succeed his father, whereas the much younger Agesilaus, who was not expected to rule, was given the traditional education provided for the youth of Sparta by the Lycurgan regime, from which only the heir apparent was exempt.[25] Unless we wish to suppose that there was some reason to doubt that Agis would succeed his father as king, such as signs of serious illness or some question about his paternity, for which there is no hint in the sources, we must therefore reject Plutarch's *post eventum* explanation of the ephors' opposition to this marriage as contrary to the facts.

The same is not true, however, for the *fact* of their opposition. Plutarch implies that Eupolia was not particularly attractive and that she came from a family which, while respectable enough, was not very affluent.[26] Given that Archidamus persisted in marrying a woman who was neither beautiful nor wealthy despite official disapproval of the match, it seems fair to conclude that he was attracted to her for other, personal, reasons, and that this was a love match. Their union produced two children, Agesilaus and a daughter, Cynisca.[27] If the suggestion of

---

[23]Plut. *Ages.* 1.1–2, cf. 3.3–5; Nepos, *Ages.* 8.1. While there may be some ambiguity in Plutarch's account about the origin of Agesilaus' deformed leg, Nepos certainly understood this deformity to be a birth defect. For discussion of treatments of childhood in classical literature, see C. Pelling, "Childhood and Personality in Greek Biography," in *Characterization and Individuality in Greek Literature,* ed. Pelling, pp. 213–44.

[24]Plut. *Ages.* 2.3.

[25]Plut. *Ages.* 1.1.

[26]Plut. *Ages.* 4.1.

[27]Xen. *Ages.* 9.6; cf. Plut. *Ages.* 20.1.

marrying for love is correct, perhaps the opposition to Archidamus' second marriage was grounded in the suspicion that his interest in a second family would have a harmful effect on Agis and would somehow disrupt the harmony of the Eurypontid line. Such a hypothesis, however, is merely speculative and is hardly germane to our principal concern here. Plutarch's explanation, which he attributes to Theophrastus, may well have been coined as a *bon mot* after the fact to allude to Agesilaus' own slightness of stature. In any case, it is more than likely that Agesilaus was aware as a child in his mother's house of a certain tension produced by the conflict between his father and the ephors over this marriage.

Agesilaus' deformity at birth presents another difficulty. According to the legislation of Lycurgus, every Spartan infant was to be examined at birth by the officials. Those infants who appeared healthy and fit were remanded to the custody of their mothers until the boys reached an age to begin their communal training. Those infants considered unfit or incapable of developing into strong, healthy warriors were to be exposed on the slopes of Taygetus for the wolves to devour.[28] This brutal custom was followed because the state had no wish to raise boys who would not one day contribute to the state as full citizens; that is, as hardy hoplite soldiers. A deformed leg that would cause a serious limp might very well have been thought sufficient to render its owner ineffective as a hoplite, and therefore cost him his life while an infant. Agesilaus' life was spared, though, and probably the reason for this was the special status of his father. In Plutarch, there is no hint of a debate over saving his life, but, unless we assume that the Lycurgan requirement had undergone some modification by the mid-fifth century, for which there is no evidence either, we must conclude that an exception was made in Agesilaus' case, probably because of his father's identity.[29] As he grew older, Agesilaus surely recognized this exception and wondered about his own status. As he came, in the course of his education, to know more about his state and its values, he must have experienced a mixed sense of gratitude and unworthiness, which led him all the more to seek to justify his existence. No other evidence has been recorded about his childhood, but it seems that he was a sensitive child, to judge

---

[28]Plut. *Lyc.* 16.1–2; cf. Michell, *Sparta,* pp. 165–66.

[29]Cartledge, *Agesilaos,* p. 22, reviews several possible reasons for the decision to spare Agesilaus and suggests that Sparta was already suffering from that oliganthropeia which would become so serious in the fourth century and thus he was reared to fill the ranks of Spartan manpower. This suggestion seems to stretch the evidence.

from his later actions.[30] Agesilaus probably felt a certain ambiguity about his identity. He was the son of a king, and therefore special, but he was not expected to reign. He possessed a physical infirmity, one that ordinarily would have cost the life of its possessor, and yet his life had been spared. His circumstances were highly unusual; he did not easily fit into the ordinary categories of Spartan society.[31] The evidence of his youth suggests that Agesilaus was well aware of his ambiguous status and that he strove to come to grips with it.

The traditional Lycurgan education, the *agoge,* given to all Spartan boys of the citizen class except the heir apparent, was designed above all to inculcate obedience.[32] Begun about the age of seven, this training took the Spartan youth through various stages of development, both physical and moral. It was austere and demanding, and its physical dimension was especially rigorous. The boys were trained in gymnastics, taught how to handle weapons and to fight, and forced to run and to march a great deal. The objective was to produce a strong and resourceful warrior, courageous in the face of the enemy, and obedient to the commands of the state and his officers. This physical training, difficult enough even for those in sound health and firm of limb, must have been even more arduous for Agesilaus because of his physical disability. Yet, we are told, he exerted himself to the utmost and surpassed many of his contemporaries.[33]

Agesilaus' response to this challenge reveals several qualities, which he must have developed during the formative period of his youth. First, he was acutely sensitive about his infirmity. He probably learned quickly the tendency of children to make fun of the misfortunes and disabilities of others, and he sought to defend himself against their taunts by joking first himself about his limp. In this way, he blunted the force of any cruel mockery directed toward his condition, and thus he controlled a situation with which he would have to live throughout his

[30]Plut. *Ages.* 25.5 *(ad fin.)* relates a story about Agesilaus' playing "horsey" with his children, and being discovered by another man, whom he requested to say nothing of the matter until he had also become a father. This seems to indicate a caring and sensitive nature, at least toward his children.

[31]On social classes and categories in Sparta, see chap. 3 below, and the interesting article of S. J. Hodkinson, "Social Order and the Conflict of Values in Classical Sparta," *Chiron* 13 (1983):239–81.

[32]Plut. *Ages.* 1.1–2; *Lyc.* 16.4–5; *Mor.* 237A4, 238E21; and Xen. *Lac. Pol.* 1.1, 2–3, 8.1–2.

[33]Plut. *Ages.* 2.1–2; see Michell, *Sparta,* pp. 40–43 and 165–74, on the nature of the Spartan educational system for young boys.

life.[34] Second, he demonstrated a fierce sense of competitiveness and
ambition, which was tied to an equally strong pride in accomplishment.
Agesilaus' disability only served to underline his ambition, according to
Plutarch.[35] Because his infirmity put him at a disadvantage vis-à-vis his
contemporaries, his strivings to excel and his frequent successes emphasized all the more his ambition and his desire to gain recognition.
Agesilaus' pride and ambition were tempered, however, by a natural
modesty; it was this quality that first attracted Lysander to him when
Agesilaus was still an adolescent.[36] Finally, Agesilaus' dogged determination deserves to be noted. Whereas another might have given up in
the face of an unequal struggle or indulged in self-pity over the cruel fate
that inexplicably denied him a sound, well-formed body, Agesilaus
manfully and resolutely accepted his condition and strove to overcome
it.[37]

Thus, the few facts that we possess about the circumstances of Agesilaus' birth, childhood, and youth suggest several key elements in the
development of his personality. First, his position and status—indeed,
the very reason for his existence—were shrouded in ambiguity, and
Agesilaus was aware of this. This ambiguity, reinforced by the daily
reminder of his disability, must have contributed to an identity crisis
more serious than usual for the young prince.[38] The need to justify
himself became increasingly important as he matured. Agesilaus met
this need in two ways. On the one hand, he exerted himself to his
utmost to fulfill the requirements and expectations of his state, as
expressed in the structure of the Lycurgan educational system. On the
other hand, he constantly sought acceptance and approval among his
fellow citizens. In both of these endeavors he found success.

There is no question of his military prowess or his personal courage
in battle.[39] In his personal habits, he demonstrated modesty and austerity, which endeared him to his subjects after he had become king; not
for him fine clothes, rich food or drink, or display of wealth, despite the

[34]Plut. Ages. 2.2.
[35]Plut. Ages. 2.1–2; cf. Xen. Ages. 10.4 on Agesilaus' ambition, and Lac. Pol. 4.1–2, on
the encouragement of rivalry and competition among the youth of Sparta, as (traditionally) instituted by Lycurgus.
[36]Plut. Ages. 2.1.
[37]Plut. Ages. 2.2.
[38]On the concept of "identity-crisis" as a significant stage in personality development,
particularly in adolescence, see E. Erikson, Young Man Luther (New York, 1958), pp. 14–
17.
[39]Xen. Ages. 6.1–3.

fact that many other Spartans coveted these during his reign, and that they were easily within his grasp had he wanted them.[40] The discipline and obedience he had learned as a youth served him well in his relations with the authorities, especially the ephors, and cloaked an ambition that might otherwise have alarmed many and contributed to a diminution of his power and influence.[41] Agesilaus also discovered diverse ways to win the affection of his fellow Spartans. He developed an outward cheerfulness of manner and a wit, which is reflected in the numerous sayings preserved by Plutarch.[42] Furthermore, Agesilaus always seems to have observed a strict fairness toward his enemies, and on more than one occasion he exerted himself to convert personal enemies into friends, especially among the Spartan citizen class.[43] He was indulgent to a fault with his friends, finding it difficult to condemn them when they erred and often associating himself with them in their misdeeds.[44] The reverse of such behavior was his ability to be deeply hurt and to bear grudges for insults to his pride and self-esteem, whether real or imagined. These attitudes toward the Spartan state and his fellow citizens, while seemingly reflecting a model Spartan citizen, in reality disguise a complex set of feelings, in which insecurity, fear of rejection, and a compulsion to win approval and renown predominate. Agesilaus' personality was scarcely simple, and he must sometimes have been driven by motives that he only imperfectly understood and over which he did not have full control. The interplay of these elements with the various historical situations Agesilaus was called upon to address did not always produce happy results either for him or for his state.

Youth and Manhood: The Peloponnesian War

The history of Greece during the four and a half decades between Agesilaus' birth and his accession as king was full of events of importance for Sparta. The sources provide no evidence of Agesilaus' involvement in any of these events. Nonetheless, it will prove useful to review them briefly in order to understand the public background of his early

[40]Xen. *Ages.* 5.1–3, 4.1–6; *Lac. Pol.* 14.2–4.

[41]Xen. *Ages.* 6.4; Plut. *Ages.* 4.1–4.

[42]Plut. *Ages.* 2.3 mentions the gaiety and cheerfulness of Agesilaus in every crisis. His sayings are collected at *Mor.* 208C–215A; cf. 190F–191D.

[43]Xen. *Ages.* 7.3; Plut. *Ages.* 20.4.

[44]Xen. *Ages.* 8.1–2; Plut. *Ages.* 5.1–2. See Xen. *Ages.* 11.13 for a summary assessment of the relations of Agesilaus with his various associates.

life and to ask what effects it may have had on him. The first decade of his life was spent in the false atmosphere of international peace and security engendered by the Thirty Years' Treaty of 446/5. By 434, however, the Epidamnus-Corcyra conflict and the crisis it provoked between Athens and Sparta's ally Corinth foreshadowed the Peloponnesian War.[45] Agesilaus would have been about twelve when, in 432/1, negotiations between Athens and Sparta broke down and the outbreak of hostilities seemed imminent.[46] His father, Archidamus, tried unsuccessfully to persuade the Spartans not to go to war with Athens, by arguing that they were ill-equipped to win such a war easily and that it would be a bitter legacy to the next generation. Very few of the fellow citizens of Archidamus adhered to his views, however, and, when matters came to a vote, the great majority of Spartans declared that Athens had broken the peace and showed themselves ready to go to war against Athenian aggression.[47]

Because Archidamus had advocated an unpopular and minority position, we might imagine that suspicions were aroused toward him and that his own prestige might have suffered as a result of his public stance. If this is so, might this situation not also have had some effect on his younger son, who, with his associates, would have followed the great public events of the day from a distance? When the war finally began, in 431, Archidamus was dispatched with a Peloponnesian army to invade Attica. He twice plundered and ravaged the enemy's territory, but he did not succeed in drawing the Athenian army into combat, and his forays failed to produce any decisive results.[48] In the next year, 429, the Spartans refrained from invading Attica while the plague raged there, but Archidamus returned at the head of an invasion force in 428.[49] When next we hear of an invasion it is Cleomenes, brother of the exiled

---

[45]See D. Kagan, *The Outbreak of the Peloponnesian War* (Ithaca, N.Y., 1969) for detailed discussion of this period; see pp. 205–50 esp. for the Epidamnus-Corcyra episode.

[46]On the question of the birthdate of Agesilaus, see my discussion in "Etude chronologique sur le règne d' Agésilas," *Ktema* 7 (1982):281–96. The dates of his reign are a matter of great dispute. His accession is linked to the Elean War, at the conclusion of which King Agis died. Agesilaus' death occurred after a period of mercenary service in Egypt, of uncertain duration, at the advanced age of eighty-four. Dates from 401 to 398 have been proposed for his accession; and from 361 to 358, for his death. A crucial passage is Xenophon's synchronism (*Hell.* 3.2.21) of events in Asia Minor with the Elean War. I have argued for an accession date of 398 for Agesilaus, and I would put his death in 359/8; thus, his birth would have occurred around 443/2.

[47]Thuc. 1.79–88. See Kagan, *Outbreak*, pp. 300–305, for discussion.

[48]Thuc. 2.12, 18–21, 47, 55, 57.

[49]Thuc. 2.71; 3.1.

King Pleistoanax, not Archidamus, who is in command. Probably in 427, Archidamus died and his son succeeded him, as expected. In 426 Agis, as king, led an invasion that was turned back at the Isthmus of Corinth because of a series of earthquakes.[50]

It was during the early years of the war that Agesilaus first attracted the attention of Lysander. The latter, noticing both the ambition and natural modesty of the young prince, and being favorably impressed by him, took Agesilaus as his young lover and sponsored his further development into maturity.[51] The relationship of lover-beloved, according to which an older man established with an adolescent boy not only a sexual union but also, more importantly, an emotional and spiritual one, was a key element of Spartan education. It was expected that the young man would pattern himself after his older lover and learn from him such qualities as strength, courage, and manliness, symbolized by the homosexual act whereby the older man literally possessed the younger one.[52] Such a relationship usually established a permanent bond between the two individuals, and it was not uncommon for one to support the other in athletic competitions, politics, and especially warfare.[53] Although little is known of Lysander's position at this time, his subsequent career in the later stages of the war suggests that he was a man of remarkable (if not necessarily admirable) qualities. Thus, his choice of Agesilaus as his lover undoubtedly singled him out as someone special and probably produced a sense of gratitude on the young man's part. Lysander's support of Agesilaus' bid for the throne some twenty-five years later, as well as his support of his career in the early years of his reign, certainly implies that the two remained on good terms during the interim, even if the sources are silent on this score.[54] Both men were intensely ambitious, and this quality may have been one

---

[50]Thuc. 3.26.2, 89.1; see D. Kagan, *The Archidamian War* (Ithaca, N.Y., 1974), pp. 147 and 193.

[51]Plut. *Ages.* 2.2; Cartledge, *Agesilaos*, dates this relationship to "somewhere between 433 and 428" (p. 29).

[52]See K. J. Dover, *Greek Homosexuality* (Cambridge, Mass., 1978), in general on the topic, and pp. 179–88 for Sparta in particular.

[53]See P. Cartledge, "The Politics of Spartan Pederasty," *PCPS*, n.s. 30 (1981):17–36; cf. Xen. *Lac. Pol.* 2.13; Plut. *Lyc.* 17.1, 18.4

[54]On Lysander in general see P. A. Rahe, "Lysander and the Spartan Settlement, 407–403 B.C." (Ph.D. diss., Yale University, 1977); and J.-F. Bommelaer, *Lysandre de Sparte: Histoire et Traditions* (Paris, 1981). Cartledge, *Agesilaos*, p. 29, makes the interesting point that Lysander was equally fortunate in his "catch" of Agesilaus, for the young prince must have been considered a highly desirable object of affection because of his family connections.

of the strong bonds between them. In any case, it is quite likely that Lysander exerted an important influence over Agesilaus at this stage and stimulated his ambition.

In 425, as Agesilaus was finishing his education and military training and was preparing to join the ranks of the Spartans as a citizen-soldier, a momentous event occurred which must have had a significant impact on him, as on many other Spartiates. Shortly before, a group of Spartan soldiers had landed on the island of Sphacteria, in the Bay of Navarino, in order to cut off an Athenian contingent on the peninsula of Pylos, which was on the adjacent mainland. The besiegers soon became the besieged, however, and as time dragged on the Spartans were unable to assist their trapped men. Ultimately, the besieged troops capitulated to the Athenians, and 292 were taken prisoner, of whom 120 were full Spartiates, citizen-hoplites.[55] The news of the surrender of these troops was a serious blow to Spartan morale. The potential loss of so many citizen-soldiers was grave, and negotiations were immediately begun to secure their return, although without initial success; the recovery of the prisoners had to await the signing of the Peace of Nicias in 421.[56] But even more important was the sense of shame and chagrin which attended the surrender. According to the Spartan ideal, citizens were to stand fast and die, if need be, where the state ordered them to, as had the heroes who had fallen with King Leonidas at Thermopylae.[57] Traditionally, when a young Spartan completed his formal training and received his shield at the ceremony that marked his entrance into the citizen body, his mother was to admonish him to "return either with his shield, or on it"; that is, victorious or dead.[58]

Desertion from duty, cowardly flight, abandonment of weapons, and even surrender were scandalous modes of conduct for the Spartans.[59] The lurid spectacle of these Spartans laying down their arms and marching into captivity in order to save their own lives was a shocking contrast to the ceremony of induction for Agesilaus' "graduating class" into the ranks as Spartan warriors. It is reasonable to assume that the news of the surrender, coming either shortly before or after Agesilaus and his peers had joined the ranks, had a profound effect upon them especially. Their zeal to prove themselves better and braver men than

[55]Thuc. 4.2–23, 26–38; see also Kagan, *Archidamian War*, pp. 218–59.
[56]Thuc. 4.39–41; Kagan, *Archidamian War*, pp. 248–49.
[57]Herod. 7.224.1, 228.2.
[58]Plut. *Mor.* 241F16; cf. 241F17. See also Hooker, *Ancient Spartans*, p. 135.
[59]See Michell, *Sparta*, p. 44; and Hooker, *Ancient Spartans*, p. 13.

those who had surrendered will have been inflamed. Although we do not know if Agesilaus served during the Peloponnesian War, his long military record as king makes it abundantly clear that he was personally brave, almost to a fault, and that he never considered surrender. If anything, his military ardor was at times intemperate,[60] and we cannot help but wonder if there was not a causal relationship between his documented career as a soldier and commander and the impression made on him by the surrender at Sphacteria at the very beginning of his life as a soldier.

The sequel to the Athenians' rejection of the Spartan peace offer was the military activity of Brasidas in the Thraceward area of northern Greece.[61] With seven hundred emancipated helots, that Spartan commander achieved some dazzling successes, most notably the winning over of Amphipolis from Athens.[62] Although his escapades in the north ultimately cost Brasidas his life, they may well have fired the imagination of young Spartans eager for a taste of war and military glory, and especially of an ambitious man such as Agesilaus. There were few additional opportunities to distinguish oneself in fighting before the Peace of Nicias brought a tentative end to the war in 421.[63]

Within three years, diplomatic pressures and military tension led to a renewal of conflict within the Peloponnesus, and in 418 King Agis twice led an expedition into Argive territory. On the first occasion he retired without engaging the enemy in battle, although he had them at a distinct disadvantage, and he narrowly missed being severely punished upon his return to Sparta. Before long, he was ordered back into the field, and he won a significant victory over his opponents at the Battle of Mantineia in 418.[64] There is no record of Agesilaus' having been among the Spartan troops on either of these occasions, but it is not unlikely that he was, because Agis marched out with a large levy of Spartiates.[65] Agesilaus thus may have had an opportunity to taste battle and to display that bravery for which he later was to be noted, but,

[60]Xen. *Ages.* 2.12–13 shows how Agesilaus risked his life, unnecessarily, at the Battle of Coroneia, because of personal bravery and, we might add, out of an almost irrational anti-Theban hatred. See chap. 4 below.

[61]Thuc. 4.78–88; Kagan, *Archidamian War,* pp. 275–304.

[62]Thuc. 4.80, 102–7.

[63]See D. Kagan, *The Peace of Nicias and the Sicilian Expedition* (Ithaca, N.Y., 1981), pp. 19–32, on the precarious nature of the Peace of Nicias.

[64]Thuc. 5.57–74; see also Kagan, *Peace of Nicias,* pp. 91–106 and, on the battle itself, pp. 107–37.

[65]Thuc. 5.64.

more importantly, he may have learned a valuable lesson from the fate of Agis after his enigmatic retirement from the Argolid. Although a Spartan king was supreme commander while in the field, he was not above criticism, and he might even be disciplined or punished by the state for his conduct, if he seemed to merit this, upon his return.[66] Agesilaus' later concern, as king, to keep on a basis of comradely relations with his troops may stem in part from Agis' experience; Agesilaus did not wish to alienate their affections, and thus to risk their displeasure with his leadership when he returned from campaign to Sparta. But, as we have seen, there were also other reasons for his constant attempts to cultivate his fellow citizens, which originated in his early need for acceptance and approval.

The decision of the Athenians to send a great expedition to Sicily in 415 found its reverberations in the Valley of the Eurotas.[67] First, the Athenian commander Alcibiades, in flight from his political enemies, sought refuge at Sparta and imparted important military advice to his erstwhile foes.[68] As a result, the Spartan Gylippus was dispatched as general to Syracuse, where he gained a great reputation for organizing the defense of the city so successfully. Then, it was rumored that Alcibiades had abused Spartan hospitality by seducing King Agis' wife, Timaia, and fathering her son, Leotychidas.[69] Agis disavowed the child and spent the last phase of the war commanding a garrison force at Decelea, in northeast Attica. Perhaps it was already at this time that Agesilaus conceived the idea of challenging Leotychidas for the succession when Agis died. Agesilaus was about thirty years old then, and his desire to achieve glory and renown had certainly not abated, although there were few opportunities to accomplish this.

During the Ionian or Decelean War, as it is variously called, from 411 to 404, many Spartans found occasion to distinguish themselves in warfare, operating from Agis' garrison outpost in Attica, or serving as harmosts in the various cities Sparta was liberating from Athens and

---

[66]Thuc. 5.63 reports that the Spartans were quite angry with Agis after his first expedition and threatened to destroy his house and impose a heavy fine on him; he barely escaped this penalty.

[67]Thuc. 6.1ff.; see also Kagan, *Peace of Nicias,* pp. 159–91, for discussion of the decision to undertake the Sicilian expedition.

[68]Thuc. 6.61; 88–93; Plut. *Alcib.* 23.1–2; Nepos, *Alcib.* 4.5–7. See J. Hatzfeld, *Alcibiade,* 2d ed. (Paris, 1951), pp. 206–14; and W. M. Ellis, *Alcibiades* (New York, 1989), pp. 65–68.

[69]Plut. *Alcib.* 23.7, *Lys.* 22.3; cf. Thuc. 8.45 for the personal enmity between Agis and Alcibiades.

putting under military occupation, or fighting under the succession of
Spartan navarchs in the Aegean theater of war.[70] But while his half-
brother was in the public eye, directing operations from Decelea, and
Lysander, his lover, was gaining fame and power as navarch, Agesilaus
apparently languished in Sparta; or, if he did achieve any notable military successes during this period, no record survives of them.[71] As the
tempo of the war accelerated after the destruction of the great Athenian
expeditionary force in Sicily and the signing of an alliance between
Sparta and Persia to crush their common foe, Agesilaus must have
yearned more and more ardently to play some role in the historic events
of this period. Denied any part other than that of an ordinary Spartan
hoplite, even that of a minor military command, as far as we can tell, he
may well have given increasing thought to the chances of becoming
king when his half-brother died. Because Agis remained unreconciled
to Leotychidas, even after the former's return to Sparta in 404, the
chances of success must have seemed reasonable. But if Agis were to die
while Leotychidas was a minor and the war was in progress, it was quite
likely that Agesilaus, as nearest of kin, would be named regent to act for
his young nephew.[72] Such a situation would have provided Agesilaus
with opportunities to distinguish himself in war, and it is possible that
he might have been content with a regency. Agis lived long enough,
however, to rule out this possibility. We cannot affirm with any certainty, therefore, that Agesilaus formulated the idea of challenging
Leotychidas for the kingship long before Agis' death.

   Lysander, Agesilaus' mentor, brought the great war to an end.[73] The
victory of Lysander over the Athenian fleet at Aegospotami in 405
crushed any hope of successful resistance to Sparta and allowed him to

[70]See, most recently, D. Kagan, *The Fall of the Athenian Empire* (Ithaca, N.Y., 1987),
for discussion of this phase of the war.

[71]The silence of both Xenophon and Plutarch about Agesilaus during the Peloponnesian War suggests that he achieved nothing of note at this time. Although Xenophon
deliberately omits any facts about the life of Agesilaus before his accession to the throne,
Plutarch does not, and it is difficult to imagine that he would have missed the opportunity to record some act of bravery or renown, had he known of such, at this stage of
Agesilaus' life.

[72]The rules of succession for Spartan kingship provided that a member of the royal
family serve as regent when the king was a minor; this had been done in several cases in
the classical period. See, for example, the case of Pausanias in 479/8 (cf. Thuc. 1.128ff.).

[73]Xen. 2.1.21–28, on Aegospotami. See C. D. Hamilton, *Sparta's Bitter Victories:
Politics and Diplomacy in the Corinthian War* (Ithaca, N.Y., 1979), pp. 40–55, for detailed
discussion of Lysander's role in ending the Peloponnesian War. See D. Lotze, *Lysander
und der Peloponnesische Krieg* (Berlin, 1964), pp. 31–37; Rahe, "Lysander," pp. 76ff.; and
Bommelaer, *Lysandre*, pp. 103–15, for further discussion.

blockade Athens and starve the city into submission. Lysander was instrumental, although with the consent of the Spartan government, in formulating the settlement of the Greek world in 404. The Athenian Empire was gone, only to be replaced by a new, Spartan organization that differed little from its predecessor.[74] Oligarchic governments were installed in the various Greek cities, harmosts and garrisons were imposed, and tribute was collected. The cities of Asia Minor were surrendered to Persia according to the treaty arrangements between Sparta and Persia. The unprecedented honors that Lysander received throughout the Greek world and the influence that he possessed upon his return home quickly stimulated opposition. In spring 403 Lysander persuaded the authorities to send him to Attica with a military force in support of the oligarchic regime there, which was threatened by a strong force of exiled Athenian democrats. After his departure, both the kings, Agis and Pausanias, decided to restrain him because of their fear of the consequences should he retake Athens. Pausanias won over three of the ephors, led out an army of his own, relieved Lysander of command, and settled affairs in Attica to his liking.[75] Where Agesilaus stood in this increasingly complex political situation is not known. There is no indication that his friendship with Lysander had diminished, although he may have experienced envy and jealousy over Lysander's success and renown. If Agesilaus had learned of Lysander's subsequent plot to revolutionize the Spartan kingship, however, he may well have been chagrined.

Checked in his foreign policy objectives by the authorities, and unable to find a permanent power base in a polis in which every magistracy was limited to a year's tenure, except for the Gerousia (to be eligible for which one must be at least sixty years of age) and the kingship, Lysander began to plot to make the Spartan monarchy elective.[76] He attempted, without success, to obtain, by bribery, an oracle that would sanction such a change in the Spartan constitution. Furthermore, the priests of Zeus-Ammon in Libya denounced him to the authorities, and he had to defend himself against their charges and to abandon his plans for the moment. Obviously, Lysander's plans were carried out in secrecy among his close supporters, and it is not clear how much of his scheme became public at his trial in 402. The probability,

[74]See Hamilton, *SBV,* pp. 58–62 for details.
[75]See Hamilton, *SBV,* pp. 69–72, pp. 77–80 for details; cf Bommelaer, *Lysandre,* pp. 160–62, and Rahe, "Lysander," pp. 213–22.
[76]Diod. 14.13.2–8, Plut. *Lys.* 24–26; cf. *Mor.* 229F14 and 212C52, and Nepos, *Lys.* 3.

however, is that the priests of Zeus-Ammon rejected Lysander's over-tures and made their complaint before learning any of the particulars of the oracle he wished to obtain, and that he was able to keep his plans a secret still at his trial.[77] Lysander revived his plans seven years later, in 395, and Agesilaus discovered them after Lysander's death, but it is unlikely that he was aware of Lysander's earlier attempt at the time.[78] Agesilaus was noted for his strict observance of the law and his respect for constituted authority in Sparta; it is extremely doubtful, therefore, that he would have continued in a close relationship with Lysander had he known of his revolutionary plotting.[79] Some of Lysander's closest associates in Sparta were clearly privy to the plot; it was probably they who were prepared to advance the money needed to bribe the priests of the several oracles. The apparent exclusion of Agesilaus suggests that he was not among Lysander's closest friends and supporters at this time.

During the last years of the fifth century, important questions were debated, and major decisions taken, in Sparta. One of the most impor-tant issues, of course, was that of imperialism.[80] The practical conse-quences of Lysander's victory in, and settlement of, the Peloponnesian War involved the establishment of a Spartan Empire in Greece, as well as grave social and economic problems. Money was needed to maintain the empire, and Spartan officers had to be sent abroad as harmosts and governors. The Spartan state was not equipped to handle such changes, and corruption soon appeared. The issues raised by this new direction in foreign policy were not settled easily or immediately. Furthermore, Sparta gave aid to Cyrus the Younger in his bid to unseat Artaxerxes, his elder brother, as king of Persia, with the result that war broke out between Sparta and Persia over control of the Greek cities of Asia Minor after Cyrus' death.[81] Finally, the Spartans made war on Elis and sent Agis in command of an army to invade their territory.[82] There is no record of Agesilaus' position on any of these issues of politics and

[77]See Hamilton, *SBV*, pp. 92–96, for discussion; see also Rahe, "Lysander," pp. 222–25; and Bommelaer, *Lysandre*, pp. 223–25.

[78]Plut. *Ages*. 20.2–3; *Lys*. 30.3–4.

[79]See Xen. *Ages*. 6.4; 7.1–3; and Plut. *Ages*. 4.1–4 for Agesilaus' respect for the law. Plut. *Ages*. 20.2–3 and *Lys*. 30.3–4 represent Agesilaus as determined to reveal the evidence of a speech that Lysander had prepared to advance his conspiracy and that was discovered in his house in 394, a year after his death. Agesilaus was deterred from doing this only by the advice of one of the ephors not to stir up dangers for the state by bringing up the conspiracy again.

[80]See Hamilton, *SBV*, pp. 55–62.

[81]Xen. 3.1.1, *Anab*. 1.2.21, 4.2.3; Diod. 14.11.2, 19.4–5; Plut. *Artax*. 6.2–3.

[82]Xen. 3.2.21–31; Diod. 14.17.4–12; Paus. 3.8.2.

foreign policy, if indeed he ever took a public stand on any of them. Presumably, he married Cleora at about this time, because the birth of his son, Archidamus, is put about the year 400.[83] Agesilaus was soon to enter the public scene with a claim to succeed Agis as king.

Agesilaus' Accession to the Throne

Upon the successful conclusion of the war against Elis, Agis went to Delphi to offer thanks.[84] On his way home to Sparta, he fell gravely ill at Heraea and was carried home to die. After his funeral, according to Xenophon, it was necessary to choose a new king, and Agesilaus came forth to challenge the right of Leotychidas to succeed. The latter professed astonishment, reminding Agesilaus that Spartan law required a king's son to succeed to the throne, and asserting that the dead king's brother would inherit the throne only if there were no son. Agesilaus did not argue the laws of succession, but he questioned the paternity of Leotychidas, claiming that Agis had denied him and citing as proof an earthquake that had driven Agis from Timaia's chamber a good ten months before Leotychidas' birth. Agis had apparently said, in the hearing of the ephors, that he did not believe that Leotychidas was his son.[85] But when he fell ill at Heraea, Agis was persuaded, in the presence of many witnesses, to retract his earlier disclaimer and to declare Leotychidas his own son. This much, at least, Pausanias asserts.[86] The point at issue, then, was whether Leotychidas was Agis' son, and conflicting evidence could be produced on this question. The decision would amount to a political choice, ostensibly based on religion.

At this point in the dispute between the two rivals, Diopeithes, a

[83]See P. Poralla, *Prosopographie der Lakedaimonier bis auf die Zeit Alexander des Grossen* (Breslau, 1913), pp. 33 and 160–61, no. 158, Archidamos III.

[84]Xen. 3.3.1.

[85]Xen. 3.3.1–2; Plut. *Alcib.* 23.7–8, *Lys.* 22.4–5, *Ages.* 3.1–2; Paus. 3.8.7–10; cf. Nepos, *Ages.* 1.2–5. See Hamilton, *SBV,* p. 122, for modern literature, to which should be added R. J. Littman, "A New Date for Leotychidas," *Phoenix* 23 (1969):269–77, who unconvincingly argues that Leotychidas' birth should be placed c. 425 and that, therefore, he could not be Alcibiades' son; and R. J. Littman, "The Loves of Alcibiades," *TAPA* 101 (1970):263–76, at 269. I owe these references to the kindness of the late Fordyce Mitchell. Hatzfeld, *Alcibiade,* pp. 217–18 and 218n.3, accepts the adultery of Alcibiades with Timaia, while reserving judgment on the question of Leotychidas' paternity. Ellis, *Alcibiades,* p. 67, declines to take a stand on the issue.

[86]Paus. 3.8.7–8; see also Plut. *Lys.* 22.4.

supporter of Leotychidas, produced an oracle to the effect that Sparta must beware lest the kingship become lame.[87] Diopeithes interpreted the oracle as a reference to Agesilaus' lameness and argued that the throne should therefore go to Leotychidas. Then Lysander entered the fray, arguing convincingly that the oracle did not refer to Agesilaus' physical lameness, but symbolically to the ambiguous circumstances of the birth of Leotychidas, which would lead to a lame kingship if he were chosen.[88] The influence of Lysander was so great that the Spartans settled the question then and there, without even referring it to Delphi for clarification, although they could have done so. They chose Agesilaus over Leotychidas, and in so doing they gave their support to the favorite of Lysander and thus also to his policies.[89]

Several aspects of this sequence of events make it quite clear that the succession was primarily a political matter in which different Spartan factions had a paramount interest. At Heraea, when literally on his deathbed, Agis was persuaded to recognize Leotychidas' claim to the throne. When Agesilaus challenged Leotychidas, Diopeithes conveniently brought forth the oracle warning Sparta to beware of a lame kingship, an all too obvious attempt to vitiate Agesilaus' claim to the throne. Then Lysander intervened with his interpretation, which the Spartan assembly found persuasive. Behind these facts there is evidence of much intrigue, of plot and counterplot, to control the succession to the throne. Why was this question of such apparent importance at Sparta, and what was Agesilaus' role in the affair?

At Sparta, of course, the kings had the very important function of conducting armies in the field.[90] In this function they often had the occasion to wield considerable influence over foreign affairs. Thus the choice of a new king, if a choice were possible, had political implications of the first order. Several political groups had been struggling for control of Spartan foreign policy for some time before this, headed by King Pausanias, King Agis, and Lysander.[91] The groups led by the latter two men generally tended to favor a more aggressive policy and had

[87]Xen. 3.3.3; Plut. *Ages.* 3.3–4, *Lys.* 22.5.

[88]Xen. 3.3.3–4; Plut. *Ages.* 3.5, *Lys.* 22.6; Nepos, *Ages.* 1.5.

[89]Plutarch, at *Lys.* 22.6, stresses the influence of Lysander in effecting the election of Agesilaus; Pausanias (3.8.10) and Nepos (1.5) agree with him. For Xenophon, this influence is minimized in the *Hellenica,* and it is ignored in the *Agesilaus.*

[90]Xen. *Lac. Pol.* 13 *passim;* see J. F. Lazenby, *The Spartan Army* (Chicago, 1985), pp. 20, 24–26, 28–29, and 37, for discussion of this function of Spartan kings. See also chap. 2 below.

[91]See Hamilton, *SBV,* pp. 79–88, for detailed discussion.

been able to combine forces against Pausanias. If a king susceptible to Pausanias' influence or ideas were to be chosen, the choice could seriously hinder Lysander's policies. In any case, there is no doubt whatsoever that Lysander was squarely behind Agesilaus. The prince was generally considered to have been under Lysander's influence, and the vote in his favor must be interpreted as a vote for Lysander's policies. We must ask, however, whether Agesilaus was anything more than a passive instrument that Lysander manipulated in the struggle for the throne.

In Xenophon's version, Agesilaus seems to take the initiative in challenging Leotychidas after Agis' death, with Lysander intervening only at the point when the meaning of the oracle of the lame kingship is debated. Plutarch, however, attributes to Lysander the original idea of urging Agesilaus to seek the throne and represents many of those who supported Agesilaus as adopting Lysander's plan. It seems improbable that Agesilaus was a mere tool, a creature of Lysander's plot; his own well-attested ambition alone would seem to rule this out. In all likelihood Agesilaus, already considering the possibility of successfully challenging Leotychidas for the throne at the news of Agis' illness, welcomed Lysander's offer of support in his endeavor. Xenophon's account—which in any event tends to downplay the role and importance of Lysander in Spartan history after his victory over the Athenians—therefore omitted this prior aspect of the support of Lysander in order to minimize Agesilaus' debt to him and his political influence. The account of Plutarch, somewhat fuller and also less biased in Agesilaus' favor and against Lysander, is likely to be closer to the truth.[92]

We should not fail to note two significant aspects of the dispute over the throne, at least as far as Agesilaus is concerned. First, Agesilaus' debt of gratitude to Lysander for his decisive support, which Plutarch comments on but about which Xenophon is silent, is important. The succession to the throne, although hardly undesired by Agesilaus, was not something he could have counted upon, not to mention achieved, without Lysander's aid. This was a great event in the life of Agesilaus, who must have experienced a marked sense of gratitude to his friend and mentor on this occasion. Second, the debate over the correct interpretation of the oracle refocused attention on the lameness of Agesilaus.

[92]The fact that Xenophon omits Lysander's role in interpreting the oracle in his *Agesilaus*, which he recounted in the *Hellenica*, seems to support my view here. Plutarch, at least in the *Agesilaus*, provides clear evidence, derived from a source other than Xenophon, that Lysander played a key role from the beginning in Agesilaus' election.

The entire body of Spartiates heard it asserted (at least by implication) that his disability made him incapable of carrying out the functions of the king and that the god had warned them about this. Even though Lysander's less literal interpretation won out, it must have been painful and embarrassing for Agesilaus to have listened to a discussion of his infirmity, which no doubt brought back much of his youthful anxiety about inadequacy and rejection. Thus, his reign began with doubts in the minds of at least some Spartans about the wisdom of their choice; years later, after the Thebans' invasion of the Peloponnesus, many Spartans attributed Sparta's setbacks to the selection of Agesilaus, which they believed had been based on an incorrect interpretation of the oracle.[93] Once secure on the throne, Agesilaus banished Leotychidas from Sparta as illegitimate and seized the estates and possessions of Agis, which he distributed in large measure to the poor relations of his own mother's family. In this way Agesilaus tried to fend off possible criticisms that he had sought the kingship because of personal greed.[94] His act, of course, had the further effect of binding his relatives even more closely to him out of gratitude for his generosity.

Within a year or two of his accession, Sparta received news that the Persians were making great naval preparations to threaten Greece.[95] The Spartans had an army in the field in Asia Minor under the command of Dercylidas, who had just recently made a truce with the satrap Tissaphernes in order to consider terms for a permanent settlement of the war.[96] The news of the naval preparations alarmed the Spartans and their Greek allies all the more, therefore, because they feared that the Persians intended to launch an expedition across the Aegean to Greece itself. Lysander conceived the idea of sending a Greek force to Asia Minor, under the command of Agesilaus, to augment the army already there and to carry the war to the enemy. He proposed his plan to Agesilaus and persuaded him. Lysander also wrote to his numerous friends in the Greek cities of Asia Minor, instructing them to request that the king be sent out to their aid. Lysander had an ulterior motive in this enterprise. Many of his former supporters and protégés in Asia Minor were being banished or even put to death by the citizens, as a result of the ephors' recent decree restoring the ancestral constitutions to these cities. Thus he wished to return to Asia Minor in order to re-

---

[93]Plut. *Ages*. 30.1.
[94]Plut. *Ages*. 4.1.
[95]Xen. 3.4.1; Plut. *Ages*. 6.1.
[96]Xen. 3.2.12–20.

establish them in power.[97] His proposal called for the establishment of thirty Spartiates as advisers to accompany the king, two thousand *neodamodeis* (freed helots), and six thousand Peloponnesian allies; he naturally assumed that he would be among the councillors. These plans succeeded, and Agesilaus prepared to sail early in 396 with his army, and with Lysander at the head of the thirty Spartiates. How Agesilaus felt about the undertaking seems clear enough. It was to be the first of his many military campaigns, and he was excited by the prospect of an independent command at long last.[98] As Plutarch suggests, he had much to thank Lysander for, and it is evident that Agesilaus recognized his debt initially: the very idea of the campaign, its organization, and the skillful maneuverings that secured its approval by the Spartan assembly were all due to Lysander.[99]

At the outset of the expedition, Agesilaus had high expectations of what he would achieve, as well as a grandiose and exalted view of his own position. In his conception, the expedition was to be a panhellenic undertaking against the common enemy, the Persian Empire.[100] Sparta had invited its various allies to contribute troops to the army, but the Thebans in particular were among those who had refused to participate. Their refusal changed the character of Agesilaus' expedition from a panhellenic enterprise led by a Spartan king to a Spartan operation to which Sparta's more submissive allies subscribed.[101] Despite this disappointment, Agesilaus still nurtured fond hopes of earning a great reputation for himself. While his forces were gathering at Geraestus, on the southern tip of Euboea, he himself determined to go to Aulis, in Boeotian territory, to sacrifice just as Agamemnon had done before sailing to Troy. The significance of this gesture could not be lost on any of the Greeks. The legendary episodes of the Trojan War were known to all of them, and the Homeric corpus formed a common body of literature at the center of Greek education.[102] Thus, both the intention and desire of Agesilaus were clear: he likened himself to Agamemnon leading a second great panhellenic expedition against the hereditary Asian foe, and he longed for the fame, glory, and prestige that Agamemnon had

[97]Plut. *Lys.* 23.1–2, *Ages.* 6.1–3; Xen. 3.4.2–3, 7. See chap. 4 below.

[98]Xen. *Ages.* 1.7–8.

[99]Plut. *Lys.* 23.2.

[100]Plut. *Ages.* 6.4. This is at least the way Plutarch depicts his views. See chap. 4 below for further discussion.

[101]Xen. 3.4.3–4.

[102]Plato, *Pol.* 606E; see W. Jaeger, "Homer the Educator," in *Paideia: The Ideals of Greek Culture,* 2d ed. (New York, 1945), 1:35ff.

acquired. It did not matter that the actual force at his disposal was only a modest one by contemporary standards and that the nonparticipation of some Greeks, such as the Thebans, diminished the panhellenic character that he hoped to impart to his expedition.[103] The ego of the king and his great ambition to achieve fame and glory stand out above all. Thus, seen in this context, the sequel at Aulis is all the more striking.

There are two accounts of the incident at Aulis; one is furnished by Xenophon in the *Hellenica* (he omits the incident entirely in his *Agesilaus*), the other by Plutarch. Xenophon relates that Agesilaus traveled to Aulis expressly in order to sacrifice where Agamemnon had sacrificed before sailing to Troy.[104] Learning of Agesilaus' arrival, the Boeotian magistrates sent cavalry to prohibit this, and they threw down from the altar the victims which had already been offered. Agesilaus called the gods to witness their impiety and then departed in anger. Plutarch's version differs in several respects.[105] He says that Agesilaus traveled to Aulis and spent the night, without giving any reason for this action. That night Agesilaus had a dream which reminded him that he was the only Greek chosen to command all the Greeks since Agamemnon and that he was setting out against the same enemy. He was then ordered to offer the same sacrifice as Agamemnon had. Upon awakening, the king related this dream to his friends and determined to offer sacrifice, but not a grisly one, such as Agamemnon had performed in immolating his daughter Iphigeneia. Agesilaus had a deer prepared and ordered it sacrificed by his own priest, instead of the one customarily appointed by the Boeotians. The Boeotarchs were angry when they heard of this and sent officers to forbid his sacrificing contrary to Boeotian custom. The envoys also cast down the victim from the altar, thus ruining the sacrifice. Agesilaus sailed away, distressed on two counts: his anger with the Boeotians and his fear that his expedition would not succeed because of this ill omen. Plutarch's account, as the more detailed and circumstantial one, deserves some credence, even though it is much later than Xenophon's abbreviated version.[106]

---

[103]Xen. 3.4.4; Plut. *Ages.* 6.4–5; Paus. 3.9.2–3.

[104]Xen. 3.4.3–4.

[105]Plut. *Ages.* 6.4–6.

[106]Could Plutarch here derive from some local Boeotian source, which would have had an interest in Boeotian religious customs, and preserved the detail about the priest? Although this would be difficult to prove, it is at least a plausible suggestion. For a discussion of the sources behind our late, extant writers, and particularly for the suggestions of a Boeotian source for Plutarch in this period, see H. D. Westlake, "The Sources for the Spartan Debacle at Haliartus," *Phoenix* 39 (1985):119–33, at 122–23.

The detail about the dream, missing in Xenophon, is reminiscent of the earlier biographical detail that Plutarch provides. In classical Greece, dreams, like oracles, were often held to represent communication from gods to human beings.[107] Thus Agesilaus' claim to have been likened to Agamemnon in a dream, a divine revelation if one wishes, tends to emphasize his own sense of self-importance with its egotistic self-pride. The episode betokens more than a little hybris on the part of Agesilaus, and his nemesis is foreshadowed. Plutarch depicts Agesilaus' choice of his own seer to perform the sacrifice instead of the one customarily appointed by the Boeotians as an insolent act rather than as a merely thoughtless one. Therefore it puts him in the wrong and virtually justifies the Boeotarchs in spoiling his sacrifice. Plutarch's account— which may well have originated in a partisan Boeotian version of the incident which was designed and released as propaganda to depict the Boeotians as innocent victims of Spartan arrogance—may nonetheless reflect what happened more accurately than the very summary version of Xenophon, which omits some aspects less flattering to Agesilaus.

The rejection at Aulis had a deep and lasting impact upon Agesilaus. He was publicly rebuffed and insulted by the Boeotian officials, and this wounded his pride. Furthermore, his sacrifice had been spoiled, with possibly serious consequences for his expedition. Perhaps even more significant was the fact that Agesilaus had no immediate means of responding to this act. He offered no resistance to the Boeotians' act, but he did call upon the gods to witness the impiety of the spoiling of the sacrifice as he sailed away to join the forces gathering at Geraestus. Agesilaus did not forget the matter, however, and ample evidence suggests that it affected him deeply.

The Rejection of Lysander

Upon the arrival of Agesilaus in Asia Minor, the stage was set for his break with Lysander. The ostensible purpose of Agesilaus in leading his army there was to protect the Greek cities from Persian aggression and to strike a preemptive blow against the Persian preparations that had been reported from Phoenicia.[108] The satrap Tissaphernes, learning of

---

[107]Cf. Homer, Iliad 2.1–34. See the issue of Ktema 7 (1982) ("Le rêve dans les sociétés antiques") devoted to the role and importance of dreams in antiquity. See also F. E. Brenk, "The Dreams of the Lives," in In Mist Apparelled: Religious Themes in Plutarch's "Moralia" and "Lives" (Leiden, 1977), pp. 214–35, at p. 228 and p. 232 esp.

[108]Xen. 3.4.2, Ages. 1.6–8; Plut. Ages. 6.1, Lys. 23.1–2.

the king's installation at Ephesus, sent him a message proposing a truce and an agreement whereby the Greek cities would be free; until Tissaphernes could secure approval from the Great King, however, he asked Agesilaus to refrain from any hostile military activity. It is at least mildly surprising, in view of the grandiose designs imputed to Agesilaus at Aulis, to find the king agreeing to a three-month truce, but there is no reason to doubt Xenophon's report or the reality of this truce. Xenophon suggests that Agesilaus realized that Tissaphernes was playing false with him, but that he wished to permit the Persian to foreswear himself in the sight of the gods. We might suppose that Agesilaus also had business enough in settling affairs among his Greek dependent allies and that he was content to enjoy a brief period of acclimatization before engaging in battle. In any case, the truce was signed, and Agesilaus continued to observe his oath even after it was quite apparent that Tissaphernes was only using the time to strengthen his forces with additional troops from the interior of the Persian Empire.[109]

Agesilaus was not idle during this time. The situation in the Greek cities was unsettled and demanded his attention. The governments were neither democracies, as in the time of the Athenians, nor decarchies, as under Lysander.[110] According to the ephors' decree of 397, the ancestral constitutions were to be reestablished, and in many cities the former partisans of Lysander, who had been left in control in 404, were being driven out or even killed by their fellow citizens because of rancor over their misconduct and harsh rule as decarchs.[111] It was to aid these very people that Lysander had planned this expedition, and, naturally enough, many of them turned to him for support and to request various favors. Agesilaus, who initially seemed unimportant because he was unknown locally and remained passive while Lysander became the center of attention, quickly grew to resent the situation. Xenophon reports that the others among the thirty Spartan councillors of the king grew angry with the pride and insolence of Lysander, who arrogated to himself the role of mediator in local quarrels and referred his clients to Agesilaus in the expectation that the king would meekly grant and approve anything he recommended.[112] Xenophon says that at first Agesilaus kept his own anger secret, acting only when the other Spartans came to him and demanded that he curb Lysander and put an end to

[109]Xen. 3.4.5–6, *Ages.* 1.10–13; Plut. *Ages.* 9.1–2; Nepos *Ages.* 2.3–5.
[110]Xen. 3.4.7.
[111]Xen. 3.4.2, cf. 7; Plut. *Ages.* 6.1. See Hamilton *SBV*, pp. 128–29 and 131–32.
[112]Xen. 3.4. 7–8.

Agesilaus' campaigns in Asia Minor

the situation, which was demeaning both to him as king and to them as councillors of equal rank with Lysander. Thus, in this version, the king's actions result from legitimate grievances, raised by his councillors, and the motif of Agesilaus' personal anger and disappointment at thus being relegated to a secondary place is downplayed.

Plutarch portrays the conflict differently.[113] His account emphasizes the contrast between the attention given to Lysander, because of his previous role in Asia Minor, and the treatment of Agesilaus, who appeared to be only the nominal commander, while the real power and influence lay with Lysander. Plutarch also points up the differences between Agesilaus' plain and unassuming behavior and Lysander's brusque, overbearing demeanor. While noting that the Spartan councillors were offended at being treated as Lysander's subordinates, Plutarch also stresses that Agesilaus himself cherished his own ambitions and feared that, if he did not check Lysander's pretensions to power, any success that the expedition might achieve would be credited to his "advisor" rather than to the king himself.[114] Thus, Agesilaus acted.

Agesilaus set about systematically checking Lysander, but it is notable that he neither confronted Lysander directly with his complaints, nor attempted to negotiate a resolution of their differences. Instead, he adopted a more circuitous course.[115] First, he opposed the advice of Lysander and ignored all of his plans or suggestions. Next, he denied any petition that he thought might have been seconded by Lysander. Finally, in any lawsuit brought before him, Agesilaus found in favor of anyone whom Lysander opposed, and against all those championed by him. When Lysander, no dullard, perceived the situation, he revealed it to his friends and advised them to pay court directly to the king. Agesilaus interpreted this approach as an attack designed to arouse anger against him, and he then decided to humble Lysander further, and now no longer by indirect means. He appointed him to the servile position of meat carver at his table. Thus was Lysander's humiliation complete.

Plutarch is always interested in character, and his assessment of the conflict between Agesilaus and Lysander is perceptive and revealing. Plutarch notes that Lysander finally took the initiative in confronting Agesilaus directly, saying "I see, Agesilaus, that you know very well

---

[113]Plut. *Ages.* 7.1–3, *Lys.* 23.3.
[114]Plut. *Ages.* 7.3.
[115]Xen. 3.4.8–10; Plut. *Ages.* 7.4–8.3, *Lys.* 23.5–9.

how to humiliate your friends." Agesilaus responded that he did, "or at any rate those who pretended to be more powerful than he." After this Lysander sought and received a command far away from the king's presence, in the Hellespont, in order to minimize the potential causes of friction between them. But, Plutarch continues, Lysander could not forgive the king for the insult done to him and continued to nurse his resentment.[116] Indeed, from that moment on, until his death, he plotted to deprive the two royal families of their hereditary right to the throne at Sparta, and he most likely would have caused a great disturbance in Spartan internal affairs by his plotting had he not died soon after at the Battle of Haliartus in 395.[117] Shortly before his death, however, upon his return to Sparta in spring 395, when his term as councillor expired, Lysander set about forming a faction of his supporters in Sparta who were opposed to Agesilaus.[118]

Plutarch clearly disapproves of Lysander's actions, adding the general remark that "ambitious spirits do far more harm than good in a state, unless they can keep their aspirations within limits." Plutarch also remarks that Agesilaus "could surely have devised some less objectionable way of correcting the faults of a man of his [Lysander's] reputation and aspiring disposition."[119] The failure of Agesilaus was his inability to suffer being ignored by his comrade; once again, his deep-seated need to achieve recognition, his great thirst for fame and glory, and his pride and ambition seem to have overwhelmed him and to have driven him to an irrevocable break with his former friend, comrade, and mentor.

The rejection of Lysander's influence was a significant turning point in Agesilaus' career. Before this, Lysander had stood at his shoulder, influencing and manipulating events in the king's public career; he played a crucial role in the struggle for the accession, as well as in the planning of the expedition to Asia Minor. Agesilaus' assertion of his own power and his mastery of the situation in Asia Minor at the expense of Lysander's enmity were cold and ruthless acts. No matter how he acted, Agesilaus might not have been able to assert his own independence and maintain the friendship of Lysander, although Plutarch's censure that he ought to have found a different way to correct Lysander's faults suggests otherwise. The more important fact is that

[116]Plut. *Lys.* 24.3–27.1, *Ages.* 8.2–3. I. Scott-Kilvert, trans., *The Age of Alexander: Nine Greek Lives by Plutarch* (Harmondsworth, Eng., 1973), p. 32.

[117]Plut. *Lys.* 24.3–27.1, *Ages.* 8.3.

[118]Plut. *Ages.* 8.3 and 20.2.

[119]Plut. *Ages.* 8.4; cf. *Lys.* 23.4–5. Scott-Kilvert, trans. *The Age of Alexander,* p. 32.

Agesilaus made no attempt to do so. His decision was calculated and final, leaving no room for accommodation between his pride and ambition and that of Lysander.[120] Agesilaus' emancipation from Lysander's influence was total, and it had its roots in his early and driving need for acceptance, recognition, respect, and, finally, fame and glory. Thus had he responded to his boyhood problems and thus he now responded to what appeared to him as a similar challenge to his first great opportunity to make his mark in history. Agesilaus could not bear to stand in Lysander's shadow and to risk having the credit for what his expedition might achieve go to his ambitious and powerful colleague; nor, now that he was king and the state's duly appointed commander in chief, did he see why he should suffer such a fate.

We should note again the differences between the accounts of this episode in Xenophon and Plutarch. Xenophon portrays Agesilaus' conduct as neither unreasonable nor unjustified. He emphasizes the complaints against Lysander lodged by his fellow Spartan officers, rather than Agesilaus' anger at being ignored and losing face. He omits any reference to Agesilaus' deliberately demeaning appointment of Lysander as his meat carver. The break between the two is played down, and Lysander is made to admit his fault and seek Agesilaus' pardon. Finally, no mention is made of the resentment of Lysander, his subsequent plotting against Agesilaus, or the Spartan faction that Lysander formed against Agesilaus. So much for the *Hellenica*. Xenophon does not record any of these events in his *Agesilaus*. Plutarch, in contrast, provides what appears to be a more balanced version, in which the characters of Lysander and Agesilaus are analyzed. It is because of Plutarch's details that we can form the less flattering picture of Agesilaus that has emerged in this analysis. Because Xenophon is patently trying to portray his hero in the best light, and because Plutarch was interested in character and moral qualities in his subjects, I find no reason not to accept the details that the latter provides as genuine and probably deriving from either Ephorus or Theopompus. While these details detract from the idealized picture of Xenophon, they allow us to view a complex and much more believable personality.

Let us attempt to summarize the principal elements of Agesilaus' personality and character as they appeared at the beginning of his

---

[120]Plut. *Ages*. 8.4. "As it was, it seems to have been due to the same passion that the one would not recognize the authority of his superior, nor the other endure being ignored by his friend and comrade." B. Perrin, trans., *Plutarch's Lives* (Cambridge, Mass., 1917), vol. 5, p. 21.

independent career, when he emancipated himself from Lysander's control. Toward his fellow citizens, Agesilaus displayed a number of qualities which endeared him to them: simplicity in his personal tastes and a disdain for material comforts; a sense of humor and laconic wit that seems to have delighted many of them; and a deep sense of loyalty, obedience, and devotion to the state, which ranked high among the Lycurgan virtues. These qualities had helped him secure the throne and the command of the expedition to Asia Minor. His abilities as a military commander were as yet unrevealed, but in the campaigns in Asia Minor he showed himself a good leader of men, genuinely concerned with their welfare and the conditions of their service while on campaign, if not a brilliant general. His personal popularity with his troops (of whom very few were at this point Spartan citizens), his bravery, and his unquestionable patriotism, formed the basis for his increasing influence in Sparta upon his return from Asia Minor in 394.[121] Behind Agesilaus' apparently modest demeanor burned a fierce ambition to achieve a name for himself through military accomplishments, if not on a heroic or legendary scale, at least equal to those of any of his contemporaries— and this ambition meant, above all, that he must emulate Lysander. Perhaps it was imperative for him to break with Lysander in order to achieve his own reputation, but certainly he was unable to brook what he took to be the latter's insolent and disdainful treatment of him among the Greeks at Ephesus. His sense of pride was linked to the obstacles he had to overcome in order to reign in Sparta, as well as to early feelings of inadequacy and fear of rejection.

Agesilaus wished above all to be noticed, to be accepted, to be approved, and he sought to achieve this not by his dress or his demeanor, but by his acts and his accomplishments, whether in athletic contests, in warfare, or in civic dealings with his fellow Greeks. His need was so great that he was capable of terminating a relationship of long duration, which had brought him many benefits, when it seemed to threaten his pride and ambition. It is doubtful that Agesilaus understood fully the nature of these forces within him. Although his treatment of Lysander was certainly a calculated response to what he perceived as threatening and provocative behavior, to an impartial analyst it seems an inappropriate and excessive reaction. And this sort of be-

---

[121]Plutarch says unequivocally (*Ages.* 21.1) that Agesilaus had become the most powerful man in Sparta within a few years of his return from Asia Minor, as a result of which he was able to arrange the appointment of Teleutias, his half-brother, as navarch.

havior was typical not only of his relations with those whom he viewed as threatening to him but also of the way he treated those who appeared useful to him. Examples abound of such curious behavior throughout his career. The tensions within Agesilaus betoken a passionate nature capable of severe overreaction to circumstances, as well as inappropriate, exaggerated responses, especially when questions of honor, esteem, and importance are at stake for him. The complexity of the personality of Agesilaus either escaped his friend Xenophon, or, more likely, the latter deliberately chose to ignore some of the more enigmatic aspects of his hero's behavior in writing about his career.[122] But no amount of omission on Xenophon's part could alter the reality of the personality of Agesilaus, and others produced versions of his career which preserved much of the less flattering side of his reign. Although these accounts are now unfortunately lost, Plutarch had read them and has transmitted enough information to us to permit at least a tentative understanding of the subject.

[122]See Higgins, *Xenophon*, pp. 76–82, for discussion of Xenophon's deliberate attempt to color his hero's life, especially in the *Agesilaus*.

CHAPTER TWO

Agesilaus as
King and Commander

For more than forty years, Agesilaus not only reigned in Sparta but also exerted extensive political influence. We have already noted Theopompus' remark that he was "the greatest and most powerful man in his day," and numerous incidental comments by other writers affirm this evaluation. For example, Plutarch tells us that Agesilaus' success in securing the title to the throne in the disputed election was due in large part to his popularity with his fellow Spartans.[1] Some years later, upon his return from the campaign in Asia Minor, Agesilaus was able to neutralize the political opposition that Lysander had formed against him,[2] and by the end of the Corinthian War he seems to have exerted dominant political influence in Sparta.[3] Throughout the 380s, again, it was Agesilaus who more than anyone else directed Spartan policy, and at the time of the celebrated Sphodrias incident his influence was of paramount importance in Sparta.[4] Even after the debacle of Leuctra and the Boeotian invasion of the Peloponnesus, Agesilaus retained enough political influence to direct Sparta's defense.[5] At the end of his career,

[1]Plut. *Ages.* 1.3; cf. 3.3: "Many of the other citizens also, because of the excellence of Agesilaus and the fact that he had been reared with them and shared the agoge, warmly supported Lysander's plan and cooperated with him" (in securing Agesilaus' election). Cf. also Xen. *Ages.* 1.5, which asserts that the state chose Agesilaus because of his birth and excellence.

[2]Plut. *Ages.* 20.2–4; cf. *Lys.* 24.1–2.

[3]Plut. *Ages.* 21.1, cf. 23.2. For detailed discussion, see R. E. Smith, "The Opposition to Agesilaus' Foreign Policy, 394–371 B.C.," *Historia* 2 (1953–54):274–88; and D. G. Rice, "Agesilaus, Agesipolis, and Spartan Politics, 386–379 B.C.," *Historia* 23 (1974): 164–82.

[4]Xen. 5.4.32–33; Plut. *Ages.* 25.1–26.1.

[5]Xen. *Ages.* 2.24; Plut. *Ages.* 31–32.7.

despite a less than impressive showing in the Second Battle of Mantineia in 362, the state chose him to go abroad as a mercenary general to Egypt in order to earn funds with which Sparta intended to hire soldiers for the attempted reconquest of Messenia.[6] Thus it is clear that his prestige and political power in Sparta were both extensive and extraordinarily long-lived; it is all the more remarkable when we recall that more than half the kings or regents of Sparta during the fifth and fourth centuries were condemned to death or exile or met with other checks to their power.[7] How can we explain Agesilaus' remarkable political success?

The ancient sources, regrettably, do not provide a full and complete analysis of this question. But they do contain enough incidental information, direct and indirect, to allow us to perform such an analysis. Agesilaus' political position in Sparta rested on two bases: an institutional one and a personal one. The institutional basis of Spartan kingship involved a series of powers and responsibilities, judicial, political, and military. These functions must be discussed in order to appreciate the institutional limits of Spartan kingship. More importantly for Agesilaus, though, was the personal aspect of his kingship. His personal power derived from a variety of factors, including his personality and charisma, his ideology, his family connections, his friends and supporters—those who constituted his faction—and the methods and tactics he employed to exercise and extend his political power. This chapter analyzes both the personal and the institutional bases of Agesilaus' power.

The Institutional Basis of Spartan Kingship

Kingship in Sparta, which was a legacy from the past, was only one part of the machinery of government and was dual; two royal houses existed, and each supplied one of the two reigning kings. From these observations, one striking conclusion seems inescapable: Spartan kingship was limited, and the power a given king might possess could not be extensive if it was derived from the institution of the monarchy alone.[8]

[6]Xen. *Ages.* 2.28–31; Plut. *Ages.* 36; Diod. 15.90.2, 92.2.
[7]See S. Luria, "Zum politischen Kampf in Sparta gegen Ende des fünften Jahrhunderts," *Klio* 20 (1926):404–20.
[8]See A. H. J. Greenidge, *A Handbook of Greek Constitutional History* (London, 1902), pp. 97–100. Aristotle, *Pol.* 1285a7, says that the power of the kings had been reduced to that of hereditary generals in his day. While Aristotle exaggerates somewhat, there is doubtless truth in his contention that the kingship had been much reduced in power from earlier days. He also says (1271a41) that the office of navarchia was a second kingship;

We shall examine the relationship of the monarchy to the other organs of government—the Gerousia, the assembly, and the ephorate—later; for the moment, let us discuss the implications of the duality of Spartan monarchy. The origins of the dual monarchy have been the subject of much scholarly debate and discussion, from antiquity until the present. It would be unprofitable to review the literature on this subject here, or even to speculate on the origins of the dual kingship itself.[9] Fortunately for us, such speculation is unnecessary.

The important fact is that classical Sparta always had two kings, or, at the least, two individuals who held royal power and exercised royal functions, one from each of the royal houses. The effect of this state of affairs was a de facto limitation of the royal power.[10] It appears that initially the two kings shared power in their collegial functions, such as the conduct of Spartan armies in the field, but by the late sixth century Sparta had decided to send only one king at a time into the field in command of an army, quite clearly to avoid the repetition of a situation in which the veto of one king over his colleague's actions would inhibit *any* direct action.[11] The likelihood is that Spartan kings from different houses often opposed one another, whether from principle or personal rivalry, in a variety of areas of activity in the early centuries of Sparta's history. Certainly, during the classical period, there is ample evidence of opposition between them, and modern scholars habitually write of the rivalry of the Spartan kings.[12]

Concerning the reign of Agesilaus—that is, the first four decades of the fourth century—several scholars have written about Spartan politics in terms of the opposition to Agesilaus' policies, most often centered around the king of the rival, Agiad house.[13] In this period it is clear

---

because the powers of the navarch were primarily military, in the naval arena, here again Aristotle would seem to limit the kings' powers to the military sphere.

[9]See C. G. Thomas, "The Spartan Diarchy in Comparative Perspective," *Parola del Passato* 38 (1983):81–104, for a somewhat speculative explanation of the nature of the dual monarchy. Older literature is cited there.

[10]See P. Carlier, "La royauté Grècque" (Thèse de Doctorat, University of Paris, 1982), in which Spartan kingship is studied in detail. I am grateful to the author for allowing me to read his doctoral thesis in manuscript.

[11]Herod. 5.75.2.

[12]Michell, *Sparta,* p. 113, writes that "the quarrels and jealousies of the two houses were notorious (Arist. *Pol.* 1271a25–27), and it is not hard to imagine the crafty ephors fostering these feelings, especially if either of the kings was young and could be induced to imagine himself slighted by the other."

[13]See Smith, "Opposition," 274–88; and Rice, "Agesilaus," 164–82; and see also J. DeVoto, "Agesilaos and the Politics of Sparta, 404–377 B.C.," (Ph.D. diss., Loyola

that rivalry did exist between Agesilaus and several Agiad kings: Pausanias first and then his sons, Agesipolis and Cleombrotus, and, finally, Cleomenes II, whose reign, though devoid of distinction, was remarkably long.[14] Most modern writers see Agesilaus as playing a leading role in Spartan politics and policymaking as king, whereas the forces of opposition (whatever the issues) tended to rally around the current Agiad, at least until the death of Cleombrotus; under Cleomenes II, there seems to have been no serious challenge to Agesilaus' dominance in Sparta. To a certain extent, Agesilaus and his rivals served as faction leaders within Sparta, and this is not surprising because the royal office gave its holder a quasi-permanent position from which to exercise power and exert leadership. Although the opposition to Agesilaus' policies was not, on the whole, terribly successful, this fact should not obscure the existence of opposition to Agesilaus. Opposition was frequently exerted through his royal rival, although also on occasion by private individuals, such as Lysander or Antalcidas,[15] and Agesilaus experienced the need to overcome this potential limitation to his power that resulted from the dual kingship. For Agesilaus, the dual kingship was an important fact of political life and a significant element in the Spartan polity. King he might be, but monarch in its literal sense, sole ruler, he surely was not.

What powers did the kings of Sparta possess? And what role did they play within the constitution and the political life of classical Sparta? We are fortunate in that we possess a detailed analysis of this topic by a contemporary witness, Xenophon, the friend, admirer, and beneficiary of Agesilaus.[16] His *Constitution of the Lacedaemonians* is of fundamental value to an understanding of the role and position of the Spartan kings. Although some scholars still debate the intention of Xenophon in writing this document, and even whether he was its author, there is little doubt that its descriptions, in particular of the kings' rights and prerogatives, accurately reflect fourth-century practice.[17] Thus this account, as

University of Chicago, 1982). Cartledge, *Agesilaos,* does not discuss Spartan internal politics to the extent that he might.

[14]See P. Poralla, *Prosopographie der Lakedaimonier,* no. 437, p. 77, on King Cleomenes II.

[15]Plut. *Ages.* 20.1–3, 23.1–2; cf. 26.2–3 and *Pelop.* 15.1–3.

[16]See Anderson, *Xenophon,* and Higgins, *Xenophon,* for discussion of Xenophon. S. Hirsch, *The Friendship of the Barbarians* (Hanover, N.H., 1985) also contains a useful discussion of Xenophon, especially in relation to the Persian Empire.

[17]See Carlier, "Royauté," 448–51; and F. Ollier, ed., *Xenophon: La république des Lacédémoniens* (Lyon and Paris, 1934), pp. vii–xi, on the question of authorship and authenticity.

well as other formal descriptions of Spartan kingship, such as that of Herodotus, and incidental references to specific events in which one or more of the kings were involved, can be used to piece together a picture of Spartan monarchy in the classical period.[18] For purposes of analysis, we may categorize the royal functions as follows (although there is some degree of overlap among these categories): religious, military, judicial, and executive-political.

The kings, according to Lycurgus, were given authority to preside over the religious sacrifices of the polis because of their divine descent.[19] They were endowed with certain privileges, including special rations, lands, and water sources, in order to allow them to fulfill these religious obligations.[20] Furthermore, while on military campaign, the king performed numerous sacrifices: before setting out, to Zeus the Conductor; at the frontier, to Zeus and Athena; before dawn, when battle was nigh; and, of course, after the battle had been fought.[21] While most of these sacrifices may seem purely perfunctory, they were not. For example, if the internal organs of the victims of sacrifice did not indicate success when they were examined, the king could declare the omens unfavorable and forgo the encounter.[22] Thus, presiding over sacrifices while in command of the army and interpreting omens gave the king significant latitude regarding when and where to give battle. For example, King Agis turned back to Sparta when, at the frontiers of Elis, an earthquake occurred, which he interpreted as an ill omen.[23] And Agesilaus learned of the impending conspiracy of Cinadon through the interpretation of the entrails of a victim that he had sacrificed.[24]

In the military sphere, the regal power is most clearly seen, and at its most potent. While on campaign, the king was the supreme commander in chief.[25] Herodotus must be mistaken when he asserts that the

---

[18]Herod. 6.56–60; Plut. *Lyc.* 5.6–7.2, 22.4; and Aristotle, *Pol.* 1271a19–27. Carlier, "Royauté," pp. 443–52, discusses the sources on the powers of Spartan kings.

[19]Xen. *Lac. Pol.* 15.2 reports that the divine descent of kings is Lycurgus' reason for granting them religious authority.

[20]Xen. *Lac. Pol.* 15.3–6.

[21]Xen. *Lac. Pol.* 13.2–5; Herod. 6.56, 57.1–2. See W. K. Pritchett, *The Greek State at War, Part III: Religion,* (Berkeley and Los Angeles, 1979), esp. pp. 67–70 for discussion of the role of religion in Spartan warfare, and the king's responsibilities in this regard.

[22]Xen. *Lac. Pol.* 13.3; cf. 4.7.2 and 5.3.14 and Pritchett, *GSaW, Part III,* pp. 78–82 for discussion.

[23]Xen. 3.2.24.

[24]Xen. 3.3.4.

[25]Xen. *Lac. Pol.* 13 is the *locus classicus* for the powers of the king while on campaign;

kings "have the power of declaring war on whom they please,"[26] for in the period discussed here the Spartan assembly, properly summoned and addressed by the ephors, declared war.[27] He may have meant, however, to emphasize the absolute power of the king while on campaign to direct his forces where he wished.[28] Furthermore, while no text directly and explicitly attests to this, disobedience of a direct order would have entailed swift punishment of any Spartan, whether *homoios* (peer), *perioecus* (free, noncitizen), or helot.[29] The Spartan regime was noted for its emphasis on loyalty and obedience, not to mention courage, and it would have been unthinkable for any Spartan to question or refuse an order from the king while on campaign.[30] Thus, the king possessed the power of life and death over his fellow citizens, at least in the military arena.

There was a host of other officers under the king, including several who bore the title of polemarch (war leader), but each took his orders from the king; as Xenophon says, "when the sacrifices were completed, the king summoned everyone around him and issued his order."[31] The polemarch does not seem to have been the highest ranking officer after the king himself; polemarchs, like colonels, were commanders of regiments. The various officers might on occasion be called together in council to advise the king, but his decision was final.[32] Even when two

---

cf. Arist. *Pol.* 1285a. See also P. Cloché, "Sur le rôle des rois de Sparte," *Les Etudes Classiques* 17 (1949):113–38 and 341–81; C. G. Thomas, "On the Role of the Spartan Kings," *Historia* 24 (1975):257–70; and Carlier, "Royauté," pp. 461–62, for modern discussions.

[26]Herod. 6.56.

[27]Cf. Thuc. 1.67, 72 and 6.88; Xen. 6.4.3. See discussion in W. W. How and J. Wells, "Appendix 17," in *A Commentary on Herodotus* (1912; Oxford, reprint, 1968) 2:349; A. Andrewes, "The Government of Classical Sparta," in *Ancient Society and Institutions,* ed. E. Badian (Oxford, 1966), pp. 1–20, discusses this point at pp. 10–12.

[28]Thuc. 8.5.3 attests that King Agis enjoyed such powers while he commanded the forces at Decelea in the Peloponnesian War, being able to send his troops wherever he wished, and to levy men and money, without specific permission from the authorities at home.

[29]See Xen. *Lac. Pol.* 13.5; cf. 9.2–6, in which the consequences of displaying cowardice in battle are detailed. See also Tyrtaeus on this topic. Similar, or worse, consequences probably attended those who deliberately disobeyed military orders. See also 8.1: "We all know that in Sparta they are obedient to the magistrates and laws to the highest degree."

[30]The refusal of the Spartan Amompharetus to follow orders to redeploy his contingent at the Battle of Plataea in 479 was highly unusual, and there were special circumstances on that occasion; cf. Herod. 9.53. See Lazenby, *Spartan Army,* pp. 105–8.

[31]Xen. *Lac. Pol.* 13.5.

[32]See Xen. 3.5.22–23 on the council that King Pausanias called soon after the death of

ephors accompanied the king, they did not interfere with his exercise of military command.[33] The ephors merely observed matters, unless the king invited them to contribute their advice. Upon their return to Sparta, they could bring charges against a king, if they deemed it fit to do so, but they could not effectively intervene against his judgment in the field. The Spartan government imposed upon King Agis a group of ten *probouloi* after his Argive campaign in 418, and these officials apparently had power to check the king's decisions while in the field.[34] Furthermore, the practice of saddling a king with such military councillors seems to have continued, for Agesilaus was given thirty Spartiate councillors for his campaign in Asia Minor in 396; these men, however, served in a subordinate capacity as commanders of specific units, governors, special envoys, or in other ways that Agesilaus directed, rather than as a restraint on his power as commander in chief.[35] In 381 King Agesipolis was also given thirty councillors to advise and assist him on his campaign to Olynthus.[36] Thus, the power of a Spartan king while in the field in command of a military force was virtually unchecked. He might be brought into court on charges upon his return to Sparta, but by then he would have accomplished whatever he had wished (or been able) to achieve.[37]

One function, not strictly military, is closely related to the king's command while in the field. It concerns the conduct of diplomacy.[38] Xenophon tells us that "the sending of embassies, moreover, either to friends or to enemies, is the right of the king;" he makes this assertion in

---

Lysander at Haliartus; and 6.4.15 for that called after the Battle of Leuctra, when the king had died, and the polemarchs took the initiative. On the status of the polemarchs, see Lazenby, *Spartan Army,* pp. 5, 6, and 10, for discussion in support of this conclusion.

[33]Xen. *Lac. Pol.* 13.5: "There are also two of the ephors present, who interfere in nothing unless the king requests it." Cf. Xen. 2.4.36: "For [as] it is customary for two of the ephors to go on campaign with the king. . . ."

[34]Thuc. 5.63, which states that this controlling measure was without precedent in Sparta.

[35]Xen. 3.4.2; cf. 8, 10, and 20 for specifics of administrative duties assigned to these councillors.

[36]Xen. 5.3.8–9.

[37]See the case of King Pausanias, on his return from Boeotia, in 395; cf. Xen. 3.5.25. There is good reason to believe that he wished to avoid a direct confrontation with the Boeotians, and he did retreat after recovering the body of the fallen Lysander. However, Pausanias was tried upon his return to Sparta for failure to execute his orders. See Hamilton, *SBV,* pp. 206–7, for discussion, and Westlake, "Spartan Debacle," 119–33.

[38]On diplomacy in general, see F. E. Adcock and D. J. Mosley, *Diplomacy in Ancient Greece* (New York, 1975); and D. J. Mosley, *Envoys and Diplomacy in Ancient Greece* (Wiesbaden, 1973).

the context of describing the king while in command of a military force.[39] The functions of a general necessarily include the reception of envoys from both enemies and friends while on campaign, and the power to conclude a truce, even if not to make a formal peace. There are numerous examples of such diplomatic activity in the classical period. Agis received envoys from Euboean and Ionian cities that were ready to revolt and made good on a promise to supply them with troops, while he commanded at Decelea, and he received pro-Spartan exiles from Elis during his campaign against that city; Pausanias received envoys from both Athenian factions during his campaign in Attica in 403, and he instructed the Athenians on what to say at Sparta if they wanted to secure an end to hostilities; and Agesilaus himself made several truces with Persian satraps in Asia Minor, Tissaphernes, and Pharnabazus, as well as sending his own envoys on diplomatic missions to various areas in Asia Minor.[40] During the Corinthian War, Agesilaus received Boeotian envoys at Perachora, and after the war he kept in touch with his partisans in Phlius while he was in the field nearby.[41] Thus, there is abundant evidence to prove that Spartan kings in the field conducted diplomacy and concluded truces through the dispatch and reception of envoys. Officially, the king could not conclude treaties or make peace without the approval of the authorities at home, but his negotiations in the field, which were, of course, linked to his conduct of military operations, could be (and usually were) quite significant in shaping the diplomatic and political results of military activities.

Two other aspects of the king's military command deserve note in that they might contribute to his political influence. First, as commander of the army, the king had control over the collection and distribution of booty.[42] In the wake of a successful campaign, he could reward his friends through enriching them with choice items of booty and thus extend and intensify his influence and the loyalty of his sup-

---

[39]Xen. *Lac. Pol.* 13.10. Many scholars have rejected this clear assertion, on the grounds that diplomacy in classical Sparta was the usual preserve of the ephors, and they have followed Weiske in emending the manuscripts so as to negate Xenophon's statement. (Ollier, *Xenophon: La republique,* p. 70, in his comment at 13.10, for example, follows Weiske's emendation.) I do not find any compelling reason to accept this emendation, however, and I follow the analysis of Carlier, "Royauté." Carlier argues (pp. 468–69) that the manuscript reading is not corrupt and that we should accept it.

[40]Thuc. 8.5.3; Xen. 3.2.29; 2.4.31, 35–36; 3.4.6, 10, 25–26, 4.1.2–3, 29–40.

[41]Xen. 4.5.6, cf. 9; 5.3.14, 17, 23–24.

[42]See Pritchett, "Booty" and "Legal Ownership of Booty," in *GSaW, Part I,* pp. 53–92, for discussions of this topic.

porters. He might also increase his personal wealth, although Agesilaus seems not to have done so.[43] He did, however, bring in significant amounts of money to Sparta, at times when the state had great need of such income. Indeed, this was one of the prime reasons for his journey to Egypt in his eighties as a mercenary commander.[44] Second, a king might increase his stature and influence while on campaign by demonstrating his personal bravery and thereby winning the respect and admiration of his fellow citizens. Agesilaus, again, scored points in this way on several occasions and thus increased his prestige.[45] The case of Agis, who narrowly missed being fined and deposed by the people because of his apparently cowardly behavior in the Argolid in 418, demonstrates the opposite side of this coin.[46] And King Pausanias was condemned *in absentia* and deposed for his failure to fight to regain the fallen bodies of Lysander and his troops in Boeotia in 395, although political motives may have outweighed judgments of bravery or cowardice on this occasion.[47] The functions of a Spartan king while in command of an army extend beyond the mere conduct of military operations and afford the ambitious ruler a variety of opportunities to turn military activities to personal and political profit. Agesilaus realized this.

The judicial competence of a Spartan king was not extensive, but it could be very significant.[48] In some cases the king himself presided over proceedings and rendered judgment, whereas in others he merely served as a member of the jury. Let us consider the former category first. The Spartan constitution provided that the kings preside over cases of adoption and of inheritance of heiresses.[49] It is clear that matters such as adoptions, wills, and inheritance were of great importance to the state because they dealt with the transmission of property and the continuity of the family.[50] The evidence does not afford us much detailed information about the functions of the kings in judicial cases such

---

[43]Cf. Xen. *Ages.* 4 *passim,* which praises the fairness of Agesilaus in financial matters and stresses his disinterest in personal enrichment, despite his numerous opportunities to achieve gain.

[44]Xen. *Ages.* 2.31; Plut. *Ages.* 36, 40.1. See Pritchett, *GSaW, Part II,* pp. 89–90, which exonerates Agesilaus of the charge of being a condottiere; Pritchett concludes, rightly, I believe, that his Egyptian expedition was primarily for the purpose of "raising money for the military establishment at home" (p. 90).

[45]At Coroneia, cf. Xen. 4.3.19 and *Ages.* 2.12, most notably.

[46]Thuc. 5.63.

[47]Xen. 3.5.25.

[48]See Michell, *Sparta,* pp. 110–11; and Hooker, *Ancient Spartans,* p. 120.

[49]Herod. 6.57.4–5.

[50]For detailed analysis of this question, see S. Hodkinson, "Land Tenure and Inheritance in Classical Sparta," *CQ,* n.s. 36 (1986):378–406.

as these, and it is likely that often their role was purely routine, amounting to the official recognition of cases of adoption or of the rights of heiresses to receive property. In the fourth century, however, Sparta was undergoing rather significant, although poorly documented, social transformation, which was linked at least in part to economic matters such as property-holding and inheritance.[51] In their capacity as judges in cases such as these, kings had a certain measure of power to influence social change. For example, the decision to reject a claim of inheritance or to ratify an adoption into a prominent Spartan family could have important consequences for the litigants. They, in turn, might feel indebted to the king who had rendered judgment. Thus, at least in principle, here, too, was a potential source of increased personal power for Spartan kings, and we would be extremely naïve to imagine that kings were, in every instance, guided only by strict principles of justice in potentially complicated legal matters. Unfortunately, the more than usually scanty nature of Spartan sources does not allow us to say much more than this.[52]

The other area of judicial activity of Spartan kings was as members of the Gerousia, the council of elders who, with the two kings, numbered thirty. The Gerousia seems to have served as a court of trial in criminal cases for Spartan citizens, and kings, as well as the other members, had a vote. This function of the kings seems to go back to the Great Rhetra itself.[53] Naturally, kings would have had the same right to question witnesses and to address the court that other members of the Gerousia possessed; the ability of the kings to sway the opinion of the gerontes would depend upon their eloquence or their personal influence. Agesilaus carried the decision in two celebrated trials for acts of unprovoked hostility against sovereign poleis, in which the outcomes had grave political and diplomatic consequences: the trial of Phoebidas in 382 after his seizure of the Theban Cadmeia, and that of Sphodrias in 378 after his abortive march on the Peiraeus.[54] Agesilaus seems to have exercised enough influence to affect the outcome of both trials. It is not absolutely clear that

[51]See P. Cartledge, *Sparta and Lakonia: A Regional History c. 1300–362 B.C.* (Boston, 1979), pp. 307–18, for discussion of Sparta's demographic decline, which is not so much a biological as a socioeconomic phenomenon, linked in all probability to matters such as inheritance and property. See also Hodkinson, "Land Tenure," for recent discussion and citations of older literature.

[52]See D. M. MacDowell, *Spartan Law* (Edinburgh, 1986), pp. 123–27, on the administration of justice by the kings.

[53]Plut. *Lyc.* 5.6–6.4; Arist. *Pol.* 1270b36–1271a6.

[54]Xen. 5.2.32–36 and 5.4.15–33; see detailed discussion of these trials in chaps. 5 and 6 below. On the Gerousia, see MacDowell, *Spartan Law*, pp. 127–29.

these trials took place before the Gerousia, but it is probable.[55] The influence of Agesilaus in each case seems based on his popularity and political
power rather than on any particular role as a member of the Gerousia.[56]

In addition, the king played a role as one of the jurors in trials
involving charges against the other king; the other jurors were the
gerontes and the ephors. In such instances, naturally, one king would
have been able to focus the opposition against the other, if the two were
rivals in politics and policy. Just such a development occurred in the first
trial of King Pausanias for failure to execute his duty in Attica, upon his
return from there in 403, when King Agis voted against him.[57] In terms
of judicial activity, a Spartan king could exercise political power and
influence policy by helping to effect the condemnation or acquittal of
his enemies or friends. Agesilaus took advantage of his prerogative on
several occasions known to us, and probably on others as well, whose
record has not survived.[58]

The final area to discuss concerns the executive-political role of the
Spartan kings. Xenophon refers to the executive functions of the kings
in broad terms when he mentions their monthly oath "to uphold the
laws of the polis."[59] Of course, Xenophon puts this in the context of the
oath of the ephors not to diminish the powers of the kingship, as long as
the kings uphold the laws, and there is little doubt that these oaths were
originally introduced to reduce friction between the monarchy and the
ephorate and to facilitate the operations of government.[60] In the classical period, however, the original antagonism that some scholars presume to have existed between these offices still continued as a potential
threat to royal power. Agesilaus made a point of courting the favor of
the ephors by subordinating his own position to theirs in order to avoid
their hostility or jealousy.[61] The royal obligation to uphold the laws

[55]See Cartledge, *Agesilaos*, pp. 136–38.
[56]This interpretation, at least, is the implication of the sources in their depiction of
these trials.
[57]Paus. 3.5.2.
[58]Plut. *Mor.* 191B8 (cf. 209E16 and 807F, and *Ages.* 13.4) relates the request of
Agesilaus that his friend Nicias be pardoned, whether guilty or innocent, of charges
against him. Obviously, this anecdote is meant to suggest that Agesilaus acted in such a
manner often, as Plutarch's comment (*Ages.* 13.3) that "indeed, although in other
matters he was exact and law-abiding, in matters of friendship he thought that rigid
justice was a mere pretext" clearly suggests. B. Perrin, trans., *Plutarch's Lives*, vol. 5, p.
35.
[59]Xen. *Lac. Pol.* 15.7.
[60]See Ollier, *Xenophon: La république*, pp. 73–74, and cf. Plut. *Ages.* 4.2, and *Lyc.*
5.6ff., 7.1ff.
[61]Plut. *Ages.* 4.2–4; cf. Xen. *Ages.* 6.4.

implies some measure of executive competence for the kings while in Sparta, and it has application beyond the tension between the two offices.

Within Sparta the ephors, representing the popular element in the constitution, exercised many executive functions: they received diplomatic envoys, presided over meetings of the assembly, and may have had a role in the meetings of the Gerousia.[62] The kings, however, may have had a role to play as executive officers or political figures in Sparta. We know, for example, that both the kings took the initiative to check the power of Lysander and remove him from command of the expedition to Attica in 403.[63] And Agesilaus, as well as some of the gerontes and ephors, seems to have seized the initiative to deal with the conspiracy of Cinadon in 397.[64] It is highly probable that a popular and prestigious king would have had the opportunity to influence policy and exercise leadership by addressing both the Gerousia and the Spartan assembly. He might also attempt to have ephors sympathetic to him elected to office. One other important role that the kings could play was in addressing the Spartan assembly, which was the army brought together in its political guise. The prime case of such activity is that of King Archidamus on the eve of the Peloponnesian War, when he argued against opening hostilities, whereas the ephor Sthenelaidas spoke to the other side of the issue.[65] Clearly, a Spartan king could wield considerable influence with the Spartan assembly, despite the failure of Archidamus to sway his fellow citizens in 432. Given that Spartan citizens were trained from an early age to give unquestioning obedience to their officers in the military, it is likely that this mentality carried over from the military to the political sphere and that the citizen-soldiers were accustomed to following the lead, in civil matters as well as military ones, of those who led them into battle. No other specific executive functions for the kings are recorded, but their powers were substantial nonetheless.

The Personal Basis of Agesilaus' Kingship

The institutional bases of Spartan kingship were available to all those who held royal power in Sparta; not all used them to best effect. The

[62]See Michell, *Sparta*, pp. 126–31, for discussion of their powers.
[63]Plut. *Lys.* 21.3.
[64]Xen. 3.3.4–8.
[65]Thuc. 1.78–88.

success of a king who dominated the politics of his state and his age, such as Cleomenes I or Agesilaus, depended not only upon the exploitation of those powers, prerogatives, and duties that adhered in Spartan kingship but also, and perhaps to an even greater degree, upon the personal basis of kingship.[66] Despite the conservative nature of his society, the citizen of classical Sparta could not say, as could the medieval Englishman, "The king is dead; long live the king!" Or if he did, it would not mean the same thing. Agesilaus reigned and ruled for forty-one years; his reign is well documented, and his personality dominated his age. Cleomenes II reigned for sixty-one years, a dozen of them overlapping Agesilaus' reign, and we know virtually nothing about him save the length of his reign.[67] Both were kings of Sparta; both had access to the same formal powers and prerogatives of monarchy; and yet Agesilaus became almost legendary in his own day, whereas Cleomenes II was a nonentity. That this should be so, in large measure, because of the nature and personality of these two men, is beyond question. It is imperative, therefore, to examine the personal basis of the kingship of Agesilaus if we are to understand what set him apart from his contemporaries and from many other kings of Sparta.

Perhaps the most striking aspect of the kingship of Agesilaus is his personality. Xenophon never tires of singing his praises, and his quasi-biographical sketch of the king is full of laudatory information about his character and personality.[68] It is abundantly clear that Agesilaus was popular in Sparta among his fellow citizens because of his personality.[69] Plutarch, who used Xenophon's writings, as well as numerous other sources, for his *Agesilaus,* reaffirms and amplifies this conclusion. At the beginning of his study, Plutarch emphasizes those qualities of Agesilaus which endeared him to the Spartans. Because he had gone through the traditional educational system, the agoge, which taught the Spartan citizen-soldier to serve and obey, Agesilaus had no pretensions about his superiority and was on equal terms with the other Spartans.[70] He

[66]On King Cleomenes I, see P. Carlier, "La vie politique à Sparte sous le règne de Cléomene Iᵉʳ: Essai d' interpretation," *Ktema* 2 (1977):65–84.
[67]See Poralla, *Prosopographie der Lakedaimonier,* item 437, p. 77, for references to his reign.
[68]Xen. *Ages.* 1.1: "I know how difficult it is to write an evaluation worthy of Agesilaus' excellence and fame. Still, the attempt must be made. For it would not be fair if, because he was so good a man, for that reason he should receive no praises, not even inadequate ones." Higgins, *Xenophon,* p. 81, wonders if Agesilaus would even have recognized himself from Xenophon's treatment in the *Agesilaus.*
[69]Xen. *Ages.* 6.4.
[70]Plut. *Ages.* 1.3 and 3.3.

possessed a good sense of humor, and his quick wit easily evoked laughter.[71] These qualities, coupled with his cheerfulness and high spirits, even in times of crisis, made him agreeable to many of his contemporaries.[72] Plutarch tells us that Agesilaus was successful in his bid for the throne on the death of his half-brother Agis because of his personal virtues and because he had been raised as an ordinary Spartan and had learned to share the disciplined life of the homoioi. While the matter was more complicated, the popularity of Agesilaus with his fellow Spartans was an important factor in the first political triumph of his career.[73] Indeed, the same virtues that contributed to his success as a leader of troops—his modest demeanor, bravery, honesty, and austerity in tastes and lifestyle—all played their role in his popularity in the political and civic life of Sparta.[74] The lines of distinction between military and civilian life in ancient Sparta were never very clearly drawn, and the Spartan soldier who was loyal and obedient would be likely to display these same attributes toward his king in civil affairs as he did to his general while on campaign.[75]

Agesilaus was aware of his strong points and appears to have used them to advance his prestige and popularity. That this was a studied and calculated pattern of behavior is suggested by the story that the ephors once fined him for deliberately diverting to himself the loyalty that the citizens properly owed to the state.[76] In any case, in commenting on Xenophon's statement that "by obeying his government's will in everything, Agesilaus became so powerful that he could do what he liked," Plutarch claimed that the truth was as follows.[77] Agesilaus took pains to display his respect for the other magistrates of the state, the ephors and the gerontes. Whenever he was summoned to the presence of the ephors, he responded on the double. When they entered his presence, he stood up out of deference to their office. Whenever a new geron was elected, Agesilaus sent him congratulations and presents, so as to win

[71]Plutarch recounts more of the sayings of Agesilaus, many of which are quite witty, than those of almost any other Greek general. See *Mor.* 208C–215A, cf. 190F–191D. This decision of Plutarch's can hardly be accidental; we must conclude that Agesilaus was noted for his wit and sayings.

[72]According to Plutarch, *Ages.* 30, the Spartans chose Agesilaus to mediate the situation of those who had displayed cowardice at the Battle of Leuctra because they trusted his justice and fairness. Furthermore, on hearing the news of the disaster at Cnidus, he cloaked his dismay in order to maintain the morale of his troops. Cf. Plut. *Ages.* 17.3.

[73]Plut. *Ages.* 3.3. But see also chap. 1 above.

[74]Plut. *Ages.* 19.4–5.

[75]See Hodkinson, "Social Order," 254–60, for a useful discussion of this point.

[76]Plut. *Ages.* 5.2.

[77]Plut. *Ages.* 4.1–4; cf. Xen. *Ages.* 6.4.

his friendship and support. Thus, in matters great and small, Agesilaus showed proper respect for the constitutional offices of the state, and thus he won over to his policies and point of view many of those who served in these offices. He exhibited a blend of simplicity, forthrightness, and loyalty which seems to have impressed a majority of his fellow Spartans, although not all fell under his charm.[78]

If the politics of Agesilaus were personal, we have a right to ask who supported him. The answer is that a combination of family members and close friends and supporters formed a core of adherents around the king, and, in this respect, politics in Sparta during the classical period differed little from those of other Greek states, including Athens and Thebes.[79] Family connections were obviously of crucial importance to Agesilaus and, most likely, to his political activities. At the outset of his career, when he had secured election to the kingship over the claims of Leotychidas, Agesilaus banished him as a bastard and confiscated his property and fortune, distributing much wealth to his own mother's family, which had been of very modest means.[80] The latter act doubtless solidified this family's support for Agesilaus and provided him with a dedicated group of political advocates. We can identify some members of the family, including Teleutias, his half-brother.

Agesilaus also sought to gratify his wife's family. It was to achieve this objective that he nominated Peisander, his wife's inexperienced brother, as navarch in 394.[81] Unfortunately, this choice proved disastrous for Sparta. Peisander stumbled into a major naval defeat at the hands of the Persian-Athenian fleet, which cost him his life, and Sparta its naval hegemony.[82] The sources make it absolutely clear that Agesilaus had made a very bad error in appointing his brother-in-law to the position of navarch, which he had done in order to ingratiate himself further with his wife's family. The suggestion is very strong that they were a powerful group within Sparta and that his misguided act had been intended to buttress his support at home. At this very time, Lysander was working to undermine Agesilaus' position in Sparta.[83]

---

[78]The case of Antalcidas comes notably to mind; see Plut. *Ages.* 23.1–2.

[79]On Athens, see B. Strauss, *Athens after the Peloponnesian War: Class, Faction, and Policy, 403–386 B.C.* (London, 1986), pp. 11–41. For Thebes, see *Hell. Oxy.* 12.1–2; I. A. F. Bruce, *An Historical Commentary on the "Hellenica Oxyrhynchia"* (Cambridge, 1967), pp. 109–12; and M. Cook, "Ancient Political Factions: Boeotia 404–395," *TAPA* 118 (1988):57–85.

[80]Plut. *Ages.* 4.1.

[81]Xen. 3.4.27–29; Plut. *Ages.* 10.5–6.

[82]Xen. 4.3.10–13; Diod. 14.83.4–7; Plut. *Ages.* 17.2–3.

[83]Plut. *Ages.* 20.2; cf. *Lys.* 24.1–2.

Consequently, Agesilaus may have taken this action in an attempt to offset political opposition at home.

A further indication of the importance of the role of his kinsmen by marriage is furnished by the career of Agesilaus' father-in-law, Aristomelidas.[84] This worthy had been one of the Spartan judges sent to try the defenders of Plataea who surrendered, at the outset of the Peloponnesian War, to the Thebans and their allies engaged in besieging the town.[85] According to Thucydides, on that occasion the Spartan judges unjustly condemned the Plataeans to death, in order to retain the good will of the Thebans, who wanted Plataean blood. Later, in early 396, before Agesilaus' expedition sailed to Asia Minor, Aristomelidas was once again sent to Thebes as an envoy to try to persuade the Thebans to join this expedition.[86] He was not successful, but it is tempting to think that he had been selected as one of the envoys precisely because he could have reminded the Thebans of his past good offices on their behalf. Again, the link with Agesilaus and his political projects is clear. Aristomelidas is likely to have been one of his suppporters, bound to him by family connections, and also a powerful and influential man in Sparta. While Agesilaus was at the height of his fame and popularity in Asia Minor because of his victories, especially at Sardis in 395, Lysander was fomenting political opposition to him in Sparta out of spite for his humiliation by Agesilaus. Peisander's appointment as navarch may be explained as an attempt by Agesilaus to cover his political base in Sparta. The absence of Agesilaus rendered him incapable of personally countering the opposition's efforts against him, but he might hope that a coalition of supporters at home, led perhaps by Aristomelidas, would defend his interests until his return. Although this reconstruction is speculative, it explains Agesilaus' act toward Peisander better than Plutarch's suggestion that it resulted from uxoriousness.

The final figures, related to Agesilaus, whom we can clearly link to his policies and activities are his half-brother Teleutias and his son and successor, Archidamus.[87] Teleutias was an excellent commander, well-

---

[84]Pausanias, 3.9.3, says that Aristomelidas was Agesilaus' maternal grandfather, but such an identification is difficult to accept because it would make Aristomelidas a man of ninety or more in 396, when he was sent on a diplomatic mission to Thebes. G. F. Hertzberg, *Das Leben des Königs Agesilaos II von Sparta* (Halle, 1856), 235n.19a, suggests that he was Agesilaus' father-in-law, and this emendation seems plausible. See Poralla, *Prosopographie der Lakedaimonier,* no. 134, pp. 28–29, for discussion.

[85]Thuc. 3.53–68; Paus. 3.9.3.

[86]Paus. 3.9.3.

[87]Xen. 4.4.19, 5.2.37–3.6; Diod. 15.21 on Teleutias. On Archidamus, see Poralla,

liked by his men, and his appointment as navarch for 391 seems to have been a political triumph for Agesilaus. The king had been in eclipse for several years following his return to Greece and his narrow victory at Coroneia in 394. Now, in 391, he and Teleutias operated in conjunction by land and sea against the Corinthian port of Lechaion and the Long Walls of Corinth.[88] For the next several years, until his death in the Corinthian War, Teleutias cooperated closely with Agesilaus in military operations.[89] They seem to have been eager to bring the war to a conclusion that would leave Sparta mistress of Greece, and their strategy led in part to this result. Teleutias therefore should be counted among Agesilaus' supporters in Sparta. Finally, Archidamus undertook a number of military campaigns in the 360s, when his father was unable to direct operations. Archidamus pursued goals and objectives similar to his father's, and he was particularly bitter in his opposition to Thebes. Thus, a continuity in policy can be traced from father to son, and it seems clear that the political formation of Archidamus came under his father's tutelage and that he formed a link in the family group that supported Agesilaus.[90]

That family members could provide ties to other political groups, and thus augment one's political power in Sparta, is well demonstrated by the incident of the trial of Sphodrias. That Spartan commander had made an unauthorized march against the Peiraeus, and his act led to a diplomatic crisis between Athens and Sparta. The Athenians demanded that he be punished for his act of hostility and, when he was not, proceeded to form the Second Athenian League. In Sparta there was much division of opinion over the issue, and Agesilaus was thought to have been inclined to vote for the condemnation of Sphodrias, because he belonged to a different political faction. But Sphodrias' son and Archidamus were lovers, and Archidamus pleaded with Agesilaus to use his influence to acquit Sphodrias. This Agesilaus did, with unhappy diplomatic consequences for Spartan-Athenian relations. The sources leave us with the impression that Agesilaus' act was rather stupid, based either on sentimentality or on cynicism about the nature of justice. It is

---

Prosopographie der Lakedaimonier, no. 158, pp. 33–34; and C. D. Hamilton, "The Early Career of Archidamus," *EMC/CV* 26, n.s. 1 (1982):5–20.

[88]Xen. 4.4.19ff.

[89]Xen. 4.8.11, 23–25; 5.1.13–24.

[90]Xen. 6.4.18, 26 for Archidamus after Leuctra; 7.1.28–32 (the Tearless Victory in Arcadia), and 7.4.20–25, Plut. *Ages.* 33; Xen. 7.5.12–13, Plut. *Ages.* 34 (activity in 362); Isocrates 6 (*Archidamus*) *passim* for his opposition to the independence of Messenia in the 360s.

equally possible, however, to argue that Agesilaus acted out of political calculation with respect to internal politics. Perhaps realizing that he was facing serious political opposition at home, he may have adopted his stance toward Sphodrias in the expectation that he would reap political profit in terms of increased support from the associates of Sphodrias. At the least, such an explanation may be seen as one of the factors that motivated Agesilaus to effect the acquittal of Sphodrias.[91]

It is fitting to discuss how Agesilaus went about extending his influence and winning supporters among those not related to him, for it is evident that family members provided no more than a nucleus, at best, for his faction. The sources emphasize that he observed a strict fairness toward his enemies, and we are told that on several occasions he exerted himself to convert personal enemies into friends, especially among the Spartan citizen class. For example, when he returned from Asia Minor he found a faction hostile to him which Lysander had nurtured during his absence. Agesilaus did not oppose the faction and attempt to crush it, but instead patiently set about persuading its members to join him. By a judicious use of favors, benefits, and other such means as were available to him as king, he systematically dissolved the opposition.[92] Agesilaus, who was much older than his fellow king, Agesipolis, son of the exiled Pausanias, deliberately courted the younger man and charmed him into agreeing with his opinion on most matters.[93] It was only after Agesipolis had matured and other Spartans approached him about political matters that he began to exhibit some degree of independence of judgment and opinion.[94] Agesilaus was indulgent to a fault with his friends. He found it difficult to condemn them when they erred, and he all too often associated himself with them in their misdeeds.[95] This policy could, of course, have negative results on occasion, as was the case with Phoebidas.

Despite all his efforts, however, Agesilaus occasionally failed to win over some Spartans. Antalcidas, an able diplomat, is reported to have been his enemy for an extensive period of time and to have opposed his Theban policies particularly.[96] This personal opposition, perhaps grounded not only in issues but also in personalities, still did not

---

[91]Xen. 5.4.25ff; Plut. *Ages.* 25–26.1; cf. Diod. 15.29.6. See the detailed discussion in chap. 6 below.
[92]Plut. *Ages.* 20.2, cf. 19.4–5, 4.1–5.2.
[93]Plut. *Ages.* 20.5–6.
[94]Diod. 15.19.4. See chap. 5 below.
[95]Plut. *Ages.* 5.1.
[96]Plut. *Ages.* 23.1–2, 26.2–3; cf. *Pelop.* 15.2 and *Lyc.* 13.6.

prevent the two from an uneasy political cooperation, as on the occasion of the negotiation and implementation of the King's Peace in 387/6.[97] Furthermore, Agesilaus' friendship could turn to bitter enmity; this had occurred with Lysander. Agesilaus seems to have possessed many personal qualities which allowed him to influence and win over a large number of Spartans. These personal qualities, coupled with his deft exploitation of the rights, prerogatives, and privileges of Spartan kingship, allowed him to exert political influence that, though not always unopposed, was virtually unparalleled in Sparta. Xenophon summed it up when he wrote: "His relatives described him as devoted to his family; his close associates, as a constant friend; those who served him, as ever mindful; those who were wronged, as a champion; and those who endured dangers with him, as a savior second only to the gods."[98]

Agesilaus as Military Commander

It was also largely through his military reputation that Agesilaus dominated the political scene in Sparta. In the military sphere, he had many difficulties to overcome to achieve this reputation. For example, in the late-fifth and early-fourth centuries, Spartan commanders were governed by committees of councillors, who supervised their activities. These commanders also found themselves limited by ever-diminishing resources. For four decades, in the face of such scrutiny and *oliganthropeia* (dwindling manpower), as the demands and nature of strategy changed, Agesilaus maintained and strengthened his personal position.

Several studies of military developments in this period have discussed the military abilities of Agesilaus,[99] and opinions of his political and military abilities have varied. G. L. Cawkwell asserts that Agesilaus was not able to answer the challenges of his day, because his mind was

[97]See Hamilton, *SBV*, pp. 301–25.
[98]Xen. *Ages.* 11.13.
[99]See P. Cartledge, *Sparta;* idem., *Agesilaos;* Hooker, *Ancient Spartans;* J. K. Anderson, *Military Theory and Practice in the Age of Xenophon* (Berkeley and Los Angeles, 1970); J. Ober, *Fortress Attica: Defense of the Athenian Land Frontier, 404–322 B.C.* (Leiden, 1985); DeVoto, "Agesilaos"; C. D. Hamilton, "The Generalship of King Agesilaus of Sparta," *Ancient World* 8 (1983):119–27. On warfare in ancient Greece in general, see V. D. Hanson, *Warfare and Agriculture in Classical Greece* (Pisa, 1983); A. Ferrill, *The Origins of War: From the Stone Age to Alexander the Great* (New York, 1985); V. D. Hanson, *The Western Way of War* (New York, 1989); and the four volumes of Pritchett, *Greek State at War.*

"numbed" by "devotion to the laws of Lycurgus"; J. K. Anderson sees Agesilaus and his fellow Spartans as limited in their strategic concepts; and P. A. Cartledge sees "the few, rich Spartiates" such as Agesilaus as responsible for Sparta's downfall.[100] Against these negative assessments, J. Ober argues that Agesilaus displayed a sound understanding for the tactical warfare of his day, and J. G. DeVoto provides a very positive evaluation of his generalship.[101] Clearly the issue is in need of further discussion; equally necessary is the establishment of parameters by which to assess the generalship of Agesilaus.

Effective generalship in antiquity demanded attention to tactics and logistics, as well as to overall strategy. In addition, the ancient general faced problems that rarely troubled his modern counterpart; in the classical world, the general led his men into battle and risked his life with them as often as not.[102] Agesilaus responded successfully to such challenges as these over a lengthy career. His earliest campaigns were waged in Asia Minor against the Persian king on behalf of the Ionian Greeks; next, he fought during the Corinthian War in Greece against the anti-Spartan coalition of Athens, Thebes, Corinth, and Argos; in the middle years of his reign, he campaigned against the Thebans as the ostensible champion of the idea of Common Peace and then in defense of the old Spartan order in the Peloponnesus; and he spent his last years as a mercenary commander fighting in Egypt on behalf of native dynasts in rebellion against Persia. Throughout the vicissitudes of a long and varied career, Agesilaus experienced and reacted to the political, military and socioeconomic changes that were shaping the fourth century.

Agesilaus was the first Spartan king to command mercenary armies, as well as the more traditional levies of Spartan troops and Peloponnesian allies.[103] He could, therefore, never take for granted the loyalty and devotion of his troops; rather, he had to cultivate their dedication to him

[100]G. L. Cawkwell, "Agesilaus and Sparta," CQ, n.s.26 (1976):83–84; Anderson, Military Theory, p. 6; and Cartledge, Sparta, p. 317.

[101]Ober, Fortress Attica, pp. 38–41, w. nn. 19 and 21; DeVoto, "Agesilaos," pp. 82–102.

[102]On the dangers and grave personal risk to the commander's life in ancient warfare, consider the following cases: King Leonidas at Thermopylae (Herodotus 7.220); the deaths of Brasidas and Cleon at Amphipolis (Thucydides 5.10); Cyrus the Younger's death at Cunaxa (Xen. Anab. 1.10ff.); and Alexander the Great's campaign and wounding in India (Arrian 6.9–11).

[103]Whatever the precise composition of the force commanded by King Agis at Decelea (cf. Thuc. 7.19.2) it appears not to have consisted of mercenaries. The same is not true of naval commanders (e.g., Lysander) in the Aegean in the Ionian phase of the Peloponnesian War. (Cf. Xen. 1.5.3–4.)

and work at maintaining their morale.[104] This situation contrasted sharply with that faced by earlier Spartan commanders. The absolute obedience and loyalty of the three hundred Spartiates who stood and fell with King Leonidas at Thermopylae, quite apart from Herodotus' heroization of their act, was considered a commonplace in the fifth century; Spartan commanders took it as axiomatic that their citizen troops would exhibit unquestioning bravery and immediate compliance with orders.[105] Even those commanders who led forces of helots or neodamodeis during the Peloponnesian War seem not to have had difficulty on this score.[106] In his first command, however, the campaign in Asia Minor, Agesilaus led a very mixed force, consisting of neodamodeis, Peloponnesian allies, Greek mercenaries (the former Cyreians, whom Xenophon had brought from Mesopotamia through Armenia to the Black Sea), and levies of Aeolic and Ionian Greeks recruited from local cities.[107]

Agesilaus managed to win the respect and loyalty of this motley array through a combination of personal traits and apparently sincere concern for his troops. His personal demeanor allowed his troops to view him as one of themselves; indeed, his modest and frugal habits provoked both consternation and derision from those in Egypt whom he went to serve as a mercenary general in his last years.[108] Although the Egyptians found his unostentatious behavior cause for mockery, his own troops loved him for it. For example, the force of Asiatic Greeks which he had recruited during 396 and 395 voluntarily chose to accompany him back to Greece when he was summoned home by the authorities, largely out of personal devotion.[109]

---

[104]The remarks of V. J. Gray, "Two Different Approaches to the Battle of Sardis in 395 B.C.: Xenophon *Hellenica* 3.4.20–24 and *Hellenica Oxyrhynchia* 11 (6).4–6," *CSCA* 12 (1979):183–200, at 187, seem apposite here: Xenophon's "most apparent purpose in writing history was to present paradigms of the good commander, and a most essential aspect of the art of command is to make your soldiers fit, skilled, keen and loyal."

[105]Herod. 7.220ff., and see the epigram for the fallen Spartans: "Go, stranger, and tell them at Sparta, / That we lie here, obedient to their command."

[106]Cf. the campaigns of Brasidas in the Thraceward region in the 420s (Thuc. 4.78–80). King Agis did encounter serious opposition from his troops because of his conduct of operations in the Argolid in 418. But the problem was not that *they* would not march into battle, rather that the *king* avoided an engagement and provoked their anger. On the political implications of this incident, see D. Kagan, "Argive Politics and Policy after the Peace of Nicias," *AJP* 81 (1962):209–18.

[107]Xen 3.4.2; cf. 3.1.4–6, 8. For modern analyses of his force, see H. Lins, *Kritische Betrachtung der Feldzüge des Agesilaus in Kleinasien* (Halle, 1914), and DeVoto, "Agesilaos," pp. 80–82.

[108]Plut. *Ages.* 36.4–5.

[109]Xen. 4.2.1–8; *Ages.* 1.38.

Agesilaus also cared about his troops. Once, when he was campaigning in the Corinthia in 390, he displayed the sort of concern for his soldiers which endeared him to them. While marching his men along the heights across the Isthmus of Corinth toward the Perachora, he noticed that the chill evening air was causing them much discomfort, and he had pots of fire sent up to warm them against the cold. Xenophon, himself a seasoned commander, remarked on this occasion that "Agesilaus won a lot of credit for displaying even in a small matter the most timely consideration for his men."[110] Such touches can win over the rank and file to their commander, as many cases in military annals demonstrate. Furthermore, on numerous campaigns, but particularly in Asia Minor, Agesilaus made it a point to allow his troops to profit from the pillaging that was so much a part of his military activity in that theater.[111] Immediately after the Battle of Sardis, when his peltasts had begun to plunder the enemy camp, Agesilaus surrounded the camp with his hoplites to prevent the peltasts from carrying off more than their fair share of the booty.[112] But Agesilaus also made it a point to provide adequate provisioning for his troops, and he appears to have been just as concerned with this aspect of his role as commander as with providing opportunities for plunder.[113] In sum, his openness and lack of arrogance, as well as his personal solicitude for the conditions of his army, made him popular and well-liked, a man who could command the respect and affection of his troops. But a positive rapport between commander and troops is hardly enough to qualify one as an effective general; much more is needed. Once assured of the loyalty and fighting spirit of his troops, the commander must know how to position them to best advantage in battle.

In the sixth and fifth centuries, Greek infantry battles had tended to be set pieces in which hoplite phalanxes faced off against one another, and cavalry and lightly armed infantry units served as scouts, skirmishers, or protectors of the flanks of the heavily armed infantry. Changes had begun to occur in the course of the Peloponnesian War, with the rise of

[110]Xen. 4.5.3–4.
[111]Xen. 3.4.12; 4.1.20–27; Plut. *Ages.* 19.3 says that the tithe alone of the spoils taken in the Asia Minor campaign amounted to one hundred talents. Ober, *Fortress Attica* (pp. 39–40), stresses Agesilaus' awareness of the economic aspect of warfare, especially in his campaigns in the Corinthia and in Acarnania in 389–88. See also Pritchett, pp. 126–32, "Profits of Generals," in *GSaW, Part II,* for a full discussion of plunder and booty and their disposition in this period.
[112]Xen. 3.4.24.
[113]See Gray, "Two Different Approaches to the Battle of Sardis," 190, for Agesilaus' concern with provisioning.

the peltasts and the use of fortified posts to raid enemy territory.[114] Although Agesilaus engaged in several battles of the classic hoplite type, particularly at Coroneia in 394 and at Mantineia in 362, he spent the major portion of his active campaigning in raiding, skirmishing, and similar "newer style" fighting, which necessitated adapting to newer tactics. We shall consider the battle of Coroneia later, but for the moment let us examine his record with regard to less "conventional" warfare.

Agesilaus showed that he was quite skillful and resourceful in responding to the challenges of his age. For example, he lacked adequate cavalry in his campaigns in Asia Minor and found that as a result he was at a serious disadvantage vis-à-vis the Persians. To remedy this defect, Agesilaus stimulated the local Greeks to raise a cavalry force. The richest men in the districts subject to him were assigned responsibility for providing the horses, and they were exempted from personal service if they paid the wages of skilled horsemen. Furthermore, by offering prizes and awards for the most skillful men and most effective units, Agesilaus not only created a new force to fill an important need but also encouraged the competitiveness of that force.[115] He made effective use of his new cavalry during 395 in ravaging much enemy territory, and this cavalry played a decisive role in the Battle of Sardis.

Agesilaus, moreover, also manifested a high degree of skill in the use of ambushes, feints, and diversionary tactics to meet the conditions in which he operated against the Persians in Asia Minor.[116] In crossing from Hellespontine Phrygia to Mysia, he encountered treachery on the part of the locals with whom he had attempted to negotiate passage of a narrow defile. He responded by laying an ambush, feigning a retreat, and drawing the hostile natives into a trap that cost them dearly and led to their seeking terms.[117] This same tactic of ambush may already have been used to good effect by Agesilaus in an earlier encounter against the satrap Tissaphernes, but on a level plain.[118] It seems quite clear that Agesilaus was adept at adjusting his tactics to both terrain and circum-

[114]See J. P. Best, *Thracian Peltasts and Their Influence on Greek Warfare* (Groningen, 1969), on peltasts; cf. Agis at Decelea on fortified positions.

[115]Xen. 3.4.15–18; *Ages.* 1.23–24.

[116]Xenophon, *Ages.* 6.5–6, speaks in general terms of Agesilaus' skill in the use of such tactics, praising even the use of deception when it seemed necessary and useful.

[117]*Hell. Oxy.* 21.1–2. See the discussion by DeVoto, "Agesilaos," pp. 91–92, and Pritchett, "Ambuscades" in *GSaW, Part II*, pp. 177–89, on the topic in general.

[118]*Hell. Oxy.* 11.2–3. But see the discussion of the problems associated with the battle in chap. 4 below.

stances. The diversionary tactic that had worked so well in Asia Minor Agesilaus repeated with variation during the Corinthian War when he captured the cattle of the Corinthians. On this occasion, in 390, Corinth was at war with Sparta and was defended by contingents of Argive and Athenian troops. Well protected by its thick walls, Corinth defied invading Spartan forces, which lacked the expertise and equipment to conduct an effective siege.[119] The surrounding territory, however, suffered the ravages of enemy invasion, and thus the Corinthians' cattle and movable property had been removed for safety to the Perachora peninsula, where they were guarded by the Athenian mercenary general Iphicrates and his force of peltasts. Agesilaus recognized that his troops, now primarily heavily armed infantry, were ineffective against the peltasts, so he resorted to a ruse to deprive those in Perachora of their military cover. He feigned a retreat as if to launch an attack on Corinth itself, thus drawing away Iphicrates' force from its defensive position in Perachora to relieve the city, supposedly under threat of Spartan attack. Keeping his men out of sight of the returning enemy force, Agesilaus was able to descend rapidly on the defenseless civilians at Peiraeon and to compel their surrender, as well as that of the cattle, foodstuffs, and other valuables.[120]

Siegecraft was the principal area of tactics in which Agesilaus proved deficient. On several occasions while in Asia Minor, he made futile attempts to take fortified towns (Leonton Kephalai and Gordion, in particular), but their defenses withstood his efforts.[121] In Greece proper, he proved unable to besiege Corinth in the 390s or Thebes in the 370s. It would be difficult to argue that Agesilaus exhibited any greater degree of technical ability in siegecraft than any of his contemporaries. However, few commanders in classical Greece were able to take a well fortified town either by storm or by siege.[122]

[119]Xen. 4.2.23; 4.4.1; 4.4.7ff.

[120]Xen. 4.5.1 and 3–5.

[121]*Hell. Oxy.* 21–22. Xenophon (3.4.12) and Plutarch (*Ages.* 9.3) contain assertions, however, that Agesilaus was occasionally successful in taking cities by force. Because few specific examples are given, I think that my judgment is, in the main, correct on his deficiency in this area.

[122]The skill of Alexander the Great in siegecraft, too often underrated, should be viewed as extraordinary in an age when effective siegecraft was the exception. And even Alexander took almost eight months to reduce Tyre by siege, whereas his successor Demetrius was dubbed "Poliorcetes" because of his expertise in a military activity that was still rare at the end of the fourth century. Arrian 2.18ff.; Plut. *Demetrius* 20; 27. On siegecraft, see F. E. Adcock, *The Greek and Macedonian Art of War* (Berkeley and Los Angeles, 1957), pp. 56–63; and A. W. Lawrence, *Greek Aims in Fortification* (Oxford,

On the matter of logistics, little need be said. Logistics were a part of the campaigning of Agesilaus, and the available evidence suggests that he rarely (if ever) experienced difficulty in this area. For example, in Asia Minor—the only area where he undertook lengthy campaigning at great distances from his major base of supply—he routinely sent instructions ahead to the cities on his line of march ordering them to prepare markets for his troops. He must have done the same on his return march to Greece. On numerous occasions he allowed his troops to plunder enemy territory, and this was done, at least in part, to augment his supplies. The sources suggest that in the campaigns in the Corinthia, Acarnania, and Boeotia, either Agesilaus took along sufficient provisions for his troops, or needed supplies were obtained en route, by purchase or plunder. In any case, the demands of the commissariat do not seem to have hampered Agesilaus' military activities.[123]

On balance, therefore, it would seem that Agesilaus exhibited skill, insight, and adaptability in meeting new military situations that demanded tactical innovation; he was at least the equal of most of his contemporaries. Two exceptions come to mind: Iphicrates, who developed peltast tactics, and the Theban generals Pelopidas and Epaminondas, who refined traditional hoplite tactics by massing strength on one wing of the phalanx.[124] Their achievements deserve note, but they do not necessarily diminish Agesilaus' well-deserved military reputation, at least in the area of tactics. His skills as a general formed yet another element of his powerful position as leader within the Spartan state. And it is worth noting that he displayed his abilities to meet the military challenges of his age at the beginning of his career, principally in the campaigns in Asia Minor and in the Corinthian War. His reputation as a general would not be diminished throughout his life.

1979). The fourth-century tract by Aeneas Tacticus, *On Siegecraft*, is also instructive in this regard.

[123]Xen. 3.4.11; 26 (on Tithraustes' provision of thirty talents to feed his army); 4.6.3ff. (on Acarnania). On the general topic of provisioning a Greek army, see Pritchett, *GSaW*, *Part I*, pp. 30–52, and D. Engels, *Alexander the Great and the Logistics of the Macedonian Army* (Berkeley and Los Angeles, 1978), which discusses the difficulties of logistics when on campaign in areas quite remote from one's supply bases. Of course, Agesilaus never undertook a campaign on the scale of Alexander the Great's odyssey, so he did not have to confront supply problems of comparable magnitude.

[124]On Iphicrates, see Hamilton, *SBV*, pp. 281–82; and H. W. Parke, *Greek Mercenary Soldiers from the Earliest Times to the Battle of Ipsus* (Oxford, 1933), pp. 50–57 and 77–83. On the Theban generals, see J. Buckler, *The Theban Hegemony, 371–362 B.C.* (Cambridge, Mass., 1980), pp. 63–64 and 110–129.

The Spartans ended the Corinthian War through negotiation with Persia. Agesilaus had established his military reputation by the end of the war. During the ensuing period of Spartan supremacy, in the face of growing opposition to Sparta by Thebes, Athens, and other states, he limited his role largely to the political rather than the military sphere, and his campaigning was restricted to a lengthy siege of Phlius in the late 380s, as well as to several skirmishes and pillaging raids, most notably in Boeotia in the 370s.[125] Although Agesilaus was clearly responsible for the political and diplomatic scenario that led to the Battle of Leuctra in 371, fortunately for him it was the other Spartan king, Cleombrotus, who led the Spartiates to death and disaster at the hands of the reformed Theban army under Pelopidas and Epaminondas.[126]

We need not examine here the military activities of Agesilaus during the 360s, when Sparta was on the defensive, for this latter phase of his career sheds no new light that would alter in any significant way our judgment of his generalship. He coped heroically with Theban invasions of the Peloponnesus, but was unable to prevent the loss of Messenia, and this event altered Sparta's position for all time. Sparta's failure in the 360s, however, was the result of its demographics, politics, and diplomacy, rather than of Agesilaus' generalship.[127] If, as is probable, Agesilaus failed to perform satisfactorily as general of the Spartan and allied troops at the Second Battle of Mantineia, we should take note that he was then eighty years of age, but also that his reputation was and remained such that within a year or two he was summoned to supervise the military activities of the rebellious Egyptian king in his war for independence from Persian rule.[128]

Agesilaus possessed many important qualities as a general. As a commander of men, whether Spartans, allies, or mercenaries, he knew how to inspire confidence and loyalty. As a tactician, he proved capable of adapting to new circumstances and situations, and he displayed skill and initiative in coping with a wide variety of military problems. As a strategist, he was at his weakest, but even here purely military solutions were rarely possible. To paraphrase a judgment often made of the

[125]See Xen. 5.4.35–41 and 47–55; Polyaenus 2.1.2, 11, 12, 21, 24–25; Diod. 15.31.3–33.4 and 34.1–2 for these expeditions.

[126]See Buckler, *Theban Hegemony*, pp. 53–68, for a discussion of the battle; see also chap. 7 below.

[127]On Spartan demographics, see Cartledge, *Sparta*, chap. 14, and E. David, *Sparta between Empire and Revolution, 404–243 B.C.: Internal Problems and Their Impact in Contemporary Greek Consciousness* (New York, 1981), chap. 2. See also chaps. 3 and 8, below.

[128]Plut. *Ages.* 36.1–2; 40.2 on Agesilaus' advanced age.

Romans, namely, that they lost most of their battles but ultimately won the war—a judgment perhaps more suitable to the Second Punic War than to other wars—it might be said that Agesilaus won most of his battles but failed to achieve lasting victory at the end of his campaigns. His principal faults were not as a general, but rather as a political leader. He lacked political vision and insight into the world outside of Sparta, which, coupled with his blinding hatred for Thebes, caused him to push his state along the road that led to Leuctra.

What, then, were the policies and objectives to which Agesilaus devoted his extensive prestige and influence? This chapter has suggested the basis on which his political power was grounded, and some of the methods he employed to exert his influence. Next, we shall consider his position toward the significant domestic and foreign issues that Sparta faced during his reign.

CHAPTER THREE

The Socioeconomic Crisis
of Fourth-Century Sparta

Within a year of his accession to the throne, Agesilaus was confronted with evidence of a serious crisis within Spartan society, the so-called conspiracy of Cinadon. The principal source for this event, Xenophon, fails to provide adequate information about its origins, its consequences, or even its purpose.[1] Despite his silence, it is clear that the authorities must have become aware of more than we are told in the *Hellenica,* and it is possible to deduce several things from this event. First, Xenophon's narrative reveals almost incidentally the existence of classes within Sparta whose identity is not well-known, as well as the existence of deep-seated social antagonism and resentment.[2] Second, the discussion of this plot suggests a connection with one of the most significant problems that Sparta was to face during the reign of Agesilaus, the ever-increasing lack of manpower, or oliganthropeia, which many ancient sources comment upon.[3] Finally, it is more than likely

---

[1]Xen. 3.3.4–11; cf. Arist. *Pol.* 1306b34.

[2]For example, the class known as the hypomeiones is not mentioned elsewhere in the sources. The antagonism between these people and the Spartiates, in particular, provides an interesting counterpoint to the helot-Spartiate conflict, which, following Thucydides (4.80), is considered by many scholars to be the most serious social tension in classical Sparta. See D. M. Lewis, *Sparta and Persia* (Leiden, 1977), pp. 26–27, and Cartledge, *Sparta,* pp. 214–22, for discussion of Spartan fears of helots. Most recently, this question has been reexamined by R. J. A. Talbert, "The Role of the Helots in the Class Struggle at Sparta," *Historia* 38 (1989):22–40, who correctly concludes that some modern scholars have exaggerated the helot threat.

[3]Arist. *Pol.* 1270a29–32; Herod. 7.234.2; Xen. 6.1.1, 15, 17, cf. 4.15, 17, *Lac. Pol.* 1.1. For discussion, see Cartledge, *Agesilaos,* pp. 37–43, which cites and evaluates earlier literature, and esp. chap. 10, pp. 160–79.

that there was a connection with another trend of the early-fourth century in Sparta, the influx of wealth and its terribly unequal distribution within the state, with increasingly deleterious consequences.[4] Thus, a discussion of the conspiracy of Cinadon and of the reaction of the Spartan authorities to it will be very instructive in our attempt to understand the nature of Sparta in the age of Agesilaus, as well as Agesilaus himself.[5]

The Conspiracy of Cinadon

Agesilaus was performing one of the state sacrifices required of the king when the seer informed him that the omens were bad. Agesilaus repeated the sacrifice twice, with similar results. The seer reported that the omens were just as bad as if they were in the midst of the enemy. Offerings were then made to persuade the gods to avert the evil, and favorable results were obtained only with difficulty.[6] Within five days, an informant who is not identified by Xenophon revealed to the ephors that a plot was being laid against the state and that the chief conspirator was Cinadon. Upon questioning, the informant further revealed that Cinadon had attempted to draw him into the plot by asking him to count the number of Spartiates in the agora and to consider them the enemy; then, to count the others there and to assume that they would join the conspiracy. The Spartiates were outnumbered, the report went, a thousand to one. When the informant asked Cinadon whether all of these men, and others who could be found outside the city on the estates of the Spartans, were actually in on the secret, Cinadon replied that they were not yet recruited, but that this would be easy to do because, whenever any mention was made of the Spartiates in the presence of helots, perioeci, neodamodeis, or *hypomeiones* (Spartans of inferior status), these individuals could hardly conceal the fact that they would gladly eat the Spartiates raw.[7]

When the ephors asked their informant whether the potential rebels were armed, he replied that those such as Cinadon who served in the

---

[4]This phenomenon has been emphasized by E. David, *Sparta between Empire and Revolution: 404–243 B.C.: Internal Problems and Their Impact in Contemporary Greek Consciousness* (New York, 1981), pp. 5–10.

[5]On this conspiracy, see E. David, "The Conspiracy of Cinadon," *Athenaeum*, n.s. 57 (1979):239–59.

[6]Xen. 3.3.4.

[7]Xen. 3.3.5–6.

army had their own weapons, and that the others could easily obtain and use a variety of tools—axes, hatchets, sickles, and so forth—or raid the iron market, where great quantities of tools and weapons were available. As for the date of the event, he replied that he had been instructed to remain in the city. The ephors appear to have become panicky at the news; Xenophon remarks that they did not even convene the "Little Assembly."[8] In any case, the ephors promptly consulted with some of the gerontes, and they decided to send Cinadon off on a mission to Aulon in Messenia, where he could be arrested well away from the city and his co-conspirators. This plan was successfully executed, and Cinadon was forced to reveal the names of his fellow ringleaders. They also were arrested, including the seer Tisamenus. When Cinadon was brought back to Sparta for further questioning and asked why he had organized his plot, he responded that he did not wish to be inferior to anyone in Sparta. He and the others were then bound, scourged, marched through the streets as a lesson to others, and executed.[9] Xenophon's account of the episode closes on this note, with no assessment of any kind regarding the causes or consequences of the conspiracy. Indeed, this is a serious failing on his part, and it is surprising that Xenophon even bothered to recount the story, because it seems to have no relationship to any other part of his history.[10] Although Xenophon failed to make a connection between this event and Sparta's general history, we are not prohibited from attempting to do so. An analysis of this account may shed much light on important aspects of Spartan history in the early fourth century.

Let us begin with the question of the purpose of the conspiracy. Although Xenophon's account does not mention this, it seems clear from the references to the arming of the conspirators, to the military metaphors, and to the hatred of many of the potential rebels toward their Spartan masters that a violent uprising was intended. At the least, attacks on, and the possible slaughter of, many Spartiates seem to have been planned; whether the survivors were to have been exiled or enslaved in some fashion is impossible to say.[11] Nonetheless, the ultimate

[8]Xen. 3.3.8. The identity of this body is questionable, for it is not attested elsewhere, but it has been plausibly suggested that it consisted of the members of the Gerousia, the ephors, and, perhaps, the kings. See P. Oliva, *Sparta and Her Social Problems* (Amsterdam and Prague, 1971), p. 193; and Cartledge, *Agesilaos*, pp. 130–31.

[9]Xen. 3.3.8–11.

[10]See G. L. Cawkwell, "Introduction" to the Penguin translation of the *Hellenica*, entitled *A History of My Times* (Harmondsworth, Eng., 1979) trans. R. Warner, p. 24.

[11]See David, "Conspiracy," 253ff.

objective of the conspiracy was probably to introduce radical changes in the nature of the Spartan polity.[12] At least one of these changes is hinted at in the response of Cinadon that he "wished to be inferior to no one in Sparta."[13] There is no way to tell whether Cinadon wanted the same thing for all those whom he planned to involve in the uprising as he did for himself, although this seems highly unlikely. Part of the answer to this question may lie in the identification of the status he possessed, that of a *hypomeion*.

This term, although recorded nowhere else in the ancient sources, is taken by a majority of scholars to refer to a distinct class within Spartan society. It is generally thought that these people were those who had once possessed the status of full citizens, but who had lost their privileges for some reason, such as failure to contribute to the *syssition* (military fraternity), or cowardice in battle.[14] It is also possible that the hypomeiones—the root meaning of "inferiors" is inescapable in the Greek—may have included others who felt that they had a title to citizenship but who were denied this for some reason; one thinks most readily of Spartan citizens' younger sons who had undergone the training of the agoge but who could not qualify for admission to a syssition because they did not possess the requisite property, perhaps because the family lot had gone to the eldest son.[15] Because we are so poorly informed about these people, any such suggestion is merely speculation, but informed speculation is necessitated by the circumstances.

The Class Structure of Classical Sparta

Classical Spartan society was divided into three major segments: the helots, whose labor provided the economic livelihood of the entire citizen class, and who themselves possessed neither citizenship nor any rights; the perioeci, free members of the state who, although lacking political rights, lived in their own communities according to their own regulations, and who were allowed to carry on trade, manufacturing, and commerce, which was considered menial work, but essential to the state and forbidden to the helots and the Spartiates; and the Spartiates,

---

[12]David, *Sparta*, p. 77, writes that "we are familiar only with the destructive aims of Cinadon's conspiracy. The constructive plans—if there were any such plans at all—remain obscure."

[13]Xen. 3.3.11.

[14]Oliva, *Sparta*, pp. 177–78; Cartledge, *Agesilaos*, p. 170; David, *Sparta*, pp. 48–49 and 75; and Kagan, *Fall of the Athenian Empire*, p. 12.

[15]See Oliva, *Sparta*, p. 170n.1, in which older literature is cited, for this suggestion.

the citizens who were called *homoioi* (peers), because of their alleged equality of education, political rights, and economic standing.[16] It was in reference to the homoioi, apparently, that people like Cinadon were judged inferior by society.

The homoioi were the Spartans *par excellence*, those whom the sources call the Spartiates.[17] Their status derived in the first instance from birth; unless one were the son of a Spartiate, he could not usually aspire to become one of the homoioi.[18] The status of some Spartans who rose to influential positions in the classical period, such as Lysander and Gylippus, bears on this question. They are called *mothakes*, and scholars view them as perhaps the sons of Spartiate fathers and helot mothers, who were marked with a stigma as a result of their birth.[19] The next essential element in the making of the homoioi was the agoge, the rigorous period of training which extended from the age of six to about twenty, during which the young Spartans were subjected to an intensive and exacting education.[20] This education emphasized physical training and fitness, and it included many athletic and military exercises intended to make excellent soldiers of the candidates. The agoge did not ignore the mind in its emphasis on the body, however, and the young Spartans had such qualities as courage, bravery, self-reliance, and obedience inculcated in them by their instructors. The youth were given only the bare essentials to survive during their years of training, and this physical deprivation served to remind them that the state expected them to observe austerity in all their dealings and in their style of life forever.[21] The ultimate objective of this sort of education was to produce a citizen-soldier who was obedient to authority, dedicated to the ideals of the state, content with a frugal existence and uninterested in material things, and, above all, an effective warrior.[22] All who passed through the agoge successfully were expected to conform to values such as these, and all who did were, in this sense, equals.

Upon completion of the agoge, the young Spartan was eligible to

[16]Plut. *Mor.* 237D10, 239D41. For analysis of these three traditional classes, see Michell, *Sparta,* chaps. 2 and 3; Oliva, *Sparta,* pp. 29–62; and David, *Sparta,* pp. 43–50.

[17]Xen. *Lac. Pol.* 10.7, 13.1, 7. See Michell, *Sparta,* p. 35; and David, *Sparta,* pp. 43–44.

[18]See Michell, *Sparta,* pp. 36–38.

[19]See Oliva, *Sparta,* pp. 174–77. The cases of Lysander and Gylippus seem to indicate that birth to both Spartan father and mother was not an absolute prerequisite for citizenship.

[20]For descriptions of the agoge, see Xen. *Lac. Pol.* 2–3; and Plutarch, *Lyc.* 16.4–18.4 and *Mor.* 237A4, 237E12–13, 238A–B. Cf. Cartledge, *Agesilaos,* pp. 25–28, and Hodkinson, "Social Order," 239–81.

[21]Xen. *Lac. Pol.* 2.3–6.

[22]Plut. *Mor.* 237A4.

enter the ranks of the military, but to do so he must first be accepted into one of the numerous *syssitia*. Here another requirement for citizenship had to be met: the possession of income sufficient to allow the soldier to contribute to the annual demands of his syssition. Each member of the syssition took his meals in common with the others, and failure to contribute one's share to the mess resulted in expulsion from the syssition and thus in loss of political rights.[23] Theoretically, therefore, all citizens must also be equal in terms of wealth in order to continue in the exercise of their political rights. Scholars generally recognize, however, that this aspect of Spartan "equality" represents a minimal qualification that has been met, rather than an absolutely equal division of wealth among all citizens.[24] There was actually inequality of wealth among the "equals" for some time before the early fourth century, although in this period, and for reasons closely linked to Sparta's victory in the Peloponnesian War and the imperialist policies that followed this victory, inequality seems to have increased considerably.[25]

The homoioi enjoyed another area of equality, that of their political rights. Every citizen had the right to attend and vote in the assembly and, in this fashion, to shape the policies of his state.[26] Furthermore, each could both vote for and stand for election as an ephor.[27] But in the area of political rights, as in that of wealth, equality meant attainment of a minimal level, rather than an absolute standard that applied to everyone. For example, the two kings of Sparta were citizens, but they came from the two royal families recognized to have descended from Heracles.[28] Thus, the vast majority of Spartans suffered in their political status vis-à-vis the kings. Furthermore, the Gerousia was composed of citizens at least sixty years of age who may have come from a select few

[23]Xen. *Lac. Pol.* 5.2–7, cf. 7.3; Plut. *Lyc.* 10, 12. Cf. Michell, *Sparta,* pp. 38–40; Cartledge, *Agesilaos,* pp. 169–70.

[24]See, on this and related questions, the substantial article of T. J. Figueira, "Mess Contributions and Subsistence at Sparta," *TAPA* 114 (1984):87–109.

[25]See Cartledge, *Agesilaos,* pp. 167–71.

[26]See A. Andrewes, "The Government of Classical Sparta," in *Ancient Society and Institutions,* edited by E. Badian, pp. 1–20 (Oxford, 1966); and W. E. Thompson, "Observations on Spartan Politics," *RSA* 3 (1973):47–58.

[27]On the powers of the ephors, see A. H. J. Greenidge, *A Handbook of Greek Constitutional History* (London, 1902), pp. 102–6. On their election, see P. A. Rahe, "The Selection of Ephors at Sparta," *Historia* 29 (1980):385–401; and the response of P. J. Rhodes, "The Selection of Ephors at Sparta," *Historia* 30 (1981):498–502. See also H. D. Westlake, "Reelection to the Ephorate?" *GRBS* 17 (1976):343–52, which concludes that reelection was not possible.

[28]Xen. *Lac. Pol.* 15.2; Plut. *Lys.* 24.3–5, cf. *Ages.* 8.3.

aristocratic families.[29] Here again the political "equality" of the citizens was more theoretical than real. The complaint of Cinadon, however, does not appear to have been directed at such inequalities as these, for the homoioi did not challenge the privileges of either royal or aristocratic families; rather, he was angry because he was *no longer* one of the *homoioi*. Before we examine the implications of his situation, let us further review the status of the two other traditional classes in Spartan society, the perioeci and the helots.

The perioeci were in many ways indistinguishable from the full Spartan citizens. In origin, it is probable that they constituted some part of the Dorian population which entered the Peloponnesus at the end of the Bronze Age. For reasons no longer clear, however, when the Spartan polis arose, the perioeci were denied citizenship by their fellow Dorians. Instead, the perioeci were left in possession of their own land and allowed to govern their own communities, as long as they did not violate those aspects of Spartan law which regulated their status.[30] The principal functions of the perioeci were to conduct the various activities, both commercial and industrial, that were essential to the survival of the state, but strictly forbidden to the Spartiates. Thus, the procurement of raw materials such as metals and their manufacture into shields, armor, swords, and spearheads, and other military equipment needed by the Spartiate warriors was the responsibility of the perioeci. They also engaged in other crafts that resulted in the production of export items, such as pottery, that could be exchanged for needed imports, as well as in various commercial undertakings, both outside the state with other communities and inside the markets of Laconia.[31]

The perioeci were permitted to live on and farm their own land, both in Laconia and in Messenia, and presumably the majority of them were not too badly off, for we have little evidence that they were dissatisfied with the system under which they lived.[32] The socioeconomic system gave them a virtual monopoly on trade and manufacturing, because both helots and Spartiates were prohibited from engaging in these

---

[29]Xen. *Lac. Pol.* 10.1; Arist. *Pol.* 1306a18–19; see the discussion in Cartledge, *Agesilaos,* pp. 121–22.

[30]See Cartledge, *Sparta,* pp. 97–99 and 178, and the other modern literature cited there.

[31]See Cartledge, *Sparta,* pp. 180–85, for a good discussion of the economic activities of the perioeci; cf. Xen. *Lac. Pol.* 7.1–2.

[32]Although Xenophon says that large numbers of them did defect from Sparta in the wake of the Theban invasions of the Peloponnesus in the 360s (7.2.2; cf. 6.5.25–29), there is little hint of dissatisfaction on their part before this time. See chap. 8 below.

activities. The perioeci were self-governing in their various communities, subject only to the requirements of observing the lead of Sparta in foreign policy and of performing military service in the army when called upon to do so by Sparta. They possessed no civic rights in the polis, but at least they were free men and seem to have been protected by law from arbitrary and abusive use of force by the Spartiates.[33] They may have resented the absence of control of their foreign policy, however, viewing it as a serious limitation, because this was one of the most essential constituents of what the classical Greeks considered autonomy, and autonomy was at the heart of the polis.[34] Therefore, perhaps the perioeci might have been induced to consider rebelling against the Spartiates in order to gain real control over their foreign policy and the autonomy of their individual communities. Such a situation is all the more likely if Cartledge is correct in his suggestion that the perioecic communities were allied to Sparta, rather than completely subject to its will.[35]

The case of the helots was different. These people, who undoubtedly represented the largest class in Spartan society, were in effect serfs on the estates of their Spartiate masters. They were divided into two groups, reflecting their separate origins.[36] Those who lived and worked in Laconia were called the *archaioi* to designate that they worked the *archaioi kleroi* (ancient allotments) of the Spartiates, whereas their neighbors to the west, in the region of Messenia, were called the Messeniakoi. The latter helots had been enslaved en masse during the wars of the Spartans in the eighth and seventh centuries, in which they acquired the rich agricultural land of southwestern Peloponnesus, Messenia. Unlike the Laconian helots, who had been reduced at an earlier stage of history and who may have been the descendants of the pre-Dorian inhabitants of the region, the Messenians were Dorian and had experienced an independent history prior to the conquest. The Messenians never forgot this tradition of independence and gave the Spartans a good deal of

[33]See D. M. MacDowell, *Spartan Law* (Edinburgh, 1986), pp. 27–31.

[34]See M. P. Ostwald, *Autonomia: Its Genesis and Early History* (Chico, Calif., 1982), for discussion of this term.

[35]Cartledge, *Sparta,* pp. 178–79. Epaminondas' retort to Agesilaus at the Peace Conference in 371 perhaps relates to this issue. When asked if Thebes was prepared to leave the poleis of Boeotia independent, Epaminondas responded by asking if Sparta was prepared to leave the perioecic cities independent. See chap. 7 below.

[36]Cf. Michell, *Sparta,* pp. 75–76; MacDowell, *Spartan Law,* pp. 31–32; and J. Chambers, "On Messenian and Laconian Helots in the Fifth Century B.C.," *Historian* 40 (1978):271–85.

trouble in the centuries following their subjugation.[37] The Messenian helots also worked estates belonging to absentee landlords and were obliged to give a proportion of their annual yield to their masters. The helots possessed no rights, not even the right to life, although right of asylum at the sanctuary of Poseidon at Taenarum was recognized.[38] This desperate situation was underscored by the fact that the ephors annually declared war upon the helots, thus legitimizing the use of force against them when it was deemed necessary and removing the stigma of religious guilt for homicide.[39] Helots could be, and often were, murdered by the Spartans, with or without reason.

The Spartans had an institution known as the *krypteia,* a sort of secret police, which enrolled young Spartiates in its ranks and closely watched the activities of the helots. Whenever there was any suspicion that one of them might be plotting to foment trouble or revolt, he was simply liquidated.[40] Thucydides remarked that the Lacedaemonians had always adopted most of their measures in order to guard against the helots.[41] While there may well be good reason to question whether he was correct in this assessment, plenty of evidence suggests that, in general, the Spartan government feared the helots and took many precautions to guard against the possibility of revolt on their part.[42] And the revolts that occurred—for example, after the earthquake of 464—are quite understandable from the helots' point of view.[43] The helots had absolutely nothing to lose by such attempts to regain their freedom, and everything to gain. The successful rebellion of the entire helot population would have meant the end of the Spartan order, because there would have been no one left to work the land of the Spartiates and they would not have been able to continue the lifestyle they had enjoyed for over two and a half centuries. Thus, it is understandable that the authorities were alarmed at the prospect of a conspiracy that aimed at raising the helots in rebellion against their masters, which is at least one of the implications of Xenophon's narrative of this episode. They had taken, however, numerous measures throughout

[37]See Michell, *Sparta,* pp. 83–84, and Chambers, "On Helots," pp. 275–76.

[38]Plut. *Lyc.* 28.4; see MacDowell, *Spartan Law,* pp. 36–37.

[39]Cf. Plutarch (*Lyc.* 28.4) who attributes this report to Aristotle.

[40]Plut. *Lyc.* 28.1–3; see H. Jeanmaire, "La kryptie lacédémonienne," *REG* 26 (1913): 121–50.

[41]Thuc. 4.80.

[42]I discuss this question in my article "Social Tensions in Late Classical Sparta," forthcoming in *Ktema* 12.

[43]Thuc. 1.101.2; Diod. 11.63.1–64.4.

their history to prevent such an occurrence; presumably, had they been faced with the prospect of a rebellion of the helots alone, they could have handled it. But this threat was much more, involving as it did virtually every class within the broad spectrum of Lacedaemonian society except for the homoioi, the elite corps of Spartiates. We have examined the identity of three of the classes mentioned by Xenophon as implicated (at least potentially) in Cinadon's conspiracy, but there was a fourth class, the neodamodeis, mentioned as potential rebels. Who were these people, and how did they fit into the scheme of things in early fourth-century Sparta?

The ancient writers mention the neodamodeis more frequently than the hypomeiones, but we are not much better informed about the former's origins or legal status.[44] Once again, the literal meaning of neodamodeis—the "new citizens" or the "new members of the *damos*"—suggests their identity. But how could one become a "new citizen" in classical Sparta, without going through the educational process of the agoge, and meeting the twin requirements of birthright and income? Obviously, one could not, and so we must look for another meaning for the term. Because the neodamodeis were mentioned as a group among the potential rebels, it is obvious that they could not have been Spartan "citizens" in any meaningful sense of the word. Fortunately for us, earlier references to them as a class, in both Thucydides and Xenophon, provide the necessary clue to their identity.[45] They were almost certainly former helots who had been freed from their original servile status and whose economic obligations had been exchanged for military ones. The neodamodeis served as hoplites, although hardly on a par with the elite Spartiate citizen-soldiers, from the early part of the Peloponnesian War until well into the fourth century. How the state had decided to emancipate some of its helots in return for the obligation to perform military service, and how the authorities had come to trust these potentially dangerous individuals, remains a mystery.[46] It is clear, however, that the authorities had come to believe it essential to the general well-being of Sparta to resort to new sources of manpower beyond the traditional ones of the homoioi and the perioeci.

---

[44]See Oliva, *Sparta*, pp. 176–82. MacDowell, *Spartan Law*, pp. 39–42 and 51, considers the neodamodeis as mothakes who had completed the agoge and were then given this status. I consider his suggestion improbable.

[45]Thuc. 5.34.1; Xen. 3.1.4.

[46]See Cartledge, *Sparta*, p. 251, for a plausible suggestion, which emphasizes the creation of the class of neodamodeis as a response to the growing scarcity of Spartan hoplites, already evident by the mid-420s in the Peloponnesian War.

The neodamodeis therefore may be considered rather like *liberti* in Roman society; that is, freed slaves who had certain obligations, although in this case they lacked civic rights. For the individuals in question, this change would have represented a marked elevation in status. No longer were they forced to labor for their masters, and no longer were they subject to the arbitrary application of force by the Spartan authorities, which might result in their death. Although not truly citizens, they did have personal freedom and, presumably, security because they constituted an important secondary pool of manpower for the state. Therefore, to a certain degree they seem to have resembled the perioeci, although there were important differences between the two classes. Both groups possessed some degree of personal freedom and were obliged to perform military service. But the perioeci possessed their own communities and lived in them according to their own regulations, whereas the neodamodeis presumably lived among the Spartiates in a dispersed fashion, and it is not clear what means of livelihood they had; they may have possessed land, or worked for others as agricultural laborers or in crafts.

The narrative of Thucydides suggests that in the late 420s the Spartans gave them land near Lepreon to hold as their own,[47] but we cannot be sure that this practice was typical of their treatment at other times and places. In any case, the principal improvement in their lives was the elimination of the oppressive aspects of helotry. They must have realized that their role as soldiers was a vital contribution to Sparta. However, the fact that they were not, and never could be, fully integrated into the citizen class undoubtedly stimulated feelings of resentment and alienation. Perhaps the agenda of the neodamodeis as potential rebels included a redistribution of wealth and privilege within Sparta, or even the total elimination of existing social distinctions. We cannot know their intentions with any degree of certainty, but history provides ample cases in which attempts at revolution occurred not among oppressed classes who had so little that they could not even conceive of change, but rather among those who had once been severely oppressed, but were given a taste of freedom or power, whether economic or political, and then began to agitate for much more.[48] Whatever the explanation, the neodamodeis were numerous. When the Spartiate commander Thibron was sent to Asia Minor in 400, he was given a force of one

---

[47]Thuc. 5.34.1.
[48]Two such cases are those of the peasants who rose in Wat Tyler's rebellion in England in 1381, and the bourgeoisie who played such a crucial role in the early years of the French Revolution.

thousand neodamodeis and four thousand Peloponnesian allies, and Agesilaus received a force of some two thousand for his expedition to Asia Minor in 396.[49] Contingents of neodamodeis are mentioned during the Peloponnesian War, especially toward the end of the Archidamian War and during the expedition of Gylippus to Sicily.[50] The entire population of the homoioi in this period may have numbered no more than two thousand, and at the time of Leuctra there may have been as few as fifteen hundred full Spartiates.[51] Thus, the neodamodeis represented a class at least equal in size to the citizen body. This fact may help to explain why the authorities adopted the policy, nowhere discussed in the sources, of creating this new social class. The incipient decline in the numbers of the homoioi, which can be detected from the early years of the Peloponnesian War at least, is surely a crucial explanatory factor. If the citizen class could not meet its military requirements, the only reasonable solution (short of cutting back on the requirements themselves; i.e., reducing the diplomatic or political objectives that produced these requirements) was either to create more true citizens or to look elsewhere for a new manpower pool. The state chose the latter alternative, and this choice is very revealing in light of later history.

To sum up: sometime early in 397,[52] the conspiracy of Cinadon came to the attention of the authorities in Sparta. Because Xenophon mentions it in connection with the sacrifice of Agesilaus, which introduces the episode, there is no doubt that Agesilaus was fully informed about its development, and he probably was the source of Xenophon's information.[53] The government responded with its traditional tactics of

[49]Xen. 3.1.4; 3.4.2–3.

[50]Thuc. 5.34.1, 67.1.

[51]Cf. Xen. 4.2.16; 6.1.1, 4.15, 17. For modern discussions of the question of Spartiate manpower, see especially A. J. Toynbee, *Some Problems of Greek History* (Oxford, 1969), pp. 297ff.; G. E. M. de Ste. Croix, *The Origins of the Peloponnesian War* (London, 1972), pp. 331ff.; Cartledge, *Sparta*, pp. 307ff.; T. J. Figueira, "Population Patterns in Late Archaic and Classical Sparta," *TAPA* 116 (1986):165–213; and S. J. Hodkinson, "Inheritance, Marriage and Demography: Perspectives upon the Success and Decline of Classical Sparta," in *Classical Sparta: Techniques behind Her Success,* edited by A. Powell, pp. 79–121 (Norman, Okla., 1989).

[52]See the chronological discussion in Hamilton, "Etude chronologique," 292, for the date of the conspiracy of Cinadon.

[53]Although Xenophon mentions Agesilaus only at the beginning of this passage (3.3.4) and speaks of the ephors as directing the measures to deal with the conspiracy of Cinadon, it is quite likely that Agesilaus was involved not only in its detection but also in its suppression. Why else would Xenophon even mention the link between his unsatisfactory sacrifices and the discovery of the conspiracy itself? See Anderson, *Xenophon,* p. 150, for the opinion that Agesilaus himself was the source of information for Xenophon about this event.

repression. There is no evidence to suggest that the authorities looked beyond the immediate causes of this disorder or that they took cognizance of a problem to be solved once the ringleaders had been arrested and executed and the conspiracy was thus crushed. They were to learn, to their distress, that the issues implicit in this crisis would not disappear as easily as those who had brought it to their attention.

The Socioeconomic Crisis of Early Fourth-Century Sparta

Why did the crisis come to a head when it did, within a half-dozen years of the end of the Peloponnesian War and of Sparta's spectacular victory over Athens, which had assured it the premier place among the Greek states? It was in large measure that very victory, or at least its consequences, that led to Sparta's dilemma. Even before the cessation of hostilities—but when there was no longer any doubt about the ultimate outcome of the war—Lysander, the architect of Sparta's victory, began to shape the postwar world. Shortly after his decisive victory over the Athenians at Aegospotami in autumn 405, Lysander dispatched his subordinate Gylippus to Sparta with an enormous sum of money. This money represented a substantial part of the war chest that Sparta had amassed with the aid of Cyrus the Younger.[54] These sums had been contributed in accordance with the Spartan–Persian treaties of 412/11, whereby Persia would provide economic assistance to Sparta for the prosecution of the war against Athens, in exchange for which Sparta agreed to the surrender of the Greeks of western Asia Minor to Persian control at the end of the war. Gylippus' delivery of these monies at Sparta represented the first of a very substantial influx of foreign capital, which would have a tremendous impact on the economy of Laconia and on the socioeconomic situation in Sparta.[55] After the final capitulation of Athens itself, and the subjugation of its last ally, Samos, Lysander returned to Sparta, bringing an additional 470 talents and other valuable gifts and donations.[56] These sums alone constituted a veritable fortune, especially for a state that traditionally forbade the possession and the use of gold and silver coins. A crisis was provoked when it was discovered

[54]Diod. 13.106.8; Plut. *Lys.* 16, *Nicias*, 28.3. The sources report the amount to have been one thousand or fifteen hundred talents.

[55]David, *Sparta*, pp. 5–6, has employed the phrase in his extremely useful and important analysis of these developments.

[56]Xen. 2.3.7–9.

that Gylippus had been guilty of peculation, and he was tried and exiled for his crime.[57]

The question then arose of how to deal with the contradiction between the Lycurgan prohibition against coined money and the obvious need and attraction of such wealth in Sparta. If Sparta were to continue to maintain a presence in the Aegean world as the dominant power— and under Lysander's influence, in the immediate aftermath of the war, there was no reason to doubt that this would happen—then the state would have to take measures to remedy one of the gravest defects in its polity, and one that had prolonged the war unduly: the lack of sufficient resources to permit Sparta to maintain a naval force and a permanent presence abroad.[58] The Spartan king Archidamus had argued at the outbreak of the conflict that this defect would make it extremely difficult for Sparta to defeat Athens, for the state possessed no regular revenue and no infrastructure to permit it to develop the financial and economic measures necessary to continue a war for a lengthy period, especially beyond the Peloponnesus; the historian Polybius made precisely the same point in his acute analysis of the reasons for the failure of the Spartans to maintain their imperial ambitions after 404.[59] The crux of the matter was simple: without an income in money to maintain a fleet—and maintenance involved not only the procurement of materials to create a fleet and to keep it in good operation but also capital to finance its operations through the payment of crews, the purchase of supplies, and so forth—and to finance the numerous Spartan garrisons abroad which had been established in many poleis by Lysander, Sparta would have to retreat from a position of empire.

A great debate took place in Sparta in summer 404 over the question of whether the ancient Lycurgan prohibition against coined money should be strictly enforced, relaxed, or abandoned.[60] The friends and partisans of Lysander, who had vested interests in maintaining the new order, argued forcefully for some exception to the old rule, whereas conservative elements in Sparta fought just as fiercely for a strict interpretation of the prohibition.[61] The result of the debate was a compromise of sorts: the state upheld the prohibition against the private pos-

[57]See Hamilton, *SBV*, pp. 55–58; and David, *Sparta*, pp. 6–8.
[58]See Kagan, *Archidamian War*, pp. 21–24.
[59]Thuc. 1.78–85; Polybius 6.49.7–10.
[60]Plut. *Lys.* 16–17; see Hamilton *SBV*, pp. 55–58.
[61]See Plut. *Lys.* 17.1–4; cf. *Lys.* 9.1–4 and 30.1 for an account of the circumstances in which Lycurgus was said to have banned the use of gold and silver coins, and the comment that its reintroduction under Lysander brought greed and corruption to Sparta; cf. also *Mor.* 239F42–240A.

session of wealth, while admitting that it was useful for public purposes and allowing its use for the common good (presumably for
purposes such as the financing of the fleet, etc.). What mechanisms
were used to enforce this rather awkward compromise are not known,
but it appears that charges of violation of the new law could be brought
before the ephors or the Gerousia. And in at least one case, that of the
harmost Thorax, the law was applied to its full extent, resulting in his
execution for the possession of private capital.[62] The influx of foreign
capital continued in Sparta's exaction of annual tribute levied on the
former states of the Athenian Empire, who now found themselves
under Spartan domination, to the tune of one thousand talents.[63]
Sparta was not equipped to deal with the regular importation of such
sums, and it was not long before the influences of corruption began to
be felt.

There is ample evidence in the ancient sources that many in Sparta
sought to enrich themselves from the new opportunities, despite the
official prohibition against possession of money.[64] One of the principal
ways in which personal enrichment could be achieved was through the
office of harmost.[65] This position, roughly equivalent to that of a
garrison commander in control of a Spartan garrison stationed in a
foreign state, had evolved during the Peloponnesian War. Originally
intended to provide protection against both internal and external enemies of pro-Spartan régimes, the post gradually took on an additional
importance as a means of retaining control of states allied or subject to
Sparta.[66] Lysander made extensive use of garrisons and harmosts in the
aftermath of the defeat of Athens, and harmosts are found in many
Greek states down to the period of the Corinthian War and beyond. The
opportunities for harmosts to enrich themselves at the expense of the
communities in which they had been installed were numerous and
varied, ranging from outright extortion and corruption to more subtle
methods, such as the acceptance of gifts and bribes in return for political
or judicial decisions favorable to local figures who wanted favors from

[62]Plut. *Lys.* 17.4–6, 19.4.
[63]Diod. 14.10.2; cf. Arist. *Ath. Pol.* 39.2, Isoc. 12.67–69, 4.132. The annual sum of
one thousand talents strikes many scholars as an impossibly high amount, but, even if
Diodorus' figure is erroneous, there is no reason to doubt that Sparta received large
amounts of tribute in the immediate aftermath of the war. See Hamilton, *SBV*, pp. 61–
62.
[64]Xen. *Lac. Pol.* 14.2–5; Plut. *Mor.* 239F.
[65]Xen. *Lac. Pol.* 14.4.
[66]See G. Bockisch, "Harmostai," *Klio* 46 (1965):129–239, for a study of the institution.

their powerful "protectors." Within a very short time after the establishment of Spartan hegemony, many men actively sought appointment as harmosts in order to acquire wealth, and the long list of complaints about the abuse of such a system in antiquity stretches back to Xenophon, who was generally a pro-Spartan ideologue and enthusiast. In his treatise on the Spartan constitution, he considers the abuse of the institution of harmost to be the chief cause of corruption in his day. "For I know that formerly," Xenophon writes, "the Lacedaemonians preferred to live together at home with moderate fortunes rather than expose themselves to the corrupting influences of flattery as governors of dependent states. And I know too that in former days they were afraid to be found in possession of gold; whereas nowadays there are some who even boast of their possessions . . . and now I have no doubt that the fixed ambition of those who are thought to be first among them is to live to their dying day as harmosts in a foreign land."[67]

It was as harmost of Samos that Thorax made his fortune, and we must not imagine that his ultimate fate prevented many others from following his example.[68] Clearchus, named as harmost of Byzantium, fell foul of the authorities at home and went into exile for similar reasons, resulting from his inability to resist temptation during his appointment.[69] Although we do not possess the specifics to substantiate many other cases, the general accusations of Xenophon, Aristotle, and Plutarch leave no doubt on this point. Imperial power had undeniably led to individual corruption.

The sources provide hardly any information on the manner in which this new wealth affected Sparta, although they make it clear that capital continued to flow into the state, both publicly and privately. It seems an inescapable conclusion, however, that the normal laws of supply and demand did not fail to operate and that, as capital became much more readily available, prices rose accordingly. The combination of the disruption in the system of distribution of materials and goods which the recent war had occasioned and the increased accumulation of capital in Sparta must have made the cost of imported items, whether raw materials or manufactured goods, more expensive as time went on. The state, whose revenues were derived in an artificial and parasitic manner, could have responded to increased costs (e.g., for materials to maintain

[67]Xen. Lac. Pol. 14.2–5. E. C. Marchant, trans., Xenophon: Scripta Minora (Cambridge, Mass., 1925), p. 185.
[68]Diod. 14.3.5; Plut. Lys. 19.4.
[69]Xen. Anab. 1.1.9; Diod. 14.12.2–9; Polyaenus, 2.2.6–10.

its fleets) without too much difficulty. But the same is not likely to have been true for individuals.

Let us consider a commodity that would have affected almost everyone in Sparta: iron.[70] Necessary as much for agricultural tools and implements as for weapons, any increase in its price would have had an impact on virtually every member of society. Gradual though such increases may have been, their cumulative effect would begin to be felt after a half-dozen years or so, particularly among those who had fixed incomes. And a large number of the homoioi had fixed incomes, which were linked to the productivity of their *kleroi* in Laconia. Even so small an increase as 2 or 3 percent, if it was a steady, annual increase, would begin to have a serious impact after a number of years. If this trend began after Aegospotami, it would have been in operation for seven or eight years by the time of Cinadon's conspiracy in 397. By then, quite a number of Spartiates may have been squeezed out of the ranks of the homoioi and reduced to those of the hypomeiones.[71] Such a development, coupled with the accumulation of capital by a relatively small number of those fortunate enough to have secured positions as harmosts, may well have pointed up the growing inequalities within Spartan society. While much of the preceding argument is admittedly based on hypothesis (in the absence of any solid ancient economic evidence, in which most ancient sources took no interest whatsoever), it is both a plausible and an instructive hypothesis. There is one corollary to this hypothesis which we must consider.

The question of land tenure in classical Sparta is a knotty problem, but one relevant to our discussion.[72] It is generally held, on the basis of a Lycurgan law reported by Plutarch, that the *kleros* inherited by a Spartiate was inalienable.[73] This allotment of land, together with the helots who worked it, formed the basis for the economic support of the homoios and his family. So long as there was a sufficient number of both kleroi and inheritors, the state would be assured of an adequate number

---

[70]Cartledge, *Sparta,* pp. 184–85, reports the great availability of iron locally. But local availability does not mean that the commodity would not be affected by general changes in the local economy more broadly conceived.

[71]For example, we know that a similar depression of individuals from one social class to another led to revolution in Corinth just a few years after this. See D. Kagan, "Corinthian Politics and the Revolution of 392 B.C.," *Historia* 11 (1962):447–57.

[72]The most recent discussion of this question is S. J. Hodkinson, "Land Tenure and Inheritance in Classical Sparta," *CQ,* n.s. 36 (1986):378–406.

[73]Plut. *Lyc.* 8.1–4; *Agis* 5.1. See R. J. A. Talbert, *Plutarch on Sparta* (London, 1988), pp. 185–86, endnote B.

of citizens. At some point in its history, however, Sparta passed a law, that of Epitadeus, which altered the rules of land entitlement.[74] This law permitted a Spartan to deed his land to anyone he wished during his lifetime and to bequeath it freely in his will. The legislation enabled individuals to sell their land in the guise of a gift, for which they might receive a "gift" of comparable value—that is, money. This convention allowed those who possessed land but needed money (or believed that they did) to exchange it for cash, and, of course, it conversely allowed those with excess cash to invest it in land. Thus, over time, a minority came to possess more and more land, while another substantial group, also perhaps a minority, found themselves without land. The dating of this law is impossible to determine absolutely from the sources, but a good case can be made for the early fourth century, shortly after the end of the war.[75] If this dating is correct, then perhaps it was this increasing awareness of socioeconomic changes—linked with the effects of the Peloponnesian War and, more specifically, with the imperialism of the supporters of Lysander—which impelled some of the hypomeiones, such as Cinadon, to plan their conspiracy. It is clear that such men were the architects of the plot, and we need not look beyond the customary arrogance and selfishness of the Spartiates, intensified by their success over Athens and by their new imperialism, to explain the apparent readiness of the other social elements within Sparta to join the conspiracy.

This analysis demonstrates several crucial points about early fourth-century Sparta. The first and most important point is the existence of deep-seated socioeconomic problems within the state. These problems became even graver and more threatening in the ensuing decades, until Sparta found itself without sufficient manpower to resist its enemies after Leuctra. The second point is the willingness of the authorities to content themselves with the suppression of the conspiracy, and their apparent blindness to the seriousness of the situation that had precipitated this crisis. Finally, we cannot escape the conclusion that Agesilaus was fully aware of the conspiracy and its outcome. Xenophon's account leaves no doubt on the matter. Therefore, Agesilaus also must bear some of the blame, along with those whom I have consistently, yet

[74]Plut. *Agis* 5.2; cf. Arist. *Pol.* 1270a21. See Toynbee, *Some Problems,* pp. 337–42; D. Asheri, "Laws of Inheritance, Distribution of Land and Political Constitutions in Ancient Greece," *Historia* 12 (1963).1–21; and Oliva, *Sparta,* pp. 188–92.

[75]See the counterarguments of Hodkinson, "Land Tenure," 390ff., who denies the historicity of Epitadeus. Older literature is cited there.

vaguely, termed "the authorities," for Sparta's failure to recognize the indications of grave social disorder. This failure resulted not from a lack of ability to effect change, but rather from a lack of will. It is ironic that this event occurred at the very beginning of Agesilaus' long reign, for no amount of success, or even brilliance, in the military or political sphere would save Sparta so long as its socioeconomic problems cried out in vain for attention.

CHAPTER FOUR

Agesilaus' Rise to Power

W hen Agesilaus came to the throne in 398, Sparta's hegemony appeared secure and widespread. Agis' expedition had just humbled Elis, and Sparta's Peloponnesian allies remained docile. Outside the Peloponnesus, the restored Athenian democracy was abiding by its obligations and had contributed a contingent to the Spartan expeditionary force in Asia Minor. Although Thebes had objected to the Spartan settlement of the Peloponnesian War, had given asylum to democratic exiles from Athens during the reign of the Thirty Tyrants, and had, moreover, boycotted both King Pausanias' expedition to Attica in 403 and King Agis' against Elis in 400, the government remained quiet and took no overt anti-Spartan action. Across the Aegean, the army under Dercylidas was holding its own against the Persians and providing protection for the Greek cities. All this changed very rapidly, and Sparta's position was shaken in 395.

In the latter half of 397, news reached Sparta of extensive Persian naval preparations to challenge its position in the Aegean. Sparta determined to send reinforcements to Asia Minor, under the command of Agesilaus himself, and the king operated successfully there for the next two years. But the Persians responded to his activities by seeking to inflame resentment against Sparta among the states in Greece proper and, in part because of contributions of Persian money, an anti-Spartan coalition was formed in Greece. In an effort to answer the threat to its hegemony posed by this coalition, Sparta recalled Agesilaus from Asia Minor to Europe in 394. Agesilaus returned to Greece and, for the next seven years, was involved in the struggle of Sparta to defeat its enemies in the Corinthian War and to reassert its hegemony.

In the decade between his departure for Asia Minor in 396 and the King's Peace in 387/6, Agesilaus rose to power in Sparta. He faced numerous challenges in these years and established his reputation and position through his response to them. First, his campaigns in Asia Minor, and then in Greece, allowed him to achieve a military reputation that would serve him well until his death almost forty years later. Second, by the time he returned to Greece in 394, his principal political opponents had been removed from the scene—Lysander by death and King Pausanias through exile. But Agesilaus did not automatically succeed to a position of dominance in Sparta; he had to work to establish his direction of policy there. Third, his relations with Thebes during this decade produced in him a "Theban obsession," a set of political attitudes which colored his policies and statecraft for the next several decades and which led to Sparta's defeat at the Battle of Leuctra in 371. This chapter examines the early years of Agesilaus' reign, the attempts by Persia and the Greek coalition to destroy Sparta's hegemony in the Corinthian War, and the results these had for Agesilaus' career.

Spartan Intervention in Asia Minor

Agesilaus' activities in Asia Minor from 396 to 394[1] constituted merely a single episode in an ongoing struggle between Sparta and Persia over the fate of the Greek communities there. The origins of the controversy lay in the treaties of 412/11 between the two powers, according to which Sparta had agreed to recognize Persia's right to control this area in return for Persian subsidies in the war against Athens.[2] Even before the Athenians had been defeated, however, the Spartan commander Lysander faced difficulties in the implementation of this agreement. It was his policy to establish decarchies in the Greek cities that were being liberated from Athenian control, supported by

---

[1]The principal sources are Xen. 3.4.1–29; 4.1.1–2.8; *Ages.* 1.6–38; Plut. *Ages.* 6–15; Diod. 14.79.1–3; 80.1–8; 83.1–3; and *Hell. Oxy.* 11–14.

[2]Thuc. 8.18, 37, and 58. For discussions of these treaties, see H. Bengtson, *Die Staatsverträge des Altertums, II: Die Verträge der griechisch-römischen Welt von 700 bis 338 v. Chr.* (Munich and Berlin, 1962), nos. 200–202, pp. 139–43; D. M. Lewis, *Sparta and Persia* (Leiden, 1977), pp. 85–107; E. Levy, "Les trois traités entre Sparte et le roi," *BCH* 107 (1983):221–41; and Kagan, *Fall of the Athenian Empire,* pp. 28–50.

garrisons commanded by Spartan harmosts.[3] The relationship of these decarchies and their attendant garrisons and harmosts to the Persian authorities, as well as their fate after the formal surrender of the cities to Persian control, is not entirely clear and has become a matter of scholarly debate.[4] What is clear is that the cities were surrendered to Persian control after 404, and that the Spartans lent support to Cyrus the Younger in his abortive attempt to supplant his brother, Artaxerxes, on the Persian throne. The Spartans subsequently responded to appeals for help from the Greeks of Asia Minor against the demands of Tissaphernes, the Persian satrap.[5]

When Cyrus was ready to march against Artaxerxes in spring 401, he sent to Sparta requesting aid and cooperation, reminding the Spartans of his good offices during the war with Athens. The Spartans decided that it was to their advantage to assist him, and they sent an order to their navarch Samius to put himself at Cyrus' disposal. Furthermore, they dispatched a force of some seven hundred troops to march with Cyrus.[6] Why the Spartans made this decision, besides the cryptic remark recorded by Diodorus about their judging it useful, is not revealed either by Xenophon or by Diodorus. Nor is there any indication that Lysander was personally involved in the negotiations for this enterprise.[7] Whatever the reasons, there can be little doubt that this aid put the Spartans at war with Persia, from a technical standpoint, because Artaxerxes was legitimate king and Cyrus' expedition resulted in military confrontation with him. After Cyrus' death, Tissaphernes returned to the coast and demanded the submission of the Greek cities there. They refused, appealing instead to Sparta for help, and Sparta came to their aid.

We must ask why the Spartans reversed their policy of cooperation with Persia and determined to engage in acts that put them at war with

---

[3]Diod. 14.10.1; 13.1 (and cf. 14.3.4); Plut. Lys. 13.3–4. See H. W. Parke, "The Development of the Second Spartan Empire (405–371 B.C.)," JHS 50 (1930):37–79; and Hamilton, SBV, pp. 58–60.

[4]See especially R. E. Smith, "Lysander and the Spartan Empire," CP 43 (1948):145–56; A. Andrewes, "Two Notes on Lysander," Phoenix 25 (1971):206–26; and Lewis, Sparta and Persia, pp. 136–41.

[5]Xen. 3.1.1ff.; Diod. 14.19.4–5; 21.1–2; 35.6–7; 36.1–3; 37.1–4.

[6]Xen. 3.1.1; Diod. 14.19.4–5.

[7]I suggested in SBV, pp. 96–97, that Lysander had been absent from Sparta at the court of Dionysius of Syracuse as ambassador, but that he might have returned by spring 401, because his influence is to be detected in the Spartan decision to assist Cyrus the Younger. I no longer think that he need have been actually *present* in Sparta for his political influence to have made itself felt on this occasion.

the empire. The Spartans became the object of scathing criticism for their abandonment of the Greeks of Asia Minor, and there is no doubt that the reputation of the state suffered from this act.[8] Thus, concern with public opinion appears to be a factor. Another consideration for some Spartans might have been the opportunity to campaign in Asia Minor and to make their fortunes as harmosts or from the booty that could result from action in this part of the Aegean. Certainly the sequel to Thibron's expedition leaves no doubt that many Spartans did profit from such activities in the next half-dozen years.[9] And, of course, we should admit the possibility of truly panhellenic sentiment; that is, the Spartans felt an obligation to protect the Greek cities of this area from Persian aggression. Numerous motives, weighing differently with different people, may well have played their individual roles in the Spartan decision.

One other event of significance occurred at this time. In summer 400, the Spartans issued an ultimatum to the Greek state of Elis to admit them to participation in the Olympic Games and to allow their dependent neighboring communities to be autonomous.[10] The ultimatum was rejected, and war resulted, with King Agis leading an invasion of Elean territory. It seems clear that this episode was part of a much longer, ongoing feud between the two states, one that involved Agis particularly. Perhaps the timing of the Elean War and the Spartan intervention in Asia Minor is not purely coincidental. Factions within Sparta with quite different agendas may have agreed to cooperate in enterprises in widely separated corners of the Greek world at this time, for their own particular reasons and objectives. This is as far as speculation over the Spartan motives in rendering aid to the Greek cities of Asia Minor should take us at this point.

In the course of his relatively short stay in Asia Minor, Thibron did some damage to Tissaphernes, in particular by cutting inland and attacking non-Greek cities that had not before been endangered.[11] But during winter 400/399 he plundered the lands of his Greek allies. Thus, in the next campaigning season, the Spartan authorities replaced him

[8]Cf. Isoc. 4.117, 123. Although these passages refer more particularly to the situation after 386, they no doubt mirror earlier criticisms of Sparta's actions in 404.
[9]See the account of subsequent activities in Asia Minor under Dercylidas, Xen. 3.1.8ff.
[10]Xen. 3.2.21–31; Diod. 14.17.4–12; Paus. 3.8.3–7. On the date of the war, see Hamilton, "Etude chronologique," 286–90.
[11]Xen. 3.1.6–7. On treatment of the Spartan campaigns in Asia Minor in this period, see H. D. Westlake, "Spartan Intervention in Asia, 400–397 B.C.," Historia 35 (1986):405–26.

with Dercylidas, who would remain in command in Asia Minor for three years, until the arrival of Agesilaus in spring 396.[12] The Spartan authorities showed great concern over the fate of their Asiatic Greek protégés from this point forward, periodically sending out commissions to survey the situation and to assure that there was no repetition of plundering.[13]

Dercylidas spent very little time in actual operations against the Persians, contenting himself with a series of truces and conducting what were essentially free-booting activities in the Chersonesus in order to support his army without burdening the Greeks of Asia Minor. Finally, in 397, when Dercylidas was instructed by the Spartan authorities, who were responding to the plea of the local Greeks, to return to Asia Minor and to attack Caria, he did so.[14] Up to that point the Spartan field armies had not inflicted substantial damage on the satraps, but their presence had apparently resulted in the protection of the Greek cities and their possessions. As a condition of the field armies operating in the area, of course, Spartan harmosts and garrisons had once again been installed in many of the cities. This was the situation in 397 when the commander Dercylidas found himself unexpectedly face to face with a superior force of Persians under the command of Pharnabazus and his chief, Tissaphernes.

At this juncture, a surprising thing occurred. Although Pharnabazus was all for engaging the enemy, and many of the Ionian troops of Dercylidas were melting away in the standing grain of the fields, Tissaphernes refused to give battle, but instead offered to negotiate with the Spartan.[15] Dercylidas eagerly seized the occasion to avoid what might have been a disastrous encounter for him, and the two sides parleyed. Tissaphernes demanded the withdrawal of the Greek army from Asia Minor and the removal of the harmosts, in return for his leaving the cities independent. A truce was agreed upon until both sides could refer these terms back to their home governments (i.e., Sparta and Susa) for discussion and approval. Thus, the fighting ceased during summer 397.

Tissaphernes was merely using the truce as a ruse to gain time. In the previous year Pharnabazus, assisted by the Greek physician to the royal

[12]Xen. 3.1.8.
[13]Xen. 3.2.6–7.
[14]Xen. 3.1.9–28; 2.6–7; and 2.12–13.
[15]Xen. 3.2.16–20. It is surprising that Tissaphernes rejected an apparent opportunity to defeat Dercylidas, but he had displayed a healthy fear of confronting Greek hoplites in battle ever since Cunaxa, and this may explain his unwillingness to fight on this occasion.

court, Ktesias, had proposed the construction of a major fleet. It was to be entrusted to Conon, the exiled Athenian admiral who had been at the court of King Evagoras of Salamis in Cyprus since 405.[16] Artaxerxes was persuaded to grant this request, and naval preparations were underway in Phoenicia and Cyprus by mid-397. As commander in chief of the Great King's forces in the west, Tissaphernes was hoping to crush the Spartans by a combined land and sea assault and to drive them out of Asia Minor for good. The Syracusan seaman Herodas, however, observed the naval preparations in Phoenicia and reported them as swiftly as he could to Sparta.

The news probably reached the Peloponnesus by late summer or autumn 397. Although the precise destination of this force was not known, it seemed clear that either the Spartan fleet and army operating along the coast of Asia Minor or even the Greek homeland itself must be the target.[17] The ephors were understandably distressed over this news, especially because Dercylidas had only a few months earlier agreed to a truce to consider terms for ending the war. They immediately called their allies together to discuss what was to be done. At this point Lysander conceived the idea of sending a new force across the Aegean, in order to take the war to the enemy before they could strike. The force was to be commanded by Agesilaus, who had not yet led an army on campaign, and who was to be advised by thirty Spartans. Lysander expected to be one of the advisers, of course, and he had his own private purposes in proposing this expedition, principally to reestablish the control of his partisans in their various cities in Asia Minor.[18] It is clear from the measures taken by Lysander and Agesilaus to win approval of their proposal that they expected to encounter opposition to it. Their assumptions were correct.

Agesilaus in Asia Minor

There is no doubt that the concept of the expedition, as well as the specific proposals regarding its commander and the force's size and composition, originated with Lysander; the sources agree on that. Furthermore, Xenophon states that Lysander "persuaded" Agesilaus to

[16]See Hamilton, SBV, pp. 114–16.
[17]Xen. 3.4.1–2; Plut. Ages. 6.1–2.
[18]Xen. 3.4.2–3; Plut. Lys. 23.1–2, Ages. 6.1–3.

agree to undertake command of the expedition.[19] In view of the ambition of Agesilaus and his desire to make a name for himself, it is unlikely that Lysander had to expend much energy in persuading him. Persuasion does imply at least some degree of reluctance, however, and we may speculate on the reasons for Agesilaus' reluctance, for none are given either by Xenophon or by Plutarch. The first reason may have been a fear on the part of the king that, even if he agreed to Lysander's plan and expressed his willingness to command such an expedition, his offer might be rejected; we have noted already that a fear of rejection was a deep-seated element of his character. No Spartan king had even taken a force to Asia Minor before; even the daring and ambitious Cleomenes I had rejected such a proposal out of hand when Aristagoras of Miletus advanced it in 500.[20] Thus, it was possible that the Spartan assembly might refuse to sanction sending one of their kings as commander, even if they approved the expedition itself. Alternatively, Agesilaus' leadership might have been challenged by the other king, Pausanias, which seems to have occurred, although the challenge was unsuccessful.[21] A second reason for the reluctance of Agesilaus is that he may already have begun to find his close political association with Lysander too confining. The two were linked by personal ties, and the king owed his mentor a debt of gratitude, but this is not to say that Agesilaus necessarily agreed with all of Lysander's political goals, especially those concerning Asia Minor. Agesilaus may already have given thought to dissociating himself from Lysander's politics, as he would do shortly after arriving in Ephesus, in order to establish his own independence of action. However that may be, he agreed to play the role for which Lysander cast him.

Lysander and Agesilaus undertook a carefully planned strategy to secure approval at Sparta for their designs. Lysander set about convincing the Spartans by several arguments that an expeditionary force should be sent across to Asia Minor. First, he observed that the Spartans still held naval superiority and that they ought to use this to attack Asia Minor and forestall any possible Persian invasion of Greece. Second, Lysander stressed that the remnant of the Ten Thousand, those Greeks who had marched with Cyrus the Younger, had made its way from the heart of the Persian Empire to the sea, thus demonstrating the vulnerability of the empire to invasion under proper circumstances. Finally, Lysander recommended a force that would not weaken the fight-

[19]Xen. 3.4.2; cf. Plut. *Ages.* 6.1.
[20]Herod. 5.51.
[21]See Smith, "Lysander and the Spartan Empire," 155 and n.87 for this suggestion.

ing strength of Sparta at home, or its ability to control the situation in Laconia and Messenia, should the need arise: two thousand emancipated helots and six thousand allied Greek troops. Only thirty full Spartan citizens would accompany the expedition, to advise the king and serve in positions of command. Thus, the allies of Sparta would furnish most of the contingent, whereas Sparta's own contribution, consisting of the neodamodeis, was considered relatively expendable.[22] We hear of no opposition in Sparta to these proposals, and understandably so. The choice of commander was another matter entirely.

Agesilaus was generally regarded to be under the influence of Lysander, and it was quite obvious that Lysander expected to be one of the thirty advisers. Thus, the entire enterprise appeared to be another example of Lysander's scheming after power. It was to be expected that the proposals of Lysander would meet opposition from his enemies in Sparta, and particularly from King Pausanias, who had effectively thwarted him in Attica in 403.[23] Lysander did not trust to his still extensive reputation and popularity alone to overcome opposition and influence the outcome of the vote on his proposals. He also wrote to his numerous friends in Asia Minor, instructing them to request that Agesilaus be sent out to their aid. The pressure of their petitions, suggesting that the expedition would encounter their willing support and cooperation if it were led by Agesilaus, aided Lysander's case.[24]

Agesilaus himself secured an oracle from Zeus at Olympia in favor of the enterprise. But even this step was not enough to overcome the opposition; the ephors demanded that Agesilaus consult the Delphic oracle as well to secure divine approval for the project. At Delphi, Agesilaus succeeded in receiving a favorable response to his inquiry by a clever formulation of his question. He asked Apollo if he shared the opinion of his father, Zeus, on the matter.[25] Having overcome the obstacles in Sparta, Agesilaus was duly appointed to lead the expedition by the Spartan state, on the conditions proposed by Lysander. The next step was to secure the allied cooperation that was necessary to assure the expedition's success.

There is no explicit mention in the sources of a congress of the Peloponnesian League at Sparta to discuss how to respond to Herodas'

[22]Xen. 3.4.2; cf. Plut. Ages. 6.1–3; Lys. 23.1–3.
[23]See Hamilton, SBV, pp. 130–32.
[24]Plut. Ages. 6.2, Lys. 23.1–2.
[25]Plut. Mor. 208F10, cf. 191B7. However, note that some scholars deny the authenticity of these oracles, arguing that they have been transferred to Agesilaus from Agesipolis (cf. Xen. 4.7.2–3).

news. Xenophon's phrasing, however, implicitly suggests such a meeting. Xenophon says that "the Spartans began to mobilize their allies and to make plans for what should be done."[26] The evidence of Pausanias makes it clear that the six thousand were initially to be drawn from all of Sparta's allies in Greece and not merely from the Peloponnesians, as had been the case with the force sent out under Thibron.[27] And, finally, Plutarch refers to Agesilaus as "the commander of all Greece."[28] Therefore, it is inherently more probable that the Spartans at least consulted their allies about this expedition than that they decided upon it independently and merely summoned contingents from them. After the Spartan decision to authorize the expedition had been taken, envoys were sent round to the various allied cities to encourage their participation. But not all of Sparta's allies agreed to participate. The Corinthians abstained, on the grounds that their city had recently experienced the destruction of their temple of Olympian Zeus through fire, which they took as an ill omen. Pausanias does assert, however, that they were eager for the expedition and only reluctantly declined to participate.[29] Because the Corinthians, like the Thebans, had also refused to participate in Pausanias' campaign to Attica, as well as in the Elean expedition, some have seen in this instance merely another refusal to cooperate with the Spartans in an enterprise to which they were opposed. Some politicians in Corinth were indeed opposed to Sparta at this time, as the Oxyrhynchus historian attests, and they may well have spoken against the participation of their city in Agesilaus' expedition.[30] But there is no reason to doubt the religious motive alleged for their act, as W. K. Pritchett has demonstrated.[31] The Athenians and the Thebans also refused, and this fact brings us to another theme of this chapter.

The embassy sent to Thebes was led by none other than Aristomelidas, who was Agesilaus' father-in-law and one of the Spartan judges at the trial of the Plataeans.[32] It is clear that Aristomelidas was selected to try to persuade the Thebans to participate because he had connections in

[26]Xen. 3.4.2.

[27]Paus. 3.9.1 mentions that envoys were sent to the Greeks north of the isthmus, as well as to those throughout the Peloponnesus.

[28]Plut. *Ages.* 6.4. The phrase is contained in the dream that Agesilaus claimed to have had while at Geraestus, awaiting the assembling of his army.

[29]Paus. 3.9.2.

[30]*Hell. Oxy.* 7.3, and see Bruce, *Historical Commentary.*

[31]Pritchett, in *GSaW: Part III*, chap. 1, pp. 1–10, demonstrates that in general the Greeks took religious omens and other signs quite seriously; see p. 136 for this particular episode: "The explanation in itself is as plausible as similar refusals on religious grounds to campaign on the part of Sparta."

[32]Paus. 3.9.3; cf. Thuc. 3.52ff., esp. 68.

their city and because the recent conduct of the Thebans suggested that they would need to be convinced to join the expedition. His close relationship with Agesilaus leaves no doubt that he was chosen expressly for this mission. Aristomelidas failed; the Thebans were having none of the expedition. And the failure of Aristomelidas' mission in winter 397/6 should have left no doubt in the mind of Agesilaus about the sort of reception he was likely to encounter in Boeotia.

As we have seen, Agesilaus traveled to Aulis to offer sacrifice in spring 396 before sailing to Asia Minor.[33] We are not told that he was either advised or required to do so by the Spartan authorities, and the likelihood is that he conceived the idea himself, in order to give his enterprise a more heroic cast. It appears that he did not seek permission of the Boeotarchs, who were the Boeotian authorities, before doing so, for the sources say that "when the Boeotarchs learned that he was sacrificing, they sent to stop him," thus implying that word of his action reached Thebes only after his arrival.[34] In addition, he had his own seer perform the sacrifice, instead of the one customarily appointed by the Boeotians. Thus, his conduct toward the Boeotians appeared arrogant and insensitive. It is, of course, possible that Agesilaus' conduct was deliberate, but his chagrin at the Boeotarchs' response suggests otherwise. He may have merely acted thoughtlessly, but the Boeotarchs did not. They not only ordered him to desist from sacrificing but also had the pieces of the victim cast down from the altar, thus spoiling the sacrifice and producing an ill omen. It is possible that their intentions in this act were to provoke Spartan aggression and to initiate warfare; only a year later, they engineered a border incident between Locris and Phocis which did indeed lead to the Corinthian War. But on this occasion in Aulis, Agesilaus was in no position to retaliate to an affront to his dignity; he could hardly turn his force aside from its appointed mission in order to launch a punitive invasion of Boeotia. Therefore, he sailed off, angry and calling the gods to witness the conduct of the Boeotarchs. He was concerned about the interrupted sacrifice, however, as well as with the rude manner in which his pretension to leadership of "all the Greeks" had been rebuffed by the Thebans.[35] The incident at Aulis became for him a public insult, an unjustified affront to his pride, which he never forgave nor forgot.

What were the objectives of Agesilaus in this expedition? How ambitious were his goals? We have more definite testimony about the goals

[33]Xen. 3.4.3–4; Plut. *Ages.* 6.4–6; Paus. 3.9.3–4. See chap. 1 above.
[34]Xen. 3.4.4; Plut. *Ages.* 6.6.
[35]Xen. 3.4.4; Plut. *Ages.* 6.6; Paus. 3.9.4.

of Lysander, and implicitly about the Spartans' in general, than we do about Agesilaus'. The king was quite eager to undertake the expedition after his initial resistance had been overcome, however, for this was his first military command and his first opportunity to achieve fame and glory.[36] And he tried to cloak his expedition in panhellenism, by likening himself to Agamemnon at the head of a Greek army sailing against the hereditary Asian foe.[37] Agesilaus did return to Asia Minor once more, in 366, to fight in the service of a satrap against the Great King of Persia, and he spent the last years of his life in service to rebellious Egyptians against the power of Persia.[38] Scholars have argued, therefore, that he was motivated by panhellenism and anti-Persian sentiments throughout his career, stemming from his early experiences in Asia Minor in the 390s.[39] We must attempt to determine, therefore, whether panhellenism was an ideal of Agesilaus.

Upon his arrival at Ephesus, Agesilaus allowed himself to be talked into a truce by Tissaphernes. One wonders why Agesilaus did so, given Tissaphernes' failure to abide by the truce with Dercylidas of the previous year. Perhaps Agesilaus welcomed the chance to familiarize himself with local conditions, for he had never been to Asia Minor before, and perhaps the nascent rivalry with Lysander was preoccupying him. In any case, he used the extra time productively. His energies were initially dedicated to asserting his own position of authority and curbing Lysander's ambition, rather than to making military preparations.[40] Agesilaus also managed to end the civil disorders that had been going on in many of the cities there as a result of the ephors' decree to restore the ancestral constitutions. Xenophon claims that Agesilaus achieved this "without bloodshed or banishment" and that he won much good will as a result.[41] By the time of the expiration of the truce, he had managed to affirm his authority and to reduce Lysander to a subordinate position, and he looked forward to engaging the enemy. By a ruse of his own, Agesilaus was able to ravage land belonging to the Persians without serious resistance or interference from Tissaphernes.[42] Agesilaus con-

---

[36]Xen. *Ages.* 1.6–8; Plut. *Ages.* 6.1, *Lys.* 23.1–2.

[37]The term *panhellenism* needs definition. S. Perlman, "Panhellenism, the Polis and Imperialism," *Historia* 25 (1976):1–30, provides a good orientation. Although anti-Persian sentiment appears to have been an important ingredient, some sense of Greek unity and cooperation was also obviously essential.

[38]Xen. *Ages.* 2.25–31; Plut. *Ages.* 36–40.

[39]Cawkwell, "Agesilaus and Sparta," 65–66.

[40]Xen. 3.4.7–10; Plut. *Lys.* 23.3–9, 24.1–2, *Ages.* 7–8.

[41]*Xen. Ages.* 1.37–38; cf. 3.4.2 and 7.

[42]Xen. 3.4.11–15, *Ages.* 1.13–19; Plut. *Ages.* 9.1–3.

ducted successful operations in the Hellespontine region, the satrapy of Pharnabazus, before returning to his headquarters at Ephesus for the winter.

In the following spring, new councillors reached Agesilaus, and Lysander and his fellows returned to Sparta. Agesilaus had spent part of the winter in raising and training a cavalry force, in which element he was clearly deficient. It is tempting to think that Agesilaus had the advice in this matter of Xenophon, who was in his service at this time, for the following reasons. Xenophon had commanded the so-called Cyreians since their return to the Asiatic seabord late in 400. Since then they had served, first under Thibron, then under Dercylidas, and finally under Agesilaus himself after his arrival in Asia Minor in 396. Furthermore, Xenophon had commanded cavalry in the army of the Ten Thousand and later wrote a tract on horsemanship.[43] When his preparations were complete, Agesilaus then tricked Tissaphernes into thinking he would march south to Caria, but he headed northeast toward Sardis. In summer 395, a skirmish near Sardis turned into a battle in which Agesilaus claimed victory. This battle is the subject of a heated conflict in historical writing. Scholars have argued for or against the two principal sources for the events: Xenophon's account in the *Hellenica* (3.4.21–25; cf. *Ages.* 1.29–34) and that of the anonymous author of the *Hellenica Oxyrhynchia* (11.4–6).[44]

Ever since B. P. Grenfell and A. S. Hunt's publication of the *Hellenica Oxyrhynchia,* a rather fierce scholarly controversy has raged over the value of this work, and particularly over its importance vis-à-vis Xenophon's *Hellenica.* To state the matter briefly, almost every commentator who has studied these two accounts of the Battle of Sardis has agreed that they are contradictory; that the contradictions can not be resolved easily, if at all; and that one must prefer one account over the other. Opinions on the trustworthiness of the account of Xenophon have depended upon whether one believes that he was an eyewitness to the battle; he himself reports that he was relieved of command at the beginning of spring 395 and that the newly arrived Spartiate staff was put in command of the various elements of Agesilaus' army, including the cavalry

---

[43]See Anderson, *Xenophon,* pp. 146–49 and 152; and Higgins, *Xenophon,* pp. 132–38.

[44]There is much scholarly debate over the actual events of the Sardis campaign. For orientation to the source problems, see the very useful discussion of Bruce, in Appendix 1 of his *Historical Commentary.* See also J. K. Anderson, "The Battle of Sardis in 395 B.C.," *CSCA* 7 (1974):27–53; and V. J. Gray, "Two Different Approaches to the Battle of Sardis in 395 B.C.: Xenophon *Hellenica* 3.4.20–24 and *Hellenica Oxyrhynchia* 11 (6).4–6," *CSCA* 12 (1979):183–200.

and the Cyreian corps.[45] Therefore, it is possible that Xenophon remained behind in Ephesus, the staging area for Agesilaus' march, when the army departed and, if so, that he obtained his information about the battle afterward, from participants. But in such a case, we would expect Xenophon to have received his information from the commander himself, Agesilaus, for they were on close terms, and Xenophon accompanied him back to Greece the next year and was with him at Coroneia.[46]

The anonymous author of the *Hellenica Oxyrhynchia,* on the other hand, is generally taken to be a historian of the first order, who took great pains to get his information straight and who, moreover, had a keen interest in political history especially.[47] But there is no agreement as to his identity and thus little can be asserted about his methods and purposes in his history, other than what the surviving fragments suggest. We have no way of knowing who or what his source (or sources) for this campaign was, and the account of Diodorus, which derives ultimately from him through Ephorus, adds nothing on this score. Although scholarly opinion had tended to favor the Oxyrhynchus historian to Xenophon on the Sardis campaign, two more recent studies have argued cogently for the plausibility, and superiority, of Xenophon's account.[48] Although I recognize the likelihood that we may never know the truth, I am inclined to accept Xenophon's version on this particular episode.

Xenophon tells us that, after making extensive preparations during winter 396/5 in his headquarters at Ephesus, Agesilaus prepared to march in spring 395. First, he made the appointments of commanders noted above, and then he announced that he would march "by the shortest route to the best parts of the country." Tissaphernes, who had been deceived by Agesilaus the previous year, when the king declared that he would march into Caria and then went north instead, this time decided that Agesilaus intended to march south to Caria, his own satrapal seat, and thus prepared to defend his territory. As J. K. Anderson has well demonstrated, Xenophon's description of the route to Sardis as taking three days, and being free from enemies, probably corresponds to one of the frequently traveled routes between Ephesus and the Hermus River Valley.[49]

---

[45]Xen. 3.4.20.
[46]Xen. *Anab.* 5.3.6; Plut. *Ages.* 18.1; Diog. Laert. 2.6.
[47]See Bruce, *Historical Commentary,* pp. 3–27, at pp. 5–8 esp., and 150–58.
[48]Anderson, "The Battle of Sardis," 27–53, and Gray, "Two Different Approaches to the Battle of Sardis," 183–200.
[49]Anderson, "The Battle of Sardis," 32–43.

Tissaphernes, having received intelligence of the actual route of march of Agesilaus, probably hastened to intercept him before he reached Sardis, crossing the mountains between the Cayster and Hermus valleys at a point farther east than where Agesilaus had crossed. Thus, Tissaphernes' advance guard, the Persian cavalry, descended into the Hermus Plain along the Pactolus River, below the city of Sardis. Meanwhile, Agesilaus was moving east. He encountered the enemy along the Hermus Plain toward Sardis. The Persians had established their baggage train and camp on the other side of the Pactolus River, and the cavalry was harassing the Greeks, who were scattered about in search of plunder. Agesilaus ordered his newly formed cavalry to attack the Persians, while the infantry moved forward on the double, the younger hoplites led by the swifter peltasts. The Persian cavalry was pinned at first by the Greek horse, and then attacked by the infantry. The Persian cavalry panicked and fled. Some Persians were cut down in the pursuit, while others succeeded in escaping. The Greeks crossed the Pactolus and found the camp undefended, and the peltasts began to plunder it. Agesilaus then arrived and surrounded the camp to prevent the peltasts from seizing undue booty. Although he could not take the city of Sardis, where Tissaphernes chanced to be (having come up with his forces behind the cavalry), Agesilaus nevertheless profited from his victory.[50] On this occasion, Agesilaus clearly demonstrated a good command of tactics, and he used the combined arms at his disposal to very good effect. Whatever the facts of the Battle of Sardis, Agesilaus and his force won a distinct victory, with important consequences in the political and diplomatic realms.

Two rather immediate results of the battle seem to have favored the

[50]Xen. 3.4.20–25, with discussions in Anderson, "The Battle of Sardis"; and Gray, "Two Different Approaches to the Battle of Sardis." Let us briefly compare the account of the Oxyrhynchus historian. Although a host of minor discrepancies has been noted (see, in particular, Ch. Dugas, "La campagne d'Agesilas en Asie Mineure," *BCH* 34 (1910):58–95, and the subsequent literature cited in Bruce, *Historical Commentary*, p. 155; and Gray, "Two Different Approaches," 183 and n. 1), two in particular stand out. The first is the difference in the march of Agesilaus to Sardis; the second is the account of the battle proper. Anderson has argued persuasively that Xenophon is likely to be correct where the march from Ephesus to Sardis is concerned (p. 42ff.). As to the second aspect, the Oxyrhynchus historian tells us that Agesilaus set an ambush, consisting of a force of hoplites and peltasts commanded by Xenocles, to trap the Persians (*Hell. Oxy.* 11.1–2; cf. Diod. 14.80.1–2). We have other evidence that Agesilaus used such tactics in his campaigns, but the problem is to explain how, or why, Xenophon would have omitted this tactic in his account of the battle. Gray notes that the Oxyrhynchus historian seems to have had a special interest in the use of stratagems such as this ambush, and she suggests that perhaps, lacking further details of the battle itself, he fell back on an established literary device to explain Agesilaus' success (196–97).

aims of Agesilaus: the execution of Tissaphernes, and his own appointment to joint command of the land and naval forces in the Aegean
theater of war.[51] When the Great King learned of the failure of Tissaphernes to protect the suburbs of Sardis and of his defeat, he dispatched
Tithraustes, a high-ranking official of the court, to remove and execute
the satrap. Thus, beheaded in his bath, perished the Persian with whom
the Spartans had had perhaps the most numerous contacts over the last
seventeen years.[52] At home, the Spartan authorities were so delighted
with the victory of Agesilaus that they took the unprecedented step of
conferring upon him command of both the army and the fleet in the war
against Persia.[53] He, in turn, delegated power as navarch to Peisander.
Agesilaus then marched again to the Hellespont, having accepted a truce
and a sum of money from Tithraustes for the purpose. In all of this,
there is little to indicate that Agesilaus yet thought of anything but what
had become the routine of this war: regular, seasonal campaigning in
which one side attempted to inflict damage on the other, whether by
ravaging, in battle, or by subverting subjects and allies. It is only after
winter 395/4 that different objectives are mentioned.

As a result, perhaps, of his success in persuading the native chieftain
Spithridates to revolt from the Great King to him, Agesilaus is reported
to have conceived the plan of marching into the interior of the empire to
inflict heavy damage upon the Great King. Xenophon says that Agesilaus hoped to detach many subject peoples from the Great King and to
make them his allies.[54] Just at this point, before Agesilaus could act on
his new strategic goal, orders reached him to return to Greece to assist
Sparta in the Corinthian War.[55] Disappointed at being summoned back
before he had accomplished the great things he yet hoped to do, Agesilaus nonetheless made preparations at once to return to Europe.

It is instructive to compare the various accounts of Agesilaus' ambitions. In the *Hellenica,* Xenophon merely indicates that Agesilaus had
this plan in mind, and he does not make clear what the king ultimately
hoped to achieve by a policy of sowing disaffection in the Persian
Empire. In his *Agesilaus,* however, Xenophon elaborates on this goal,
claiming that war was "not to save Greece, but to subdue Asia" and that
he had hoped "to crown his achievement by dissolving the empire that

[51]Xen. 3.4.25, 27.
[52]Xen. 3.4.25, *Ages.* 1.35; Diod. 14.80.6–8; Polyaenus 7.16.1.
[53]Xen. 3.4.27; Plut. *Ages.* 10.5.
[54]Xen. 4.1.41; Plut. *Ages.* 15.1.
[55]Xen. 4.2.1–2; Plut. *Ages.* 15.2.

had attacked Greece in the past."⁵⁶ These are extravagant claims indeed, and they are made at a safe time; that is, when Agesilaus has been forced to turn back to Greece and cannot possibly attempt to execute his plans. And this book, unlike the *Hellenica,* was written after Agesilaus' death. Plutarch makes Agesilaus' objective even more impressive, "to march into the interior of the empire and to fight for the person of the Great King himself, and for the wealth of Susa and Ecbatana."⁵⁷ It is quite clear that Plutarch is writing here with the benefit of hindsight, as his comparison between Agesilaus and Alexander indicates. But how accurate are these descriptions of Agesilaus' plans and objectives in 394? This question is all the more important because Agesilaus never had the opportunity to implement such plans, and because these passages are fundamental to any argument that he was a panhellenist throughout his career.

It is, of course, very difficult to resolve this question. We are dependent upon the sources for our knowledge of Agesilaus' motives and ambitions, and there is no means to verify their evidence. But an examination of the development of their accounts may help us. The version in the *Hellenica* presents the simplest set of goals for Agesilaus, and, although there is considerable scholarly debate over the relationship between this account and that of the *Agesilaus,* I believe that the former account is more accurate and that the elaborated objectives of the latter work represent Xenophon's attempt to portray his deceased hero as a panhellenic figure. Of course, Plutarch's account is the latest, although it may well be based on other fourth-century sources, such as Ephorus or Theopompus, which are not extant. It is possible to trace a development in the surviving literature of the treatment of Agesilaus' goals in 394 from an originally modest proposal to spread disaffection among the Great King's subjects to a full-blown crusade to destroy the empire itself. The latter plan was never fully developed by Agesilaus in 394, although Xenophon may have suggested it to him. Xenophon's experience of the expedition of Cyrus the Younger, and of the march back to the sea from the heart of Mesopotamia, may have convinced him that it was possible for a Greek army of moderate size to attempt the conquest of the Persian Empire. It is very easy to see how his eulogistic work might have attributed such plans to Agesilaus at this

⁵⁶Xen. *Ages.* 1.8; 1.36; cf. 2.29. E. C. Marchant, trans., *Xenophon: Scripta Minora,* pp. 65 and 79.
⁵⁷Plut. *Ages.* 15.1–3.

point in his career. But could Agesilaus have been receptive to such a plan?

None of the Spartan commanders before Agesilaus had ever attempted, or even proposed, a march into the interior of the Persian Empire in an attempt to destroy its King's power. The idea must have appeared novel, then, if it was actually mooted in 394. The orders of Agesilaus, as far as we know them, also gave him no licence to embark on such an undertaking. To have marched into the interior of the empire might have put the Greek cities at risk, not to mention his own lines of communication and supply, and his mission was to protect those very cities. In his absence, Pharnabazus, Tithraustes, and other Persian dignitaries would have had a free hand to operate against the Greek communities.

We must also consider the question of logistics. It is one thing to march several days inland from the coast (and from the sea, whereby links with Greece were maintained), but quite another to march for three months or more into the heart of hostile country. Agesilaus always seems to have been aware of the problems of supply for his army in his campaigning near the coast, and he surely would have given serious thought to the problems of obtaining food for his troops, fodder for his animals, and material at great distances from the seaboard and friendly territory. Xenophon *could* have told him, if he did not, of the difficulties in this regard which the Greeks had occasionally faced while they marched as part of Cyrus' army. Last, but not least, there was the question of Agesilaus' army itself. This was a motley group, consisting of several thousands of neodamodeis, of even more numerous Peloponnesian allied troops, of Greek mercenaries (many of whom were remnants of the Ten Thousand), and of local Greek units raised in one fashion or another. Whether such a force could have been held together on such an expedition, and how it would have been paid and supported, were questions that no competent general could afford not to ask. In short, it is extremely unlikely that Agesilaus ever contemplated the extravagant objectives that the sources attribute to him and, if he ever did contemplate them, that he must have quickly realized that they were beyond his abilities. A somewhat more limited goal of establishing a band of territories between the coastal strip, protected by Sparta, and the interior of the Persian Empire, governed by local rulers in revolt from the Great King, has been proposed.[58] Although such a strategic

---

[58]See R. J. Seager, "Agesilaus in Asia: Propaganda and Objectives," *LCM* 2 (1977):

objective cannot be proved without a doubt, it is at least a possibility. In any case, this objective is quite different from the grandiose plans that Xenophon and Plutarch ascribed to Agesilaus. To claim that Agesilaus was a panhellenist because he entertained plans of invasion deep into the Persian Empire with the object of destroying it is to ignore a number of practical and relevant aspects of his situation in 394. To explain how such an idea came about is easy enough, given Xenophon's tendency to heroize Agesilaus, and his desire in the *Agesilaus* to exonerate him from the hostile charges in Plutarch's account.

The withdrawal of Agesilaus from Asia Minor in summer 394, and the disastrous naval defeat at Cnidus shortly before his arrival at the borders of Boeotia, ended an epoch for Sparta. Theopompus chose to end his *Hellenica* at this juncture, for he believed that the Spartan defeat represented a major turning point in Greek affairs. Agesilaus did not return to Asia Minor for a quarter-century, despite the hopes that he had expressed to his Greek allies from the area.[59] Now the attention of Agesilaus, from the point of his recall to Greece, was focused elsewhere than on the Greeks of Asia Minor or on panhellenism and patriotism: his enmity was turned, once again, toward Thebes.

The Corinthian War

The Thebans had failed in their gambit to provoke a hostile reaction from the Spartans at Aulis, but Ismenias' faction continued to plot to reduce Sparta's might in Greece. Fear and alarm over Spartan aggression had also been growing in other Greek states—especially Athens, Corinth and Argos—and Persian diplomacy, reinforced with ample sums of money, stimulated them to open hostility by 395. At Haliartus in Boeotia in that year, Lysander met death and his allied army met defeat at the hands of the Thebans.[60] Whether Agesilaus felt any loss at his former friend's death, or remorse for the way he had treated him at Ephesus in 396, one can only surmise. It is virtually certain, however, that he would have experienced both shame and anger over the defeat of a Spartan force by the Thebans, as did many in Sparta. When King Pausanias, arriving at Haliartus the day after the battle, elected to re-

---

183–84; and D. H. Kelly, "Agesilaus' Strategy in Asia Minor, 396–395 B.C.," *LCM* 3 (1978):97–98.

[59]Xen. 4.2.3–4.

[60]Xen. 3.5.17–20; Plut. *Lys.* 28; Paus. 3.5.3.

cover the dead by truce instead of by fighting, the Spartans were outraged and brought charges of misconduct against him. Pausanias fled to Tegea and was condemned *in absentia*.[61] As more and more states joined the anti-Spartan coalition during 395, the situation became more and more dangerous, and eventually the ephors determined to summon Agesilaus home.

When the order reached him, Agesilaus dutifully obeyed and prepared to return, despite his great disappointment. The sources underscore his readiness to obey the authorities, one of the qualities they most admire in him, by emphasizing the high hopes he had at this time of achieving even greater victories over his enemies in Asia Minor, and his acute disappointment at losing the opportunity to do so.[62] The great expedition, which had engendered such expectations in the king but which had begun so inauspiciously at Aulis, was now brought to a premature end, and precisely when Agesilaus was supposedly planning to crown his victory at the Battle of Sardis in 395 with even more daring exploits. The reason for his recall to Greece was clear: war threatened the state at home, and, because Pausanias had been banished and his sons were still minors, Sparta had need of Agesilaus. The cause of the war was Theban intrigue and corruption at the hands of Persian agents; this was widely believed.[63] Therefore, Agesilaus had good reason to intensify his hatred of the Thebans, who once again had intervened decisively in his affairs.

We cannot know when precisely Agesilaus' attitude toward Thebes hardened; perhaps it was a gradual process, beginning with the incident at Aulis, continuing through the news of the outbreak of the war in Greece and of Haliartus, and culminating on the return march to Boeotia. In any case, the behavior of Agesilaus at the Battle of Coronea in late summer 394 shows him in the grip of intense and powerful emotions—anger, hatred, and revenge—which almost make his actions irrational, and his subsequent dealings with Thebes reveal a similar pattern. It is easier to recognize the reasons for his anger and hatred, however, than it is to understand the depth and intensity of those emotions and the way in which they seem to have dominated, even obsessed, him over the next quarter-century.

When Agesilaus announced to his allies that he had been ordered home by the Spartan government, the contingents of Greeks from Asia Minor declared their willingness to march with him. In turn, he pledged

[61]Xen. 3.5.21–25; Plut. *Lys.* 29.1–3, 30.1; Paus. 3.5.4–6.
[62]Xen. 4.1.41–2.1–4, *Ages.* 1.35–36; Plut. *Ages.* 15.1–6.
[63]Xen. 3.5.1–5; *Hell. Oxy.* 7.2–3, 13.1–3, 18.1–5; Plut. *Ages.* 15.6.

to return to Asia Minor as soon as he could, and he left behind garrisons under harmosts in many of the cities. He marched from the Hellespont through Thrace, Macedonia, and Thessaly to the borders of Boeotia without much difficulty. In Thessaly he made use of his cavalry to defeat the renowned Thessalian horsemen who were harassing his column, and then at Narthacium he proudly erected a trophy in celebration of this victory. He was particularly proud that his victory was over a people that prided itself for its excellent cavalry, the Thessalians, and that he had won it with the force that he himself had raised and trained in Asia Minor.[64]

At Thermopylae, Agesilaus planned to collect reinforcements before invading Boeotia, for his army was composed almost totally of allied contingents and neodamodeis, and virtually bereft of Spartan hoplites.[65] The ephors sent orders for him to proceed immediately, however, and he did so, remarking to his closest associates that the day for which they had returned from Asia Minor was at hand. When he reached the border at Orchomenus, he was joined by one regiment of Spartan troops which had crossed over from Corinth to his aid, and half a regiment which was stationed in Orchomenus. The ephors had also allowed any young Spartan to volunteer to join Agesilaus, and fifty such were sent to him. Thus bolstered by his own elite troops, Agesilaus prepared for battle.[66] When he reached Boeotia, where he was to encounter the enemy coalition, news of the defeat at Cnidus arrived. In that naval engagement, Conon and Pharnabazus had crushed the Spartan fleet, and Peisander, Agesilaus' brother-in-law and the navarch in command, had perished. The defeat was devastating, but Agesilaus deliberately suppressed this information and told his men that the engagement had been a Spartan victory; the deception seems to have had the desired effect of uplifting the morale of his troops on the eve of battle, and they won a skirmish with the enemy before the main engagement.[67]

---

[64]Xen. 4.3.3–9, Ages. 2.2–5. In the Agesilaus, Xenophon comments that the trophies of Agesilaus were as numerous as his campaigns (6.3), but this is no doubt a bit of hyperbole.

[65]Xen. 4.2.5; Plut. Ages. 17.1–2.

[66]Xen. 4.3.10, 15–16, cf. 4.2.5; Plutarch, Ages. 17.1–2, mentions two regiments crossing over from the Peloponnesus, but he is contradicted, and disproven, by the eyewitness report of Xenophon, Ages. 2.6, who says clearly that he had "one regiment and a half of Lacedaemonians."

[67]Xen. 4.3.10–14. In Ages. 6.5–6, Xenophon speaks in general terms of Agesilaus' skill in the use of the ruse, praising even the use of deception when it seemed necessary and useful. On deception by Spartans, see A. Powell, "Mendacity and Sparta's Use of the

Xenophon remarks that the Battle of Coroneia was unlike any that had been fought in his time.[68] Some scholars have taken this comment as proof that Xenophon must have written this account in the *Hellenica* (and that in the *Agesilaus*) before the Battle of Leuctra in 371, because that was unquestionably the most important battle of the entire period, but this interpretation need not be correct. It is most likely that Xenophon was present at Coroneia, having accompanied Agesilaus on his march home, whereas he clearly was not at Leuctra. Furthermore, the peculiar development of the battle may well have caused him to record this remark.

The Battle of Coroneia was a classic hoplite encounter, in which neither cavalry nor peltasts played any considerable role; both sides were roughly equal in numbers.[69] The anti-Spartan coalition was drawn up with its back to Mount Helicon and its flank near the town of Coroneia. Agesilaus' army had crossed the Cephisus River and faced the coalition on the plain. The two lines advanced, with the Thebans opposite the Orchomenians, the Argives facing Agesilaus' contingent, and the other troops of the coalition in the center, across from the Asiatic mercenaries under Herippidas. The Thebans moved forward more swiftly than the rest of their line and put the Orchomenians to flight, rushing on to the baggage train in the Spartan rear; but Herippidas' forces overwhelmed their opponents, and the Argives are said to have fled before they crossed spears with Agesilaus. Except for the Thebans, the allies were beaten all along the line. Xenophon says that Agesilaus could have permitted the Thebans to file past his Spartans and then attacked them on the flank, which would undoubtedly have inflicted severe casualties on them. Instead, he chose to block their withdrawal and thus force, in effect, a second, frontal confrontation, which was tantamount to a new major engagement.[70]

The Thebans came on gamely and bravely and began to cut their way through the Spartan lines. Agesilaus fought furiously in his own front

Visual," in *Classical Sparta: Techniques behind Her Success,* edited by A. Powell, pp. 173–92 (Norman, Okla., 1989).

[68]Xen. 4.3.16; cf. *Ages.* 2.9.

[69]Xen. 4.3.15–21, *Ages.* 2.6–16, and Plut. *Ages.* 18.1–19.3 provide the main accounts; summary versions in Diod. 14.84.1–2; Paus. 9.6.4; Nepos *Ages.* 4.5; Polyaenus 2.1.3–4; Frontinus 2.6.6; and Justin 6.4.13. On the battle itself, see W. K. Pritchett, *Studies in Ancient Greek Topography, Part II: Battlefields* (Berkeley and Los Angeles, 1969), pp. 85–95, which gives full references and evaluation of the ancient sources. See also Lazenby, *Spartan Army,* pp. 143–48.

[70]Xen. 4.3.19, *Ages.* 2.12.

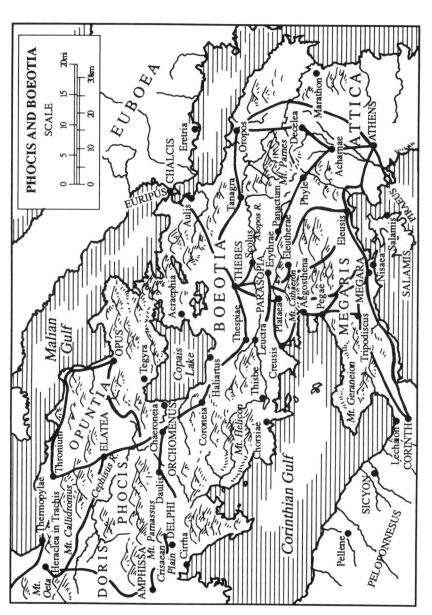

The Battle of Coroneia

PHOCIS AND BOEOTIA

SCALE

0   5   10   15   20mi

0   10   20   30km

EUBOEA

CHALCIS

EURIPUS

ATTICA

ATHENS

PIRAEUS

Marathon

Decelea

Acharnae

Oropos

Mt. Parnes

Phyle

Eleusis

Eleutherae

Panactum

Erythrae

Salamis

SALAMIS

Aulis

Tanagra

Scolus

Asopos R.

Mt. Cithaeron

Aegosthena

Pegae

Tripodiscus

MEGARIS

MEGARA

Nisaea

Mt. Geraneion

THEBES

PARASOPIA

Plataea

Leuctra

Creusis

Thespiae

Thisbe

Chorsiae

Mt. Helicon

Haliartus

Coroneia

BOEOTIA

Acraphia

Copais
Lake

Tegyra

OPUS

OPUNTIA

ELATEA

Thronium

Mt. Callidromus

Heraclea in Trachis

Thermopylae

Malian
Gulf

Mt.
Oeta

DORIS

AMPHISSA

Mt. Parnassus

Crisaean
Plain

Cirrha

DELPHI

Daulis

PHOCIS

Cephisus R.

Chaeroneia

ORCHOMENUS

Corinthian Gulf

Lechaion

CORINTH

SICYON

Pellene

PELOPONNESUS

line and suffered numerous wounds inflicted by the Thebans. He fell, and his bodyguard found it difficult to carry him to safety. Eventually, the Thebans broke through and made their way, still in good order, up Mount Helicon. One group, however, sought refuge in the nearby temple of Athena Itonia. When their plight was reported to Agesilaus, he gave orders that they be permitted to escape to safety. On the day following the battle, Agesilaus ordered his forces once more into the field in order to see if the Thebans wished further combat. They did not, asking instead for permission to recover their dead under truce. Agesilaus granted this, set up a trophy to mark his victory, and then went to Delphi to dedicate the tithe of his booty from Asia Minor before returning to Sparta.[71]

Two things stand out about the conduct of Agesilaus at this battle: his desire to crush Thebes militarily, and his concern to appear to have done so honorably and bravely, without resorting to any tactics that might seem at all questionable and thus detract from the significance of his anticipated victory. The sources note that he took an unnecessary risk in engaging the retreating Thebans in frontal combat, and Xenophon seems at a loss to explain Agesilaus' conduct on this occasion, which he describes as "unquestionably courageous, but hardly the safest plan."[72]

Despite the technical victory that Agesilaus won, symbolized by the request of the Thebans to recover their dead and his erection of the trophy, the outcome of the battle was in no way decisive. The Theban contingent in particular had distinguished itself, fighting through the Spartan lines to safety, and the Spartan casualties, while not enumerated by Xenophon, could not have been light, as his description of the intense fighting around the king indicates. Thus, the victory at Coroneia was much less than Agesilaus had hoped. He had not soundly defeated the Thebans, or punished them for the wrongs he imagined they had done him. Furthermore, the battle had not given the Spartans the victory they had hoped would impel their enemies to negotiate. Finally, Agesilaus suffered painful wounds. The stalemate at Coroneia contributed even more to his developing ire toward Thebes.

There is a final note on this episode. If the chief objective of battle is to obtain victory, then Agesilaus attained his goal with undue and unnecessary risk. For he not only endangered his own life but also risked the entire campaign. Had he been killed, as Lysander had been at Haliartus a year earlier, or as Cleombrotus would be at Leuctra in 371, his force

---

[71]Xen. 4.3.19–21, *Ages.* 2.13–16; Plut. *Ages.* 18.1–19.3.
[72]Xen. *Ages.* 2.12, cf. 4.3.19.

might have withdrawn from the field in dismay, leaving the Thebans victorious. Only a small contingent of Agesilaus' army were Spartans, and even their discipline might have faltered if their commander had been killed. To be sure, ancient commanders routinely risked their lives in battle; Alexander the Great was almost killed at the Granicus at the beginning of his invasion of Asia.[73] But the need for the commander to take an active role does not diminish the fact that the risking of his life endangers the entire campaign; consider the results of the death of Cyrus the Younger at Cunaxa in 401.[74] It is one thing for a commander to risk his life in order to carry the battle, and quite another for him to do so unnecessarily, as Agesilaus apparently did. Had he died at Coroneia in 394, much of subsequent Greek history would have been different.

Little is known of Agesilaus' activities during the two years following his return to Sparta late in summer 394. He may simply have been recuperating from the wounds sustained at Coroneia, but another explanation is equally likely. R. E. Smith suggests that the failure of the state to entrust any campaign to him reflects its dissatisfaction with his recent performance.[75] Several reasons may be adduced for this dissatisfaction. First, the disastrous naval defeat suffered at Cnidus in August 394, under the command of Peisander, his brother-in-law, must have had grave repercussions in Sparta, and it is likely that his enemies laid much of the blame for this defeat at Agesilaus' door. The Spartans might have returned to Asia Minor to wage further war effectively against Persia had they maintained control of the sea. But the Spartan fleet suffered a devastating defeat at Cnidus, from which they never fully recovered. Plutarch's criticism of Agesilaus for appointing the inexperienced Peisander to this critically important post for personal reasons, when other, more seasoned candidates were available, is just as pertinent today as when Plutarch (or his source) made it in antiquity.[76] Nothing of enduring value, save perhaps to his own military reputation, resulted from the campaigns of Agesilaus in Asia Minor, and he must bear the blame for Cnidus, at least indirectly, because of his judgment in the selection of the naval commander. Second, his failure to win a decisive victory at Coroneia and thus force the anti-Spartan

---

[73]Cf. Arrian, *Alex.* 1.14–15.

[74]Xen. *Anab.* 1.10ff.

[75]See Smith, "Opposition," 274, for this suggestion.

[76]Xen. 4.3.10–12, cf. 3.4.27–29; Plutarch, *Ages.* 10.5–6, reports that Agesilaus was criticized for appointing an inexperienced commander such as Peisander, his brother-in-law, which he had done to gratify his wife.

coalition to the bargaining table may well have provided ammunition for his domestic foes. Finally, he had to face a hostile faction's organized opposition when he returned to Sparta. Agesilaus had deliberately humiliated Lysander and therefore incurred his undying anger. In retaliation, Lysander plotted to change the Spartan constitution by making the monarchy elective, and in 395 strove to build an effective political opposition to Agesilaus in Sparta.[77] Before his plans to modify the method of succession and then perhaps to challenge Agesilaus personally and work to have him deposed could be put into effect, Lysander died in the Battle of Haliartus.

After the Battle of Coroneia, Agesilaus had to exert continuous efforts to neutralize the effects of Lysander's work. He had to go to Lysander's house in search of a state document, and he found there a copy of a speech that Lysander had had prepared to aid in his proposed constitutional change. Agesilaus immediately realized that he could ruin Lysander's reputation, and undercut what remained of his political influence, if he published this document. One of the ephors advised against this, however, arguing that Agesilaus' plan would result in more harm than good. Agesilaus followed his advice and decided to "bury the document with the dead Lysander."[78] The political faction that Lysander had formed against Agesilaus continued to work against his interest, and Plutarch relates that he had to devote a fair amount of time and effort to diffuse this opposition and to win over (or at least to neutralize) his political enemies.[79] It is probable that the supporters of the exiled King Pausanias also opposed Agesilaus, and he worked to cultivate the friendship of Pausanias' son Agesipolis.[80] It is impossible to tell how much time this process of political reconciliation took, but the evidence suggests that it was a lengthy undertaking. Therefore, it is unlikely that Agesilaus had consolidated his political position and had recovered from his battle wounds before momentous shifts in Spartan policy occurred in 392.

---

[77]Plut. *Lys.* 24–26, *Ages.* 20.2.

[78]According to Plutarch's *Agesilaus* (20.3), it was an unnamed geron who advised Agesilaus not to make public Lysander's speech, whereas in the *Lysander* (30.4) it was Lacratidas, the chief ephor, who gave this advice; this discrepancy suggests that Plutarch used at least two sources for this episode and that he did not take the trouble to reconcile their conflicting information. In any case, the concern with making the document public was that it might stir up trouble by influencing the Spartans to consider making a change from hereditary to elective monarchy.

[79]Plut. *Ages.* 20.2–4.

[80]Plut. *Ages.* 20.5–6.

After a fruitless year of trench warfare in which the Spartans fought no further pitched battles in Greece, they turned their efforts to a diplomatic resolution of their dilemma, and it seems quite clear that the diplomatic overtures were not to Agesilaus' liking. The early years of the Corinthian War had exposed the limits of the strength of Sparta and demonstrated its incapability to conduct the war successfully on two widely separated fronts. By the beginning of 392, the balance sheet told against Sparta. In Greece, Sparta had lost not only its commander Lysander but also much prestige at Haliartus, which had led to the formation and expansion of the anti-Spartan coalition. Thebes, Athens, Corinth, Argos, and a host of less powerful states had rebelled against Sparta and, with Persian subsidies, were fighting to overthrow its hegemony in Greece. The allied coalition formed a solid block of territory stretching from central Greece to the very borders of Laconia, and Sparta was effectively isolated within the Peloponnesus by the occupation of Corinth at the isthmus. The victories of Sparta in 394 at Nemea and Coroneia were insufficient to incline its enemies to negotiate. The situation was even worse in the Aegean. Cnidus cost Sparta its recently acquired naval supremacy, and Pharnabazus and Conon followed up their victory with a diplomatic campaign to win over the Greek cities from Spartan control. Sparta's insufficient resources precluded a victory in such a war, and its serious losses in the Aegean theater, as well as its natural inclination to protect its immediate interests in Greece, led to the mission of the Spartan diplomat Antalcidas.

In spring 392, Sparta sent Antalcidas to Sardis to attempt to arrange a peace with the satrap Tiribazus. Antalcidas proposed a settlement that, first, would have recognized the Persian claim to the cities of Asia Minor and, second, guaranteed the autonomy of all other poleis. Although the offer to relinquish the Greeks of Asia Minor to Persian control may have struck many Greeks as a callous abandonment of Sparta's commitment to protect them, the plan was, after all, really only a return to the policy of the Ionian War. Furthermore, when Conon and Pharnabazus had swept through the Aegean in the aftermath of the Battle of Cnidus, they had proclaimed freedom to any Greek city that would admit them. The majority of cities did so, driving out those Spartan harmosts and garrisons that Agesilaus had left in place, and regaining their independence.[81] This independence must mean that, in the short run, these cities were free to govern their own affairs without

[81]Diod. 14.84.3–4; Xen. 4.8.1–5.

being garrisoned by, or paying tribute to, the Persians. Such a situation would have allowed Antalcidas to argue that the cities no longer needed Spartan protection and that they had elected to revert to the Persian sphere of interest. The second clause of the proposed treaty was a novel idea that would become a central aspect of Greek diplomacy in the fourth century. The concept of a common peace that guaranteed the autonomy of every polis could hardly be offensive to any except those who wished to dominate their neighbors, or so at least it could be made to appear. Therefore, the goal of Antalcidas' diplomacy—to relinquish the unprofitable war in Asia Minor and to establish an international order in which the sovereignty of every polis would be guaranteed—was in keeping with the non-interventionist policies that King Pausanias had pursued. It is likely that Antalcidas had emerged as a leading spokesman for those who had supported Pausanias. But the proposals were not successful. Learning of Antalcidas' mission, the allies sent envoys of their own to Sardis, and they refused to sanction the peace terms. They undoubtedly suspected that Sparta would try to employ the principle of autonomy to its advantage, and against theirs. Tiribazus agreed to the terms, but his decision was later reversed by his master, Artaxerxes, and the negotiations came to nought.[82] Later in 392, a second conference was held at Sparta in which there was no Persian participation. On this occasion, the Spartans apparently offered lenient terms to their Greek foes in the hope of settling affairs in Greece so that they could turn their attention once again to the war in the Aegean. But the Athenians rejected these terms, the negotiations broke down, and war resumed in 391.[83]

It is difficult to imagine that Agesilaus would have willingly embraced the principle of the surrender of the Greeks of Asia Minor to the Great King of Persia in 392, just two years after he had left there with a promise to return to aid them when all was well at home.[84] Indeed, in speaking of the negotiations that ultimately led to peace in 387 on precisely the terms that Antalcidas proposed first in 392 and then again in 387, Plutarch insists that Agesilaus had no part in the abandonment of the Greeks of Asia Minor.[85] It is curious that Xenophon is silent on the matter. Plutarch asserts, in justification of his remark, that Antalcidas

[82]Xen. 4.8.12–17; cf. Hamilton, *SBV,* chap. 8.

[83]Andoc. 3.20; cf. Hamilton, *SBV,* pp. 252–59; see also J. DeVoto, "Agesilaus, Antalcidas, and the Failed Peace of 392/1 B.C.," *CP* 81 (1986):191–202.

[84]Xen. 4.2.3, cf. 4.3.1–3.

[85]Plut. *Ages.* 23.1–2.

was the bitter enemy of Agesilaus. And the opposition of the two men at other times over relations with Thebes is documented.[86] Plutarch's strong assertion that Agesilaus had nothing to do with the terms of the King's Peace in 387/6 is a bit disingenuous, and it fits with his view of the king as a thoroughgoing panhellenist. Nonetheless, it is difficult to imagine that Agesilaus supported Antalcidas' efforts in 392. Therefore, it seems likely that events had worked against Agesilaus when Antalcidas was dispatched to Sardis. His loss of prestige upon his return home, the opposition of Lysander's followers, and the successes of Conon in the Aegean may have contributed to a situation in which the Spartan authorities—that is, the ephors, but undoubtedly with the assent of a majority of the assembly—decided to seek peace with Persia even at the cost of abandoning the Greeks in Asia Minor. Such a decision surely pained Agesilaus, who probably blamed the Thebans once again for this state of affairs. The only comfort Agesilaus could find in such terms was the hope of a new command against the Thebans.

Agesilaus had to strike a compromise when terms were offered at the conference in Sparta. The price of peace in Greece so that Sparta could renew the war in the Aegean was the granting of terms to its Greek foes which conceded certain matters to them. The union of Corinth and Argos, which had been inaugurated in 392, was to be guaranteed, and these states were willing to make peace.[87] Moreover, the Thebans were eager to accept the terms offered at this point, which they did not find punitive.[88] The treaty would recognize the independence of Orchomenus from the Boeotian Confederacy, but the federal structure was otherwise left intact, with Thebes continuing to dominate Boeotian affairs. Again, Agesilaus would not have been pleased to allow Thebes to escape any punishment for its offenses, but this concession seemed necessary in order to end the conflict at home and to permit the marshaling of effective forces at sea for the resumption of the war against Persia. Clearly, neither of these choices would have satisfied everyone in Sparta, least of all Agesilaus, but the need for compromise was evident, and Sparta was faced with the necessity to salvage what it could from the war. Two opposite desires beset Agesilaus: on the one hand, the wish to return to Asia Minor to complete his unfinished business there; and on the other, the desire to humble and reduce Theban power. Thus,

[86]Plut. *Ages.* 26.2–3; cf. *Pelop.* 15.2 and *Lyc.* 13.6, in which Antalcidas criticizes Agesilaus for teaching the Thebans the art of war, when they had no wish for it.
[87]See Hamilton, *SBV,* chap. 9.
[88]Andoc. 3.20.

his state's dilemma must have produced an agonizing internal conflict, which intensified his hatred for Thebes.

In spring 391, Agesilaus was once again in command of a Spartan army. He invaded and ravaged the Argolid and then, in concert with Teleutias, his half-brother, fell upon the Corinthia.[89] It is evident that Agesilaus had restored his fortunes with the Spartans by this time, not only because he had been given another command but also because it was through his influence that Teleutias had been named navarch.[90] Apparently the misfortune of Cnidus had been forgiven, if not forgotten. Teleutias captured the Corinthian port of Lechaion at the same time that Agesilaus captured the Long Walls, which linked the port to the city of Corinth. These walls had been captured and destroyed by the Spartans in the previous year, then evidently rebuilt.[91] No doubt as a result of this achievement, Agesilaus was sent out in the following year, 390, to conduct further operations in the Corinthia. During these operations, he displayed his feelings toward the Thebans.

Agesilaus had scored a minor triumph at the Isthmus of Corinth. He arrived while the Corinthians and Argives were celebrating the Isthmian Games and sent them fleeing to the protection of the city. Corinthian exiles in his army then celebrated the games anew.[92] After this celebration, Agesilaus marched across the isthmus to Perachora, where he succeeded in capturing a large amount of booty and numerous prisoners at Peiraeon and the Heraeon. While he was contemplating the display of his booty, Theban envoys arrived, seeking an audience with him. In view of the reported eagerness of the Thebans to secure peace at the conference at Sparta in 392, and their virtual withdrawal from military activities after that date, it is not surprising that the object of the embassy was to approach Agesilaus about the possibilities of securing peace. The king pointedly ignored the envoys although Pharax, the Spartan who served as *proxenos* (diplomatic representative), tried to present them to him.[93]

In the meantime, news reached the king that the Spartan army had suffered a serious reverse: near Corinth, Iphicrates, the Athenian mercenary commander, had engineered the destruction of nearly half a regiment of Spartan troops. Agesilaus immediately ordered his troops

[89]Xen. 4.4.19, *Ages.* 2.17.
[90]Plut. *Ages.* 21.1.
[91]Xen. 4.4.13; 4.4.18. See discussion in Hamilton, *SBV,* pp. 280–81.
[92]Xen. 4.5.1–2; Plut. *Ages.* 21.2–3.
[93]Xen. 4.5.6; Plut. *Ages.* 22.1.

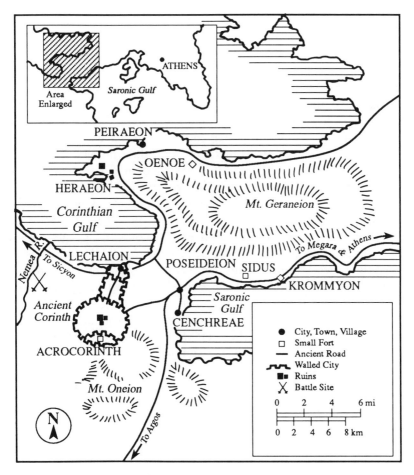

Agesilaus' campaigns near Corinth

to march, but, when he recognized that there was nothing to be done, returned to the Heraeon. Then he summoned the Theban envoys and asked them what they wanted, but their mood had changed. Barely able to contain their jubilation over the Spartan setback, the envoys merely requested permission to journey on to Corinth. Agesilaus became quite angry, seeing through their dissimulation, and replied that he would show them that he was still master of the situation. He did so by marching back to the Corinthia and ravaging the surrounding countryside, while the allied contingents looked on, not daring to venture

out beyond the walls to confront him. He then sent the envoys home to
Thebes via Creusis.[94]

It is, of course, possible that the envoys would have changed their
mind about the advisability of discussing peace in any event, as soon as
they had learned of the defeat of the regiment. But it is undeniable that
Agesilaus lost an important psychological advantage by insulting the
envoys while he was triumphant. Had he received them at that point,
before the news of the defeat arrived, he might have sent them back
home to discuss terms of his dictation with their home government.
Instead, his vengeful and spiteful behavior alienated the envoys and
caused an opportunity to negotiate peace terms to be lost. It is difficult
to say what the authorities in Sparta thought about the king's behavior,
but it is probable that the Theban proxenos, if no one else, lodged a
complaint against it. Perhaps the choice of the young King Agesipolis to
lead an expedition two years later against Argos, while Agesilaus received the much less interesting command of an expedition across the
Corinthian Gulf in support of the Achaeans against the Acarnanians,
resulted from displeasure at Agesilaus' mishandling of the Heraeon
affair.[95] But this suggestion is only speculative. In any case, the Thebans
appear to have taken no further part in the war. Only the Athenians
continued to play an active role, reestablishing contacts in the Aegean
and attempting to revive the influence that they had once exercised
there. In time, their efforts would alarm Persia and create a climate
favorable to a diplomatic resolution of the war.

In the meanwhile, Agesilaus enjoyed one last military adventure. In
389 Sparta was asked by its allies in Achaea to launch a campaign against
the neighboring Acarnanians. Sparta sent Agesilaus with an army to
respond to the situation. In his invasion, the king advanced slowly
through enemy territory, systematically ravaging the land as he went.
There was no resistance because the Acarnanians had retreated to
mountainous areas, taking their cattle and some other possessions with
them. The slow advance of Agesilaus deceived the Acarnanians into
thinking that they could bring their cattle back down to the valley and,
when they did so, he force-marched his army to seize the booty. His
army beat off an attack by the enemy, and Agesilaus completed his
ravaging of the territory. His object, short of defeating the Acarnanians
in outright battle—which he seems to have considered too risky—was
to bring them to their knees by harming their agriculture and livestock.

---

[94]Xen. 4.5.7–10; Plut. *Ages.* 22.2–4.
[95]Xen. 4.6.1–7.1; 4.7.2–7.

In 388 Agesilaus invaded Acarnania once again and threatened to resume his ravaging. He had apparently deliberately avoided destroying any cities, and he had allowed the Acarnanians to sow their fields late in the previous year so that they would use their seed corn and hope for a harvest, despite his initial ravaging. Faced with the threat of a second destruction of the crops, this time without any seed corn to sustain them for another season, the Acarnanians capitulated.[96] Thus, Agesilaus proved to have had more insight into the nature of warfare than the Achaeans, who complained about the way in which he had conducted his initial invasion. Although this tactic may be reminiscent of the Spartan strategy of invasion of Attica practiced during the Archidamian War, Agesilaus demonstrated that such economic pressure could be quite effective, perhaps even more so than outright military confrontation. Despite his successes, however, his state was weary of the war.

In 387 the Spartans appointed Antalcidas navarch and instructed him to negotiate a settlement with Persia. This time he was more successful, having persuaded Artaxerxes, the Great King of Persia, to end the war on condition that the Greeks of Asia Minor be surrendered to him and that all the other cities remain autonomous. Representatives of the various belligerent states were summoned to Sardis to hear the Great King's pleasure, and later they assembled at Sparta to ratify the terms.[97] Although the allies were far from satisfied with this formula for peace, they were weary of the fighting by then, and the prospect of having to wage war against the combined might of Sparta and Persia drove them to accept the terms of the agreement. At the Peace Conference called at Sparta to ratify the agreement, Agesilaus singled out the Thebans as recipients of his wrath. There is evidence that almost all of the allies were disinclined to accept the agreement initially, but Agesilaus directed his intense anger only toward the Thebans.[98] He clearly presided over the conference, and he had clearly determined in advance how he was going to interpret the autonomy clause of the agreement. This clause declared that every polis, great or small, was to be autonomous. While

[96]Xen. 4.6.1–7.1; Polyaenus 2.1.10. See the good discussion of this campaign in Ober, *Fortress Attica*, pp. 39–40.

[97]Xen. 5.1.25, 29–31; Diod. 14.110.2–4; cf. Plut. *Ages.* 23.1–3; *Artax,* 21.4–5. See Hamilton, *SBV,* chap. 11; and T. T. B. Ryder, *Koine Eirene: General Peace and Local Independence in Ancient Greece* (Oxford, 1965), chap. 2, esp. pp. 34–36.

[98]See Hamilton, *SBV,* pp. 310–23, for the negotiations leading to the King's Peace. Plutarch, *Ages.* 23.3, comments explicitly on Agesilaus' desire to reduce Theban power in the peace; cf. also Xen. 5.1.32–33 for the story of Agesilaus' mobilization to force Theban compliance; and cf. *Ages.* 2.21.

there is some room for debate over the meaning of this term, the most general interpretation is that it means "self-governing"; that is, subject to no outside power, either in determining the form of internal constitution or in foreign policy.[99] The Athenians therefore were forced to relinquish control of those Aegean states that they had regained some power over since Conon's victory at Cnidus, except three islands awarded to them: Lemnos, Imbros, and Skyros. The Argives and Corinthians—who had entered into a novel union of isopolity in 392, only to have this degenerate into an outright Argive takeover of Corinth by 389—were forced to dissolve their association, and the Argive troops had to evacuate Corinth, where those exiled and given refuge by the Spartans now returned. The compliance of these states seems to have been gained by no more than stern warnings, and each state only surrendered something gained during the Corinthian War.[100]

The situation was totally different with regard to Thebes. When the Thebans came forward to swear the oaths in support of the King's Peace, Agesilaus refused to accept the oaths, arguing that they amounted to a violation of the autonomy clause.[101] In his interpretation, individual representatives of each and every polis that belonged to the Boeotian Confederacy must sign for their polis, or be excluded from the treaty. This interpretation was no less than a demand for the dissolution of the confederacy. The Theban envoys replied that they had no instructions to do as Agesilaus requested. He then ordered them to return to Thebes to seek authorization to sign for it alone, and, to give his demand credibility, he summoned the allies of the Spartans to march at his orders. Before he had gone beyond Tegea, however, the Theban envoys returned with new instructions and agreed to leave all the poleis, including those of Boeotia, free; the confederacy was thus dissolved.[102] Xenophon leaves no doubt about Agesilaus' role in all of this. Agesilaus insisted on the interpretation of the clause whereby the Boeotian Confederacy ended, and he won the ephors over to his way of thinking so that he could summon the allied forces against Thebes. When Xenophon, a contemporary and usually a strong supporter of Agesilaus, reports these facts, there can be no reason to doubt their accuracy. Agesilaus finally saw Thebes humbled and its control of Boeotia brought to an end.

[99]On the question of the meaning of autonomy, see Ryder, *Koine Eirene,* chap. 1; and M. P. Ostwald, *Autonomia: Its Genesis and Early History* (Chico, Calif., 1982).

[100]Xen. 5.1.32 and 34. See Hamilton, *SBV,* chap. 9, for Corinth and the domination by Argos.

[101]Xen. 5.1.32.

[102]Xen. 5.1.33.

When the agreement was ratified, it appeared that peace had finally come to Greece. Sparta posed as the champion of the King's Peace and carefully watched to ensure that its interests were not threatened by any new political moves. Sparta had met the first challenge to its hegemony, and, even if the state exerted direct control over less territory in 386 than it had in 395, its dominance seemed assured. Agesilaus emerged from the Corinthian War with his military reputation enhanced, his political position secure, and his hostile feelings toward Thebes intensified. And when Agesilaus was criticized because the Spartans were "medizing" by surrendering the Greeks of Asia Minor to the Persians, he cynically replied that it was rather the Great King who was "laconizing."[103]

[103]Plut. *Ages.* 23.2.

CHAPTER FIVE

From the King's Peace
to the Seizure of Thebes

The signing of the King's Peace in 387/6 opened a new chapter in the history of Sparta, the second phase of its hegemony, which lasted until the fateful Battle of Leuctra in 371. The major provisions of this agreement—which ended the hostilities of the Corinthian War and provided for the autonomy of all poleis, whether great or small—ostensibly established a new order in Greek international affairs. But from the outset, there was one serious defect in the agreement: Who was to enforce it? Although the rescript to the peace treaty itself stipulated that Artaxerxes, the Great King of Persia, would make war with ships and money against whichever of the two (i.e., the Greek belligerents on either side in the Corinthian War) that refused to accept the terms, it soon became clear that Persia was not interested in active intervention in the politics of the mainland.[1] We must also distinguish between the process of ratification of this treaty, which brought hostilities to a conclusion, and future situations in which the principles of this peace might be invoked. In the treaty itself, there is no evidence of the establishment of any mechanism, whether process of appeal or formal court proceedings, whereby alleged violations of the autonomy clause could be addressed.[2]

The Spartans had first negotiated the King's Peace, and, quite natu-

---

[1]Xen. 5.1.31; Diod. 14.110. See T. T. B. Ryder, *Koine Eirene* (Oxford, 1965), pp. 34–36 and 40; R. Seager, "The King's Peace and the Balance of Power in Greece, 386–362 B.C.," *Athenaeum*, n.s. 52 (1974): 36–63; and G. L. Cawkwell, "The King's Peace," *CQ*, n.s. 31 (1981):69–83.

[2]Ryder, *Koine Eirene*, pp. 39–40.

rally, they chose to act as its interpreters and enforcers. Of course, inherent in such a procedure was the danger that they might abuse their trust. Had the Spartans acted in an impartial and just manner, they might have been able to convince their fellow Greeks that they were worthy of the title *prostates tes Hellados* (protector of Greece). Instead, they appear to have employed their self-appointed position as enforcers of the peace to their own advantage, as they perceived it, and in so doing they gradually alienated more and more of their neighbors until, in 371, few remained loyal after the shock of the Battle of Leuctra. This chapter examines Spartan politics and policy in this crucial period in order to trace Sparta's developing relations with the other Greeks and to understand especially the part of Agesilaus in influencing his country's role in foreign affairs.

Politics in Sparta after the King's Peace

Our knowledge of this period depends primarily on the accounts of Xenophon and Diodorus; Plutarch affords some additional information, and occasionally Isocrates and other writers, as well as epigraphical evidence, fill out the picture. The two principal sources are in agreement about the Spartans' general objectives in the immediate aftermath of the King's Peace. These sources tell us that the Spartans were eager to reassert their control of Greece and to reestablish their hegemony, which had been challenged in the Corinthian War. Xenophon tells us that the Spartans "turned their attention to those of their allies who had been against them in the war or who had been more inclined to the side of their enemies. These, the Spartans decided, should be punished or reorganized in such a way that disloyalty would become impossible."[3] The account of Diodorus generally agrees with this assessment; he asserts that "the Lacedaemonians, however, who by their nature loved to command and by policy preferred war, would not tolerate the peace which they considered to be a heavy burden, and longing for their past dominance over Greece, they were poised and alert to begin a new movement."[4] Thus, Sparta took a number of steps to impose its will on various other Greek states. Xenophon does not explic-

[3]Xen. 5.2.1. R. Warner, trans., *Xenophon: A History of My Times* (Harmondsworth, Eng., 1966), p. 257.
[4]Diod. 15.5.1. C. H. Oldfather, trans., *Diodorus of Sicily* (Cambridge, Mass., 1954), vol. 6, p. 337.

itly associate any particular Spartan leader with specific policies or programs in this period, beyond naming the kings who commanded in specific campaigns (although he cannot disguise Agesilaus' antipathy toward Thebes), but Diodorus does. After having related a series of incidents which led to a reassertion of Sparta's primacy in Greece, and not only in the Peloponnesus, he states that the two Spartan kings, Agesipolis and Agesilaus, disagreed on matters of principle: "Agesipolis, a peaceful and just man, who excelled in intelligence, declared that the Spartans should abide by their oaths not to enslave the Greeks, contrary to the common agreements. He indicated that Sparta was in ill repute because it had surrendered the Greeks of Asia Minor to the Persians and had organized the cities of Greece to its own advantage, although it had sworn in the Common Peace to preserve their autonomy. On the other hand, Agesilaus, by nature a man of action, was fond of war and desired dominance over the Greeks."[5] It is quite clear that Diodorus, or his source, viewed the dynamics of Spartan politics as revolving around two leaders, the two kings, who differed in character and policy. He may not be far wrong in this.

In a passage that refers to events some five years later, Xenophon mentions the partisans of Agesilaus, the partisans of King Cleombrotus (who succeeded Agesipolis), and those between the two groups.[6] This tripartite division of factions does not necessarily contradict Diodorus' picture; the situation may have become more complex in the intervening period. The similarity between these two views, in which each king is the leader of his own group, is striking. Therefore, it is very likely that Diodorus is correct in discerning two factions in Sparta by 383. But is his characterization of the kings and their goals also correct?[7]

Agesipolis was a far younger man than Agesilaus. In 394, while Agesilaus was still in Asia Minor and the Spartans needed to field an army against the Greek coalition at the Nemea, Agesipolis was too young to command, and a regent was appointed in his place.[8] The first recorded military command of Agesipolis was in 388 in the campaign against Argos, and his next in 385 in the campaign against Mantineia.[9] Thus, he may have been no older than his early thirties in 383. Agesilaus

[5]Diod. 15.19.4.
[6]Xen. 5.4.25.
[7]For discussions of Spartan political factions in this period, see Smith, "Opposition," 274–88; Rice, "Agesilaus, Agesipolis," 164–82; and DeVoto, "Agesilaos."
[8]Xen. 4.2.9.
[9]Xen. 4.7.2–7; 5.2.3.

made a point of cultivating him by small kindnesses and acts of friendliness.[10] These actions by Agesilaus tend to suggest that he was able to influence his younger colleague. And they call into question whether Agesipolis could have been an effective opponent of his in foreign policy, as Diodorus suggests. Agesipolis' father, King Pausanias, however, had been opposed to Lysander, and possibly to Agesilaus, before his exile in 395.[11] The policy of Pausanias while king, and presumably after his exile, had been one of reason and negotiation, rather than of force, toward other Greek states; indeed, his decision to recover the bodies of Lysander and the other fallen Spartans at Haliartus by truce rather than by battle had led to his exile.[12] Furthermore, Pausanias was not averse to the existence of democratic governments in other Greek states, as his actions in Attica in helping to effect the restoration of democracy in 403 attest. To judge by what we know of him, Pausanias would have approved of the attitude of honesty and integrity which Diodorus attributes to his son, and it is likely that Agesipolis was influenced by his family tradition in this matter.[13] It is plausible to believe that, in his early years as king, Agesipolis fell under the sway of Agesilaus but, as he matured and came to play a more independent role in the state, especially as a military commander, may have developed his own ideas in foreign policy and formed a sort of rallying point for those who were opposed to Agesilaus' policies.[14]

The assessment of the political situation in Sparta in 383 by Diodorus follows immediately upon his narrative of the Spartan interventions in the affairs of Mantineia, Phlius, and Olynthus, and just before the treacherous seizure of the Theban Cadmeia. His analysis quite clearly anticipates that event, which is the principal example of violation of oaths and of aggressive behavior by Sparta in this period. Diodorus asserts that Phoebidas, the Spartan commander, accomplished this seizure with the secret instructions and approval of the Spartans.[15] Although Diodorus does not mention Agesilaus by name in this context, other ancient sources implicate him, either directly or by complicity

[10]Plut. Ages. 20.5–6.
[11]See Hamilton, SBV, pp. 79–83; 123–24; 194–96.
[12]Xen. 3.5.25.
[13]See Xen. 5.2.6 for the influence of Pausanias over his son as late as the campaign against Mantineia, when Agesipolis acts in an upright fashion toward the Mantineians who surrendered.
[14]This is essentially the argument developed by Smith, "Opposition," 274–88; and Rice, "Agesilaus, Agesipolis," 164–82.
[15]Diod. 15.20.2.

after the fact.[16] Therefore, Agesilaus seems to fit Diodorus' portrayal of him. This observation leads us to examine the question of what exactly Agesilaus' policies were. Did Agesilaus represent the opposite of Agesipolis, in Diodorus' characterization? Or is this assessment too schematic?

Agesilaus clearly was "a man of action," who "was fond of war" and "desired dominance over the Greeks." His record during the expedition to Asia Minor and in the Corinthian War establishes the first two points, and his attitude toward Thebes, Argos, Corinth, and Athens in his implementation of the King's Peace proves the third point. But was Agesilaus disdainful of Sparta's oaths to preserve the autonomy of the other Greek cities? And was he unmindful of the poor opinion that the actions of Sparta since 386 had earned it among them, as Diodorus says? Xenophon stresses Agesilaus' piety and strict observance of oaths, and Plutarch reaffirms these characteristics.[17] If Diodorus' statement is taken literally and is generally applied to Agesilaus' actions, it is contradicted by Xenophon's statement and ought to be rejected because it lacks the authority of a contemporary witness. But if Diodorus is thinking in this statement of a particular instance, such as Agesilaus' conduct toward Thebes on the occasion of the seizure of the Cadmeia, then his assessment rings true.

Agesilaus was almost blinded by his hatred of Thebes and his enemies there, and he certainly scorned public opinion in Greece in his cynical remark that Sparta ought not to consider whether the seizure was justified, but merely whether it benefited Sparta.[18] Moreover, there may well have been legitimate differences of opinion about the interpretation of the oaths guaranteeing autonomy, and Agesilaus might not have agreed with Agesipolis' attitude toward the issue. In any case, the opposition of the two kings on the question of Thebes, as well as on the more basic issues of foreign policy which underlay it, is undeniable. We must attempt to discover whose policies and views governed Spartan actions after the King's Peace, and how soon the opposition between the two crystallized. To do so, we shall examine the series of incidents which involved Sparta in the affairs of Mantineia, Phlius, Olynthus, and Thebes from 386 to 379.

[16]Xen. 5.2.32; Plut. *Ages.* 24.1.
[17]Xen. 3.4.5–7, 11, *Ages.* 1.9–13; cf. 11.1–2; Plut. *Ages.* 9.2–3.
[18]Xen. 5.2.32.

Mantineia

Sparta had no sooner settled Greek affairs to its liking at the conclusion of the Corinthian War than it turned its attention to its neighbors within the Peloponnesus. The occasion for Sparta's intervention in the internal affairs of Mantineia was the expiration of the thirty-year truce that had been established between Sparta and that city after the Battle of Mantineia in 418.[19] Although Xenophon is mistaken when he writes that "it was being said that this was the year when the thirty-year truce between Sparta and the Mantineians would no longer be in effect," for the truce would have expired before the King's Peace was ratified in 386, this much is clear: the expiration of the truce removed the protection that Mantineia had enjoyed and rendered the state vulnerable to Spartan demands. And the Spartans had demands to make, based on a list of alleged grievances. Among these were Mantineia's supplying of grain to Argos during the Corinthian War; the refusal of the Mantineians to serve with the Peloponnesian levy on the pretext of the celebration of a sacred truce; and their unsatisfactory service when they had grudgingly responded to Spartan summonses.[20] In more general terms, the Spartans alleged that the Mantineians were not trustworthy allies and that they were envious of Spartan successes and gleeful over Spartan setbacks. A recent case in point was when Agesilaus had been obliged to escort the survivors of the mora defeated by Iphicrates in 390 back to Sparta at night in order to avoid the scorn and ridicule of Mantineia.[21] To this catalog, we may add the reason recorded by Diodorus; namely, that Mantineia had prospered since the end of the war, was full of proud and valiant men, and was situated uncomfortably close to Sparta, just beyond its northern border.[22] The Spartans demanded, therefore, that the Mantineians tear down their city wall.[23] The additional demand that the Mantineians disperse into the constituent villages that had coalesced to form the city—mentioned by Diodorus as part of the initial demands, but not by Xenophon until after the capitulation of the city—

---

[19]For discussion of the chronology of the Mantineian War, see K. J. Beloch, *Griechische Geschichte,* 2d ed., 4 vols. in 8 (Strassburg, Berlin, and Leipzig, 1912–27), vol. 3, pt. 2, pp. 230–31. The ancient sources are Xen. 5.2.1–7; Diod. 15.5.1–5, 12.1–2; Isoc. 4.126.

[20]Xen. 5.2.1–2.

[21]Xen. 4.5.18.

[22]Diod. 15.5.3.

[23]Xen. 5.2.1; Diod. 15.5.4.

was probably added afterward to punish the Mantineians for their stubborn and lengthy resistance.[24]

In this episode, so reminiscent of the Elean War, the Spartans were clearly acting out of spite and vengeance to humble a neighboring polis that was technically a member of the Peloponnesian League.[25] Their objective seems to have been to punish an ally who was no longer considered trustworthy, thereby removing a potential threat on the northern border and, at the same time, sending a message to other states that might have contemplated policies not to Sparta's liking. It is a telling point that, in issuing this demand, the Spartans demonstrated that they had learned little from the lesson of the Corinthian War. Furthermore, it is arguable that, in demanding the destruction of the walls of Mantineia, the Spartans were meddling in the internal affairs of their neighbor and therefore guilty of a violation of its autonomy. Who in Sparta was behind the ultimatum to Mantineia?

Diodorus gives no indication of who among the Spartans urged the punishment of Mantineia, and he does not even name the commander of the Spartan forces in the ensuing war. But Xenophon provides quite an interesting account. After the Mantineians had refused the Spartans' demand, the government ordered mobilization against them. Xenophon reports that Agesilaus asked the authorities to excuse him from undertaking the command, on the grounds that the Mantineians had given his father much help in the wars against the Messenians.[26] Agesipolis took over the command, even though, as Xenophon comments, his father was on excellent terms with the leaders of the democratic party in Mantineia. This section in Xenophon is very instructive. The fact that Agesilaus asked to be excused from the command strongly implies that he expected, or had already been directed, to assume leadership of the army. It is tempting to think that Agesilaus had been nominated to command not only because of his military reputation but also because he had been instrumental in instigating the entire affair. But if this is so, why did he decline to conduct the expedition against Man-

[24]We should not preclude the possibility, however, that Diodorus' account is correct and that Xenophon deliberately omitted this initial demand in order to soften the harshness of the Spartans.

[25]On the Elean War, see Xen. 3.2.21ff., Diod. 14.17.4–12, and Paus. 3.8.3–6. See discussions in Hamilton, *SBV,* pp. 109–12; and Cartledge, *Agesilaos,* pp. 248–53.

[26]Xen. 5.2.3. The wars in question were those following the great earthquake and the Messenian rebellion that occurred in 465/4 in the reign of King Archidamus; cf. Thuc. 1.101ff.; Diod. 11.63.5–7; Plut. *Cimon* 16.6ff.; Polyaenus 1.41.3. See Cartledge, *Sparta,* pp. 216–20.

tineia? D. G. Rice has made the very plausible suggestion that Agesilaus wanted Agesipolis in control of the army for his own purposes. If Agesipolis were successful, then Agesilaus' goals toward Mantineia would have been accomplished, and the young king would have been implicated in Agesilaus' policies. But if Agesipolis should prove incompetent or unsuccessful in the field, his prestige would have been much diminished, and Agesilaus, in any case, could have been sent out to redeem the situation.[27] The link between Agesipolis' father, who was Agesilaus' old opponent, and the democratic leaders in Mantineia provides another clue to the complexities of this situation.

The sources do not state that Sparta demanded the end of the democratic government of Mantineia. Nonetheless, Diodorus' account makes it clear that in the aftermath of the Corinthian War the Spartans undertook to support their partisans in the various cities of Greece and that this support often involved direct intervention in the internal politics of these cities.[28] In some instances, in which the friends of Sparta were exiled as a result of the free flow of politics after the war and because of their responsibility for what had occurred under their rule, the Spartans were given a ready made opportunity. They often dispatched forces to restore their exiled friends and in this manner brought the weaker cities under their indirect control.[29] Thus, it is probable that the Spartans had this object in mind in their intervention against Mantineia. In any event, Sparta's successful military operations certainly resulted in a change in the constitution of Mantineia.

When King Agesipolis led his army into Mantineian territory, the Mantineians sent an appeal for aid to Athens.[30] Although not stated, the reasons for this appeal can readily be ascertained. Because Mantineia alone was no match for its Spartan foes, and because most of the Peloponnesus had been cowed into submission by Sparta's enforcement of the King's Peace, the aggrieved state had to look elsewhere for potential aid. Both Mantineia and Athens were democracies, and it is doubtless that the Mantineian government counted on support from Athens on ideological grounds. Also, Athens was a maritime power, and the Mantineians may have thought it capable of landing troops in the Peloponnesus. Finally, Athens had allied with Mantineia after the

[27]Rice, "Agesilaus, Agesipolis," 168–69.
[28]Diod. 15.5.2. "At once then they stirred up the cities and, with the aid of their own friends, they established factions in them."
[29]Diod. 15.5.2–3.
[30]Diod. 15.5.5.

Peace of Nicias, and the Mantineians may have hoped for a similar success in the diplomatic realm on this occasion. The Athenians, however, chose not to become involved in what they regarded as a breach of the King's Peace. Thus, Mantineia prepared to resist the Spartan invasion by itself. King Agesipolis first ravaged the land, and then he laid siege to the city, employing half his troops to encircle it by constructing a ditch and then a wall, while they were protected by the remainder.[31] But as the siege wore on, through the summer and into the ensuing winter, Agesipolis learned that Mantineia was well supplied with foodstuffs, and he became concerned about the consequences of keeping the Spartans and their allied contingents under arms for an extended period of time. He then ordered that the river that flowed through the city be dammed. This tactic caused the river to flood inside the city walls, and, as the water level rose, the mud bricks began to dissolve. The Mantineians at first tried to shore up their crumbling walls with timber but, when this proved impractical, sued for peace.[32]

The Spartans demanded that the population disperse to the villages that had been their homes before the synoecism that had produced the walled urban complex. In desperation, the Mantineians were forced to agree. But the pro-Argive faction and the democratic leaders feared for their lives, and it was only through the intervention of Pausanias that they were permitted to go safely into exile.[33] In the end, the fortifications and houses were demolished, the population was dispersed among four villages, and a new, aristocratic government was established. Although the landowning classes at first resented this arrangement, they rapidly came to terms with it, because their dwellings were now closer to their lands and because they enjoyed power in the new government. Henceforth, the Spartans sent not one officer to mobilize the Mantineians, but one to each of the constituent villages.[34] Thus the episode ended, with the effective dissolution of the city of Mantineia and the reduction of its population to subservience to Sparta through its dispersal and the establishment of aristocratic government. Although effected by King Agesipolis, it was a settlement with which King Agis or King Agesilaus would have been delighted. The outcome was remarkably similar to Agis' settlement of the Elean War in 398, and, even if the

[31]Xen. 5.2.4.
[32]Xen. 5.2.4–5; Diod. 15.12.1–2.
[33]Xen. 5.2.6.
[34]Xenophon (5.2.7) mentions four villages, whereas Diodorus (15.5.4) speaks of five. I prefer the contemporary evidence.

sources fail to remark on this, it could not have escaped the notice of contemporary Greeks. Under the guise of the peace, Sparta was using force to regulate affairs in the Peloponnesus to its liking, and the role of Agesilaus in this policy was undeniable.

Phlius

It was not long before the news of the Mantineian affair began to have effects. A group of exiles from the Peloponnesian city of Phlius arrived in Sparta, seeking support in their desire to return to their city. The exiles alleged before the ephors that, while they had been in their city, Phlius had opened its gates and received the Spartans within and had cooperated in all endeavors with Sparta. But since their exile, the situation had changed, and the Phliasians were far less well disposed toward Sparta. The implication was clear: if the exiles were restored to Phlius, they would bring about a return to the cordial relations that had previously existed between the two states.[35] Accepting at face value what the exiles told them, the ephors sent at once to Phlius, stating that the exiles were friends of the Spartans who had been unjustly driven out. The ephors said that the exiles should be restored, not on threat of force, but rather in goodwill. The Phliasians decided to comply with this request because the exiles had many relatives still within the city, and they had the support of others who shared their views, as well as a faction that wanted to change the constitution.[36] To reject the Spartan request, the Phliasians reckoned, would run the risk of some of these people opening the gates to the Spartans, should they decide to use force against Phlius. The Phliasians agreed that the exiles would receive back any property that had unquestionably been theirs, with public compensation to those who might have acquired such property; any disputed property was to be recovered through proper channels in the courts.[37] Although the matter was settled on this basis, it would erupt into a burning issue within a few years, and Agesilaus and the Spartans would be drawn into Phliasian affairs once again. But this chapter of the business makes it plain that the Spartans were more than willing to meddle in the internal politics of allied cities and, moreover, that knowledge of this willingness

[35]Xen. 5.2.8. See R. P. Legon, "Phliasian Politics and Policy in the Early Fourth Century B.C." *Historia* 16 (1967):324–37, for discussion of this episode.
[36]Xen. 5.2.9–10.
[37]Xen. 5.2.10.

impelled disaffected elements in Greece to seek similar Spartan intervention in their own interests.

This Phlius affair is illustrative in other ways. Although the circumstances in which the exiles were originally expelled are not known, it is
likely that their expulsion occurred during the Corinthian War. Phlius
appears to have enjoyed a democratic constitution from some point in
the 390s, and the exiles were clearly oligarchs.[38] The exiles had probably been driven out by their democratic opponents in a factional struggle, and the exiles sought Spartan intervention in the post-Mantineian
climate in order to attempt to regain their position at home. The exiles'
allegations against Phlius are difficult to substantiate in the historical
record, but the ephors apparently made no effort to verify them. During the latter part of the Corinthian War, Phlius appears to have been
cooperating with Sparta: the Athenian general Iphicrates cut a Phliasian
column to pieces in 391, and Phlius gladly accepted a Spartan garrison
for protection after that; and in 388 Phlius was the staging point for
Agesipolis' invasion of the Argolid.[39] On the other hand, the Phliasians
declined to fight with Sparta at the Battle of Nemea in 394, alleging that
a sacred period of truce prevented them from undertaking war.[40] And
prior to their defeat by Iphicrates in 391, they had refused to admit the
Spartans within their walls, for fear that a garrison would restore those
who claimed to have been exiled for pro-Spartan sympathies.[41] The
ephors seem to have acted on the basis of the following considerations:
Phlius enjoyed a democratic constitution, which was a form of government generally not to the Spartans' liking; the exiles claimed that they
had been expelled for pro-Spartan sentiments, and their leaders were
tied by friendship to Agesilaus; and Phlius had a lukewarm record in the
Corinthian War, although in its latter years Phlius had cooperated with
the Spartans. For all of these reasons, the ephors deemed it appropriate
to recommend to Phlius that it take back its exiles; the unwritten agenda
undoubtedly involved the expectation that the exiles would be able to
work to restore oligarchy to Phlius and to reinstate themselves to
effective control of the state. This agenda could not be accomplished
without direct military intervention on the part of Sparta.

Our sources do not speak of further disturbances in Phlius until
several years later, and two signal events occurred in the interval: the

---

[38]See Legon, "Phliasian Politics," 326 and n.12.
[39]Xen. 4.4.15; 4.7.3.
[40]Xen. 4.2.16.
[41]Xen. 4.4.15.

expedition against Olynthus, and the seizure of the Cadmeia. These incidents shall be examined later in this chapter, and we need only note one connection between them and Phlius at this point. When the Spartans dispatched Agesipolis to take command of the Olynthian expedition, the Phliasian government made a substantial contribution to his war chest. The king commended them for their prompt and generous assistance.[42] The act of the Phliasian government in supplying money so willingly to Agesipolis was evidently intended not only to demonstrate the loyalty of Phlius to Sparta but also to ingratiate Agesipolis to them. The Phliasians are likely to have known that there was division of opinion in Sparta over foreign policy, and particularly over the manner in which to treat its allies, with Agesilaus favoring direct intervention, if necessary, in the affairs of allied states in support of his friends, and Agesipolis inclined not to intervene, if such action could be avoided. In this, Agesipolis was following his father's policies, and he was probably supported by others in Sparta such as Antalcidas. But the Phliasians miscalculated the situation in Sparta.

Xenophon writes that the Phliasian government had not restored the rights of the returned exiles and that it insisted that any claims about disputed property be submitted to its courts. The former exiles responded that they could hardly expect justice from partisan courts, empaneled from among their opponents, and they determined to appeal the matter once again to Sparta. The Phliasian government displayed confidence that the Spartans would not intervene, at least not by force, for it felt certain that the other king, Agesilaus, would never be sent into the field while his colleague was away in Chalcidice.[43] Nonetheless, the former exiles, together with others from Phlius who agreed with them, set out for Sparta and secured an audience with the ephors. They pointed out, once again, that they were being treated unfairly. When the Phliasian government learned of the delegation, it angrily fined all who had dared to appeal to Sparta without permission.[44] The government may have felt justified in doing this, but by the same token its act was a partisan one. The former exiles and their friends who had been fined now feared for their lives, and they remained in Sparta, lodging a further appeal. They again claimed that the people in Phlius who refused them their rights and who had fined them were the very same

---

[42]Xen. 5.3.10.
[43]Xen. 5.3.10.
[44]Xen. 5.3.11.

who had shut the Spartans out of the city. The former exiles also claimed that the goal of the government was to prevent anyone in the future from coming to Sparta to report on what was happening in the city. This case was clearly a persuasive one, for the ephors ordered mobilization against Phlius.[45]

Xenophon reports no discussion at Sparta over this issue and does not say if the Spartan authorities made any attempt to reason further with the Phliasian authorities. The entire episode indicates that the Spartans were just as guilty of partisan politics toward the former exiles, in accepting their side of the story, as was the Phliasian government. It is possible that the ephors saw this episode as an open and shut case, but the fact that they ordered mobilization, and assigned Agesilaus to command the force, suggests that there was more to the matter than that. Xenophon's report about the Phliasians' reasoning that they would not have to fear Agesilaus' marching against them indicates their awareness of the political situation in Sparta. They knew that Agesilaus was their enemy, but they hoped that the supporters of Agesipolis would prevail in any situation potentially dangerous to them. But the inability of Agesipolis to plead personally weakened his case and Agesilaus carried the day, no doubt prevailing upon the ephors to act as they did. Throughout this period, despite opposition, he appears to have wielded decisive influence in Spartan politics, and this can have occurred only if he exercised influence over successive boards of ephors.

As Xenophon reports in what must be considered a classic piece of understatement, Agesilaus was not displeased by the ephors' decision, for the friends of his father, Archidamus, were in the faction of Podanemus, and his own friends were in that of Procles, the son of Hipponicus.[46] What clearer statement that Agesilaus' view of foreign relations was based on personal and factional connections could be desired? Agesilaus set out as soon as the sacrifices proved favorable, and he was met by envoys from Phlius, who urged him not to invade their territory and pressed bribes upon him. Agesilaus replied that he did not come to do harm, but rather to undo injustice. When the envoys begged him not to invade, promising anything to avoid this, Agesilaus replied that promises had been violated in the past and that action was now needed. And the specific action he demanded was the occupation of their acropolis by Spartan troops.[47] Although the Spartans had occupied the

---

[45]Xen. 5.3.12–13.
[46]Xen. 5.3.13. Cawkwell, "Agesilaus and Sparta," 71–77, considers Agesilaus' politics of *philhetaireia* not only proper but also to Sparta's advantage. I could not disagree more.
[47]Xen. 5.3.14–15.

Phliasian acropolis after the victory of Iphicrates in 391, and they had departed leaving Phlius free and independent after the Phliasians had regained strength and courage—as Agesilaus pointed out—the government refused to agree to his demand on this occasion. The king lost no time in invading their land, putting the city under siege, and throwing up a circumvallation. The siege lasted for twenty months.[48]

Not all in Sparta, or in Agesilaus' army, approved of the undertaking. This disapproval is evidenced by the remark of some of the soldiers that they were making themselves hated by a city of some five thousand for the sake of a handful of former exiles. The Phliasians continued to convene their assembly within sight of the besiegers, thus underlining this idea.[49] Agesilaus responded to this situation by encouraging the exiles to persuade any friends or relatives who might slip out of the city to visit them to desert, and to form these people into a military force. Ultimately, they amounted to one thousand strong, and, when well-trained and well-armed at the expense of the exiles, with Spartan loans, they won over the critics in the Spartan army, who said that they were just the kind of allies with whom they would like to serve on campaign.[50] The siege now continued with no further complaints among the Spartans, even though the self-discipline of the Phliasians and the existence of stockpiles of food caused it to drag on. It is telling that Agesilaus made no attempt to assault the city walls, expecting rather that he would eventually reduce the defenders through starvation. While he was conducting the siege, news arrived that Agesipolis had died while on campaign in the north. Xenophon says that Agesilaus publicly mourned the death of his colleague, with whom he had been close. But it is more than likely that Agesilaus secretly rejoiced at the elimination of a political rival, all the more if Diodorus' description of the antipathy between the two kings is correct.[51]

Delphion led the resistance in Phlius. The Phliasians had voted to go on half-rations, thus prolonging the siege far beyond what Agesilaus had anticipated. Eventually, however, they were driven to ask for terms by the want of provisions. They requested permission to send envoys to negotiate with the ephors, and Agesilaus granted this, although he was miffed at being treated as if he had no authority. He actually *had* no such authority, but his self-esteem was nevertheless wounded. He sent to his friends in Sparta to arrange that the ephors would leave the final disposi-

---

[48]Xen. 5.3.16, cf. 25 *ad fin.*
[49]Xen. 5.3.16.
[50]Xen. 5.3.17.
[51]Xen. 5.3.19–20; cf. Plut. *Ages.* 20.5–6; Diod. 15.19.4.

tion to his judgment.[52] When the Spartans finally informed the Phliasians that Agesilaus was empowered to settle affairs there, they had no choice but to accept his orders. He decided that a commission of one hundred—fifty from the former exiles and fifty from those in the city—should be set up to decide who should be executed and who spared among the besieged, and next to establish a new constitution. In order to guarantee that this was accomplished as he wished, Agesilaus left behind a garrison with six months' pay. He then marched his army off and dismissed the allied contingents.[53] Phlius became an oligarchy, and Agesilaus' friend Procles controlled the government, speaking for his city on several crucial occasions over the next decades.[54]

The lessons of Phlius for Greek politics were clear. In the factional rivalry between the oligarchic exiles, led by Procles, and the democrats, headed by Delphion, both sides had to contend with the possibility of Spartan intervention. Procles and his associates actively sought Spartan aid, first to be restored to their city and then to secure fair treatment. But their ultimate goal was to reestablish an oligarchy, and Agesilaus was more than willing to assist them in this. Delphion and his supporters necessarily tried to win over Agesipolis, in the hope that his influence would be a sufficient counterweight to that of Agesilaus; thus, they contributed to his fund for the Olynthus campaign. Unfortunately for them, they miscalculated Agesilaus' influence in Sparta in the absence of Agesipolis. Then, when the news of Agesipolis' death in Chalcidice reached them, they realized that they could no longer hope to avoid Agesilaus' wrath. The Spartans seem to have regarded it as perfectly natural that they should intervene in the internal affairs of an allied city. To be sure, they were asked to do so by the exiles, but the provisions of the King's Peace, assuring the autonomy of every polis, prohibited such behavior. Once again, Spartan hypocrisy could not be disguised.

Olynthus

In spring 382, envoys came to Sparta from an unexpected quarter, northern Greece. The Greek poleis of Acanthus and Apollonia, located in the Chalcidic peninsula, as well as the neighboring kingdom of Mace-

---

[52]Xen. 5.3.23–24. The handling of these negotiations is quite reminiscent of the negotiations between the Athenians, Lysander, and the Spartans in spring 404. Perhaps Agesilaus took a page out of the book of his former mentor.

[53]Xen. 5.3.25.

[54]Xen. 6.5.38 and 7.1.1.

don, sent envoys to ask for Spartan intervention in their part of the world. It seems that the Greek city of Olynthus, having formed a confederacy of several nearby cities, was actively engaged in expanding its power and control by forcing many smaller cities to join.[55] The confederacy had been formed in or before the Peloponnesian War, and it had either survived the King's Peace or, if it had been dissolved in fact as it theoretically should have been in 386, it had been revived by the Olynthians since then. Early in his reign, around 393, King Amyntas III of Macedon had surrendered a number of the cities he controlled to Olynthus for safekeeping when he was threatened by the Illyrians.[56] Now that he had recovered his position, he had requested that the cities be returned to him, but the Olynthians refused. Thus Macedon sent to Sparta, presumably asking it to intervene and force Olynthus to return the disputed areas. Diodorus writes of an alliance between Macedon and Sparta at this time, which led to Spartan military intervention on behalf of King Amyntas.[57] Diodorus believed that the appeal of the Macedonian king was the principal reason for Sparta's decision to intervene in the politics of northern Greece. The Spartans determined to extend their influence into the area around Thrace and seized this opportunity to do.

The appeal of the Greek cities of Acanthus and Apollonia, according to the account of Xenophon, which does not mention an appeal by Macedon, was made by the Acanthian envoy Cleigenes.[58] Cleigenes' speech was a carefully calculated one, designed both to appeal to the Spartans' self-interest and to alarm them, rather than to stress their self-assumed obligation as upholders of the principle of autonomy to forestall further Olynthian violations of the King's Peace. It was certainly arguable that Olynthus violated the principle of autonomy by pressuring weaker, neighboring states to join its confederacy, even if a defense of the existence of the confederacy could be made on a legal basis. But Cleigenes does not seem to have argued this way, at least insofar as we can tell from his speech. It is possible that Xenophon modified the original speech in order to eliminate the embarrassing picture of Sparta cynically violating the autonomy principle one moment for its advantage, as in the case of Mantineia, and hypocritically upholding it the

---

[55]Xen. 5.2.11–19; for discussion of the earlier history of the Olynthian Confederacy, see A. B. West, *The History of the Chalcidic League* (Madison, Wis., 1918; reprint, New York, 1973); and J. A. O. Larsen, *Greek Federal States* (Oxford, 1968), pp. 58–78.

[56]Diod. 14.92.3.

[57]Diod. 15.19.2–3.

[58]Xen. 5.2.12–19.

next, with Olynthus. If Cleigenes did not appeal to the autonomy principle, and, in Xenophon's version of his speech, he did not, then the reader of Xenophon's account would not have to confront the evidence of Sparta's hypocrisy on this score.[59] Whatever the case may be, Cleigenes' speech had the desired effect.

Having ascertained the object of the envoys, the ephors introduced them before an assembly of the Spartans and their allies. Cleigenes argued that the Spartans had been neglecting the growth of a serious threat to themselves in northern Greece. The Olynthians had expanded their power by forcing the adherence of many smaller poleis to their league, and they also controlled numerous Macedonian cities, including Pella, the capital. The Olynthians were well supplied with timber, grain, and other materials with which to sustain a war effort. Cleigenes asserted that they had also recently entered into negotiations with the Thracian tribes on their eastern boundaries, and this could lead to their gaining control of the rich mineral resources of Mount Pangaeus. In addition to all of this, envoys had come to Olynthus from Thebes and Athens to discuss treaty arrangements, and the Olynthians had just voted to dispatch their own envoys to both those states. Finally, Olynthus had demanded that both Acanthus and Apollonia join the confederacy and send military detachments to the Olynthian forces. Cleigenes said that these states wished to remain independent and to preserve their autonomy, but they could not withstand the pressure of Olynthus alone. They needed immediate military assistance. They had come to Sparta in order to seek such assistance.[60]

After this speech, the ephors called upon their allies to give their opinions. After many had come forward and urged action, in order to gratify the Spartans, they put the matter to a vote and decided to send out an expeditionary force to aid the Acanthians, Apollonians, and Macedon.[61] Xenophon does not mention two distinct votes, but, on the analogy of the events of 432, there was probably a separate vote of the Spartan assembly following the vote of the allied representatives.[62] The remark that many of the allies spoke to gratify the Spartans suggests

[59]We have no statement from Xenophon comparable to Thucydides' elaboration of the principles that he followed in composing the speeches in his *History* (1.22), and such an omission would hardly be unusual in Xenophon's account. See J. Buckler, "Xenophon's Speeches and the Theban Hegemony," *Athenaeum,* n.s. 60 (1982):180–204; and V. J. Gray, *The Character of Xenophon's Hellenica* (London, 1989), pp. 137–40.

[60]Xen. 5.2.12–19.

[61]Xen. 5.2.20.

[62]Thuc. 1.88, 119. See Kagan, *Outbreak of the Peloponnesian War,* pp. 286ff., for discussion of the situation in 432.

quite clearly that the latter consulted and lobbied before the allied vote. How else would the allies know what to say to please the Spartans? Let us examine the probable Spartan motives in this undertaking. First and foremost, the threat that the potential alliance of Thebes, Athens, and Olynthus posed to Sparta should be noted. As Cleigenes observed, it was very shortsighted of Sparta to allow a powerful coalition of these three states to develop after having striven to dismantle the Boeotian Confederacy and to remove its potential threat to Spartan interests.[63] There is no doubt about the hostility of Thebes to Sparta in this period. We do not know for certain that the proposed alliance between Thebes and Olynthus was concluded, but the former not only declined to take part in the Spartan expedition against Olynthus in an official capacity but also passed a decree forbidding any Thebans to serve with the Spartans as volunteers.[64] There is epigraphical evidence that Athens had already entered into an alliance with Olynthus;[65] thus, Xenophon may err in his report of the speech, unless Cleigenes himself was unaware that the treaty was a *fait accompli*.

The prospect of such an alliance of powerful states would have been deeply disturbing to a majority in Sparta, for it could well have threatened Sparta's settlement since 386. For Agesilaus in particular, the specter of a hostile and dangerous Thebes, allied to the powerful Olynthian Confederacy, was abhorrent. And for those who sincerely viewed Olynthus' aggressions as a violation of the principle of autonomy, the appeal for aid was well within Sparta's legal stance. Thus, for different reasons, Spartans of various factions could have supported intervention on this occasion. Those who favored the moderate and conciliatory policies of King Pausanias and Antalcidas, and perhaps now of King Agesipolis as well, would have voted in the conviction that Olynthus was acting in contravention of the King's Peace. Agesilaus and his supporters, perhaps the majority, would have needed no further motive than their well-attested desire to keep Sparta dominant throughout Greece, the objective that Agesilaus had pursued since 386. If the Ly-

[63]Xen. 5.2.16.
[64]Xen. 5.2.27. If this assertion, reported by Xenophon in the speech attributed to Leontiades in his overtures to Phoebidas to seize the Theban Cadmeia, is correct, then it seems to prove either that Thebes was at this time not a member of the Peloponnesian League, or that, as a member, it was acting in a rebellious fashion. In either case, Thebes' action in refusing to take part in the expedition against Olynthus was clearly hostile to Sparta.
[65]M. N. Tod, *A Selection of Greek Historical Inscriptions,* 2 vols. (Oxford, 1946–48), no. 119, 2:53–54. The inscription is fragmentary, however, and the archon's name is not certain; thus, we should not press this evidence too far.

sandreans still retained any independent influence at this time,[66] the prospect of campaigning far off in the north with opportunities for fame and fortune may have been appealing. Besides, because a majority of the allies had voted in favor of an expedition, few in Sparta could have been concerned that this enterprise would cost Sparta the goodwill of its allies.[67]

Xenophon's account reveals that at least some of the allies expressed concerns about the prospect of lengthy service in the field. After the vote had been taken that each city would send its proportionate contingent for an army of ten thousand, a proposal was made to allow any city to commute its military obligation from a contingent of soldiers to a cash payment. The rate was set at three Aeginetan obols per day for a hoplite, and four times that for a horseman. If any state failed to send its contingent or to pay its assessment, the Spartans were authorized to fine said state at the rate of two drachmas per man per day.[68] This decision, reported so matter-of-factly by Xenophon with no comment or explanation, demands discussion because it sheds important light on the development of the relations of Sparta with its allies in this period. It also underlines a significant shift in military practice in the early fourth century.[69] The Olynthian War was to prove a long and expensive undertaking. The distances involved in marching from the Peloponnesus to the Chalcidice were great, and the probability was that the troops originally dispatched might not be home for a long while. Beginning in 382 and lasting until 379, it consumed portions of four campaigning seasons. The Spartans suffered substantial losses in manpower, including three commanders (two to battle wounds and one to a fever). Of course, the allies could not have known in advance that the war would last this long and be this costly, but they could well have anticipated more than the usual summer campaign. Therefore, it is likely that the very same allies who urged the Spartans to respond to the appeal of Cleigenes proposed a novel measure to lessen the burdens of military service upon themselves.

[66]I have suggested in *SBV*, pp. 255–56, and 321, that this faction may still have been active in 392, but that it had lost its influence by 386. There is no clear evidence that they maintained an independent activity in the late 380s.

[67]Xen. 5.2.20.

[68]Xen. 5.2.21–22.

[69]The employment of mercenary troops in lieu of citizen hoplites had become more common ever since the end of the fifth century, but the increasing use of such soldiers by the Spartans was a particularly revealing aspect of social change within the state. On these developments, see Parke, *Greek Mercenary Soldiers*, pp. 83–90. See Lazenby, *Spartan Army*, pp. 3–40, on the nature of the military in the age of Xenophon.

For several decades the Spartans had been employing mercenaries, especially for service in Asia Minor.[70] The proposal to allow states to commute their military obligation into a cash payment is consonant with this practice and intended to permit the Spartans to hire mercenaries in lieu of allied troops in cases in which the allies found it too burdensome to serve in person. The proposal doubtlessly came from the allies, but the Spartans do not appear to have objected to it. Sparta apparently found this practice perfectly satisfactory in the conduct of its military operations. Indeed, one wonders if it may not have seemed preferable in those instances in which its allies had not served satisfactorily when called into the field (e.g., the charge against the Mantineians). As for the stipulation that the Spartans could fine any state that refused to assume its obligation, it is likely that they requested this in order to guarantee that they would have recourse against any recalcitrants. One final point is worth noting: Sparta showed itself flexible in the matter of the military obligations of its allies. Although the Spartans tended to be conservative in their policies, this innovation is proof that, on occasion, they could adopt new policies to meet the changing conditions of the day. And their willingness to accept this change in their military structure simply serves to emphasize their unwillingness to recognize the need for social and economic changes within Spartan society itself, such as was suggested by the conspiracy of Cinadon.

When the Spartans and their allies had decided to send off a force of ten thousand under these conditions, the Spartan Eudamidas was instructed to gather the army. Cleigenes now spoke up again, thanking the Spartans for their assistance, but pointing out that it would take a long time for the army to be collected and march to Chalcidice. He pleaded that the Spartans must move quickly in order to save Acanthus and Apollonia from Olynthian compulsion. Eudamidas was instructed to march at once with a small force while Phoebidas, his brother, was to collect the full army and follow him at a later date. In this way the Spartans hoped to stiffen the will of their new allies in the north and to forestall further Olynthian expansion.[71] Eudamidas marched to Chalcidice, where he apparently was killed in battle against the enemy in 382. Meanwhile, his brother—who had marched out with the rest of

---

[70]For example, Thibron seems to have recruited mercenaries in Asia Minor in late 400, and his successor, Dercylidas, took over command of the Ten Thousand, who had fought for Cyrus the Younger, in 399 (cf. Xen. 3.1.4–6, 8ff.). And Agesilaus, of course, inherited this same army upon his arrival in 396.

[71]Xen. 5.2.23–24.

the army—grasped the opportunity to seize the Theban acropolis while encamped in Theban territory. This act created a crisis in Sparta, and Phoebidas' troops never reached their destination. Instead, Teleutias, Agesilaus' half-brother, who had achieved a fine reputation as a commander during the Corinthian War, was dispatched by the Spartan government to assume command of the army in the north.[72] He operated during 382 and into summer 381, when he was slain in combat. At this point, the Spartans deliberated again and resolved to send out one of the kings to redeem the situation. They chose Agesipolis, and we must ask why.

It is clear that the first three commanders of the campaign against Olynthus were supporters of Agesilaus. Phoebidas was saved from severe punishment after his seizure of the Cadmeia through Agesilaus' intervention, and suspicions arose that he had been acting on Agesilaus' orders.[73] We may assume that his brother was also one of the king's friends and political supporters. Teleutias' record of close military and political cooperation with Agesilaus during the Corinthian War makes it plain that he also was one of the king's close supporters within his faction. If, then, the Olynthian expedition had initially been commanded by Agesilaus' supporters, and if it had been largely sponsored by Agesilaus himself, it is surprising that he did not work to win the command for himself after Teleutias' death. Perhaps the reason behind this turn of events is that Agesilaus wanted his rival Agesipolis well away from the Peloponnesus so that he could intervene in the internal affairs of Phlius.[74] Furthermore, if Agesipolis were victorious, he would only have accomplished a goal that Agesilaus shared; if he were to die on the campaign, as happened, then a rival to Agesilaus' power would be eliminated. Such a gamble worked at Mantineia, and Agesilaus may well have been willing to try it once again. In any case, Agesipolis' absence left Agesilaus free to intervene in Phliasian affairs.

The outcome of the military operations in the north is of interest to us. The circumstances of Eudamidas' death are not detailed, and Teleutias' command did result in some successes against Olynthus. But Teleutias was caught against the city walls in hot pursuit of the Olynthians, where he was killed. His death caused panic among his troops,

---

[72]Xen. 5.2.37; cf. 5.1.13–24 and H. D. Westlake, "Individuals in Xenophon, *Hellenica*," in *Essays on the Greek Historians and Greek History* (Manchester, 1969), pp. 203–25, esp. 208–9.

[73]Plut. *Ages.* 24.1.

[74]This is the suggestion of Rice, "Agesilaus, Agesipolis," pp. 177–78.

who scattered in search of safety to several different friendly cities.[75] This action by his troops set back whatever success he had achieved to that point, and, upon learning of his death, the Spartans determined to send out Agesipolis. The king took a cautious stance at first, but eventually he defeated a substantial force of Olynthians in battle. But he fell ill with fever and was carried to the shrine of Dionysus at Aphytis, where he died. His body was preserved in honey and brought home for burial in Sparta.[76] The final commander in the war was Polybiades. King Cleombrotus, Agesipolis' brother, was as yet untried, and Agesilaus at this time was conducting the siege of Phlius. Polybiades campaigned from the latter part of 380 into 379, and he succeeded in forcing the Olynthians to come to terms by reducing their supplies and starving them into submission. They capitulated on terms that made them subservient allies of Sparta and dissolved their confederacy.[77] The northern adventure was finally brought to a satisfactory conclusion for Sparta, although at the cost of many lives, including those of Agesipolis and two other commanders. The defeat of Olynthus occurred at approximately the same time as the surrender of Phlius to Agesilaus.

Thebes

The treacherous seizure of the Theban Cadmeia by the Spartan commander Phoebidas, in time of peace and without any obvious provocation, was a gross violation of the principle of autonomy, and it shocked the sensibilities of the Greek world. The sequel to this act, including the decision to garrison the Cadmeia permanently, the establishment of pro-Spartan oligarchs in power, and the trial and execution of the anti-Spartan Theban polemarch Ismenias cost Sparta heavily in public opinion. The sources make it evident that there was widespread chagrin at Phoebidas' act, in Sparta as well as elsewhere in Greece, so the resolution of the affair is all the more puzzling. In order to determine what was at stake, and who was behind these events, we must examine the ancient evidence closely.[78]

According to Xenophon, whose account of this episode is the most

[75]Xen. 5.3.1–6; Diod. 15.21.1–3.
[76]Xen. 5.3.8–9, 18–19; Diod. 15.22.2 and 23.2. Pausanias, the father of Agesipolis, erected a monument to his memory at Delphi; cf. Tod, no. 120, 2:54–56.
[77]Xen. 5.3.20, 26; Diod. 15.23.2–3.
[78]The principal accounts of these events are Xen. 5.2.25–36; Plut. Ages. 23.3–7, 24.1; Diod. 15.20.1–3.

complete of the ancient sources, the Spartan commander Phoebidas was ordered by his state to collect the contingents authorized by the allied vote for the war against Olynthus and to march them north to the relief of his brother, Eudamidas. While Phoebidas was encamped before the city of Thebes, the Theban polemarch Leontiades came to his camp and opened a dialogue. Leontiades had long been a partisan of the Spartans and the head of a pro-Spartan faction in Thebes; his principal opponent was Ismenias, who led a faction of his own supporters. Before the Corinthian War, these two rival factions had disputed for control of Boeotian affairs, and Ismenias' faction set off the Corinthian War by engineering the Phocian-Locrian incident.[79] During the war, some Thebans were exiled, apparently for pro-Spartan sympathies, but Agesilaus had forced their restoration after the King's Peace.[80] It seems likely that these exiles would have become members of Leontiades' faction upon their return, if they had not already belonged. Since 386 Thebes had been divided politically between these two factions. The reported negotiations between Thebes and Olynthus, as well as the Theban decision prohibiting any Theban from joining the Spartan-led army to northern Greece,[81] strongly suggest that Ismenias' faction had the upper hand in Thebes in 382. Thebes' status vis-à-vis the Peloponnesian League in this period is not clear. Although several ancient sources either assert (Isocrates) or imply (Plutarch and Pausanias) that Thebes had become once again subject to Sparta as a member of the league after the King's Peace, some scholars have denied this relationship.[82] I am inclined to accept the evidence in favor of Thebes' renewed membership in the Peloponnesian League after 386. If this is indeed the case, then the refusal of the Thebans to join the Olynthian expedition, as well as their obstruction of Sparta's aims in this enterprise, presents a challenge to Sparta and Agesilaus.

It was against such a background that Leontiades approached Phoe-

[79]Hell. Oxy. 18.1–5; Xen. 3.5.1–6; cf. Hamilton, SBV, pp. 182ff.

[80]Xen. Ages. 2.21 reports that Agesilaus restored Theban and Corinthian exiles after the King's Peace.

[81]Xen. 5.2.27.

[82]Isoc. 14.27–28 and 29 asserts this; Plut. Pelop. 4.4–5 represents Pelopidas and Epaminondas as fighting at Mantineia, and the occasion in question can only be that of Agesipolis' campaign; Paus. 9.13.1 also mentions these two Theban heroes at Mantineia (and necessarily in 386/5). For discussion, see H. M. Hack, "Thebes and the Spartan Hegemony, 386–382 b.c.," AJP 99 (1978):210–27 at 217–19, with n.21, in which Theban subordination to Sparta as a member of the Peloponnesian League is argued; for the contrary view, see J. Buckler, "The Alleged Theban-Spartan Alliance of 386 b.c.," Eranos 78 (1980):179–85.

bidas with the request that he occupy the Theban acropolis and lend the support of his troops to a coup d'état that Leontiades and his group were planning. Of course, the Theban leader stressed the advantages that Phoebidas and the Spartans would enjoy from such an act: instead of having the Thebans hostile, the Spartans could be assured that Thebes would willingly send troops to the allied army, and the city would be well disposed to Sparta for the future. Leontiades suggested that Phoebidas would be a hero, having accomplished in the overthrow of Thebes a greater deed than his brother hoped to accomplish at Olynthus. He succeeded in persuading Phoebidas, who was known rather for his ambition than for his good sense or reflection.[83]

Leontiades and Phoebidas agreed that the Spartan would break camp and resume his march, as if en route to the north, and Leontiades would join him and lead him up to the acropolis. On the appointed day, the Theban senate was meeting in the agora, rather than as usual in the Cadmeia, because the women of Thebes were celebrating the Thesmophoria there. The streets were deserted at that hot midday, and the Spartan troops had no difficulty in seizing the acropolis, where Leontiades gave Phoebidas the key to the gates. Leontiades then set off for the senate meeting, where he informed the members that the Spartans were in control of the acropolis, but that there was no cause for concern if they were peaceably minded. Next he ordered the arrest of his rival Ismenias for instigating war, and his co-conspirators placed him under arms. Ismenias' friends dispersed in panic, some to flee the city immediately, and others to their homes. As word spread of what had happened, and particularly of the arrest of Ismenias, eventually some three or four hundred of his partisans went into exile to Athens, apparently to avoid a similar fate. Another polemarch was chosen in place of Ismenias, and Leontiades set off at once for Sparta. The coup seemed assured.[84]

The reception of Leontiades in Sparta was not what he had expected. He had anticipated elation and celebration at the news of the coup, but found that the ephors and a majority of the citizens were angry with Phoebidas because he had acted without authorization of the city. Agesilaus, however, came forward to argue that the state ought to consider only whether the result of Phoebidas' act was beneficial to Sparta; if so, this bold act could be excused, for custom allowed a commander to take

[83]Xen. 5.2.28.
[84]Xen. 5.2.28–32; Androtion, *FGrH*, 324F50.

the initiative when circumstances warranted.[85] So Leontiades addressed
the Spartans with this question in mind, and he persuaded them that the
coup was to their advantage, by reminding them of various hostile acts
that the Thebans had performed prior to this. Interestingly, the three
acts to which he made reference were the Theban refusal to march
against the Athenian democrats at the Peiraeus in 403, Thebes' aggression against the Phocians in 396, and the Theban alliance with Olynthus, which had only just been concluded. The first two acts would
have reminded the Spartans of the discredited policies of the exiled
king, Pausanias, whereas the alliance with Olynthus could only have
been seen as a deliberately hostile, and dangerous, anti-Spartan act.
Leontiades concluded that the new regime in Thebes was more than
willing to demonstrate its loyalty and support of Sparta, provided that
there was reciprocal support from Sparta. His arguments proved persuasive, and the Spartans voted not only to maintain the garrison in the
Cadmeia but also to prosecute Ismenias.

Given that a majority of the Spartans had been angry with Phoebidas,
it is difficult to imagine that Leontiades' speech alone had changed their
minds. Rather, it is probable that Agesilaus used his influence and that
of his faction to sway the assembly to the position that it ultimately
adopted.[86] The decision to prosecute Ismenias in particular smacks of
Agesilaus' influence, because he and his faction were probably responsible for the insult to Agesilaus at Aulis, as well as for working to start the
Corinthian War, which resulted in Agesilaus' recall from Asia Minor
before he had achieved his goals there.[87] The temptation to exact vengeance from his enemy, now held under arrest in Thebes by Leontiades'
government, was more than Agesilaus could resist.

The Spartans sent out a court empaneled of three Spartans and one
judge from each of the other allied states; in this way, they probably
hoped to legitimize its kangaroo nature. Only when the court had
convened in Thebes were the charges against Ismenias lodged. Ismenias
was accused of having acted in the interests of barbarians; of having
become a guest-friend of the Persian to the detriment of Greece; of
having accepted bribes from the Great King of Persia; and, together
with his colleague Androcleidas, of having been chiefly responsible for
all the disturbance in Greece—that is, for the Corinthian War. Although

[85]Xen. 5.2.32; cf. Plut. *Ages.* 23.3–4.
[86]Xen. 5.2.33–35.
[87]See Hamilton, *SBV,* pp. 154–60 and 192–95 for discussion and sources.

Ismenias defended himself against all the charges, he failed to persuade his judges, and he was convicted and put to death.[88]

The hypocrisy of these charges, brought in this sham of a trial, must have been apparent to many in Greece. It was no secret that the Spartans themselves had been allied with the Persians and had accepted money from Persia on more than one occasion; namely, during the last phase of the Peloponnesian War, in 392 for a short time, and then in 387. As for the allegation that Ismenias had been a friend of Persia to the detriment of Greece, how could those who engineered the King's Peace and abandoned the Greeks of Asia Minor to Persian control expect to be taken seriously when they indicted another for such acts? The tragedy was that the charges stood, the judges convicted the defendant, and Agesilaus probably smiled in grim satisfaction at his victory over an old opponent. Xenophon concludes that thereafter Leontiades and his group held control of Thebes and gave the Spartans whatever support they requested.[89] Although Thebes appeared safely under the control of a solidly pro-Spartan oligarchy, Leontiades' regime would fall within a short time, with dire consequences for Agesilaus and Sparta. Such is Xenophon's account of the seizure of the Cadmeia and its sequel.

Diodorus' version of this event differs from Xenophon's in substantial ways.[90] Diodorus begins his account with the concern of the Spartans that Thebes could become a serious threat if, for example, it formalized its alliance with Olynthus, and he reports that the Spartans (otherwise unidentified) gave secret instructions to their commanders, if the occasion presented itself, to seize the Cadmeia. There is no mention of Leontiades and his planned coup, and the seizure appears as the work of Phoebidas alone. Another point of difference concerns the Theban response: Diodorus reports that the Thebans resented the seizure, gathered under arms, and were defeated. At that point, Phoebidas expelled three hundred of them. Now finding itself in ill-repute among the Greeks for this act, Sparta fined Phoebidas, but would not remove the garrison from the acropolis. Finally, Sparta removed Phoebidas from his command and replaced him with his brother Eudamidas; in Diodorus' version there had been no division of the army and no rapid deployment of a small field force, as Xenophon reports, under Eudamidas' command. This account is clearly unfavorable to Sparta and

[88]Xen. 5.2.35–36.
[89]Xen. 5.2.36.
[90]Diod. 15.20–1.3.

serves to exculpate Thebes by omitting all mention of Leontiades and his coup or of the trial of Ismenias. Furthermore, those who fled into exile did so only after a brave attempt at military resistance to Phoebidas' men, and Diodorus describes them as "most eminent." The fine of Phoebidas is mentioned to underline the Spartans' recognition that he had acted wrongly, even if they hypocritically refused to evacuate the Cadmeia.[91] Diodorus' account was probably derived from a pro-Theban version of events, which sought to minimize the factional division within Thebes, to portray the exiles as brave men who would one day return to liberate their homeland, and to lay the blame squarely upon the Spartans, and not just on Phoebidas. Recognizing its partisan nature, we must ask whether its differences with the equally partisan account of Xenophon can be resolved.

The placing of the account of the seizure of the Cadmeia within book 15 should be noted. Although chapter 20 opens a new archon year (382/1), it follows immediately the passage in which Diodorus discusses the political differences between Agesipolis and Agesilaus. Thus, there is a logical link between Diodorus' analysis of Spartan internal politics and the Phoebidas incident, and it is tempting to link Agesilaus with the Spartans who gave secret instructions to their commanders. Xenophon's insistence that the Spartans were angry with Phoebidas because he had acted without authorization of the state does not necessarily contradict Diodorus' report. If the instructions came from a powerful and influential figure, Agesilaus, but not from any formal decision of state in which ephors and assembly had taken part, the interpretations that Xenophon and Diodorus give to the event become explicable.

Is there any more direct evidence that Agesilaus was implicated in the act? While Agesilaus is not mentioned in Diodorus' account, Xenophon admits that Agesilaus' intervention allowed Leontiades to persuade the Spartan authorities not to withdraw the garrison from the Cadmeia. Xenophon says nothing further about Phoebidas, and it is certainly possible that Xenophon merely failed to mention that the Spartans had fined him. After all, a fine was a mild penalty compared to such alternatives as reduction or loss of civic rights, exile, or death. Is it not possible that the Spartan authorities originally contemplated punishing Phoebidas more severely but, after having been persuaded that his act had benefited Sparta, decided on a mere slap on the wrist? He had certainly

[91]Diod. 15.20.2.

exceeded his authority, and, even if his act seemed beneficial, Spartan military discipline demanded that some punishment be meted out for this breach. He may also have been removed from his command, as Diodorus says, for Xenophon's narrative of the Olynthian campaign makes it plain that Eudamidas commanded there until Teleutias replaced him. It is possible to resolve the apparent discrepancies between these two accounts in this manner. But what of Plutarch?

Plutarch's account sheds some interesting additional information on this episode. Plutarch recounts the Phoebidas incident in the context of the enmity of Agesilaus toward Thebes, as reflected especially in his harsh interpretation of the King's Peace. Agesilaus forced the Greek cities, particularly Thebes, to abide by the peace, in order to weaken it by dissolving the Boeotian Confederacy.[92] When Phoebidas had seized the Cadmeia, Greece was indignant, and the Spartans were displeased. Those especially who were opposed to Agesilaus' policies demanded of Phoebidas by whose command he had acted, thus turning suspicion on the king. Agesilaus spoke up at this point, declaring that they ought to determine whether the act was beneficial, for, if it was, the advantage to Sparta would justify an independent and unauthorized act.[93] Plutarch then digresses to note how Agesilaus always spoke of the necessity of honest and upright acts, whereas in his dealings with Thebes he was guilty of acting out of ambition and contentiousness. For, Plutarch continues, Agesilaus not only saved Phoebidas but also persuaded Sparta to assume responsibility for the seizure of the Cadmeia and to install Leontiades and Archias in power in Thebes.[94] This intervention gave rise to the suspicion that though Phoebidas had carried out the deed, Agesilaus had counseled him to do so, and the king's subsequent acts made the belief general.[95]

Plenty of circumstantial evidence implicates Agesilaus. First, his well-documented hatred for Thebes long predated this event, and there is no particular reason to imagine that his animus toward Thebes had been satisfied by the dissolution of the Boeotian Confederacy in 386. Second, the recent Theban negotiations with Olynthus, coupled with the Theban decree forbidding participation in the Spartan undertaking against Olynthus, must have refired the anger of Agesilaus and convinced him that some more permanent solution to the Theban problem

[92]Plut. *Ages.* 23.3.
[93]Plut. *Ages.* 23.4.
[94]Plut. *Ages.* 23.5–7.
[95]Plut. *Ages.* 24.1.

must be devised. Finally, he is likely to have been in contact with his partisans in Thebes, the faction of Leontiades and the exiles whom he restored in 386, throughout this period. Even if Agesilaus and Leontiades had not planned the coup in advance, the former's intervention in the Spartan assembly to mitigate the Spartans' anger with Phoebidas and to convince them to make the most of the occasion by retaining control of the Cadmeia and by prosecuting Ismenias made it seem to many that he had engineered the act. Plutarch reports as much, whereas Xenophon, needless to say, downplays the incident in the *Hellenica* and omits it in the *Agesilaus*. It was public knowledge that Agesilaus had raised the question of the expediency of Phoebidas' act, so Xenophon could not omit this fact; it was the point on which the debate in Sparta over Phoebidas' guilt turned. Plutarch credits Agesilaus with persuading the Spartans to retain control of the Cadmeia and to accept the new government of Leontiades, whereas Xenophon's account attributes this to Leontiades' speech at Sparta. It is probable that both accounts contain part of the truth; that is, both Leontiades and Agesilaus played decisive roles in shaping the outcome of the debate in Sparta.

The coup at Thebes had a considerable impact on the Greeks. Both Plutarch and Diodorus explicitly attest the ill repute that Sparta suffered from the seizure of the Cadmeia, and the same may be inferred from Xenophon's account.[96] Among contemporary sources is Isocrates, who chastises the Spartans in his *Panegyricus*.[97] To have seized the acropolis of a neutral city, in time of peace, whose autonomy had been guaranteed by the very peace upon which Agesilaus had been so insistent, as well as to support the overthrow of the legitimate government and the establishment of a narrow pro-Spartan oligarchy, inevitably sullied Sparta's reputation.[98] The fact that the garrison which occupied the Cadmeia was composed of allied as well as Spartan troops, or that the court which tried Ismenias contained judges who represented Sparta's allies, did nothing to alter the basic feeling that Sparta had imposed its will on another polis, in blatant violation of the principle of autonomy. Not only had Thebes received a government acceptable to Sparta, but its citadel remained garrisoned. All that remained lacking from the unpopular settlement Lysander had imposed upon the Greek world after the Peloponnesian War was the exaction of tribute, and it could be

[96]Plut. *Pelop.* 6, *Mor.* 576a; Diod. 15.20.2; Xen. 5.4.1.
[97]Isoc. 4.126.
[98]See also Nepos, *Pelop.* 1 and Polybius, 4.27.4.

argued that the military contributions demanded of Thebes for the Olynthian campaign were tantamount to such. Thus, in the eyes of many in Greece, but particularly among the Athenians and the Theban exiles, Sparta's treatment of Thebes in 382 amounted to a return to the most high-handed tactics of the period just before the Corinthian War. And that war had been fought to prevent even further encroachments by Sparta against the autonomy of the other Greek states. But there was no effective challenge to Sparta's settlement of the Theban issue in 382, and in the ensuing years Sparta went on to subdue Olynthus, dissolve the Olynthian Confederacy, and install a pro-Spartan oligarchy in Phlius. Sparta accomplished these events by 379, when it appeared to be at the acme of its power.

Sparta's fortunes were in full flow, and the tide had not yet begun to ebb. Both of the surviving formal histories of this period choose this point to comment on Sparta's successes. Xenophon, after narrating the capitulation and reduction of Olynthus to the status of a subservient ally, writes that "the Spartans had now been so successful that the Thebans and the rest of the Boeotians were completely in their power, the Corinthians had become absolutely faithful, the Argives had been humbled because their plea of the sacred months no longer protected them, and the Athenians were left destitute of allies, whereas those among the allies of the Spartans who had been unfriendly to them had been chastised (e.g., Mantineia and Phlius), and it seemed that they had established their empire safely and soundly."[99] Diodorus similarly mentions that with the reduction of the Olynthians many other states were eager to enlist under Spartan leadership. At this point, Sparta reached its greatest power and exercised hegemony both on land and at sea. Thebes was secured by a garrison; Corinth and Argos were held in check through previous wars; the Athenians, because they still colonized the lands they occupied, were in ill repute among the Greeks; and the most powerful rulers, such as the King of Persia and Dionysius of Syracuse, sought alliance with Sparta.[100] There is no doubt that Sparta's writ ran throughout most of Greece and that its power was at its zenith. But what were the bases for that power, and who orchestrated it in Sparta at this time?

Sparta's power rested on several things. Although it is not explicitly attested, Sparta presumably claimed that its mandate to direct the affairs

[99]Xen. 5.3.27.
[100]Diod. 15.23.3–5.

of Greece derived from its self-appointed role as enforcer of the King's Peace. But few could have taken such a claim too seriously, especially after the affair of the Theban Cadmeia; Sparta's willingness to (mis)interpret the principle of autonomy to its own perceived advantage was all too obvious. Still, the appeal of Acanthus and Apollonia for Spartan aid against Olynthus was grounded on the autonomy principle. One of the cardinal points of its foreign policy was the reliance on governments sympathetic to its own values and ideals; that is, oligarchies in its allied states. The well-attested cases of Mantineia, Phlius, and Thebes leave no doubt on this score. And some scholars believe that this was a wise and sensible policy, in which a community of interest between states, based on ties of social class and political friendship, makes for stable and sound interstate relations.[101] But to achieve such governments, the Spartans had been willing to use force and even, as in Thebes, to garrison an allied state. Whether such tactics would produce stable and loyal allies would be a question for the future. Another underpinning for the new order of Sparta was, of course, its military system. Here I mean not only the Spartan army,[102] but also the impressive machine that the Spartans had forged from the resources of their allies. Sparta's military reputation was still strong, despite some setbacks in the course of the Olynthian campaign, and Agesilaus was still considered the premier general of his age. But this military system itself rested on a fragile socioeconomic foundation, and the system might prove unable to cope with future stresses. Finally, we must mention diplomacy, for the Spartans did not ignore this area in attempting to settle Greece to their own designs. Rather, they seem to have been quite skilled in some aspects of negotiation, as the history of the fourth century suggests.[103]

At the conclusion of the Olynthian campaign, Agesilaus was unquestionably the dominant political figure in Sparta. With signal success, he had been striving to direct the foreign policy of his state ever since the conclusion of the King's Peace. He, above all, wanted to control Greece through the establishment of pro-Spartan oligarchies in states allied to Sparta, or once close to it, as Thebes had been. Control of the Pelopon-

[101]See esp. Cawkwell, "Agesilaus and Sparta," 71–84. But see A. Missiou-Ladi, "Coercive Diplomacy in Greek Interstate Relations," CQ, n.s. 37 (1987):336–45, for an analysis of Sparta's coercive approach to other states, which makes clear that such tactics engendered resentment among the Greeks.
[102]For the most recent study of this topic, see Lazenby, Spartan Army, pp. 3–40.
[103]See esp. D. J. Mosley, "Diplomacy by Conference: Almost a Spartan Contribution to Diplomacy?" Emerita 39 (1971):187–93.

nesus, for the security of Sparta, was central to his goals, but he was not averse to adventuring into central or northern Greece if need be. His direct, interventionist policies had produced opposition at home, in men such as Antalcidas and Agesipolis, but after the latter's death at Olynthus in 380, effective opposition to Agesilaus' political dominance evaporated for the moment. The position of Agesilaus depended upon his personal rapport with his fellow citizens and subjects, his military reputation, a devoted circle of friends and relatives who would serve in military positions at his direction, and, of course, his regal status. Just as Sparta was at the apex of its power in 379, so also was Agesilaus at the peak of his career. Fresh from his successful siege of Phlius, with his friends in control of Thebes, the state that had been so irksome to him, he might well have considered that he had served his state well in establishing Spartan hegemony throughout Greece. He had passed his sixtieth year and thus was exempt from further military service. But if Agesilaus thought that he might spend the rest of his years in quiet enjoyment in Laconia, he was much mistaken. His Theban nemesis was yet to come.

CHAPTER SIX

The Liberation of Thebes
and Its Aftermath

The years from 379 to 371 were fateful ones for Sparta. Its hege-mony—secure, to all appearances, following the capitulation of Phlius and Olynthus in 379—was first challenged by the liberators of Thebes, and seriously shaken at the Battle of Leuctra in 371. When we discuss the events of this period, we are tempted, following Xenophon, to concentrate on Theban-Spartan relations. After all, the two principal events that open and close this period involve primarily these two states, and there were several Spartan military campaigns in Boeotia in the interval. But Xenophon omits too many events, and important ones, in his account. For example, there is no mention of one of the signal developments of the early fourth century, the founding of the Second Athenian League,[1] or of the striking Spartan defeat at Tegyra in 375, at the hands of Pelopidas, which presaged that at Leuctra,[2] or of the diplomacy that resulted in the Peace Conference in 375/4, where nu-merous Greek states attempted to put an end to the hostilities of the Boeotian War.[3] Although we cannot ignore the importance of relations between Thebes and Sparta in the 370s, we must recognize the limita-tions of Xenophon's treatment of these years. We must not only exam-ine the evidence of Diodorus, Plutarch, the Attic orators, and especially epigraphy in order to fill in events but also use these sources to correct the distorted picture of Spartan politics and diplomacy which emerges

---

[1]See C. D. Hamilton, "Isocrates, IG ii² 43, Greek Propaganda and Imperialism," *Traditio* 36 (1980):83, and see 83n.3 for references to modern comments.
[2]Plut. *Pelop.* 16–17.
[3]Diod. 15.38.1–4.

from Xenophon's account alone. This chapter analyzes the events surrounding the liberation of Thebes in winter 379/8, and their immediate aftermath, because it was in this context that the first overt challenge to Sparta's hegemony occurred.

The Liberation of Thebes

Agesilaus' settlement of the Phlius affair to his liking, and Polybiades' defeat of the Olynthians with the resultant break-up of the Chalcidic Confederacy, brought the Spartan hegemony to its acme. But the moment of triumph was not long-lived. In December 379, a small group of Theban exiles returned to their native city, assassinated the leading members of the pro-Spartan oligarchic regime, and negotiated the withdrawal of the Peloponnesian garrison from the Cadmeia, thus liberating Thebes from Spartan control. The exiles set out from Athens, and they enjoyed the private encouragement and support of many Athenians, and probably at least the tacit consent of the Athenian government. Xenophon, Diodorus, and Plutarch all provide versions of the liberation of Thebes, and, although these versions often differ in details, they agree on substantial points. Let us examine what led to the return of the Theban exiles and to the success of their efforts to liberate their fatherland.

Leontiades had planned the coup to overthrow the legitimate government of Thebes in 382 and to introduce the Spartans to the Cadmeia. He was not only a polemarch but also the leader of a pro-Spartan, oligarchical faction. Others of his group included Archias and Philip, polemarchs in 379, and Hypates, who was assassinated with them; there were surely others, but they are unnamed. Plutarch describes the entire faction as "oligarchical, rich, and immoderately ambitious."[4] Although Leontiades was not serving as polemarch in 379, he was high on the list of the liberators, thus suggesting that he was still powerful and influential with his faction. But shortly after the coup in 382, Leontiades took the initiative in plotting the murder of the political associates of Ismenias, who had fled into exile in Athens. The plot was only partially successful, however, because only Androcleidas fell victim to unknown assassins at that time. Leontiades and his group also prevailed upon the Spartans to send to Athens, ordering the expulsion of the exiles on the

[4]Plut. *Pelop.* 5.2.

grounds that they had been declared common enemies by the allied cities.[5] Thus, the pro-Spartan government in Thebes seems to have done all in its power to eliminate any potential future threat from the exiles.

Although we are not informed in detail about the conduct of their government in Thebes itself, the use of the terms "tyrants" and "tyranny" in reference to them, by Xenophon as well as Plutarch, implies that they ruled in a despotic manner.[6] The fact that the jail in Thebes held 150 political prisoners in 379 suggests that the government muzzled opposition, and the report that many Theban women defiled the corpse of the prison warden, after his murder by the liberators, also attests to their hatred for a man who must have played a prominent role in the repressive politics of the tyrants.[7] The tyrants did not crush all opposition within Thebes, however, for the exiles were in contact with friends inside the city, who helped them plan their return. Therefore, the most appropriate conclusion is that the faction of Leontiades initially took severe measures to destroy their opposition, killing and driving into exile several hundred of their most ardent opponents. Thereafter, relying upon the garrison in the Cadmeia and their domination of the organs of government, they took no further measures to root out potential enemies beyond the arrest and imprisonment of outspoken opponents. As a result, elements remained within Thebes who were, or became, disaffected with their rule and entered into secret negotiations with the exiles in Athens.

Chief among such men was Phillidas, who contrived to have himself appointed secretary to the polemarchs. He identified a number of others, including Charon and Hipposthenidas, who agreed to play a role in the plot to overthrow the government.[8] And there were others, such as Epaminondas, who objected to the tyranny of Leontiades and the Spartan occupation. Although probably not privy to the plot, they quickly joined in the movement of liberation and did their part to help the insurrection to succeed.[9] But, despite the willingness of many within Thebes to work for the overthrow of the tyranny, the architect of the rebellion was Pelopidas, a young exile. According to Plutarch, Pelopidas inspired his fellow exiles with patriotism and enthusiasm, and his

[5]Plut. *Pelop.* 6.2–3.
[6]Xen. 5.4.1; Plut. *Pelop.* 6.1–2.
[7]Plut. *De Genio Socratis* 33.
[8]Plut. *Pelop.* 7.3, 8.3.
[9]Plut. *Pelop.* 7.3, 12.2–4.

rhetoric produced the decision to attempt a coup of their own.[10] Xenophon makes no mention of Pelopidas, focusing instead on his co-conspirator Melon, as chief of the rebels. But Xenophon's antipathy toward Pelopidas and Epaminondas is so well known as to require little comment here; the omission of the name of Pelopidas is merely the product of Xenophon's bias and does not constitute proof that he played no role in these events.[11] In contrast, Plutarch's highly detailed and circumstantial account clearly derives from the circle of the liberators themselves and perhaps from a Boeotian source.[12]

The plot of Pelopidas and Melon was straightforward.[13] A small band would slip, unobserved, into Thebes. Upon reaching the city, the conspirators, numbering a dozen, were met by men from within the city who were privy to the plot and conveyed to the house of Charon. There others joined them to the number of forty-eight. Phillidas, the polemarchs' secretary, was prepared to introduce them, disguised now as courtesans, to a drinking party at Archias' house. The conspirators expected that Archias and the others would be drunk and off-guard and that Pelopidas and company would quickly cut them down with swords hidden beneath their garments.

Phillidas duly introduced the conspirators into the polemarchs' dinner party. There were different versions of how exactly this was accomplished, as Xenophon writes,[14] but probably three of them were dressed as courtesans, and three others as their maids. When these conspirators had been seated next to Archias and the others, they stabbed them to death. Next, Phillidas led them to Leontiades' house. According to Xenophon, they gained entrance because Leontiades trusted Phillidas and suspected no foul play, but Plutarch asserts that the door was opened to them when they claimed to have a message from the Athenian Callistratus.[15] Leontiades also was murdered, and then the

[10]Plut. *Pelop.* 7.1–2.

[11]Xen. 5.4.2–9. For discussions of Xenophon's tendency to ignore the role and achievements of the two Theban generals, see G. S. Shrimpton, "The Theban Supremacy in Fourth-Century Literature," *Phoenix* 25 (1971):310–18; and G. L. Cawkwell, "Epaminondas and Thebes," *CQ*, n.s. 22 (1972):254–78.

[12]See Shrimpton, "Theban Supremacy," 315–18, and Westlake, "Spartan Debacle," 119–33, at 122–23, for such a suggestion.

[13]Xen. 5.4.3–7; Plut. *Pelop.* 8.1ff. Xenophon says there were seven conspirators; Plutarch mentions twelve.

[14]Xen. 5.4.7. Does the mention of three men dressed as courtesans provide a clue to the number of polemarchs at Thebes? We do know of two in 382, Ismenias and Leontiades, but there may have been a third.

[15]Xen. 5.4.7; Plut. *De Genio Socr.* 32, *Pelop.* 11.3–6.

liberators went finally to the house of Hypates, who was also dispatched. Having eliminated, presumably, the heart of the tyrannical opposition leadership, Pelopidas, Melon, and the others next made proclamation in the streets of Thebes, announcing the death of the tyrants and calling upon the citizens to come out to the support of their coup.

There was apparently a good deal of noise and confusion during the night, but the majority of the Thebans awaited dawn before venturing forth. Epaminondas, Gorgidas, and a small group of men rallied to the cry for freedom immediately. In the meantime, Phillidas led a group to the prison, where he tricked the warden, slew him, and succeeded in opening the gate. Then Phillidas armed the prisoners, some 150, and set them to be ready to act.[16] As the noise of the hubbub reached the Spartan harmost in the Cadmeia, he sent in alarm for aid to the garrisons in the neighboring cities of Plataea and Thespiae, according to Xenophon, and probably also to Sparta, as Diodorus says.[17] A number of those in Thebes who favored Sparta fled to the Cadmeia. The garrison there numbered 1,500, and the commander was later criticized for failing to strike at the conspirators during the night, when they had not yet secured the aid of the majority of the Thebans, and when a swift blow might have reversed the coup.[18] Meanwhile, the remaining Theban exiles in Attica were sent for, and those in the Cadmeia were put under siege by the liberators. Here the sources diverge, and we must attempt to answer three different, but interrelated, questions: How long did the siege last? What role exactly did the Athenians play in these events? How did the Spartans respond to this challenge to their power?

According to Xenophon, the returning exiles were also joined by an Athenian force on the border under two Athenian generals, who had not been authorized to act by the Athenian government, but who took the initiative privately. As if to stress the private initiative of these Athenians, in a later passage Xenophon relates that the Athenian people brought them to trial and punished them.[19] On the morrow, reinforcements from Plataea were detected and beaten off by the liberators, who then attacked the defenders of the Cadmeia, in concert with the Athenians. Xenophon gives the impression that the allies in the garrison, by far the most numerous, pressured the Spartans and their commander to

[16]Xen. 5.4.8–9; Plut. *Pelop.* 12.1–2; cf. *De Genio Socr.* 33.
[17]Xen. 5.4.10; Diod. 15.25.3; cf. Plut. *Pelop.* 13.1.
[18]Plut. *Pelop.* 12.3.
[19]Xen. 5.4.9–12 and 19.

The area of Thebes

surrender very quickly; indeed, he seems to imply that the surrender occurred on the day following the coup against the Theban tyrants. Despite a safe conduct given to the occupiers of the Cadmeia, some Thebans set upon and mistreated their bitterest enemies; only the intervention of the Athenians saved a few of them. The Spartan-led force then marched off to the Peloponnesus. Xenophon says next that "when the Spartans had learned what had happened, they put the harmost to death, and then called out the ban against Thebes."[20] Agesilaus declined to lead the expedition, which was now clearly punitive and no longer relief, and the recently installed King Cleombrotus was put in charge.

Diodorus had a different story to tell of the siege of the Cadmeia.[21] At daybreak an assault was made upon the acropolis, and its defenders sent to Sparta for aid. Anticipating that a large army would be sent to the relief of the defenders, the Thebans immediately sent envoys to Athens. These men reminded the Athenians of the assistance they had received from Thebes in the time of the Thirty Tyrants, and besought the Athenians to send all aid to help in the siege of the Cadmeia before the

[20]Xen. 5.4.12–13. The harmost is unnamed, although Xenophon surely knew, or could have learned, his name.
[21]Diod. 15.25.3–4, 26.1–27.2.

Spartans could retaliate. The Athenians voted to assist the Thebans and sent the general Demophon, with a force of five thousand infantry and five hundred horsemen, to reach Thebes as soon as possible. Demophon hastened there and joined his forces to the Thebans, who were augmented by other Boeotians to the number of some fourteen thousand. This force assaulted the acropolis continually, day and night. The attacks on the acropolis continued for some time, and the besieged garrison, although stoutly defending its position, only gave thought to surrender when the Spartans were slow in marching to their relief and when their provisions began to give out. Whether this was a matter of days or weeks is guesswork, although the narrative of Diodorus suggests a much longer siege than that of Xenophon. Furthermore, the Theban embassy to Athens, which Diodorus records, puts the Athenian action in an entirely different perspective. He says this embassy reminded the Athenians of the aid the Thebans had given to Thrasybulus in 403.[22] On the motion of Cephalus, the Athenians voted to send a substantial force—five thousand hoplites and five hundred horse under Demophon—immediately to aid the Thebans.[23] The evidence of Deinarchus alleges that the Athenians gave aid to the Thebans and dislodged the garrison from the Cadmeia within a "few days." But can we trust this account? Note that there was no question of acting under a preexisting treaty obligation here. Another very late source, Aristeides,[24] claims that the Athenians played a leading role in the liberation of the Cadmeia while there was still no treaty between the states.

According to the version of Diodorus, supported by Deinarchus and Aristeides, this force, then, participated in an official manner in the siege of the garrison in the Cadmeia. Moreover, many troops came to Thebes from the other cities of Boeotia. The garrison eventually capitulated, however, but only a short time before relief arrived. At this point, Diodorus mentions that *three* harmosts had been in command, indicating that two were put to death for their action, and the third heavily fined while he himself went into exile.[25] Plutarch's account agrees with that of Diodorus in several details; for example, the size of the garrison, fifteen hundred, and the fact that three commanders were punished, two by death and one by a fine, although Plutarch supplies the names of all three. He also agrees that the surrender occurred just before the

[22]Diod. 15.25.4.
[23]Deinarchus 1.38–39.
[24]*Panathenaicus* 294–96.
[25]Diod. 15.27.3.

arrival of help, for the troops who had evacuated the acropolis were
intercepted by Cleombrotus at Megara (no more than about a day's
march from Thebes).[26] One final point in Plutarch's account needs to be
noted. Plutarch asserts a bit further on that the Athenians renounced
their alliance with Thebes, when panic set it, following the invasion of
Cleombrotus.[27] No other source suggests that the Athenians had made
an alliance with Thebes at this point, merely that they voted to send
official aid. Perhaps Plutarch is confusing events with the sequence in
395, when Theban envoys succeeded in persuading the Athenians to
make a treaty with them before sending aid to Boeotia.[28] All of these
similarities suggest that these two accounts go back to a common
source for their story here, perhaps Ephorus (or perhaps a Boeotian
source?). And, of course, the account of Deinarchus contains elements
that agree with the accounts of Diodorus and Plutarch: the Athenian
assistance was official, moved in a decree by Cephalus, and it came
before the surrender of the Cadmeia.

In the late-nineteenth century, G. Grote asserted that we must choose
between the account of Xenophon and those of Diodorus and Plutarch
for the siege and surrender of the Cadmeia and for the nature of the
Athenian participation in that act, and many scholars who have since
examined these problems agree that it is almost impossible to reconcile
their contradictions. In order to attempt to determine the truth of these
apparently contradictory versions, we must examine the situation in
Athens before 379.

The Athenian Reaction

From the conclusion of the King's Peace until the intervention in the
liberation of Thebes, Athens had maintained a very low profile politically. Athens had recognized the impossibility of continuing the struggle against Sparta in 387, especially after Antalcidas had closed the
Hellespont to Athenian shipping and had reestablished an alliance with
Persia.[29] The political and diplomatic efforts that Conon began and

[26]Plutarch (*Pelop.* 13.2) says that Pelopidas' capture of the Cadmeia came just before
the arrival of Spartan reinforcements; the garrison that surrendered had only progressed
as far as Megara when it encountered the Spartan relief force. The harmosts were
Herippidas, Arcisus, and Lysanoridas.
[27]Plut. *Pelop.* 14.1.
[28]Xen. 3.5.7–17.
[29]Xen. 5.1.25ff. See Hamilton, *SBV,* pp. 308–10, for discussion.

Thrasybulus continued in the Aegean—to restructure an Athenian alliance system—had perforce been abandoned in 386. Athenian foreign policy thereafter was cautious and circumspect, and those alliances that the Athenians did make, for example with Chios in 384, were carefully drafted to observe the terms of the King's Peace, as P. Cloché has demonstrated.[30] The Athenians were reportedly negotiating with Olynthus at the time of the Spartan decision to intervene in affairs in the north, and scholars presume that the diplomacy between Athens and Olynthus came to nought, perhaps because the Athenians did not want to risk Spartan displeasure.

About 380, at Persian request, Athens recalled Chabrias, its general, from Egypt, where he was serving as a mercenary commander for a rebellious local ruler against Persia, and sent out Iphicrates to serve in Asia for the Persians.[31] There is no record of action against Sparta at the time of the seizure of the Cadmeia in 382, although Athens gave refuge to Theban refugees. We can attribute the Athenian refusal to honor a Spartan demand to expel the exiles, which Diodorus reported, not so much to defiance of Sparta as to a desire to assert Athenian autonomy. Thus, until 380, the record of Athenian relations with other states is characterized by scrupulous observance of the principles of the King's Peace, and by avoidance of conflict with Persia or Sparta. At the same time, the Athenians were by no means subservient to Spartan demands. There seems to have been no strongly pro-Spartan faction in Athenian politics, and Athens had little reason to fear a coup similar to Leontiades' in Thebes. But despite criticisms of Sparta's record since 386 such as Isocrates voiced in his *Panegyricus* (and earlier voiced by Lysias in his *Olympic* oration), there was no strongly anti-Spartan group either.[32] It was against such a background that Athens gave its support to the Theban exiles in their attempt to overthrow the tyrants in 379.

The domestic political situation in Athens is rather more difficult to determine in this period. Many scholars believe that there had been three prominent political factions in Athens during the Corinthian War.[33] The first faction, which Cephalus and Epicrates led, had been willing to risk conflict with Sparta as early as 396 by sending aid to

[30]P. Cloché, *La politique étrangère d'Athènes de 404 à 338 a.C.* (Paris, 1934), p. 51.

[31]Diod. 15.29.2–4. For discussion of the chronological questions, see C. L. Sherman, *Diodorus of Sicily* (Cambridge, Mass., 1952), vol. 7, p. 25n.3.

[32]See Hamilton, "Isocrates," 95–96, for discussion and references.

[33]See Hamilton, *SBV*, pp. 168–74; and Strauss, *Athens after the Peloponnesian War*, pp. 89ff., for discussions of this topic.

Conon, the refugee Athenian admiral, then in service with the Persians against Sparta.[34] A second faction was led by three men—Thrasybulus, the hero of the overthrow of the Thirty Tyrants in 403, Aesimus, and Anytus. They seem to have represented a more moderate socioeconomic class of Athenians than did Cephalus and Epicrates, but they were not opposed to war with Sparta when the moment was right: Thrasybulus carried the motion for alliance with Thebes in 395, which plunged Athens into the Corinthian War. Furthermore, he took an active role in pursuing Athenian maritime interests in the Aegean in 389, where he was killed by the Greeks whom he was pressuring to contribute to the support of his fleet.[35] The demagogue Agyrrhius, who had gained popular favor in Athens by introducing ecclesiastic pay, led the third faction.[36] His nephew Callistratus of Aphidna was associated with this third faction when he made the motion to exile those members of the Athenian embassy that negotiated peace (either in 392, as some scholars hold, or in 386, after the King's Peace, as I have argued, following the suggestion of I. A. F. Bruce.)[37] Among those exiled were Andocides, who has been associated with the Thrasybulus group, and Epicrates, the associate of Cephalus.

After 386, the political factions in Athens were in flux, with many of those who had played a leading role during the Corinthian War gone from the scene: Thrasybulus and Conon were dead; Epicrates was in exile; and Agyrrhius had been condemned to prison for debts. In the period from 386 to 379, Cephalus was still active, and two Athenian mercenary generals who had risen to prominence in the war, Iphicrates and Chabrias, were available for service and potentially influential politically. Both seem to have been absent from Athens from about 386 to 380.[38] Among those only coming to prominence in this period were Callistratus and Timotheus, the son of Conon, who began a career as a commander.

Although there were influential Athenian leaders who would, in the period after the liberation of Thebes, play a role in urging their city to resist Sparta militarily, and in striking an alliance with Thebes subsequently, the question is whether they were prepared to risk war before

[34]*Hell. Oxy.* 7.1–3; see Hamilton, *SBV,* pp. 172 and 175.
[35]See G. L. Cawkwell, "The Imperialism of Thrasybulus," *CQ,* n.s. 26 (1976):272–77, on Thrasybulus, and Strauss, *Athens,* pp. 150–57.
[36]See Strauss, *Athens,* pp. 157–61, on Agyrrhius.
[37]See Hamilton, *SBV,* pp. 237–39 and 320–22.
[38]See Parke, *Greek Mercenary Soldiers,* pp. 55–57 and 76.

such an alliance had been accomplished. The evidence of Deinarchus makes Cephalus the mover of the decree that sent Athenian troops to aid the Theban exiles in their siege of the Cadmeia, and Callistratus was certainly quite active throughout the 370s in opposing Sparta. Did these men actually involve their state in hostilities against Sparta before the Spartan relief expedition arrived in Boeotia just after the surrender of the Cadmeia by the ill-fated harmost? The choice must be between the account of Xenophon and that of Diodorus, corroborated to some degree by the evidence of Deinarchus, Plutarch, and perhaps Aristides; attempts to harmonize these accounts, like that of Cawkwell, are not very satisfactory and have generally not won favor among scholars.[39] What, then, are the arguments for accepting one version of events over the other?

Xenophon was a contemporary of the events he describes, unlike the other authors in question, and the most telling criticism that can be brought against him is that he too often *omitted* crucial events from his history.[40] In this instance, however, it is not an omission with which we have to deal, but rather with an alternate, and contradictory, version of events. Let us ask whether Xenophon or his source, most probably someone in the circle of Agesilaus, if not the king himself, could have had any reason to deny that the Athenian aid to Thebes was official. In his subsequent account, Xenophon makes it quite clear that the raid of Sphodrias was the event that caused Athens to break relations with Sparta, and he spares no pains to censure both Sparta and Agesilaus for the way in which they handled this incident. If Xenophon knew that the Athenians had voted to send an official contingent to aid the Thebans in the assault on the Spartan-led occupants of the Cadmeia, one might expect him to have reported this, for such a fact would have legitimized Sphodrias' raid on the Peiraeus. Given his pro-Spartan bias, we would expect Xenophon to suppress (or omit) facts that reflect badly upon Sparta. And yet, in this instance, by suppressing, or omitting, the supposed fact of an official Athenian vote to attack the garrison, he achieves just the opposite effect: to exonerate the Athenians from blame for breaking the peace and to inculpate Sphodrias for a reckless, un-justified, and fateful deed. Xenophon's version is the one that he be-

[39]See G. L. Cawkwell, "The Foundation of the Second Athenian Confederacy," *CQ*, n.s. 23 (1973):47–60.

[40]See Cawkwell's remarks in his "Introduction" to the Penguin translation of the *Hellenica*, p. 35ff.: "One may address oneself to the most astonishing thing about the *Hellenica*, its omissions."

lieved to be correct. Moreover, it is internally consistent, for later he claims that the Athenians panicked after the expedition of King Cleombrotus and put the two generals who had acted on their own initiative on trial, condemning the one to death and the other, who had fled, to exile.[41]

One further point deserves note. We know from Plutarch that one of the harmosts who surrendered the Cadmeia was Herippidas, a Spartan who had served on several occasions with Agesilaus and may be presumed to have been one of his supporters.[42] Xenophon may have chosen to omit his name in order to spare Agesilaus the embarrassment of having his associate named in this shameful episode. Furthermore, if the Cadmeia fell after just a day, the blame that attaches to its commanders is all the more keen. In Diodorus' version, the garrison held out for some time, fighting valiantly and only capitulating when provisions had given out and its men despaired of help from Sparta. This account is clearly more favorable to the defenders, tending to heroize them, and unfavorable to Sparta, whose summary execution of the commanders seems more difficult to understand. In contrast, Xenophon's version of events quite correctly blames the commander for failure of nerve and for a too hasty capitulation; his execution by the Spartan authorities appears reasonable, or at least comprehensible. In sum, there is no reason to doubt Xenophon's version, and good reason to accept it. What of Diodorus' version?

As is well known, the method of Diodorus causes him occasionally to repeat events, and some scholars have seen in his report of the Athenian force under Demophon a doublet of the later Athenian expedition to thwart Agesilaus.[43] There is also a certain inconsistency in the account of Diodorus, because he writes that even after the Athenian aid to the Theban exiles, the peace between Athens and Sparta still remained unbroken; it is difficult to see how this could be so if Athenian troops had assisted officially in the assault on the Cadmeia. In addition, Diodorus' version of the events subsequent to the liberation of Thebes is muddled, and Diodorus may well have transposed a later vote to assist

---

[41]Xen. 5.4.19.

[42]See Poralla, *Prosopographie der Lakedaimonier*, no. 349, p. 62, for sources. Herippidas served with Agesilaus in Asia Minor, returned with him and fought at Coroneia, and then served with him in the Corinthian War; cf. Xen. 3.4.6, 20; 4.1.20–27, 2.8; 3.15–17; 4.8.11.

[43]Diod. 15.32.2. See R. M. Kallet-Marx, "Athens, Thebes, and the Foundation of the Second Athenian League," *CA* 4 (1985):127–51, at 129–30, with 129nn.13 and 14, on the question of accuracy of dates in Diodorus. Older literature is cited there.

Thebes to the immediate aftermath of the murder of Leontiades. The error in antedating an official Athenian decree to aid the Thebans, confused perhaps with an alliance that had certainly been made between Thebes and Athens before the time of the Aristoteles Decree in February 377, may have crept into the record in the fourth century. In any case, it was clear that Athens had given military support in the siege, and it would be convenient to forget that this support had been privately supplied and that the two commanders who had organized it had been punished for their unauthorized act. Thus, it seems best to accept Xenophon's account for the Athenian aid, although recognizing that events were moving swiftly and that there was a reaction in Athens against the act of the two generals, which threatened to embroil it in war with Sparta.

The Spartan Reaction

Xenophon provides the fullest account of the Spartans' reaction to the news of the Theban coup.[44] When the Spartans learned of the murders of the pro-Spartan oligarchs and of the surrender of the Cadmeia, they executed the harmost and called out the ban against the Thebans. Agesilaus declared that he ought not to be sent out in charge of the expedition, because he had passed his sixtieth year, and the law exempted from service outside of Laconia all who had reached that age. Xenophon asserts that the real reason for the reluctance of Agesilaus to command was his fear that, if he did lead out the army, his critics would accuse him of stirring up trouble for the state on behalf of tyrants. Instead, Agesilaus allowed them to make such dispositions as they wished, and they chose Cleombrotus, the brother of the recently deceased King Agesipolis, as commander. This was his first command, but Agesipolis appears to have involved himself politically in Spartan affairs, for within a few months he and his faction were opposed to Agesilaus. Despite the plausibility of the reason that Xenophon alleges, it seems strange that Agesilaus would willingly decline a golden opportunity to chastise the Thebans, his long-time enemies. We should, therefore, examine the situation in Sparta somewhat more carefully.[45] Diodorus has nothing to say on the matter, whereas Plutarch, who

[44]Xen. 5.4.13–18.
[45]See D. G. Rice, "Xenophon, Diodorus and the Year 379/378 B.C.: Reconstruction and Reappraisal," *Yale Classical Studies* 24 (1975):95–130, for such an investigation.

follows Xenophon closely here, amplifies on Xenophon's statement by saying that Agesilaus, after having just made war upon the Phliasians, did not want to appear to be harrying the Thebans over their tyrants.[46]

Xenophon makes clear that the decision to march out could not have been in relief of the garrison, because it had already surrendered, or in support of the tyrants, because they were already dead. It was a punitive expedition, designed to inflict damage upon the Thebans and, if possible, to coerce them once again under Sparta's sway. Of course, the Spartans might have chosen to respond differently. Having recognized that their control over Thebes was at an end, they might have attempted to negotiate a settlement with those now in power there.[47] But the prestige of Sparta was at stake, and it took the decision to employ military means. Because this was almost certainly Agesilaus' preferred response, we must ask if there was another motive for his refusal to lead the expedition. If Cleombrotus had become the head of a faction opposed to Agesilaus' policies since his brother's death,[48] then he and his followers might well have wished to refrain from further involvement in Theban affairs. They might have viewed Athens as a greater potential threat to Sparta's position in Greece than the newly liberated Thebes, especially in view of the Athenian assistance. Thus, the command of the expedition to Thebes would give Cleombrotus an opportunity to signal his intentions. But why would Agesilaus be willing to risk putting his opponent in charge of the expedition? If Cleombrotus succeeded in punishing the Thebans, then he would have achieved the goal of Agesilaus and become implicated in his policies. But if Cleombrotus failed to achieve anything in Boeotia (as indeed occurred), he would be discredited and his influence in Sparta much diminished. Agesilaus may have reasoned that he had little to lose by putting Cleombrotus in command, and much to gain, politically.

However that may be, Cleombrotus set out, in the dead of winter, and only succeeded in reaching Theban territory with difficulty. The Athenian commander Chabrias was holding the border fort of Eleutherae to prevent Spartan access to Boeotia by that route, and Cleombrotus had to cross Mount Cithaeron by the road to Plataea, which was held by the prisoners freed from the Theban jail. Cleombrotus defeated

---

[46]Plut. *Ages.* 24.2.

[47]Isocrates (14.29) reports that the Thebans attempted to negotiate a settlement with the Spartans at about this time, but some scholars reject his evidence.

[48]For this opinion, see Smith, "Opposition," 280; and Rice, "Xenophon, Diodorus," 105–9.

and killed most of them and reached bases still loyal to Sparta, Plataea and Thespiae. From these cities, he marched into Theban territory, where he encamped for sixteen days without doing any damage to the region. The Thebans refused to come forth to fight, and Cleombrotus eventually returned home. On the way, his men were battered by a violent wind on the slopes above Creusa. When they returned to Sparta, they grumbled, saying that their commander's behavior left them wondering if they were at peace or at war with Thebes.[49] It seems clear that Cleombrotus chose not to inflict damage on the territory of Thebes, probably in the hope of effecting a reconciliation between the two states. But this was not to be, despite Theban overtures for peace.

With the removal of Archias, Leontiades, and the other pro-Spartan tyrants, and the evacuation of the Cadmeia by the Spartan garrison, the liberators had apparently accomplished their major goals: their city was free, and they controlled the government (Plutarch asserts that Pelopidas, Melon, and Charon were elected Boeotarchs by the citizens of Thebes on the day following the coup).[50] Isocrates provides the information that, immediately after the seizure of the Cadmeia, the Thebans deserted their Athenian allies and sent to Sparta, saying they were prepared to abide by the old agreements with Sparta. The Spartans demanded that they take back their exiles and punish the murderers; that is, Melon, Pelopidas, and company.[51] Clearly, Agesilaus' role is to be seen in the Spartan response: harsh terms for hated enemies. The expectation of Agesilaus was that the return of the exiles would lead to a renewal of a pro-Spartan government at Thebes, just as had happened at Mantineia and Phlius. Needless to say, the new government rejected these demands, and its diplomatic overture came to nought.

The Theban government probably dispatched the embassy to Sparta only after Cleombrotus' army had taken the field against them, in an attempt to avoid a further escalation of hostilities. They were prepared to rejoin the Peloponnesian League, in return for autonomy in local government. Aware that an embassy had been sent to Sparta, Cleombrotus preferred to do no harm to Theban territory pending the outcome of this embassy. Agesilaus, however, would accept nothing less than retribution for the murders of his partisans, and the de facto

[49]Xen. 5.4.14–18.
[50]Plut. *Pelop.* 13.1. See J. Buckler, "The Re-establishment of the *Boiotarchia* (378 B.C.)," *AJAH* 4 (1979):50–64.
[51]Isoc. 14.29. Isocrates' statement proves that the Cadmeia had already been surrendered (cf. Xen. 5.4.12, 14 on the exiles, with Plut. *Pelop.* 12.3 on pro-Spartans joining the garrison).

overthrow of the new regime in Thebes. Even after the refusal of the Thebans to accept the Spartan demands, Cleombrotus refrained from ravaging their territory, perhaps to show them that not all Spartans agreed with Agesilaus. Indeed, all the sources agree that Cleombrotus and Agesilaus belonged to opposing factions at this time. If we accept the view that the embassy arrived only after the departure of Cleombrotus' army, then the outcome demonstrates that Agesilaus was in control of the situation there. And if that is so, it may help to explain the allegation that Cleombrotus was behind the march of Sphodrias on the Peiraeus. Did the Theban overture occur before or after the alleged Athenian renunciation of the two generals? Xenophon puts the latter event after Cleombrotus' arrival in the field. It is possible, then, that two motives caused the Thebans to seek accommodation with Sparta: fear of the desertion of Athens and the desire to avoid Spartan reprisals.

The Sphodrias Incident

According to Xenophon, before returning to Sparta, Cleombrotus put Sphodrias in command of a garrison at Thespiae, and left him a third of the troops that the king had led forth, as well as all of the money that he had, with instructions to hire mercenaries.[52] Some time later, the commander was persuaded to attempt a night march on the port of Athens, the Peiraeus. His apparent objective was to capture the Peiraeus, perhaps to garrison it, and thus to emulate the act of Phoebidas at Thebes. The attempt failed, for Sphodrias and his force were quite some distance from their objective when dawn broke and they were seen by the Athenians; the plot probably misfired through a miscalculation by Sphodrias of the time needed to cover the distance. Instead of proceeding, he turned his troops back toward Thespiae, plundering the Attic countryside as they went.

The Athenians were furious over the incident. Xenophon mentions a Spartan embassy in connection with the Sphodrias incident, but its purpose is not divulged. Etymocles, who was a close associate of Agesilaus, and two others had come to Athens, and they were arrested when the news of Sphodrias' attempt became known. They disclaimed any knowledge of the event, arguing cogently that if they had known about it they would hardly have chosen to stay at the home of the Spartan proxenos in Athens, where they were easily apprehended. This defense, coupled with the assurance that the home government in

[52]Xen. 5.4.15.

Sparta would soon take Sphodrias to task for his unwarranted act, convinced the Athenians to allow them to return to Sparta. The Spartans did bring Sphodrias to trial. Not only was he acquitted, however, through the influence of the two kings, but he was also praised for his daring. When the Athenians learned of the outcome of the trial, they declared that the peace had been broken and began preparations for war against Sparta.[53] The sources agree on these basic facts, but there is no agreement about who was ultimately responsible for putting Sphodrias up to the raid, and serious questions concerning why the trial ended as it did remain.[54] Because it is evident that the outcome of the Sphodrias incident had major repercussions on Spartan-Athenian relations, it is fitting to explore the issue of responsibility for the raid and the reasons for the outcome of the trial.

Xenophon states clearly that the Thebans were responsible for suborning Sphodrias by a bribe; Plutarch agrees with him. They made overtures to him to attempt the seizure of the Peiraeus because, quite simply, the Athenians had experienced a change of heart following the expedition of King Cleombrotus into Boeotia and had become fearful of a war against Sparta. The Athenians therefore put on trial the two generals who had led the Athenian forces in assisting the liberators of Thebes, condemning one to death and the other, who had already fled, to exile.[55] This turn of events undoubtedly occurred under the influence of those in Athens who feared Sparta and wished to maintain the status quo, if possible. It is probably this act that Plutarch had in mind when he wrote, rather inaccurately, that the Athenians, fearful of the Spartan invasion of Boeotia, "renounced their alliance with Thebes" and prosecuted those who favored the Boeotian cause, executing some, exiling others, and fining still others.[56] However that may be, it was because they feared that they would have to stand alone against the Spartans that the Thebans intrigued to induce Sphodrias to commit his hostile act.

Once again, Diodorus tells quite a different story.[57] He imputes the responsibility for the raid not to the Thebans, but to King Cleombrotus, who acted without the consent of the ephors, and therefore, presumably, in secret. It is easy enough to see whence Diodorus' version may have derived. Because Agesilaus' group in Sparta was clearly

[53]Xen. 5.4.20–24; 34.
[54]See Rice, "Xenophon, Diodorus," 112–18, and A. G. MacDonald, "A Note on the Raid of Sphodrias," *Historia* 21 (1972):38–44.
[55]Xen. 5.4.19–20; cf. Plut. *Pelop.* 14.1.
[56]Plut. *Pelop.* 14.1.
[57]Diod. 15.29.5–6.

surprised by the raid, they had no part in it. In the ensuing discussions over Sphodrias' punishment, it became clear that he belonged to Cleombrotus' circle,[58] and it was simple to believe that the king had instructed him to undertake his enterprise. Cleombrotus had shown little interest in punishing the Theban liberators or in recapturing Thebes during his expedition in winter 379/8, and he may well have belonged to a faction that opposed Agesilaus on the issue of Thebes and felt that a resurgent Athens was a much more serious threat to Sparta.

It seems possible to suggest that both accounts of the incident may contain a kernel of truth. Cleombrotus left Sphodrias as harmost of Thespiae with instructions, perhaps more general than specific, to seek to thwart any Athenian attempt at anti-Spartan activity. Then, when the Theban leaders had come to believe that the Athenians were no longer going to support them against Sparta, they sent to Sphodrias to encourage him to undertake a daring deed that would emulate Phoebidas' at Thebes. Of course, their motivation was to provoke Athens into confrontation with Sparta. Had Sphodrias succeeded, their plan might have backfired, but they took the gamble, which worked.[59] To all appearances, a Spartan commander had, in time of peace and without provocation, invaded the territory of an independent state and thus committed a hostile act, tantamount to war. But was the raid without justification?

Cawkwell has argued that the Athenians had already begun the process of establishing their Second League before the raid of Sphodrias.[60] In this reconstruction, the raid is presented as both comprehensible and justified as an attempt to forestall the growth of Athens' maritime ambitions. The difficulty is that our sources are not clear on this process. Xenophon omits any reference to the establishment of the Second Athenian League, or indeed to its operation in the 370s. Diodorus does provide an account of its establishment, in two separate passages, and the former occurs prior to his narrative of Sphodrias' raid.[61] Thus, Diodorus seems to date the early stages of the league's foundation before the raid.

But there are several problems with his account. First, Diodorus'

---

[58]Xen. 5.4.25.

[59]This intrigue is reminiscent of the Thebans' staging of the Phocis-Locris incident, which provoked the Corinthian War, and of the attempt to provoke Agesilaus at Aulis.

[60]Cawkwell, "The Foundation of the Second Athenian Confederacy," discussed and expanded by Kallet-Marx, "Athens, Thebes, and the Foundation of the Second Athenian League," 129–40.

[61]Diod. 15.28.1–4; 29.7–8.

absolute chronology is erroneous and, more seriously, his account is internally inconsistent.[62] In any case, he makes it quite clear that it was the raid of Sphodrias, or, more precisely, the sequel to that raid at Sparta, which led Athens to vote that Sparta had broken the peace. In other words, even if Athens had begun to solicit allies for the league during the incipient phases of development, before the raid of Sphodrias, Diodorus states plainly that such activity did not constitute a breach of the terms of the King's Peace. Diodorus also fails to mention Athens' punishment of the errant generals, an act that Xenophon surely did not invent and that clearly indicates that the Athenians were prepared to acquiesce to Spartan demands in order to maintain the peace. As Xenophon shows, this event occurred before the raid, and it surely must have been viewed in Sparta, as it was in Thebes, as a sign that the Athenians had abandoned their hostility toward Sparta. The suggestion that the raid of Sphodrias was *fully* justified as a preemptive strike against nascent Athenian naval aggression is unacceptable. At best, we can admit that some people in Sparta might have remained convinced that Athens was becoming a threat, even after the trial of the generals, and they might have sought to exploit what they perceived as Athenian indecision by instigating Sphodrias' raid. Let us examine the Spartan reaction to news of the raid.

Initially, the Spartan authorities reacted vigorously. Shocked by the report of Sphodrias' unauthorized act, the ephors recalled him to stand trial. He failed to respond, fearing that he would be convicted of a crime, despite whatever support he may have hoped for from Cleombrotus. And yet, although he did not return to stand trial, he was acquitted. All the sources note the injustice of this verdict, and Xenophon provides an instructive, if not wholly convincing, explanation of it.

Xenophon relates that Agesilaus' son, Archidamus, was the lover of Sphodrias' son Cleonymus, though Sphodrias belonged to the political circle of Cleombrotus.[63] When Cleonymus begged Archidamus to intercede with his father on Sphodrias' behalf, the young prince did so, but reluctantly. At first Agesilaus replied that he could not declare a man

---

[62]The method of moving from topic to topic, which causes Diodorus to insert an account of the war of the Persians to reconquer Egypt between the two chapters dealing with Spartan-Athenian affairs, may have resulted in some confusion in the presentation of the sequence of events leading up to the establishment of the league. See C. D. Hamilton, "Diodorus on the Establishment of the Second Athenian League," *Ancient History Bulletin* 3 (1989):93–102, for detailed discussion of these points.

[63]Xen. 5.4.25.

innocent who had enriched himself by harming Sparta (a reference to the Theban bribe) without laying himself open to criticism.[64] Indeed, in this regard, Agesilaus was quite correct. However, Archidamus returned again and asked his father to consider forgiving Sphodrias, guilty though he was, for Cleonymus' and his own sake. The appeal was based on personal favoritism, but no doubt it reminded Agesilaus of the rather similar circumstances of Phoebidas' trial. On that occasion, Agesilaus had argued for acquittal on the grounds of expediency, and he might do so again in the present instance. His reply, "Well and good, if it should turn out honorably for us," discouraged Archidamus, who could not conceive how such a verdict could turn out honorably. But Agesilaus had changed his mind. His friend Etymocles, in a conversation with one of Sphodrias' friends, reported that Agesilaus averred to all of his associates that there was no doubt of Sphodrias' guilt, but that it was difficult to put to death one who in childhood, boyhood, and youth had always acted well and honorably, for Sparta had need of such soldiers.[65] As a result, he was acquitted. Plutarch's account of this incident is obviously closely based on Xenophon's, and adds little to it, whereas Diodorus merely notes that Sphodrias, who had the support of the kings, was acquitted by a miscarriage of justice.[66] All three sources, however, reflect the widespread feeling that the outcome of the trial represented a gross injustice, and there is no doubt that the entire episode became a cause célèbre. Let us examine more closely the political aspects of the trial.

That it was a political trial is made clear by Xenophon's report that King Cleombrotus' friends, who moved in the same circles as Sphodrias, were inclined to acquit him, but were afraid of Agesilaus and his friends, and of those who did not belong to either faction.[67] There were three distinct groups, and they differed over the issue of Sphodrias' guilt, but doubtless on many other issues as well. It is equally clear that Agesilaus held the decisive power at the trial, although how exactly this power was exercised is not so clear. One theory is that he influenced the votes of members of the Gerousia, assuming that the trial took place among them, or conversely that he influenced the assembly, if that is where the trial occurred.[68] In any case, his concurrence with the opinion

[64]Xen. 5.4.30.
[65]Xen. 5.4.31–32.
[66]Plut. Ages. 25; Diod. 15.29.6.
[67]Xen. 5.4.25.
[68]Cartledge, Agesilaos, pp. 137 and 157, states that the trial took place before the Gerousia, and that the political groups mentioned in Xenophon refer to groupings

of Cleombrotus was sufficient to determine the outcome of the trial. The real question for us, then, is to ascertain why Agesilaus adopted the opinion that he did.

A number of reasons come to mind. First is Xenophon's allegation that he acted to oblige his son, who thereby was able to assure himself of Cleonymus' loyalty and affection. This is certainly a plausible factor in Agesilaus' decision, but, as Xenophon implies, it is hardly a sufficient one in and of itself. A second reason may have been one that Plutarch stressed, in discussing Agesilaus' political abilities: he tried, whenever possible, to do favors for his political opponents and thereby obligate them to him.[69] Plutarch emphasizes that Sphodrias was an opponent of Agesilaus, who belonged to the opposing faction.[70] Although we know little about the subsequent career of Sphodrias, there is at least no evidence that he continued in his opposition to Agesilaus, and this may have been one of the king's objectives in deciding to vote for his acquittal. As an extension of this idea, Agesilaus may have wished to reduce the degree of opposition to himself and his policies from Cleombrotus' faction, and even to have indebted them to him. Indeed, shortly after the trial Agesilaus agreed to undertake an expedition into Boeotia to wreak vengeance on the Thebans. He had declined to lead the expedition that Cleombrotus directed immediately after the liberation of the Cadmeia, precisely because he feared the criticism of his enemies. If these enemies included Cleombrotus' faction, Agesilaus might have been aiming to blunt their criticism, if not to win their active support, with regard to future interventions he was probably already planning against Thebes. Yet a fourth motive may have been, as recently suggested,[71] related to an ever-growing awareness of the diminishing supply of Spartiates. When Agesilaus said that Sparta had need of such soldiers as Sphodrias, he may have meant that the state needed every single hoplite it could muster in a period of declining manpower, and he may have meant it quite literally. In any case, Xenophon makes a point of mentioning that Sphodrias, one of the king's tent companions, died fighting with Cleombrotus at Leuctra.[72]

---

within the Gerousia. I think this view is not entirely clear. I believe that Xenophon, in referring to the "friends of Cleombrotus, those of Agesilaus, and those in between," does not mean to restrict his remark to members of the Gerousia, but rather to influential Spartans in general. It is probable, however, that the trial occurred before the Gerousia; cf. chap. 2 above.

[69]Plut. Ages. 20.4; cf. Xen. Ages. 7.3.
[70]Ages. 24.3.
[71]Cartledge, Agesilaos, p. 158.
[72]Xen. 6.4.14.

It is, of course, possible that all of these motives, and others as well, were factors in Agesilaus' decision. But he must have been aware that to fly in the face of justice for reasons of expediency such as these was to run the risk of public censure of his act, outside of Sparta if not within. And the Athenians had made it quite clear to Etymocles, one of Agesilaus' close friends, and the other Spartan ambassadors that punishment of Sphodrias was a *sine qua non* for further good relations between the two states. Thus, in throwing his influence behind the acquittal of Sphodrias, Agesilaus knowingly rebuffed Athens. Perhaps he calculated that the Athenians would not respond to this act of provocation; after all, had they not recently condemned their generals as a token of their submissiveness to Sparta? But if this were so, Agesilaus miscalculated badly. The Athenians immediately voted that the Spartans were guilty of breaking the peace, and they took measures to prepare for war. Despite Spartan diplomatic attempts to counter those of Athens (if the activities mentioned by Diodorus are to be dated to this period), it was successful in its recruitment efforts of allies. The result was the formal establishment of the Second Athenian League, as well as warfare at sea between Athens and Sparta.

The linkage between the handling of the Sphodrias affair in Sparta and the establishment of the league is absolutely clear. Whatever the outcome of the political maneuverings of Agesilaus within Sparta on this occasion, there is no doubt that his policy resulted in a major disaster for Sparta in foreign affairs. The question that has engaged the attention of so many modern historians—namely, why Xenophon made no mention whatsoever of the founding of the Second Athenian League—is less puzzling when viewed in this light. Contemporaries of Xenophon must have recognized that the Athenian decision to go forward with the diplomatic efforts to establish a second maritime alliance was the result of Agesilaus' decision about Sphodrias, and thus it represented for him a foreign policy failure of great proportions. To have reported the establishment of the league, as a result of the trial in Sparta, as Diodorus did (following Ephorus), was too painful for Xenophon, Agesilaus' admirer and champion. Rather than call attention to this colossal blunder on Agesilaus' part, Xenophon omitted any reference to the league, although he was honest enough to record that the angry Athenians "built gates for the Peiraeus, fitted out ships, and did all they could to assist the Boeotians."[73] Linking the acquittal of Sphodrias to the Athenian decision to go to war, Plutarch reports that it led to

[73]Xen. 5.4.34.

Agesilaus' becoming very unpopular,[74] and his observation doubtless reflected widespread contemporary opinion on this issue.

Agesilaus' Boeotian Campaigns in 378 and 377

Upon the conclusion of the Sphodrias affair, the Spartans determined to call out the ban and to make war again on the Thebans. This time, they appointed Agesilaus as commander, and he agreeably accepted the command. He sent orders ahead to put an end to local fighting which had broken out in Arcadia between Orchomenus and Cletor. The city of Cletor had hired a mercenary army, and Agesilaus arranged with its commander to employ this force to occupy the pass over Mount Cithaeron in order to facilitate the passage of the Spartans into Boeotia.[75] The expedition that he led involved a very substantial number of troops, some eighteen thousand in all, drawn from the allies of Sparta and its own ranks.

It was apparently on this occasion that allied dissatisfaction with the war in Boeotia resulted in a restructuring of the Peloponnesian League army. Plutarch tells us that Sparta's allies were grumbling over the constant demands made on them to prosecute Spartan campaigns in Boeotia. Agesilaus responded to this criticism by demonstrating that Sparta contributed more than its share of soldiers through a clever ploy. He separated the Spartan troops from the allied ones, then had his herald summon all to stand as he called various occupations aloud: smiths, potters, carpenters, and so forth. Eventually, not a single allied soldier remained seated, whereas not a single Spartan had arisen; in this way Agesilaus graphically demonstrated that only the Spartans devoted themselves fully to the profession of arms and that the allies' complaints should be ignored.[76] But Diodorus informs us of a reorganization of the league forces into ten military districts, each of which apparently made an equal contribution to levies of the army. Ratios were set between hoplites and peltasts, and between horsemen and hoplites, apparently so that obligations could easily be recalculated in money payments for those who wished to commute their service obligations into cash to hire mercenaries. This arrangement was related to the earlier change, enacted in the course of the Olynthian campaign, which permitted the

[74]Plut. *Ages.* 26.1.
[75]Xen. 5.4.35–37.
[76]Plut. *Ages.* 26.3–5; cf. Polyaenus 2.17.

commutation of military obligations into money payments; and it apparently occurred in connection with the summoning of the allies of Sparta to march into Boeotia in summer 378.[77]

When Agesilaus finally marched his army over Cithaeron into Boeotia, he encamped before Thespiae, which had a Spartan garrison, and planned his campaign.[78] In anticipation of a Spartan invasion, the Thebans had constructed a defense system consisting of a trench and a palisade, from a point on the border of Thebes and Thespiae in the west, along the northern side of the Asopus River to the border of Thebes and Tanagra in the east. This fortification was designed as a screen, to protect Theban territory from the penetration and devastation of an invading army. The fortification took advantage of the natural terrain when possible, as far as we can tell, and a combined force of Thebans, under Epaminondas, and Athenians, under Chabrias, patrolled Theban territory behind it. Agesilaus' army surely considerably outnumbered the forces that the Thebans could martial, even with the aid of Chabrias' five thousand, and they would refuse to give battle. But Agesilaus' first problem was to get behind the barrier in order to attempt to engage the enemy.

Over a period of days, Agesilaus shifted his camp frequently, watching the movements of the enemy forces behind the palisade. On one occasion, the Theban cavalry made a sortie from one of the numerous sally ports in the stockade and inflicted light casualties on Agesilaus' troops. When he had taken the measure of their movements and established a pattern of routine, much as Lysander had with the Athenian fleet at Aegospotami, Agesilaus acted. He marched his army at daybreak to a point east of his camp, where he managed to cross the stockade before the enemy could impede him. He was then able to move about, unopposed, almost up to the city itself.[79] On one occasion, after his penetration of the stockade, Agesilaus encountered the enemy forces, drawn up on a defensible height. Chabrias was in command, and he ordered his soldiers to stand at ease, with their spears upright and their shields resting at their knees. Clearly, the defiant posture was meant as a challenge, and an insult, to Agesilaus, but the

---

[77]Diod. 15.31.1–2; cf. Xen. 5.2.21–22.

[78]Xen. 5.4.38–41; Diod. 15.32.1–33.4. See M. H. Munn, "Agesilaos' Boiotian Campaigns and the Theban Stockade of 378–377 B.C.," *CA* 6 (1987):106–38, with plates. This is an excellent study, both in terms of historiographical and topographical analysis, and I follow it in the main here.

[79]Xen. 5.4.41. Munn, "Agesilaos' Boiotian Campaigns," 111 and 116–17.

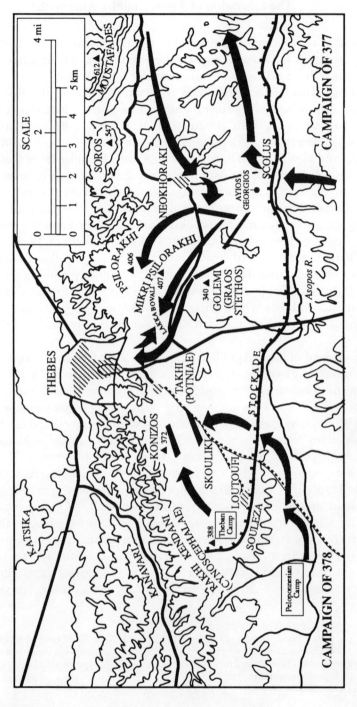

Agesilaus' Boeotian campaigns of 378 and 377

Spartan did not attempt to assault the enemy position.[80] Rather, he contented himself with marching toward Thebes and plundering as he went. Once within Boeotian territory, he conducted operations that put the Thebans on the defensive and resulted in extensive ravaging of their land, but these operations did not produce a decisive end to the conflict. Strategically, they were counterproductive, because the Boeotians fought on with ever-greater determination after Agesilaus had withdrawn and returned to the Peloponnesus.

After Agesilaus' departure, the garrison at Thespiae continued to plunder Theban territory, and eventually the Thebans seized the initiative and attacked Thespiae. There, following an encounter in which the Thebans were first put to flight by the peltasts in Spartan service, but then rallied bravely, the Thebans won a victory over the Spartan garrison forces in which the harmost Phoebidas was killed.[81] Encouraged by their success, they began to extend their control over other cities of Boeotia and to reestablish the old Boeotian Confederacy, which Agesilaus had dissolved in 386. Many democrats had fled to Thebes from their various cities at this time, because the rest of the Boeotian towns were governed by Spartan-installed and -supported oligarchies. It is not possible to gauge the degree of success which Thebes enjoyed in extending its control in this season, but over the next several years more and more of the Boeotian cities fell once again under Theban sway.[82] Because the Thebans had succeeded at Thespiae, the Spartans determined once again to dispatch Agesilaus to Boeotia in 377.[83]

On this occasion, as he had done in 378, Agesilaus sent orders to the polemarch at Thespiae to occupy the heights of Cithaeron, and he easily crossed into Boeotia again. Then he duped the enemy concerning his intentions, by requesting that a market be prepared at Thespiae, but instead marched off eastward to Erythrae and Scolus.[84] In this way, he managed again to slip behind the stockade at an unguarded point and to ravage the territory east of Thebes, in the direction of Tanagra. When the Theban army took up a position on an elevation and waited to give battle, Agesilaus ignored them and turned toward Thebes. This feint drew off the Thebans, who feared for the safety of their city, and who

[80]Diod. 15.32.3–33.4. See Munn, "Agesilaos' Boiotian Campaigns," 117–21.
[81]Xen. 5.4.42–45; Diod. 15.33.5–6.
[82]Xen. 5.4.46.
[83]Xen. 5.4.47; Diod. 15.34.1.
[84]Xen. 5.4.47–49. This tactic of Agesilaus is reminiscent of a much earlier deceit that he practiced against Tissaphernes when in Asia Minor; cf. 3.4.11–13.

withdrew on a course parallel to that of Agesilaus. As a result, Agesilaus was able to harry the retreating Thebans, and to inflict some casualties on them. He failed to assault Thebes, however; when he turned back to Thespiae, he found the citizens in the midst of stasis. He imposed a settlement upon them and then retreated to Megara.[85]

The effect of Agesilaus' two invasions of Boeotia was that the Thebans had lost their harvests for two years and were in dire need of imported grain. The activity shifted to the sea, where the Thebans attempted to import grain purchased in Pagasae. Unfortunately for them, the Spartan harmost in Oreus on Euboea, Alcetas, intercepted the fleet, capturing the grain and imprisoning the crews in Oreus. But not long afterward, the prisoners managed to seize the acropolis of Oreus, and thereafter Thebes was able to import grain with no difficulty.[86] Thus, his Boeotian campaigns proved fruitless in terms of their ultimate aims. The Thebans suffered from the ravaging of their land, and this helped to dispose them to make peace in 375, but they remained in control of their city and their government, and they retained their ambitions to regain control of most of Boeotia, which they did in the late 370s. From the tactical point of view, both Agesilaus and the Thebans enjoyed limited successes from these activities. Agesilaus managed to breach the defenses of the stockade and to ravage Theban land, but he failed both to bring the enemy army into a major engagement and to force Thebes to Sparta's will. Similarly, the Thebans failed to protect their territory from plundering by their system of defense, but, more importantly, they held Agesilaus at a standstill and thwarted his real objectives.[87]

Meanwhile, Agesilaus was taken ill on his journey home. He had paused at Megara and, while going up from the shrine of Aphrodite to the government offices, he ruptured a vein, which caused severe swelling in his good leg. A Syracusan surgeon opened his leg below the ankle and alleviated the pressure, but then it proved difficult to staunch the flow of blood for a considerable period, until Agesilaus lost consciousness. His men carried him back to Sparta, and he was unable to take an active role for the rest of the summer and all through the winter. Not only was he not able to assume the command of the force sent to invade Boeotia again in 376, but we hear virtually nothing more about him

[85]Xen. 5.4.49–55, *Ages.* 2.22; Polyaenus 2.1.11; Diod. 15.34.1–2. See Munn, "Agesilaos' Boiotian Campaigns," 121–33.
[86]Xen. 5.4.56–57.
[87]See Munn, "Agesilaos' Boiotian Campaigns," 133–38.

until the Peace Conference in Sparta in 371.[88] In the interim, the war had shifted to the sea, and others in Sparta must have taken the lead in directing it.

The Second Athenian League and the War at Sea

During spring and summer 378, the Athenians undertook a vigorous diplomatic campaign to forge a new maritime alliance. They had enjoyed a bilateral treaty with Chios since 384, and at this time they began to attract other Aegean states into alliance as well. The end product of this activity was what scholars call the Second Athenian League.[89] We are imperfectly informed about its origins and early development, and the most important sources of information are a series of Athenian treaties and decrees, most of them surviving as fragmentary inscriptions, and a narrative account provided by Diodorus.[90] Xenophon ignores the rise of the league, and the other literary sources reveal very little. Nevertheless, it is possible to trace the stages in the development of the league until February/March 377, when the passage of the Aristoteles Decree marked the establishment of the principles and organization of the league. Diodorus portrays the league as developing through some four stages, from its origins at some point in 378 to the passage of the decree in 377, but there is good reason to dispute details of this presentation. At first, the Athenians sent envoys to various cities to persuade them to revolt from the Spartans.[91] This is an inaccurate description of the early phase of the league, for none of the six "charter member" states of the league—Chios, Mitylene, Methymna, Byzantium, Rhodes, and Thebes—was allied to Sparta, and thus it is incorrect to speak of their rebellion, as Diodorus does. Leaving aside the inac-

[88]Xen. 5.4.58; Plut. *Ages.* 27.1–2. On the nature of Agesilaus' illness, see M. Michler, "Die Krankheit des Agesilaos in Megara," *Sudhoffs Archiv für Geschichte der Medizin* 47 (1963):179–83.

[89]For the most recent treatments of this topic, see J. Cargill, *The Second Athenian League: Empire or Free Alliance?* (Berkeley and Los Angeles, 1981); and Kallet-Marx, "Athens, Thebes, and the Foundation of the Second Athenian League."

[90]The dating of the initial steps in the formation of the Second Athenian League is a matter of considerable scholarly controversy. I have examined Diodorus' account of the origins of the league in *AHB* 3 (1989):93–102 and have concluded that his account is confused and contradictory. More particularly, the various steps that Diodorus records before the Sphodrias incident could not have taken place in the brief span of time necessitated by the narrative.

[91]Diod. 15.28.2.

curacy of this statement, which fits more properly the period after 377, when allies of Sparta such as the Chalcidian League and Acarnania did indeed join Athens, we may admit that Athenian diplomacy scored successes in the Aegean among former members of the Delian League. Athens then moved to convert a series of bilateral alliances into a new league, with the appointment of representatives of the various states to a common council that met in Athens. From this point forward, all decisions were taken in common.[92]

There were guarantees of independence for each of the states, although from the first they all accepted Athens as the hegemon. By summer 378, the basic principles of the league had been spelled out, and it was then a question of how successful the Athenians could be in expanding their organization. Its purpose would be enunciated clearly in the Aristoteles Decree: "So that the Lacedaemonians shall leave the Greeks free and autonomous, to enjoy tranquillity, possessing their own territory in safety."[93] The aim of the Athenians was to recruit allies in a common effort to preserve freedom and autonomy from Spartan aggression, and the Spartans could not fail to attempt to defend themselves and their conduct from such an assault.

In response to initial Athenian successes, the Spartans apparently sent out their own envoys to attempt to forestall the recruitment of additional cities. These activities were no doubt designed to stress the dangers of involvement with Athens, and we may imagine that the Spartan envoys greatly emphasized the pretended abuses of the fifth-century Athenian Empire, which had developed out of the Delian League.[94] But the envoys' efforts were in vain. It is likely that Athens responded to the Spartan efforts with further diplomacy of its own, and the end result of the propaganda of each side is reflected in the decree. This document clearly states that the league is established in accord with the terms of the King's Peace of 387/6, which guaranteed the autonomy of every polis, large or small. This concern is specifically detailed by a

[92]Diod. 15.28.3–4. Actually, Diodorus does not spell out the bicameral nature of the organization, whereby each member state except Athens had a vote in the synedrion, and that body stood on an equal footing with the Athenian assembly. Decisions taken by either one of these bodies had to be ratified by the other before becoming binding on the league members. See Cargill, *SAL*, p. 115ff., for discussion and sources.

[93]Cargill's trans., *SAL*, p. 17.

[94]See Hamilton, "Isocrates," 103–4, for detailed discussion of this point. For a recent discussion of Athens' fifth-century empire, see M. F. MacGregor, *The Athenians and Their Empire* (Vancouver, 1988), although this book makes no pretense of being more than an excellent introduction to the subject. The standard work remains R. L. Meiggs, *The Athenian Empire* (Oxford, 1972).

series of clauses, in which prospective allies are guaranteed the right to remain independent, to enjoy their own constitutions, and to be free from garrisons and commanders. Many modern scholars take these explicit guarantees to be references to past practices of the Athenians in the fifth-century empire, but they are just as likely, or even more so, to be intended as references to more recent practices of the Spartans toward their allies and subject states.[95]

From the days of Lysander, down to the period of Agesilaus' influence in the 380s, the Spartans had imposed harmosts and garrisons, changed constitutions to their liking, and, from time to time, exacted tribute. Athenian diplomats and propagandists may well have intended such explicit guarantees against such practices to lay stress on current Spartan practices in an effort to win away states from Sparta, or to attract others who might feel threatened by it. In contrast, the rather lengthier set of provisions against Athenian land-holding in states allied to Athens probably responded to very real fears of many Aegean poleis. Many of the cleruchs whom Lysander had driven out of the Aegean in the last year of the Peloponnesian War had not yet given up the desire to regain their possessions.[96] The Spartan envoys may have emphasized this area in their diplomatic efforts, and the Athenians, in turn, voted to prohibit any return to such fifth-century policies of territorial expropriation in allied states.[97] However that may be, the Athenian propaganda effort was successful, and scores of states accepted the invitation of the Aristoteles Decree and became members of the league in and after 377. As a result, Athens was able to prosecute a vigorous maritime policy, aimed at reducing Sparta's influence even more.

By summer 377, when Agesilaus fell ill on his return from his second invasion of Boeotia, the situation for Sparta in Greece had changed dramatically. Merely two years before, in winter 379/8, Sparta had stood at the height of its power, dominating an alliance system that stretched from the Peloponnesus to the Chalcidice. The chain of events which began with the return of Pelopidas, Melon, and the other exiles to liberate Thebes in December 379 changed the situation drastically. Thebes was not only liberated from Spartan control, but also the new government there became bitterly anti-Spartan and dedicated to the establishment anew of the old Boeotian League. Indeed, by 377 the first steps toward the elimination of Spartan control of the Boeotian cities

[95]Hamilton, "Isocrates," 104–6.
[96]See ibid., 94–96, for discussion and sources, particularly the rhetoricians Andocides and Isocrates.
[97]Diod. 15.29.8; IG ii² 43, 11.

and their incorporation in the league had already been taken. Moreover, through the blunder of Sphodrias, and even more the maladroit handling of his trial, Athens had become alienated from Sparta. Athens had also taken the first steps toward the establishment of a new maritime league, founded specifically to guarantee the autonomy of member states against Spartan aggression. The Spartan reaction had been too little, too late. Diplomatic efforts during 378 failed to reassure prospective allies of the Second Athenian League that they were better off in the Spartan sphere. Indeed, the Athenians were able to capitalize upon and to turn Spartan propaganda to their own advantage, as the guarantees of the Aristoteles Decree demonstrate. Sparta's armed interventions in Boeotia were also to little avail. Despite some minor victories in skirmishes with the Thebans, Agesilaus had little to show for his two invasions of Boeotia. Perhaps his opponent Antalcidas summed it up best when he chided the wounded king with the words "the Thebans are paying you well for teaching them to fight, when they had neither any wish for it, nor any skill either."[98]

That Agesilaus and his policies were largely responsible for this turn of events is undoubtedly true. In the short run, it was his insistence on retaliation against Thebes in the wake of the liberation, and his impossible demands in response to the Theban overtures for peace, which drove the Thebans into their position of entrenched hostility to Sparta. And, of course, the reason for this was that unreasoning obsession to crush Thebes which stretched back almost two decades to the incident at Aulis. As for Athens, it is clear that, despite the desire of some Athenians to reclaim their former position of power, the outcome of the Sphodrias incident spelled the end of any possibility to peaceful accommodation between the two powers. Here again, Agesilaus must bear the blame for this fateful development. In the long run, as well, Agesilaus' policies of intervention and oppression had alienated many poleis and prepared the way for the massive defections from Sparta's leadership, which were only beginning in 377. The lessons of Mantineia and Phlius, of Thebes and Olynthus, had not been lost on the Greeks. Sparta, under Agesilaus' influence, had interpreted the King's Peace and the principle of autonomy in too selfish a fashion. Now, many states were ready to heed Athens' call to guarantee their autonomy by other means. Just how far they were prepared to go, and what this would mean for Sparta's position in international affairs, the future showed.

[98]Plut. *Ages.* 26.2; cf. *Pelop.* 15.2 and *Lyc.* 13.6.

CHAPTER SEVEN

The Road to Leuctra

The liberation of Thebes and the establishment of the Second Athenian League in 378 had weakened Sparta's position in the Greek world considerably. In the following years, Sparta waged desultory warfare in a valiant, but vain, attempt to reaffirm its hegemony in the Greek world. Fighting occurred in two theaters: in central Greece, where Sparta and the poleis that it still controlled battled Thebes at the head of the new Boeotian Confederacy; and elsewhere in Greece, primarily at sea, between Sparta and the allies of the ever-expanding Second Athenian League. The costs of this warfare proved difficult for all combatants to bear, and, as Sparta in particular came to recognize that it was losing ground, an attempt at negotiations was made in 375. But the peace that was concluded did not last for long, and once again the belligerents found themselves at war. After a few further years of fruitless hostilities, the situation seemed ripe for another attempt at a diplomatic resolution. But the resultant conference only led to a confrontation between the Theban leader, Epaminondas, and King Agesilaus, and to the resumption of hostilities. Another Spartan invasion of Boeotia was to have fateful consequences at the Battle of Leuctra. The events of the 370s, the road to Leuctra, are the subject of this chapter.

The War from 377 to 375

While Agesilaus was engaged in his second invasion of Boeotia in 377, the Athenians seized the initiative and launched a vigorous offensive at sea. The first overseas activity in which they engaged was the

freeing of Euboea. All of the Euboean cities except Hestiaea came over
to Athens, and Athens decided to send an expedition to conquer that
city. Euboea was crucial to the allied cause because it could be used by
the Spartans to attack grain convoys from the Hellespontine region on
their way to the Peiraeus. Chabrias took Hestiaea by storm, fortified its
acropolis, and left a garrison in possession. He also ravaged the neighboring territory of Oreus, where the Spartan harmost Alcetas had just
been overthrown. The seizure of Oreus was particularly important, for
the Spartans there had preyed upon a small squadron of grain ships
destined for Boeotia from Pagasae, capturing both crews and cargo.[1]
With the northern coast of Euboea now in allied hands, Thebes and
Athens could hope to receive shipments of grain unperiled. Chabrias
then sailed off to the Cyclades, where he won over Peparathos, Scia-
thos, and some other islands subject to the Spartans.[2]

In the next year, 376, the Spartans determined to invade Boeotia once
again. Agesilaus still lay disabled from his illness of the previous year,
and King Cleombrotus was ordered to undertake the expedition. He
proved unsuccessful in crossing Cithaeron, however, because he failed
to secure the heights in advance, and a mixed force of Athenians and
Thebans routed the advance guard of peltasts he sent on to hold the
pass. Thinking that he would not be able to enter Boeotia by this route,
Cleombrotus led his army home and disbanded it.[3] In this setback,
Cleombrotus gave clear proof of what many had been saying of him: he
was not the commander that Agesilaus was. After all, had Agesilaus not
crossed Cithaeron twice, in 378 and 377, despite the possibility of
enemy opposition?[4] For the next several years, Spartan policy seems to
have drifted without strong leadership. We hear nothing more about
Agesilaus until the Peace Conference of 371, presumably because of his
weakened condition and his age; and Cleombrotus' failure to invade
successfully in 376 may have diminished his prestige and influence
accordingly. Perhaps Antalcidas, whose opposition to Agesilaus over
the question of Thebes is a matter of record, worked in these years to
reduce and eliminate further direct confrontation between Sparta and
the Boeotian League, although we cannot know for sure. For the

---

[1]Xen. 5.4.56–57.
[2]Diod. 15.30.3–5. According to Plutarch (*De Gloria Atheniensium 8*), Timotheus freed
Euboea from Spartan control.
[3]Xen. 5.4.59.
[4]Xenophon, 6.4.5, records just such a criticism of Cleombrotus prior to the Battle of
Leuctra, but it is clear that suspicions of his abilities had been developing long before 371.

moment, the Thebans had a relatively free hand to extend their influence and power over Boeotia, and they would soon win a signal victory over a Spartan force at Tegyra, in 375.

Although little occurred on land during 376, there was much activity in the Aegean, culminating in the Battle of Naxos. The allies of Sparta, after the abortive expedition of Cleombrotus to Boeotia, complained about the progress of the war and urged the Spartans to outfit a fleet and put pressure upon Athens and Thebes. This decision was taken, and the navarch Pollis operated in the waters off southeastern Attica, and in the Saronic Gulf, thus threatening the grain ships to Athens. As a result, Chabrias was dispatched with a fleet to interdict Pollis, and a naval battle was fought round Naxos, which the Athenians won resoundingly. Chabrias returned to Athens with a large amount of booty and eight captured ships, much to the delight of his countrymen.[5]

In 375 the Spartans were planning another invasion of Boeotia. But the Theban allies of Athens prevailed upon it to send Timotheus on a voyage round the Peloponnesus, in order to threaten that area and force the Spartans to keep their troops at home. The strategy worked, and no invasion of Boeotia occurred, either in 376 or in 375, with the result that the Thebans continued with their policy of attempting to revive the Boeotian League under their own hegemony.[6] Timotheus then sailed on to Cephallenia and Acarnania, where he succeeded in persuading some cities to revolt from Sparta to the Second Athenian League, and eventually he reached Corcyra.[7] There he won over the island, "neither enslaving the inhabitants, nor banishing anyone, nor changing the constitution," as Xenophon says. This may be an oblique reference to the guarantees of the league decree; in any case, an inscription of 375 records the adherence to the league of Corcyra, Acarnania, and Cephallenia, hard proof of Timotheus' intentions in this area.[8] The Spartans sent out a fleet under Nicolochus, a man of great energy and daring, as

[5]Xen. 5.4.60–61; Diod. 15.34.3–6, 35.1–2; Plut. *Phocion* 6; Polyaenus 3.11.2.
[6]Xen. 5.4.62–63. For Theban ambitions in this sphere, see Buckler, *Theban Hegemony,* pp. 18–23.
[7]Diod. 15.36.4–6; Xen. 5.4.64–65. For the adherence of these cities, see the stele of the Aristoteles Decree, 11. 106ff., and Cargill, *SAL,* pp. 27 and 43; see also pp. 99–114.
[8]See Bengtson, *Die Staatsverträge des Altertums II,* no. 262, p. 217, and the discussion in Cargill, *SAL,* pp. 103–6. Cargill denies that Corcyra joined the league at this time, arguing instead that the negotiations for membership alluded to in this inscription were only partially successful. He presents the arguments in his chapter "Allies of Athens and the League." Even if Corcyra were not technically a member of the league, however, it seems clear that it became subject to Athenian control in 375, and an ally shortly after 375.

navarch. An indecisive battle at Alyzia was claimed as a victory by both admirals, who had roughly equal fleets. But Timotheus was constantly in need of money to maintain his fleet, and both sides were beginning to tire of the war.[9] The growing power of Thebes—which had enjoyed two years free of Spartan invasion in which to proceed with plans to reconquer the cities of Boeotia and to reconstitute the Boeotian League as well—was beginning to worry Athens, just as it was Sparta.

The Spartans in particular had suffered an especially bitter defeat at the hands of the Thebans at the Battle of Tegyra in Boeotia in 375.[10] On that occasion, which Plutarch describes as a sort of prelude to Leuctra, the Theban Sacred Band, under the leadership of Pelopidas, defeated a contingent of Spartans in a hoplite encounter. The situation was the following. The city of Orchomenus had taken the Spartan side in the war and had received two regiments of Spartans as a garrison. This action, of course, was reminiscent of Orchomenus' decision to break with Thebes and the Boeotian League and fight on the Spartan side at the outbreak of the Corinthian War, in 395.[11] When Pelopidas learned that the garrison was away on an expedition to Locris, he decided to attack Orchomenus in the hope that he could capture the city. His intelligence proved faulty, however, for other Spartans had replaced the garrison, so he turned back, marching through the district of Tegyra. The path was relatively narrow, skirting the bordering hills on the one hand, and the plain that had been flooded and turned into marsh by the Melas River, on the other.[12] At this point, Pelopidas encountered the returning Spartans, who greatly outnumbered him, on their march back from Locris to Orchomenus. When one of his men announced in panic that they had fallen into their enemies' hands, Pelopidas replied coolly, "Why not say that they have fallen into ours?"

He had only the three hundred hoplites of the Sacred Band and some horsemen with him, whereas the Spartan force numbered two full regiments; the regiment encompassed at least five hundred men, and thus he was clearly outnumbered at least three to one.[13] Undaunted, however, Pelopidas ordered his cavalry to move to the front of his force, while he drew up the hoplites in massed formation. The Spartan

[9]Xen. 5.4.65–66.
[10]Plut. *Pelop.* 16.1–17.5; *Ages.* 27.3 and Diod. 15.81.2.
[11]Xen. 3.5.6; see Hamilton, *SBV*, pp. 194–96.
[12]Plut. *Pelop.* 16.1–3.
[13]Plut. *Pelop.* 17.1–2. See Lazenby, *Spartan Army*, pp. 5–10, for discussion of the strength of a Spartan mora. He concludes that its strength was 1,280 (p. 10). The ancient sources put the size of a regiment variously at from 500 to 900; cf. Plut. *Pelop.* 17.2.

polemarchs Gorgoleon and Theopompus, confident of an easy victory, advanced against them. In the ensuing melee, the fiercest fighting developed where the respective commanders stood in the front lines, and both the polemarchs fell fighting. As those about them began to be seized with fear, they opened a lane to allow the Thebans to pass through, which they supposed was their objective. Instead, Pelopidas exploited the gap in the Spartan line to assault those of the enemy who still held their places, and thus he slew many and routed the rest. The Thebans pursued their fleeing foes for a little distance but soon broke off the pursuit out of fear of the Orchomenians and the relief force from Sparta which was in the city. But there could be no doubt that Pelopidas had carried off a signal victory, against superior odds: an achievement virtually unique in Spartan military annals. He stripped the dead, erected a trophy, and returned home triumphant.[14]

Xenophon does not mention the Spartan defeat at Tegyra, but Diodorus referred to it in his eulogy of Pelopidas as the first occasion when the Thebans erected a trophy over the Spartans.[15] And Plutarch gave it a prominent place in his *Pelopidas*. He mentions specifically that this victory was achieved, unlike others that the Thebans had won in the 370s, in a pitched battle fought in open and regular array. The Spartans had been unsettled by the losses they had sustained in sallies and skirmishes at Plataea, Thespiae, and Tanagra in the preceding few years, and we may well imagine the effect upon them when they learned of this defeat. For a regular force of Spartans to sustain a defeat in hoplite warfare, at the hands of a numerically inferior enemy, must have been a shocking blow. It is small wonder, then, that the Spartans showed themselves ready to consider a negotiated peace later that year.

The Spartans had been overextending their resources, as two incidents that also occurred in 375 seem to prove. In Thessaly, Jason of Pherae was consolidating his power in the 370s and bringing more and more of the Thessalian cities under his control. When he threatened Polydamas of Pharsalus, that ruler appealed in person at Sparta for armed assistance. The speech of Polydamas reveals that Jason was in the process not only of bringing all of Thessaly under his control, but also of looking beyond the borders of Thessaly toward a weak and vulnerable Macedon in the north.[16] Jason claimed to be allied with the Boeotians, Sparta's enemies, and the others who were at war with Sparta. He

---

[14]Plut. *Pelop.* 17.3–5.
[15]Diod. 15.81.2.
[16]Xen. 6.1.11. See the discussion in C. D. Hamilton, "Amyntas III and Agesilaus: Macedon and Sparta in the Fourth Century," *Ancient Macedonia* 4 (1986):239–45.

boasted that he could easily win over the Athenians, should he choose to do so.[17] Furthermore, he had recruited a large mercenary army of some six thousand, whom he kept in good condition, and whom he would match against a citizen army at any time. Thus, Jason represented a great threat to Polydamas, whom he invited to submit and become his second in command. But Polydamas, who was both proxenos and benefactor to Sparta, sought and received his permission to seek Spartan aid. Polydamas asked for a Spartan army, to be commanded by no less than a royal figure; a force of neodamodeis, led by a private individual, he said, would be of no use, and the Spartans ought to decline his request if that was what they might consider dispatching to his aid.[18]

The Spartans did not answer him immediately, but instead spent the next two days in reckoning how many regiments they had serving abroad, and how many would be needed to guard Laconia from attacks by Athenian warships. They then replied that they could not send an adequate force and told him to return home and make the best arrangements that he could. In the event, Polydamas submitted to Jason and helped him to achieve the position of *tagus,* whereby all of Thessaly was subject to his authority and he could count on a large army and cavalry drawn from the entire land.[19] Two aspects of this episode merit note. The first is to ask why Jason permitted, indeed encouraged, Polydamas to seek military aid at Sparta. This would seem a foolish and potentially dangerous step for Jason to have taken, unless we conclude that he was quite confident that the Spartans would decline to aid Polydamas, as they actually did. It is probable that Jason's intelligence was good and that he knew that the Spartans had recently sent their King Cleombrotus to Phocis at the head of a force numbering no less than four regiments of their own troops, and a corresponding number of allied contingents. This action had occurred in response to a Boeotian expedition into Phocis,[20] where, in all probability, the Thebans had undertaken an aggressive policy in the wake of their recent victory at Tegyra. Now Agesilaus was still very ill from the malady that had struck him at Megara on his return from Boeotia in 377. As a consequence, neither of the two kings was available to take service in a new field of endeavor

[17]Xen. 6.1.10.

[18]Xen. 6.1.4–6, 15. The reference seems to be to the sort of force that the Spartans had sent to Asia Minor, first under Thibron and then under Dercyllidas, from 400 to 396, or at first against Olynthus, where, only eventually, they sent out a king in command.

[19]Xen. 6.1.17–18. See H. D. Westlake, *Thessaly in the Fourth Century B.C.* (London, 1935), pp. 76–83.

[20]Xen. 6.1.1. Xenophon reports nothing more of the military activities of this force. It was presumably withdrawn after the Common Peace of 375 was signed.

such as Thessaly. And as for Spartan manpower, the four regiments serving in Phocis amounted to two-thirds of the Spartan army. Therefore, Jason may well have known that the Spartans were in no position to commit the kind of military assistance that Polydamas sought.

The other aspect of the situation concerns the lapse in time over the Spartan response to Polydamas. Xenophon would have us believe that it took the Spartans two full days to count up the number of contingents serving abroad, and those needed for home defense. It is inherently improbable that the Spartan authorities did not have such military information immediately available to them; after all, the fundamental aspect of Sparta was its military character, and to suppose that it would take them two days to find out where their contingents were, and what their additional forces, available for service elsewhere, amounted to, stretches the imagination. It is more likely that the authorities devoted the time in question to a political debate over the wisdom and feasibility of undertaking another potentially serious commitment in northern Greece. Faced with the threats posed by Theban expansion in Boeotia and central Greece, where they had just dispatched a large army under Cleombrotus, and by Athenian expansion on the sea, which included raids on the Peloponnesus, the Spartans concluded that they could not begin new adventures in Thessaly.[21]

A by-product of this decision was that King Amyntas of Macedon turned to Athens for support in his struggles against his neighbors. The Spartans had assisted him earlier, as recently as in their expeditions against Olynthus, his expansive neighbor, from 382 to 379,[22] but now he reasoned that they were either uninterested or unable to help check Jason of Pherae. He could not have helped but feel himself threatened by the expansion of Jason on his southern borders, and Sparta's decision not to intervene in Thessaly on behalf of powers threatened by Jason, however reluctantly adopted, must have sent a clear signal. In any event, Amyntas went on to cultivate good relations with Athens, and Macedonian timber, pitch, and other naval materials came to supply a good deal of what Athens needed for shipbuilding.[23] Thus, Sparta lost an opportunity to maintain its influence in the north. It is likely that

[21]See Hamilton, "Amyntas III and Agesilaus," 242–43.

[22]Diod. 15.19.3; Xen. 5.2.11–19. Cf. Xen. 5.2.20–24, 37–43; 3.1–9, 18–19, 26, and Diod. 15.20.3–21.3, 23.2–3.

[23]On the rich timber resources of ancient Macedonia, see the valuable study by E. N. Borza, "The Natural Resources of Early Macedonia," in *Philip II, Alexander the Great, and the Macedonian Heritage,* ed. W. L. Adams and E. N. Borza (Washington, D.C., 1982), pp. 1–20 at 2–8.

Amyntas became an ally of the Athenians in or shortly after 375.[24] Therefore, the decision to commit a substantial portion of their military resources to the defense of Phocis against Theban aggression, as well as the refusal to send aid to Polydamas, represents clear evidence that the Spartans had strained their resources to the limit. In such a climate, then, peace negotiations were begun in 375.

The Peace of 375

There are two major sources for the Peace of 375: Xenophon and Diodorus.[25] Xenophon makes only a brief reference to it, stating that the Athenians decided to send envoys to Sparta and there secured peace. Diodorus provides a fuller, and more intelligible account, in which it appears that the initiative was taken by the great King of Persia, Artaxerxes, for purposes of his own, and that a general peace resulted, similar to those of 387/6 and of 371. Because Diodorus reports that Epaminondas demanded that Thebes sign for Boeotia and was therefore excluded from the peace, some scholars have concluded that his account is confused with the Peace of 371.[26] On that latter occasion, there is no doubt that Thebes and Epaminondas were excluded from the treaty on this very issue and that their exclusion led to the Spartan decision to invade Boeotia once again. But it is clear that the Thebans intended from the moment of the liberation of their city to reestablish the Boeotian League,[27] and it is quite likely that Epaminondas voiced sentiments in 375 similar to those which he expressed in 371. The Thebans, after all, had been very successful in their efforts to expand their power in Boeotia; they were undefeated in 375; and doubtless they saw no reason to relinquish the gains they had recently made in the treaty before them.

[24]See Hamilton, "Amyntas II and Agesilaus," 243–44 and Cargill, SAL, pp. 84–86 for full discussion of the epigraphical evidence bearing on the alliance between Macedon and Athens in the 370s.
[25]Diod. 15.38.1–4 and Xen. 6.2.1. The numerous problems connected with this Peace, including its dating, have been the subject of much research. See, in particular, T. T. B. Ryder, Appendix II, "The Peace of 375," in Koine Eirene, pp. 124–26, which contains older literature; and G. L. Cawkwell, "Notes on the Peace of 375/4," Historia 12 (1963):84–95; J. Buckler, "Dating the Peace of 375/4," GRBS 12 (1971):353–61; and V. J. Gray, "The Years 375 to 371 b.c.: A Case Study in the Reliability of Diodorus Siculus and Xenophon," CQ, n.s. 30 (1980):306–26.
[26]See Ryder, Koine Eirene, pp. 124–25.
[27]See J. Buckler, "The Re-establishment of the Boiotarchia (378 b.c.)," AJAH 4 (1979): 50–64.

But whether they were excluded from the Peace of 375 is quite another matter; the evidence seems to suggest that they were not. As T. T. B. Ryder has suggested, the factual cause for the confusion in Diodorus may be reflected in Isocrates' *Plataicus,* in which the orator alleges that the Athenians *threatened* to exclude the Thebans from the peace if they did not abandon attempts to coerce the Boeotian cities to join in the newly refounded Boeotian League.[28] Faced with this threat, the Thebans appear to have capitulated and signed the Common Peace Treaty; they also withdrew their garrisons from the cities that they had occupied in Boeotia.[29]

We must now analyze several aspects of this peace. First, who initiated the negotiations, and where were they held? Second, were there one or several stages in the negotiations? And, finally, why did the various principals respond as they did? To the first of these questions, there is no difficulty with accepting Diodorus' account of the initiative of the Great King. Diodorus records that Artaxerxes needed mercenaries for his war in Egypt, and thus he decided to promote peace in Greece, sending envoys to the various states. So had he done before, in accepting Antalcidas' overtures in 388/7, and so would he do again in 371.[30] Xenophon's remark about the Athenians sending envoys to Sparta in no way contradicts this testimony, and they may well have merely been responding to the initial Persian approach, after having determined themselves that peace would best serve their interests. The Great King had been planning the Egyptian expedition since 376, and his decision to send envoys to Greece to enforce a peace may well have been made in the winter of 376/5, as has been suggested.[31] The Spartans may have sent themselves to seek Persian intervention after the Battle of Naxos in September 376.[32] In any case, it is possible that the Persian initiative came to Greece before summer 375 and that the Athenian

[28]Ryder, *Koine Eirene,* p. 124; cf. Isoc. 14.37.
[29]Diodorus (15.38.2–4) recounts the altercation between Thebes and Athens, but he states that the Thebans were excluded from the Common Peace. Isocrates' remark makes it probable that the Thebans capitulated for the moment, rather than face pressure from both Athens and Sparta.
[30]See Xen. 5.1.25, and Diod. 14.110.3–4 for 387, and Diod. 15.50.4 for 371. See, in general, the useful discussions in Ryder, *Koine Eirene,* pp. 34–38 and 64–69.
[31]Cawkwell, "Notes on the Peace of 375/4," 90.
[32]D. G. Rice, "Why Sparta Failed" (Ph.D. diss., Yale University, 1971), suggests that Antalcidas may have taken the initiative in contacting Artaxerxes to reestablish the conditions of the peace that bears his name, that of 387/6 (p. 146). I find this suggestion plausible; Cawkwell, "Notes on the Peace of 375/4," 90, also makes this suggestion of the Spartans, but without mentioning Antalcidas.

victory at Alyzia, which seems to have occurred toward midsummer,[33] was a fortuitous event further disposing the major Greek states to determine on a Common Peace, as the Great King wished. Certainly not only the major states, such as Athens, Sparta, and Thebes were signatories to the treaty, but also smaller states, as Isocrates' oration proves with regard to the Plataeans. The peace to which Isocrates makes the dispossessed Plataeans refer, about 373, can be no other than this treaty, signed sometime in 375.[34]

It is quite likely that the meeting of Greek states took place in Sparta: Xenophon speaks of Athens sending men there, and the analogy with the Peace of 371 (as well as of 387/6), when the general conference was held in Sparta, makes this probable. We cannot be sure that the negotiations were protracted, over several stages, but the following scenario seems sensible. First, Persian envoys arrived in the principal belligerent states—that is, Athens, Sparta, and (possibly) Thebes—to open negotiations. Next, the Athenians, no doubt after consulting with their allies in the league, sent off to Sparta to discuss conditions for peace. The Athenians would have invited the Thebans to accompany them. In Sparta the conference met and deliberated, deciding on the peace. Because the Great King does not seem to have been an official signatory to this peace, there is no need to postulate further travel to Asia to obtain his ratification. For example, in 386 the final ratification was made in Sparta on the basis of a Persian proposal.[35] But even if we imagine that the Great King swore to the peace, this could have been done after the conference at Sparta. Thus the peace would still be dated to 375, probably in the month of Hecatombaion.[36] Finally, there is the question of why the various states responded as they did to this initiative.

It is clear that the Athenians had achieved major gains in the preceding three years. They had reestablished their naval alliance, which had grown to include perhaps as many as fifty states thus far.[37] Sparta had been defeated in several battles, most notably at Naxos and at Alyzia,

---

[33]Xen. 5.4.65–66. Cawkwell, "Notes on the Peace of 375/4," writes: "Each summer's campaign is carefully enough described and the narrative is plain sailing down to the battle of Alyzia in mid-375" (89).

[34]Isoc. 14.37; cf. 1, 5, 10, and 14, and see Ryder, *Koine Eirene,* p. 124.

[35]See Ryder, *Koine Eirene,* pp. 34–36, and Hamilton, *SBV,* pp. 310–23, for detailed analysis and discussion of these events.

[36]See Cawkwell, "Notes on the Peace of 375/4," 88–91; and Gray, "The Years 375 to 371 B.C.," 307–15, esp. 314.

[37]On the question of the ultimate size of the league, see Cargill, *SAL,* pp. 45–47 and my remarks in "Problems of Alliance and Hegemony in Fourth Century Greece Reconsidered," *EMC/CV* 26, n.s. 1 (1982):310–13.

and it was no longer a serious threat to Athens' hegemony at sea. Offsetting factors included the growing recognition that the expenses of the league were ever more troubling; Timotheus in the west had been sending urgent messages for more money to support his fleet. This deficiency of the league would be perennially frustrating, as F. S. Marshall stressed,[38] and the Athenians must have become aware of this limitation on their potential to conduct further maritime activities. The opportunity to make peace while preserving their gains, thus alleviating the economic pressures of keeping the fleet at sea, would have been welcome. Furthermore, there was growing concern over the behavior of their Theban allies. Not only did they not contribute their fair share to league expenses for naval operations,[39] but they were also expanding their own power in Boeotia in a quite alarming manner. The Athenians had no wish to see their power increase further to the point where it might actually threaten Athens itself. Already a dispute over Oropus on the Boeotian-Attic border promised to become a bone of contention between the two powers.[40] Thus here also the prospect of a Common Peace, guaranteeing the autonomy of all states, was welcome to Athenians who wished to see Thebes' expansion curtailed.[41] Athens was so delighted with the signing of the peace that it formally established a religious cult in celebration of Eirene (Peace, personified as a goddess), and ordered the erection of a statue of Timotheus next to that of his father, Conon.[42]

The Spartans had their own reasons for wanting peace. First and foremost, the war had gone badly for them. Three invasions of Boeotia had been attempted, and the two successful incursions of Agesilaus had

[38]See F. S. Marshall, *The Second Athenian Confederacy* (Cambridge, 1905), pp. 37–42, on the finances generally, and p. 64 on Timotheus' difficulties: "This is the first occasion upon which we hear of that deficiency in monetary resources which was the bane of the Second Confederacy."

[39]Xen. 6.2.1.

[40]Isoc. 14.20, cf. 37; see Xen. 7.4.1 and Diod. 15.76.1 on the Theban seizure of Oropus in 366.

[41]Rice, "Why Sparta Failed," 147, argues that the pro-Spartan, anti-Theban faction of Callistratus had come to power in Athens by 375, and that this group worked for the peace. His interpretation lacks any specific documentary evidence, but is nonetheless suggestive. See also B. R. Sealey, "Callistratus of Aphidna and His Contemporaries," *Historia* 5 (1956):178–203, for discussion of his career.

[42]Aesch. 3.243; Nepos *Tim.* 2.3. See also Cawkwell, "Notes on the Peace of 375/4," 90 and 90n.58; and Gray, "The Years 375 to 371 B.C.," 314 and 314n.41. On the significance of special honors, see C. D. Hamilton, "On the Perils of Extraordinary Honors: The Cases of Lysander and Conon," *Ancient World* 2 (1979):87–90. On the use of religious cults as propaganda, see B. R. Sealey, "*IG* II², 1609, and the Transformation of the Second Athenian Sea-League," *Phoenix* 11 (1957):95–111, at 110.

resulted in nothing more than a temporary discomfiture of the Thebans, through the loss of ravaged crops. At the end of his expedition of 377, Agesilaus had fallen seriously ill, and he was unable to play a vigorous role, either in military affairs or in political ones, for the next several years; there is no hint in the sources that he took part in the conference of 375, although it was held in Sparta.[43] At sea, the war had gone equally badly, and numerous states had gone over to the Athenian League. Spartan diplomacy was ineffective in attempting to stem the tide of defection, and the losses of Acarnania and the Chalcidian League[44] must have rankled particularly. These areas had formed two of the ten military districts established in the reform of the Spartan military alliance of 378. Their loss would naturally have reduced the military potential at Sparta's disposal, and there is other evidence to suggest that the Spartans were finding it difficult to meet their military commitments in this period: Xenophon relates an appeal to Sparta for aid from Polydamas of Pharsalus in Thessaly at just about this time.[45] In the end, the Spartans declined the appeal, saying that "at the present they were not able to send out a sufficient force to aid him."[46] This decision had far-reaching implications because it hastened the drift of the Macedonian king, Amyntas, away from Sparta toward Athens. Finally, we must not forget the victories that the Thebans had won over Spartan forces in Boeotia, culminating in Pelopidas' signal defeat of two Spartan regiments near Tegyra in 375.[47]

Thus, with the two principal belligerents disposed to make peace, a treaty was concluded. Its terms reaffirmed those of the King's Peace of

[43]According to Xenophon, 6.4.18, Agesilaus had still not fully recovered from his illness after the Battle of Leuctra. Rice, "Why Sparta Failed," 146, has suggested that Agesilaus joined with the conservative faction, led by Antalcidas, in arranging this peace, just as the two had cooperated before in 387/6. Again, while there is no direct evidence for this interpretation, it is at least plausible. I would emphasize, however, that, as Rice says, it was Antalcidas (or someone else in Sparta) who took the initiative, not Agesilaus.

[44]See West, *Chalcidic League*, p. 108; and Cargill, *SAL*, p. 42, on the Chalcidians.

[45]I reject K. J. Beloch's dating of this event to 371 (*Griechische Geschichte*, 2d ed., 3:237); his reasoning is that the report in Xenophon of the dispatch of Cleombrotus and the Peloponnesian army to Phocis in 375 must be erroneous, for there is no mention of their return, and they could not have remained there for four years, until 371; and because the report of Polydamas' mission is given by Xenophon as "almost at this time" (6.1.2), it also must have been misplaced to 375 from 371. See Gray, "The Years 375 to 371 B.C.," 308, and Sealey, "Transformation of the Second Athenian Sea-League," 102–4, on this point.

[46]Xen. 6.1.17.

[47]Diodorus (15.37.1–2) seems to be referring to this Battle of Tegyra when he speaks of the Theban expedition against Orchomenus. See chap. 6 above.

387/6, laying down the principle of autonomy for all poleis as its fundamental provision. There was apparently an additional, new proviso, namely that all garrisons should evacuate occupied cities as part of the guarantee of autonomy. That this provision was implemented is shown quite clearly by the fact that, a year or two later, the Thebans were able to take Thespiae, Tanagra, and Plataea.[48] These cities, and others, had been garrisoned at least since 382, if not since 386, and they had served as bases for Spartan operations in Boeotia in 378 and 377. If they were among the cities Thebes had already subjugated, they must also have lost their Theban garrisons, as did the other cities of Boeotia. It is doubtful they had been taken yet. Now, devoid of Spartan-commanded troops, they were left to their own devices and fell easily to Theban pressure in 374 or 373. The Spartan army in Phocis under King Cleombrotus was also withdrawn at this time, and the Athenians notified Timotheus to return with his fleet from western waters.

Diodorus records that Athens and Sparta gave mutual recognition to each other's aspirations, Athens acknowledging Sparta's hegemony on land, and Sparta acknowledging Athens' at sea. Whether this was a formal aspect of the peace is doubtful, but there was clearly a de facto recognition of the situation on the part of the two major powers.[49] The difficulty with making this peace endure came, in part, from Thebes, who wished to be acknowledged as hegemon in Boeotia. But neither Athens nor Sparta would accept this, and the Thebans backed away from their demand rather than be excluded from the peace. Thus, toward the end of 375, the Greek world embraced its second Common Peace. But much had changed since 387/6, and not least the position of Sparta. Although still powerful, Sparta had been forced to acknowledge the existence of the Second Athenian League, as well as a powerful and independent Thebes. Furthermore, Sparta's resources had been strained to the utmost, and it had been forced to realize that it could no longer dominate mainland Greece as it wished. In short, the events of 378 had brought military, political, and diplomatic setbacks to Sparta which should have caused it to rethink its position on the international scene.

The Failure of the Peace and the Road to Leuctra

Xenophon intimates that the Peace of 375 was shortlived, but modern scholarship has demonstrated that his account is somewhat mislead-

[48]Isoc. 14.1 and 9; cf. 14.110. Cf. Diod. 15.46.4–6 and Paus. 9.1.4–8.
[49]See Ryder, Koine Eirene, pp. 60 and 125–26.

ing.[50] He notes that upon his return from the west Timotheus landed some Zacynthian exiles on their island. These men in turn pressured the Spartan inclined oligarchy in the city, who sent an appeal for aid to Sparta. The Spartans sent out the admiral Mnasippus, who conducted operations against Corcyra, and, when the Athenians dispatched a fleet commanded by Iphicrates, the peace ended. Xenophon's narrative implies that the Zacynthian affair occurred immediately after the signing of the peace and the recall of Timotheus to Athens. But Xenophon has foreshortened his account, and omitted several key events.[51] It is clear that Mnasippus was Spartan navarch for 374/3 and that the expedition of Iphicrates sailed for western waters after midsummer 373.[52] Not until the operations around Corcyra were undertaken, then, did the peace fail. Xenophon not only syncopates his account but also provides a less than satisfactory explanation of why the peace broke down.

Diodorus devotes a chapter to a discussion of the effects of the peace on various states.[53] In general, he observes that the granting of autonomy led to factional disputes in many cities, and he cites case studies both in the Peloponnesus and in the northwest. This passage of Diodorus, incidentally, would seem to prove that the return of exiles was one of the clauses of the peace, even if it is not explicitly mentioned. Presumably these repatriated exiles were partially responsible for the civil strife that ensued. As a result of this strife, both Athens and Sparta tended to intervene in favor of their partisans in the various states. There is no reason to doubt that such internal disputes took place; Xenophon has one of the Athenian speakers at Sparta in 371 describe the existence of pro-Spartan and pro-Athenian factions in all of the states, with the implication of intervention by the two major powers.[54] Indeed Diodorus' report here lends weight to the probability that the Peace of

[50]See Cawkwell, "Notes on the Peace of 375/4," 85 and 88–89: "The whole discussion has been bedevilled by the Xenophontic account of Mnasippus; . . . if the peace were to fall in 374, it would be necessary to stretch Xenophon's account uncomfortably." See also Gray, "The Years 375 to 371 B.C.," 308: "Xenophon is wrong in connecting Mnasippus' expedition so closely to the Zacynthian affair." See also C. Tuplin, "Timotheus and Corcyra: Problems in Greek History, 375–373 B.C.," Athenaeum, n.s. 62 (1984):537–68.

[51]As Cawkwell, "Notes on the Peace of 375/4," 84–85, has demonstrated.

[52]See Gray, "The Years 375 to 371 B.C.," 316–17, on this dating; contra Cawkwell, "Notes on the Peace of 375/4," 86, who suggests a date of 373/2 for Mnasippus' navarchy. In both systems, however, the key event of Iphicrates' voyage would be after midsummer 373.

[53]Diod. 15.40.1–5. See J. Roy, "Diodorus Siculus XV.40—the Peloponnesian Revolutions of 374 B.C.," Klio 55 (1973):135–39.

[54]Xen. 6.3.14.

375 included a clause calling for the return of exiles, as well as for the elimination of garrisons. The events in question are reported as happening as a result of the peace, and consequently soon after its implementation. They probably filled 374. After detailing events in several Peloponnesian cities, including Phlius and Corinth, Diodorus turns his attention to the northwest.

Diodorus relates that Timotheus not only landed the Zacynthian exiles but also gave them aid in their attempts to take control of their city.[55] As a result, the Spartans sent Aristocrates with a fleet of twenty-five ships to aid their partisans. This event, together with another, probably occurred during 374. In Corcyra, party strife broke out and the pro-Spartan faction sent for aid. The Spartans dispatched Alcidas, with twenty-two ships.[56] Upon his arrival, he made an abortive attempt to seize the city, then sailed away. Thus, two events took place that involved a prelude to the breakdown of the peace. Eventually, the situation in Corcyra worsened, and partisans of these states within the city made appeals to both Athens and Sparta. The Athenians voted to send their general Timotheus, and he prepared to sail from the Peiraeus in Mounichion (April/May) of the archonship of Socratides (374/3).[57] Instead of proceeding directly to Corcyra, Timotheus spent some time cruising in the Aegean, visiting the Thracian region as well as the islands of the Cycladic group. His explanation of this activity was that he was in need of crews for his ships and additional revenues. Be that as it may, the Athenians became angry with him "because he was wasting the best part of the sailing season" and deposed him from office.[58] Because the height of the sailing season would be around midsummer, the deposition probably occurred in July.

Iphicrates was then elected to succeed him, and he sailed as quickly as he could, after having added ten additional ships to the sixty already under Timotheus' command (by scraping together what ships he could at Athens). When Iphicrates arrived in Corcyraean waters, Mnasippus had just been killed a short time before in a battle against the besieged townspeople of Corcyra.[59] Iphicrates contented himself with the interception and capture of nine out of ten ships sent by Dionysius of Syracuse to aid the Spartans. Iphicrates then put his crews to work in the

[55]Diod. 15.45.1–4.
[56]Diod. 15.46.1–3.
[57]The date is furnished by Ps.-Dem. 49.6.
[58]Xen. 6.2.11–13; cf. Ps.-Dem. 49.9–10 and 22 for the date.
[59]Xen. 6.2.14–26, cf. 31.

fields of the Corcyraeans, where much-needed work had to be accomplished for the following year's planting. During Mnasippus' blockade, it had been impossible for the Corcyraeans to perform their normal agricultural tasks. Iphicrates also took his troops, hoplites and peltasts, over to Acarnania on the continent, where they carried out various activities against hostile neighbors of their allies. Finally, he took his forces to Cephallenia, where he planned a campaign against the Peloponnesus, which apparently was carried out in the next fighting season, that of 372.[60]

It is clear from these events, then, that the Athenians and Spartans were pulled back into conflict through their affiliations with other states. As internal conflicts broke out in states in which they had interests, opportunities arose for intervention. As a result of intervention on behalf of friendly factions in places such as Corcyra and Zacynthus, the two major powers came once again to combat each other. But neither state gained much from these activities, and the cost to each must have caused them to wonder if the war was worth the effort. Therefore, by 371 they were disposed once again to consider a negotiated settlement. Events in one other area made them quite eager to conclude peace again: Boeotia.

Forced to abandon their efforts to reestablish the Boeotian League by the Peace of 375, the Thebans nonetheless began to pursue their own objectives as they saw the Athenians and Spartans become involved in supporting their partisans. Thebes was quick to take advantage of the withdrawal of Spartan garrisons from the Boeotian cities, and the Thebans began to pressure Plataea, Thespiae, and other poleis to rejoin the league. Indeed, in 373 the Thebans made an unexpected sortie against Plataea, with the result that they shut out many Plataeans from their city, capturing and enslaving them, and imposed a settlement upon those within the walls whereby they withdrew to Athenian territory, abandoning all they possessed. The Thebans then dismantled the city and incorporated Plataea's territory into their own. The Plataean exiles sought aid from Athens, but instead of a military expedition to restore them to their city, the Athenians voted to grant them equal citizenship. The destruction of Plataea took place in the archonship of Aristeus (373/2); that is, in summer 373.[61]

---

[60]Xen. 6.2.31–39; Diod. 15.47.1–7; Polyaenus, 3.9.55.
[61]Diod. 15.46.4–6; Paus. 9.1.4–8. Pausanias, 9.1.8, mentions the archon year of the capture of Plataea, which he says occurred two years before the Battle of Leuctra.

Isocrates produced a speech, the *Plataicus,* which purports to be an appeal by a Plataean for Athenian protection before the city's destruction at the hands of Thebes. The document in question is more likely to be a political pamphlet written by Isocrates to urge Athenian assistance to Plataea.[62] Despite a spirited defense of Plataean conduct, and a strong case that the Athenians had an obligation to defend the freedom and autonomy guaranteed to all cities by the Peace of 375 as well as by the principles of their league, Isocrates failed to convince the Athenians to intervene effectively against Thebes. Timotheus, his political associate, already in disgrace because of his deposition and trial in this year, was not elected general again until 366. The Thebans also ravaged the territory of Thespiae at about this same time, and, in the following year, they seem to have begun to threaten neighboring Phocis once again.[63] As a result of these developments, both the Athenians and the Spartans began to fear the continued growth of Theban power. Thus, when an opportunity arose to negotiate a peace once again in 371, the two major powers were inclined to consider this.

The Peace of 371

Artaxerxes sent again to Greece in 371 to impose a peace. His Egyptian expedition had failed in 373, but he had not abandoned the project of reconquering Egypt.[64] Thus, he needed Greek mercenaries, and the resumption of hostilities in Greece after 374 was an impediment to his intentions: while the Greeks were fighting among themselves, they could not be available for service with Persia. For example, Mnasippus had a force of some fifteen hundred mercenaries with him on Corcyra, and Ctesicles took some six hundred mercenaries when he went to relieve the besieged city of Corcyra; Iphicrates, after his return from the Persian expedition to Egypt, was immediately selected to succeed Timotheus as general of the expedition to Corcyra in 373. No doubt there were other opportunities for mercenary service in and after 373.[65] As for the Greeks, we have seen that both Athens and Sparta were disposed

---

[62]See Ryder, *Koine Eirene,* pp. 61–62 for discussion; Cawkwell's remarks, "Notes on the Peace of 375/4," 84, are also apt: "It is more natural to regard the speech as a piece of propaganda to support the actual Plataean appeal."

[63]See Xen. 6.3.1; Diod. 15.46.6 and 51.3; Paus. 9.14.2 for Thespiae.

[64]Diod. 15.50.4, cf. 41–43.

[65]Xen. 6.2.5 and 10; Diod. 15.47.1 and 4; and 43.6. For discussion, see Parke, *Greek Mercenary Soldiers,* pp. 86–87 on Mnasippus, and pp. 105–7 on Iphicrates and Timotheus in service to the King of Persia.

to negotiate peace in 371. Thus, the Athenians decided to send envoys to Sparta, and they invited the Thebans to accompany them. A peace conference was once again held in Sparta, in late June 371.[66]

Representatives of most of the Greek states attended the conference in Sparta, which was held in response to the Great King's order. We know the names of some seven Athenian ambassadors, as well as those of Epaminondas of Thebes and of Agesilaus, who took an active part. Xenophon tells us that the Athenians addressed the Spartans and their allies and also that the Athenians and their allies ratified the treaty by oath, city by city. This suggests that the conference was general, and that its purpose was a third attempt at a Common Peace, in accord with the agreements made formerly (in 387/6 and 375).[67] Xenophon attributes speeches to three of the Athenian ambassadors.[68] Callias asserted that he had twice before successfully come to negotiate peace, and he stressed the common concern over Plataea and Thespiae; that is, over Theban expansion.[69] Then Autocles criticized the Spartans for their hypocrisy in constantly insisting upon autonomy for all the cities, while forcing their allies to go to war against other cities, often when they had no quarrel with Sparta's intended victims. Autocles also castigated Sparta for the imposition of narrow oligarchies in other states.[70] Finally, Callistratus gave a milder, more conciliatory speech, in which he claimed that everyone makes mistakes and that taking the Cadmeia was Sparta's most serious blunder. However, he argued that peace could now be made with Athens and Sparta sharing hegemony, the one on the sea and the other on land, to mutual advantage.[71]

The Spartans voted to accept peace on these conditions: first, that all governors (here the word *harmosts,* usually employed for Spartan garrison commanders, is used) were to be withdrawn from the cities; second, that all forces, naval and military, were to be disbanded; and third, that all the cities were to be left autonomous. There was a fourth condition; namely, that if any state violated the terms of this treaty, any

---

[66]Diod. 15.50.4; Xen. 6.3.2–3; Plut. *Pelop.* 20.1. For the background, see Ryder, *Koine Eirene,* pp. 63–65.

[67]Xen. 6.3.3–20; cf. Diod. 15.50.4.

[68]See the discussions of these speeches in D. J. Mosley, "The Athenian Embassy to Sparta in 371 B.C.," *PCPS,* n.s. 8 (1962):41–46; T. T. B. Ryder, "Athenian Foreign Policy and the Peace-conference at Sparta in 371 B.C.," *CQ,* n.s. 13 (1963):237–41; and C. J. Tuplin, "The Athenian Embassy to Sparta, 372/1," *LCM* 2 (1977):51–56.

[69]Xen. 6.3.4–6.

[70]Xen. 6.3.7–9.

[71]Xen. 6.3.10–17.

other state so desiring could go to the aid of an injured party, but no state would be legally obligated to do so.[72] The Spartans took the oaths on behalf of themselves and their allies, whereas Athens and its allies swore, city by city, to the treaty. Xenophon says that on the next day the Thebans requested that the name "Thebans" be changed to "Boeotians." Agesilaus refused to alter the treaty, but he was willing, if the Thebans wanted, to strike their name from the agreement.[73]

Other accounts add more on this last point. Plutarch tells us that Epaminondas challenged Agesilaus on the general issue of swearing the oath on behalf of one's allies. He made a well-received speech in favor of justice and equality, and, when Agesilaus asked him whether he considered it just and equal for the Boeotian cities to be independent of Thebes, he responded by asking the same question concerning the Laconian cities and Sparta. When Agesilaus demanded if Thebes would leave the Boeotian cities independent, Epaminondas again answered the question with a question: Would Sparta leave the Laconian cities independent? Agesilaus gladly seized this pretext to strike out the name of the Thebans from the treaty.[74] Nepos, in his *Life* of Epaminondas, praised his subject's rhetorical ability by asserting that Epaminondas had shaken Sparta's power as much by his speech at the conference as by his subsequent victory at Leuctra.[75]

Of course, Xenophon omitted this altercation, partly because he chose to mention Epaminondas as little as possible in his *Hellenica,* and partly because he must have recognized that Agesilaus' intransigence on this point led to the debacle of Leuctra.[76] Clearly, Epaminondas had the better of Agesilaus in this verbal contest, as Nepos notes when he says that "it was then, as became apparent afterward, that he succeeded in depriving the Lacedaemonians of the support of their allies." Thus, Xenophon played down Agesilaus' role as much as possible. The exchange reported by Plutarch, which is not to be doubted, probably occurred on the occasion noted by Xenophon, when the Thebans returned on the day after the swearing of the oaths to request that "Boeotians" be substituted for their name. Both Plutarch's and Xenophon's

---

[72]Xen. 6.3.18. See Ryder's discussion of these terms (*Koine Eirene,* pp. 67–69), in which he greatly stresses the innovative clause providing for *voluntary* enforcement of the terms.

[73]Xen. 6.3.19.

[74]Plut. *Ages.* 27.4–28.2; cf. Paus. 9.13.2.

[75]Nepos, *Epam.* 6.4.

[76]On the general neglect of Epaminondas, Pelopidas, and the Theban hegemony in historical writing of the time, see Shrimpton, "Theban Supremacy," 310–18.

accounts are tendentious in their own ways. There is no reason, however, not to accept the bitter confrontation between the two leaders. It is perfectly consonant with what is known of Agesilaus that he should have seized a golden opportunity to isolate Thebes diplomatically, and then to threaten it militarily. This had been his objective since the liberation of the Cadmeia in 379. He probably regarded Epaminondas' argument as specious, mere sophistry, for he did not believe that the two situations were comparable. Sparta had ruled the cities of Laconia for centuries, and they had not had an independent existence since at least as far back as 700. And, he would have reasoned (if he could reason at all in the height of passion) that surely the other Greeks would not equate Sparta's dominance of Laconia with Thebes' dominance of Boeotia. Perhaps Agesilaus ought to have made such a case, coolly and logically, instead of imperiously striking the Thebans out of the peace. But he seems to have been glad of a pretext to exclude Thebes and to make it the object of a "righteous" attack on behalf of the independence of the Boeotian cities. Thebes' destruction of Plataea in 373 lent some weight to his case. In any event, under the impetus of Agesilaus' wrath, Sparta prepared to march against Thebes. As Xenophon reports, the Thebans went away in a state of profound discouragement, feeling themselves politically isolated and militarily vulnerable. The outcome of the resultant battle at Leuctra was no doubt a great surprise to both parties.[77]

The Battle of Leuctra: Preliminaries

Agesilaus had achieved what had doubtless long been a prime objective: for the first time since its liberation in 378, Thebes was isolated politically and vulnerable militarily. It is clear that Agesilaus intended to follow up on his exclusion of the Thebans from the Peace of 371 by an attack upon their city. The only question was, when and from what direction? At this time, King Cleombrotus was in Phocis at the head of a Lacedaemonian army. Xenophon tells us that he had been sent out early in 375 to counter Theban threats against Phocis,[78] but he never relates the recall of Cleombrotus to Sparta and his subsequent return to Phocis.

---

[77]For an attempt at explaining the object of the Thebans on this occasion, see the analysis of D. J. Mosley, "Theban Diplomacy in 371 B.C.," REG 85 (1972):312–18. He argues that the Thebans had a reasonable chance of gaining the one concession from Athens and Sparta of permitting Thebes to control Boeotia, rather than these two states' forfeiting all the other gains of the conference.

[78]Xen. 6.1.1.

Some scholars have concluded that he must have remained there for the intervening four years, but a majority reject this interpretation on several grounds. First, the Peace of 375 required the withdrawal of garrisons and armies, and, because Sparta signed this accord, Cleombrotus' remaining in Phocis would have been a violation, which is nowhere noted in the ancient sources. Second, the expenses of maintaining a large army abroad for four years would have been exorbitant, especially at a time when the Spartans were forced to devote more and more of their resources to the naval war against Athens. Finally, there is no record of military activities in Phocis between 375 and 371, although Thebes moved to attack both Plataea and Thespiae in 373. Had Cleombrotus been available for service in Phocis at that time, it is more than probable that he would have taken some action on behalf of these formerly pro-Spartan cities. Thus, it seems best to surmise that Cleombrotus had returned to Sparta following the Peace of 375 and that, in the wake of renewed Theban threats against Phocis, he had been sent out once again, in 372 or 371, and that Xenophon, as so often, has simply omitted any mention of this.

In any case, the king sent to Sparta for instructions upon news of the results of the Peace Conference of 371. When the Spartan assembly met to decide how to deal with the situation, Prothous argued that Sparta should withdraw its forces from the field, as the peace required, and then take action. Such a course would have put Sparta in favor with the gods, and in compliance with the treaty.[79] It would also, of course, have cost Sparta the element of time in striking at Thebes. To have withdrawn the army from Phocis, disbanded it, and then called it up again would have taken weeks, at least, and would have involved additional expense. And there was the further consideration of how Sparta's allies would have responded to such a development. Xenophon indicates that the Athenian Autocles' speech at the Peace Conference made it clear that many of its allies were tiring of its policies. If the army was disbanded, it might have been difficult to reassemble it easily, while, with the troops in the field, action could be taken with far less risk of allied disaffection.[80] Xenophon does not mention who at Sparta urged the sending of Cleombrotus' army directly against the Thebans, but it seems highly

<hr />

[79]Xen. 6.4.2–3.

[80]Xen. 6.3.7–8; cf. 6.4.15, in which Xenophon says that some of Sparta's allies were not displeased with the outcome of the Battle of Leuctra. Cf. Paus. 9.13.9, which reports that some of Sparta's allies at the Battle of Leuctra had been disaffected for some time. Thus it is quite clear that there was substantial displeasure, if not outright opposition, on the part of the allies of Sparta toward its policies in this period.

likely that Agesilaus was behind this policy, and it prevailed. Cleombrotus was ordered to send an ultimatum to Thebes to leave the Boeotian cities independent and, if the Thebans refused, as was expected, to march into Boeotia and engage them in battle.[81]

Of course, the ultimatum was rejected by Thebes, and Cleombrotus marched by the major route from Phocis into Boeotia, by way of Coroneia. But the Thebans had had time to anticipate his move. They had dispatched one Boeotarch to guard the pass over Cithaeron, by which Agesilaus had previously invaded their land, and a much larger force under six Boeotarchs, including Epaminondas, to intercept Cleombrotus in the narrow defile between the town of Coroneia and Lake Copais in western Boeotia.[82] Faced with this resistance, Cleombrotus turned around and made his way into Boeotia from the southwest, by way of the difficult coast road. He proceeded to Creusis on the Corinthian Gulf, which he captured, as well as a dozen Theban triremes, having taken several small towns en route. This he did, no doubt, to secure a line of reinforcement or retreat, if necessary, through the gulf to Corinth. Thence he marched north into the plain of Leuctra, where he took up camp on the slopes of a hill on the southern side of the plain.[83] Meanwhile, the Thebans had received intelligence of his movements. A small force under Chaireas, sent to hold Mount Helikon, south of Coroneia, had detected Cleombrotus' march to the south and tried to intercept him, meeting destruction at the hands of his much larger force.[84] But reconnaisance was undoubtedly sent to the main Theban force under Epaminondas, which marched east toward Thespiae, skirting Helikon, and then south into the plain of Leuctra, where they took up a position on a hill opposite that of the Spartans. Thus, the two armies were in position for the fateful fight.[85]

The Battle

There are four ancient accounts of the Battle of Leuctra, each with its own faults: Xenophon, Diodorus, Plutarch (*Pelopidas*), and Pausanias.[86]

[81]Xen. 6.4.3.
[82]Diod. 15.52.1 and 7; Paus. 9.13.7.
[83]Xen. 6.4.4; Diod. 15.53.1; Paus. 9.13.3. On these maneuverings, see W. K. Pritchett, "III: The Battle of Leuctra," in *Studies in Ancient Greek Topography, Part I*, 2 vols. (Berkeley and Los Angeles, 1965–69), 1:49–58.
[84]Paus. 9.13.3.
[85]Xen. 6.4.4; Diod. 15.53.2.
[86]Xen. 6.4.4–15; Diod. 15.52–56; Plut. *Pelop.* 20–23; Paus. 9.13.3–12.

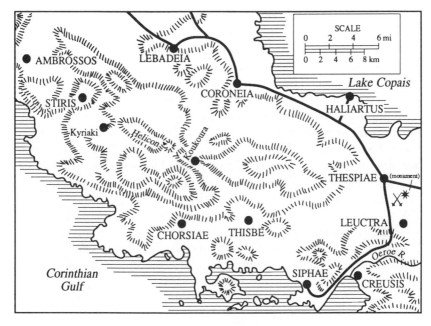

The Battle of Leuctra

These accounts have recently received considerable discussion,[87] and much is now generally agreed about their relative value and importance for Leuctra. Xenophon's account, the only contemporary one, is clearly not concerned with giving a complete version of events. Rather, Xenophon is intent upon providing an explanation of the Spartan defeat and, as we have seen, his antipathy to Epaminondas and Pelopidas causes him to ignore their roles in the battle. But he affords an account that, limited though it is, can be supplemented by details from other sources, notably Plutarch and Pausanias, where these authors do not contradict him. As for Diodorus, it is agreed that his account of the battle is of little value because he contradicts Xenophon on several crucial facts. For example, he relates that Jason of Pherae, Thebes' ally, arrived *before* the battle and arranged a truce between the

[87]See, for example, Anderson, *Military Theory*, chap. 10, pp. 192–220; Buckler, "Leuktra," in *Theban Hegemony*, pp. 46–69; G. L. Cawkwell, "The Decline of Sparta," *CQ,* n.s.33 (1983):385–400, at 397–99; Lazenby, *Spartan Army*, pp. 151–62; J. Buckler, "Plutarch on Leuktra," *Symbolae Osloenses* 55 (1980):75–93; C. J. Tuplin, "The Leuctra Campaign: Some Outstanding Problems," *Klio* 69 (1987):72–107; and V. D. Hanson, "Epameinondas, the Battle of Leuktra (371 B.C.), and the 'Revolution' in Greek Battle Tactics," *CA* 7 (1988):190–207.

two sides. Cleombrotus thus withdrew from the plain of Leuctra and was met by Archidamus, Agesilaus' son, with a second army. The combined Spartan force then returned to Leuctra and engaged the Thebans. Because Diodorus believed that two royal commanders were present, he described the Spartan army as advancing crescent-shaped, a tactic contradicted by all the other versions.[88] According to Xenophon, Jason arrived after the battle and then arranged a truce, and Archidamus arrived with a relief force, after news of the disaster had reached Sparta, to conduct the survivors homeward.[89] There can be no question of the superiority of Xenophon to Diodorus on these points, and we shall therefore reject his account of the battle proper, as do those who have investigated it in detail.

Much depended on the outcome of the battle, particularly for the respective commanders. Epaminondas and his fellow Boeotarchs, some of whom had spent the years 382–79 in exile, felt that they must engage and defeat the Spartans. To refuse to fight, even in the face of superior odds, might have meant the failure of their control of Boeotia, the capture of Thebes, and the loss of everything they had struggled for since the liberation of their city. Thus, they preferred death in battle to such disaster and to the possibility of exile. But the six Boeotarchs were divided equally in their opinion on how to respond to the Spartans. Epaminondas, Malgis, and Xenocrates were in favor of fighting, but Damocleidas, Damophilus, and Simangelus opposed battle, urging instead that their wives and children be sent to Athens for safety and that they prepare to withstand a siege of Thebes. Only when Brachyllides, the seventh Boeotarch who had been summoned with his force from Cithaeron to stiffen the army at Leuctra, gave his vote in support of Epaminondas did the Thebans decide to stand and fight.[90]

As for the Spartans, Cleombrotus himself was beset by political problems. His friends urged him to engage the enemy, lest he be tried and exiled upon his return to Sparta, and his political foes waited to see if he really was pro-Theban in his sympathies. No doubt they would have immediately brought charges of treason against him had he failed to engage the enemy, as he had done in 378 and again in his abortive invasion of Boeotia in 376. In such a politically charged climate within the Spartan camp, King Cleombrotus had little choice but to come to

---

[88]Diod. 15.54.5–7, 55.1. See the remarks of Lazenby, *Spartan Army,* pp. 155–56.
[89]Xen. 6.4.17–18, 20.
[90]Xen. 6.4.6; Diod. 15.53.3; Paus. 9.13.6–7 (which records the names of the seven Boeotarchs); Plut. *Pelop.* 20.2.

battle.[91] But his force appears to have outnumbered the Boeotians; the level plain at Leuctra provided classic terrain for a hoplite encounter; and he had been ordered by the government to do precisely this: to give battle. The one factor that might have weighed on Cleombrotus' mind was the realization that he had not yet commanded in a full-scale hoplite encounter, but, if this gave him any pause, there is no record of it in the sources. There seems to have been something like exuberance in the Spartan camp at the approach of battle. With their morning meal, the Spartans drank wine (apparently not an uncommon practice); as a result, they went into battle slightly intoxicated.[92]

Things were different in the Boeotian camp. There, with the numerical odds against the Boeotians, not even the memories of recent victories, such as Tegyra, could keep the troops from fearing the coming encounter. Epaminondas, realizing that only his Theban troops were really trustworthy, gave leave to any who did not wish to fight to withdraw, and the Thespians did so. He and the other commanders apparently publicized various oracles and omens that had occurred in an effort to encourage their troops. Among these was the report that the arms from the Temple of Heracles had disappeared, supposedly taken up by the god himself in order to fight with them, and an old oracle purporting to promise destruction to the Spartans for the long-past rape of two Boeotian girls at Leuctra.[93] Xenophon says that he had reason to believe that these various signs had been manufactured for the occasion by the Theban commanders, and J. Buckler has also been skeptical of their authenticity.[94] Be that as it may, the desired psychological effect was achieved, and the troops of Epaminondas were heartened in their resolve in the face of the enemy. Epaminondas was able to convince them not to be concerned at their inferiority in numbers by the following device. He caught a snake and likened it to the enemy. Then he

[91]Xen. 6.4.5; interestingly, only Xenophon comments on the political tensions within the Spartan camp, while he fails to note the initial division among the Boeotarchs which the other sources record. No doubt the explanation of these divergences lies in the ultimate sources employed by these writers; the information of Xenophon came from the Spartan side, whereas that of Diodorus, Plutarch, and Pausanias came from a Boeotian source, or at least one more interested in the Theban point of view, possibly Ephorus. For an excellent discussion of the possible sources of information of these writers (although on another topic), see the valuable study of Westlake, "Spartan Debacle," 119–33.

[92]Diod. 6.4.8.

[93]Diod. 15.53.4–54.4; Paus. 9.13.4–6 and 8; Plut. *Pelop.* 20.3–22.2.

[94]Xen. 6.4.7; see J. Buckler, "The Thespians at Leuktra," *Wiener Studien,* n.s. 11 (1977):76–79, at 77.

crushed its head, which represented the Spartans. The troops understood that they had only to beat the Spartans in order to sweep the field
in victory.[95] Not so the camp followers, who attempted en masse to
escape to Thespiae, but the Spartan mercenaries, Phliasian and Her-
acleote horse, and Phocian light armed troops drove them back into the
Boeotian camp.[96] Thus, the stage was set for battle.

I have repeatedly referred to the Spartans' numerical superiority, but
without indicating what it was. None of the sources provides reliable
numbers for the battle. Xenophon only indicates that Cleombrotus had
four of the six Lacedaemonian regiments with him, as well as various
allied contingents; but, of the latter, only those noted above are specifically named by him.[97] It is probable that the allied forces represented the
same proportion of their total commitment that the Spartans did, that
is, two-thirds (four out of six morai [regiments]); they had served in
Phocis in 375 in that proportion, according to Xenophon.[98] The only
reliable total provided by an ancient source is the ten thousand, plus one
thousand cavalry, given by Plutarch.[99] As regards the Boeotians, the
only figure provided is six thousand, given by Diodorus, for the force at
Coroneia. If we reckon this at one thousand hoplites per Boeotarch, and
we add an additional one thousand for the force with Brachyllides that
came up from Cithaeron, there were some seven thousand Boeotians
present initially, of whom four thousand were Thebans. That number
must be reduced to account for the defection of the Thespians and
others before the battle, as well as for the force under Chaireas which
had been massacred by Cleombrotus.[100] It is likely then that the Boeotians were outnumbered by about three to two, and that perhaps the
Theban and Spartan forces were more or less evenly matched.[101]

The basic order of battle of both sides is clear enough. In the Spartan

[95]Polyaenus 2.3.15.

[96]Xen. 6.4.9.

[97]Xen. 6.1.1, 4.9; cf. 6.4.17. Pausanias reports (8.6.2) that Arcadians were present
with the Spartans, although he suggests that they were at Leuctra under compulsion.

[98]Xen. 6.1.1. Estimates of the size of the allied force will depend upon the size one
imagines the mora to have been, and estimates range from four hundred to nine hundred
in antiquity, and up to almost thirteen hundred by modern scholarship. See Lazenby,
Spartan Army, p. 155.

[99]Plut. Pelop. 20.1. Eleven thousand appears more reasonable than the twenty-four
thousand given by Frontinus, or the forty thousand given by Polyaenus (Front. Strat-
egemata 4.2.6; Polyaenus 2.3.8 and 12). Diodorus (15.51.3) merely characterizes the
Spartan army as "huge."

[100]Diod. 15.52.2; Paus. 9.13.3 and 8.

[101]This is the conclusion of Lazenby, Spartan Army, p. 155.

army, the Lacedaemonians themselves held their right wing, with their allies on the left. This was in accord with the Spartans' normal deployment. The four morai were grouped on the right, drawn up "not more than twelve deep," as Xenophon says. The king, with the *hippeis* (royal bodyguard), was probably positioned between the first and second mora from the right. In the Boeotian army, the Thebans held their left wing, opposite the Spartans, with their Boeotian allies on their right, facing the Spartan allies.[102] The Thebans were massed "not less than fifty deep," a tactic that they had employed as early as the Battle of Delium in 424, as well as at the Battle of Nemea and probably at Coroneia and Tegyra.[103] The sheer weight of such a column was designed to crush the enemy line and to carry all before it. Epaminondas apparently positioned his men such that they would engage the Spartan line at the point where King Cleombrotus and his force stood, for the fiercest fighting was there, as well as the greatest losses for the Spartans. Although Plutarch makes clear the important role of the Theban Sacred Band under Pelopidas, the sources do not specify where this force was placed in the line. It is unlikely to have been placed behind the main Theban column, as has been suggested, for then Pelopidas would have had great difficulty in determining what was happening so that he could move his men into the fray at the critical moment, as he did. It is more likely that the Sacred Band formed the first several ranks of the Theban hoplite line, thus becoming literally its "cutting edge."[104] The dispositions of the two armies are thus likely to have been such before the battle.

The engagement opened with a cavalry action. Xenophon says that the Spartans deployed their cavalry in front of their phalanx because the ground was level there.[105] Usually, in Greek warfare cavalry served as scouts, to identify enemy positions, or as auxiliary troops, to protect the flanks from enemy movements, and occasionally in pursuit of fleeing troops. Rarely, though, were they in front of the phalanx, instead of behind or beside it. Thus we must ask why the cavalry was

---

[102]Xen. 6.4.12; Plut. *Pelop.* 23.1.

[103]Lazenby, *Spartan Army*, p. 156.

[104]Anderson, *Military Theory*, p. 217, places the Theban Sacred Band behind the phalanx. Lazenby's conclusion, *Spartan Army*, p. 157, seems much more likely: "It makes much more sense of what Plutarch says about Pelopidas and his command if the Sacred Band was stationed somewhere in the front of the Theban phalanx, and perhaps it made up the front three or four ranks of the whole phalanx, forming in a very real sense its 'cutting edge.'"

[105]Xen. 6.4.10.

positioned there. The Boeotian cavalry also operated in front of the phalanx, and they closed with the Spartans. The latter were not very well trained; the horses belonged to the rich, and the riders were those hired for service. Therefore the Spartan horse were not up to grade. On the contrary, the Theban horse had been given a good deal of practice in operations against Orchomenus and Thespiae, and they were in superb condition. As a result, the Thebans drove the Spartan horse back in the engagement, and many of the Spartan cavalry fled into their own lines, fouling the hoplite phalanx. Those who could retreated to the rear through the gap that had opened in the Spartan line between the Spartans' right and the allies on the left.[106] It appears that Cleombrotus ordered his horse to operate in front of the phalanx to screen the movement that he had ordered in response to his realization that the Thebans were opposed to him, and that they had presented him with a very deep phalanx.[107] Under the cover of the dust raised by the cavalry, and in the midst of the confusion caused by the horsemen, Cleombrotus was attempting to respond to Epaminondas' oblique advance. The Theban general had moved his phalanx forward in oblique fashion, toward his left, in order to draw the Spartans away from their allies in the line as far as possible, as well as to produce a gap in the phalanx. Some of the Spartan horse escaped through this gap.

When Cleombrotus realized the Theban tactic, he decided to wheel part of his line around behind the phalanx, in order to encircle the enemy on his own left flank. Thus, units from the left of the Spartan portion of the line were being moved toward the rear, in preparation for a flanking movement.[108] It was at this juncture that Pelopidas saw his opportunity and dashed forward with the Sacred Band at a run. He engaged the Spartan front while the line was still disordered, which was a result both of the cavalry that had fouled the first ranks, and of the units that were being moved around the phalanx. Pelopidas caught Cleombrotus by surprise, and bitter fighting developed in the front of the Spartan line. Before long the king himself fell, and his men carried him off the field to die. Those around him must have fiercely contested the fallen king's body, but they bore the full brunt of the massed Theban phalanx. Many of them fell, including the infamous Sphodrias, and his son Cleonymus.[109] The Thebans literally swept the field, carrying all

---

[106]Xen. 6.4.10–11, 13; Plut. *Pelop.* 23.1.

[107]For this view, see Anderson, *Military Theory*, p. 216; and Lazenby, *Spartan Army*, pp. 158–59.

[108]Anderson, *Military Theory*, pp. 218–19; and Lazenby, *Spartan Army*, pp. 158–59.

[109]Xen. 6.4.13–14; Plut. *Pelop.* 23.1–4; Diod. 15.55.4–56.2; Paus. 9.13.9–10.

before them. On the other flank, there was little action, neither the Boeotians nor Sparta's allies having much of an appetite for battle. The Spartans eventually gave way, and they retreated, but in good order, to their camp, which was protected by a small ditch. Epaminondas did not pursue them, but waited until the morrow to see what the enemy would do.[110]

After the king had died and the Spartans had retreated to their camp, the polemarchs took counsel about the best course of action. Some urged a return to battle, but others noted that they had suffered severe losses and that their allies were not displeased with how things had gone, and they thought they could not count upon them to fight loyally. The next day, the polemarchs sent heralds to take up the dead under truce, thus signaling their acceptance of defeat. Epaminondas insisted that Sparta's allies collect their dead first, so that the numbers of Spartan dead would be apparent to all. As it turned out, about one thousand Lacedaemonians had been slain, including four hundred of the seven hundred Spartiates present.[111] The allied casualties were light, not surprisingly because their part in the action was minimal. The Thebans may have lost as many as three hundred, but their victory was undeniable.[112] It was some time, however, before the extent of the Spartan defeat became apparent.

The Aftermath of Leuctra

After their defeat, the Spartan commanders sent a messenger with the news of the disaster to Sparta. The report was greeted with distress, but the ephors decided to continue with the celebration of the Gymnopaidiae. The names of the dead were divulged to their relatives, but the ephors ordered them not to exhibit evidence of mourning. On the following day the relatives of those who had fallen went about with

---

[110]Xenophon (6.4.14–15) describes the orderly retreat of the Spartans to their camp after their defeat; Diodorus (15.56.2–3) describes a panicked flight of Spartans and a hot pursuit by Epaminondas. Xenophon's account is probably the more accurate one.

[111]Xen. 6.4.15; Paus. 9.13.11–12; Diod. 15.56.4 relates the impossible figure of more than four thousand Spartan dead.

[112]Diodorus (15.56.4) mentions "about three hundred" Theban dead; Pausanias (9.13.12) claims, rather precisely, that only forty-seven of the Thebans and loyal Boeotians died. Xenophon and Plutarch give no figures for the Theban casualties. See Tod, *GHI*, no. 130, 2:92–94, for an inscription honoring several victorious Theban leaders on this occasion; cf. H. Beister, "Ein thebanisches Tropaion bereits vor Beginn der Schlacht bei Leuktra. Zur Interpretationen von IG VII 2462 und Paus. 4.32.5f.," *Chiron* 3 (1973): 65–84.

cheerful mien, while those whose men had survived seemed gloomy and downcast.[113] Spartan law required that those who had displayed cowardice in battle be severely disciplined as a lesson to others, and on this occasion this law raised a dilemma for the Spartans: many had fled before the enemy at Leuctra, but the state was in desperate need of soldiers; furthermore, the authorities feared that to have disgraced these people might cause them to stir up a revolution.[114] To deal with the emergency, the authorities appointed Agesilaus law-giver, and he proved adequate to the task. Wanting neither to change any of the existing laws, nor to cause anger or offense among those who would be affected by the application of the law against the *tresantes* (tremblers), he declared that "the laws must be allowed to sleep for a day, to be sovereign once again from the morrow." In this fashion, Agesilaus saved both the laws and the men from disgrace.[115] It is also worth noting here that, according to Plutarch, many in Sparta blamed Agesilaus when they heard the news of Leuctra, claiming that they were now being repaid for making the wrong choice of kings and for interpreting the oracle about the lame kingship incorrectly. Despite this open criticism, Agesilaus still had enough influence in Sparta to be named lawgiver at this crucial juncture.[116]

The ephors then called out the ban of the remaining Spartan soldiers, including the two regiments that had remained at home, and all those up to forty years beyond the minimum military age, as well as those who had originally been excused because they were serving in various magistracies. Archidamus, Agesilaus' son, was put in command of this force, for his father had not yet fully recovered from his illness. The allies were also called out, and the Tegeans, Mantineans, Corinthians, Sicyonians, Phliasians, and Achaeans all turned out to assist the Spartans. Archidamus held the sacrifices at the frontier, while the Spartans, Corinthians and Sicyonians prepared ships to transport the army across the gulf to the shores of Boeotia.[117]

Meanwhile, the Thebans sent a garlanded messenger to Athens to announce the glad tidings of their victory. He met with a less than cordial welcome, however, and the Athenian *boule* (council), which was in session, gave him no reply and did not even invite him to partake of-

[113]Xen. 6.4.16; Plut. *Ages.* 29.
[114]Plut. *Ages.* 30.2–3.
[115]Plut. *Ages.* 30.4, *Mor.* 191C, 214B, *Comp. Ages. et Pomp.* 2; Polyaenus 2.1.13.
[116]Plut. *Ages.* 30.1–2.
[117]Xen. 6.4.17–19.

their hospitality.[118] This response was tantamount to a diplomatic re-
buff, especially because Thebes and Athens were allied at this time, and
it is clear proof that the Athenians were distressed at the news of the
Theban victory. It was also a harbinger of things to come, for before the
summer was over, the Athenians would organize another peace conference, this time in Athens itself, at which they tried to minimize the
effects of the Theban triumph.[119] The Thebans had also sent to their
ally, Jason of Pherae, urging him to come to their aid, because they
anticipated that the Spartans would dispatch another army to Boeotia.
Jason marched swiftly, so swiftly indeed that the Phocians, through
whose territory he moved, were not able to organize a force to contest
his passing; for the Phocians were at war with him at that time.[120]

When Jason arrived in Boeotia, the Thebans pressed him to attack the
Spartan army with his peltasts from the heights while they made a
frontal assault on the position. But Jason persuaded them otherwise,
arguing that fortunes change, and pointing out that the Spartans, hard-
pressed and in difficult straits, would be likely to fight to the bitter end.
Jason then adopted the role of mediator and persuaded the Spartans to
accept a truce by reminding them that many of their allies were already
discussing friendship with the enemy. He stressed his role as proxenos
of the Spartans, a position he had inherited from his forefathers, and
succeeded in resolving the situation. A truce was arranged whereby the
Spartan army was permitted to evacuate Boeotia. The army withdrew
south to Creusis and then proceeded along the coastal route to Aegosthena, where Archidamus and the relief force from the Peloponnesus
met it. Archidamus bowed to the inevitable and led the combined
armies back to Corinth, where he dismissed the allies before marching
the Lacedaemonians back to Sparta.[121]

Leuctra was one of the great turning points of history. Although the
actual military defeat suffered by the Spartans was something less than
catastrophic, if unprecedented, the political and diplomatic results of
the Theban victory were far-reaching indeed. To what extent contemporaries recognized the potential significance of this battle for the diplomatic and political situation in Greece is difficult to gauge. Xenophon,
however, took pains to exonerate Agesilaus, his hero, from any respon-

[118]Xen. 6.4.19–20.
[119]Xen. 6.5.1–2.
[120]Xen. 6.4.20–21.
[121]Xen. 6.4.22–26; cf. Diod. 15.54.5–6, who misrepresents the time and circumstances of Jason's arrival at Leuctra, as well as those of Archidamus' expedition.

sibility for Leuctra, claiming that "up to this time he and his city enjoyed unbroken success; and though the following years brought a series of troubles, it cannot be said that they were incurred under the leadership of Agesilaus."[122] Xenophon is writing of the period following Agesilaus' return from Boeotia in 377, until the Battle of Leuctra, and he is technically correct. Agesilaus did not command in any of the battles in Boeotia between 376 and 371. But we must not fail to recognize that those battles were fought, regardless of who commanded on any given occasion, in pursuit of policies that Agesilaus had shaped and urged on his state for years. The outcome of Leuctra was the price Sparta had to pay for Agesilaus' Theban obsession. At least Plutarch understood this. In his *Comparison of Agesilaus and Pompey,* he condemns Agesilaus for his anti-Theban policies, which Plutarch claims led to the loss of Spartan hegemony in Greece.[123] Although Plutarch was capable of reasoning to such a conclusion on the basis of the information at his disposal, it is equally likely that this criticism was leveled against Agesilaus in his own lifetime, and it was probably to be found in Ephorus' history. Perhaps Xenophon's encomium of the king responded to such charges. To determine whether they will stand scrutiny, we shall review the course of events after Leuctra.

[122]Xen. *Ages.* 2.23. E. C. Marchant, trans., *Xenophon: Scripta Minora,* p. 93.
[123]Plut. *Comp. Ages. et Pomp.* 1.4 and 3.2.

CHAPTER EIGHT

The Collapse of
Spartan Hegemony

In the aftermath of the Battle of Leuctra, shock waves rippled through Greece. At first there was consternation as the news of the battle traveled from city to city, and then activity burst forth. The decade that followed is generally known as that of the Theban hegemony, to indicate that Thebes had succeeded to the place that Sparta had occupied in the affairs of Greece for the preceding fifteen years. Much diplomatic activity took place, and a good deal of warfare as well. For Sparta and for Greece, the outcome was not necessarily preordained, and the responses of the various states—principally Sparta, Athens and Thebes—to the momentous event at Leuctra and its sequel must be studied in detail in order to trace the course of the failure of the Spartan hegemony after the battle. One useful index to measure the decline of Sparta's hegemony is the state of the so-called Peloponnesian League, or what the Greeks referred to as "the Lacedaemonians and their allies." I trace the defections from Sparta's alliance as one particularly helpful way to gauge this process. Thus, the focus of this chapter will be on Sparta and its relations with the other Greek states, particularly within the Peloponnesus, although not exclusively there. For example, I discuss affairs in northern Greece, in Thessaly and Macedonia, but only as they relate to our major consideration.

The Peace Conference at Athens

After the return of the Spartan army to the Peloponnesus, the Athenians invited to Athens all the cities who wished to participate in the peace which the Great King had decreed.[1] When the representatives had assembled, they resolved to take the following oath: "I will abide by the treaty which the King sent down, and by the decrees of the Athenians and their allies. And if anybody takes the field against any one of the cities which have sworn this oath, I will come to her aid with all my strength."[2] This latter provision, as Ryder has stressed, was an important innovation; it made obligatory what had been a voluntary aspect of the Peace of 371 in Sparta. The difficulty with this provision, however, was to determine "who was to decide when action was needed and who was to direct the action?"[3] The Athenians were attempting to quell the rising tide of Theban aggression, and anti-Spartan feeling, by thus involving all states in a common obligation to uphold the Common Peace. It seems that the Athenians' objective was to prevent Thebes from exploiting its victory at Leuctra, but troubles arose in another part of the Greek world.

The Eleans argued that the peace did not affect the cities of Margana, Scilluntis, and Triphylia, which properly belonged to them. These cities, of course, had been wrested from Elean control by the Spartans in 398,[4] and the Eleans now attempted to exploit Sparta's weakness after Leuctra to their own advantage. Their interpretation was not accepted, however, for the Athenians and the others present voted that all cities, small as well as great, should have their freedom guaranteed. They then sent out officers charged with administering the oaths to do so to the highest authorities in each city, and Elis was excluded from the peace.[5]

The Mantineians also determined to act on their newly guaranteed freedom and to exploit Spartan weakness. They resolved to reconstitute themselves into a single polis, thus reversing the dissolution that King

---

[1]Xen. 6.5.1ff. For discussion, see Ryder, *Koine Eirene,* Appendix IV, pp. 131–33.

[2]Xen. 6.5.2. C. L. Brownson, trans. *Xenophon: Hellenica, Books VI & VII* (Cambridge, Mass., 1921), p. 77. The mention of "the decrees of the Athenians and their allies" is presumably a reference to the Aristoteles Decree; cf. Ryder, *Koine Eirene,* p. 71: "The 'resolutions of the Athenians and their allies' are best explained as being those which at the foundation of the confederacy had defined the freedom and autonomy which it was formed to protect."

[3]Ryder, *Koine Eirene,* pp. 72–73.

[4]Xen. 3.2.30–31; Triphylia and Margana are mentioned here, but not Scilluntis; cf. Diod. 14.17.4–12, and 34.1; and Paus. 3.8.3–5.

[5]Xen. 6.5.2–3. The practice of sending officers to administer the oaths in each of the individual cities is a novel aspect of Common Peace treaties, probably modeled on the Athenian practice of sending emissaries to administer oaths in the various cities which became allied to Athens. See Ryder, *Koine Eirene,* pp. 132–33.

Agesipolis had carried out in 385.[6] Of course, these acts constituted a direct challenge to Sparta's dominance of the Peloponnesus and thus represented a failure of its policies there. And they were merely a harbinger of things to come. The Spartans sent Agesilaus to Mantineia as ambassador, in order to prevent the synoecism without Spartan approval. He was unable, however, to persuade the Mantineians to desist, even though he gave his word that, if they gave up their work for the present, he would see to the construction of a city wall for them, with Lacedaemonian approval, and without great expense.

The Mantineians were understandably suspicious of such an un-characteristically generous offer from Sparta, and the government re-plied that it was impossible to stop the wall's construction, for it had been authorized by a decree of the people. In the meanwhile, other Arcadian cities sent to help with the work, and Elis contributed three talents to its expense. Agesilaus went off in anger, and Sparta had to watch the undoing of its Arcadian policy.[7] The fact that Agesilaus was sent to Mantineia indicates both that he had recovered from his long illness and that he was still influential at Sparta, as his appointment as law-giver shortly before this also suggests. He must have returned to Sparta eager to take action to redress the situation, but even worse was yet to come.

In Tegea, factionalism had developed, with Callibius, Proxenus, and their supporters working toward the unification of all the peoples of Arcadia, while Stasippus and his followers, the pro-Spartan faction, opposed them. When negotiations broke down, both sides armed themselves. During the ensuing fighting, Proxenus and some others were killed, and Callibius and his men fled to a position beside the city gate toward Mantineia. They had long before sent for aid to Mantineia, and now a force arrived to succor them. Stasippus' followers then fled to the temple of Artemis, outside the walls in the direction of Pallantium, where they became trapped. The refugees surrendered to the faction of Callibius, who bound them, transported them to Tegea, and put them to death after trial, presumably on charges of treason.[8] In the mean-while, some eight hundred of the partisans of Stasippus had fled to Sparta, where they agitated for Spartan intervention on their behalf.

Of course, this had been the time-honored story in the Peloponnesus:

[6]Xen. 6.5.3; cf. 5.2.7. See chap. 5 above.
[7]Xen. 6.5.3–5.
[8]Xen. 6.5.6–10.

pro-Spartan political exiles could always count upon Spartan intervention to reestablish them in power, and Cawkwell considers this a sound
policy for Sparta and Agesilaus to have followed.[9] The Spartans determined to send out a force against Mantineia, on the grounds that the
Mantineians had transgressed their oaths by marching against Tegea
and thus violating the autonomy of that city. It is tempting to think that
the Spartans were glad of a pretext to punish the Mantineians for their
assertion of independence in rebuilding their city and its walls against
Sparta's wishes. The ephors called out the ban and instructed Agesilaus
to lead the army; this affords clear proof that Agesilaus was now
sufficiently recovered in health, for it is the first campaign that he led
since 377. Agesilaus was able to count upon Arcadian Orchomenus,
which was hostile to Mantineia and refused to join the Arcadian Confederacy that was being formed. A mercenary force under Polytropus,
first collected at Corinth, was there, and others, such as the Lepreans
and Heraeans, were ready to serve with Sparta. While Agesilaus was
occupied at Eutaea in Arcadia, where he busied his men with repairs to
the city wall, the Mantineians attacked Orchomenus. They were beaten
off in their attack and pursued in their retreat by Polytropus and his
peltasts. In an encounter, the Mantineians killed Polytropus and drove
off his troops, whom they would have hunted down and killed, had not
some Phliasian horsemen arrived to force them to desist. Accordingly,
they returned home.[10]

Reckoning that he could no longer count on the support of the
mercenaries, Agesilaus marched forth through the territory of Tegea
toward Mantineia, ravaging and plundering the land as he went. The
Arcadians who had gathered at Asea now marched to Tegea, and from
there toward Mantineia, where they hoped to join the Mantineians.
They had with them some Argives, but hardly the full Argive comple-
ment. In conjunction with Elis and Argos, the Arcadians at this point
sent envoys to Athens seeking aid but, when the Athenians refused to
heed them, they sent to Thebes.[11] Meanwhile, Agesilaus was caught
between two enemy forces, the Mantineians to his north, and the
Arcadians and Argives to the south, in the plain between Tegea and
Mantineia. So he declined the advice to attack the force from Tegea, lest

[9]Cawkwell, "Agesilaus and Sparta," 75. With regard to Mantineia, he writes: "The
repressive policy had worked. For Spartan power, a broad girdle across the Peloponnese
of so-called autonomy, which was in fact imposed landed aristocracy, was best" (76).
[10]Xen. 6.5.10–14; Diod. 15.59.4, 62.1–2.
[11]Xen. 6.5.15; Diod. 15.62.3.

he himself be attacked from the rear, and he allowed the Arcadians to link up with the Mantineians. At the same time, the Orchomenian peltasts and the Phliasian horse also effected a juncture with Agesilaus. The next morning, Agesilaus was encamped in a valley behind Mantineia, with the enemy occupying the heights to his rear. He managed to extricate his force by an interesting maneuver. He first turned his line of march into phalanx position, facing the heights from which an attack might come. Then he marched the other units around behind the protective cover of his phalanx until they had emerged from the dangerously narrow valley into the plain, where battle could be engaged, if necessary, on favorable terms for the Spartans. The Mantineians refused to engage the Spartans, on the advice of the Eleans. These latter urged them not to give battle until the Thebans had arrived, which they expected to happen soon, because Elis had advanced Thebes ten talents for the expenses of the expedition to aid them. Agesilaus remained for three days in position, in order not to seem to be frightened of the enemy, even though it was midwinter and he was eager to disband his troops. Eventually he marched back to Laconia, by way of Eutaea, confident that he had scored a moral victory in that he had invaded Arcadia, ravaged the enemy's land, and no one had come forth to confront him.[12]

If Agesilaus celebrated his homecoming, the celebration was brief indeed, for an invasion of the Peloponnesus, and of Laconia itself, such as had not been seen for centuries, was about to occur. The result of the events of the year following Leuctra and the Peace Conference at Athens was the collapse of Sparta's Peloponnesian alliance. Mantineia had been once again reconstituted and fortified as a city, and it had joined many of the other Arcadian cities in forming a new federation; only some Tegean exiles, and Orchomenus and a few smaller Arcadian communities, remained loyal to Sparta. Elis had also gone over to the enemy, and Argos had taken up arms once again in the attempt to gain advantage against its inveterate foe. The Thebans also had determined to march into the Peloponnesus in response to pleas for aid from various cities, especially Elis and Mantineia. It is not clear how much of this would have occurred if Agesilaus had not taken the field against Tegea, in favor of the exiles. Of course, Tegea was Sparta's oldest ally in the entire Peloponnesus; its treaty with Sparta, dating from the mid-sixth century, was the cornerstone and model for those with other states that had

[12]Xen. 6.5.16–21, *Ages.* 2.23; Plut. *Ages.* 30.5.

subsequently formed the league.[13] Thus, Sparta no doubt felt justified in aiding its friends from Tegea. But Agesilaus' action nonetheless helped to speed along a movement that had begun shortly after the Peace of Athens at the end of 371, in the wake of Leuctra.

The Invasion of the Peloponnesus in 370/69

The architects behind the Theban invasion of the Peloponnesus were not the Thebans themselves, but rather the Eleans and Mantineians.[14] Lycomedes of Mantineia had taken the lead in the reconstitution of his polis, under a democratic government, and in the formation of the Arcadian federal union.[15] His object was to free Arcadia from Spartan domination, and to that end he needed to find allies. Stymied in its attempt to regain recognition of its right to control its border communities in the Athenian conference after Leuctra, Elis was more than ready to join with the Arcadians in alliance.[16] Argos was also prepared to join them, as it had done in 418, in another attempt to curtail Spartan influence within the Peloponnesus.[17] Xenophon makes only a casual reference to the presence of Argives with the Mantineians at this point, providing no explanation of why they may have chosen to take an active part in Peloponnesian affairs. But Diodorus relates that a serious disorder had occurred in Argos just after the conference at Athens. Apparently some demagogues had instigated trouble against some of the wealthier citizens, and these latter retaliated by plotting against the government. Arrests, confessions under torture, and summary executions followed, and mob rule led to the murders of over twelve hun-

---

[13]Herod. 1.66–68; cf. Hooker, *Ancient Spartans,* pp. 111–13, on the Spartan-Tegean treaty of alliance, which formed the cornerstone of Sparta's Peloponnesian League; see F. Jacoby, *Abhandlungen zur griechischen Geschichtschreibung* (Leiden, 1956), pp. 342–43, on the treaty itself.

[14]Diod. 15.62.3; Dem. 16.12, 19; cf. Xen. 6.5.19 on Elis' role. There is scholarly debate on the chronology of the events of the 360s, including that of the several Theban invasions. For discussion, see J. Wiseman, "Epaminondas and the Theban Invasions," *Klio* 51 (1969):177–99; and G. L. Cawkwell, "Epaminondas and Thebes," *CQ,* n.s. 22 (1972):254–78.

[15]Diod. 15.59.1–2; cf. Paus. 8.27.2 Also see Larsen, *Greek Federal States,* pp. 180–95, for detailed analysis and discussion of the Arcadian Confederacy. J. Roy, "Arcadia and Boeotia in Peloponnesian Affairs, 370–362 B.C.," *Historia* 20 (1971):569–99, is useful on this topic, among others. Buckler, *Theban Hegemony,* p. 108, admits that Epaminondas is unfairly credited with the achievements of Lycomedes.

[16]Xen. 6.5.5; Diod. 15.62.3.

[17]Xen. 6.5.16; Diod. 15.62.3.

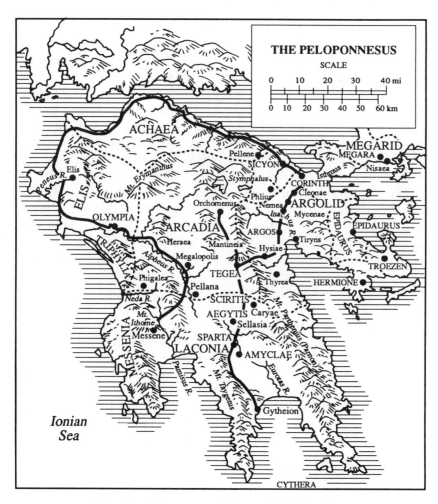

Epaminondas' invasion of the Peloponnesus, 370

dred. In the event, even the demagogues themselves fell victims to the
mob that they had instigated.[18] Although there is no hint of it in
Diodorus' account, the original victims, men of wealth and influence
and apparently of oligarchic leanings, may have sought help from
Sparta. This certainly had been the pattern for decades within the
Peloponnesus. Although speculative, such a hypothesis might explain
why the Argives suddenly took the field against the Spartans. It appears

[18]Diod. 15.58.1–4; Isoc. 5.52; Plut. *Mor.* 814.

to be the Arcadians who took the initiative in sending envoys first to Athens and then to Thebes to seek to recruit them into the anti-Spartan Peloponnesian alliance. Of course, Athens had nothing to gain from such a move, and it rebuffed the envoys.[19] In Thebes, however, it was another story. Although there was opposition to such involvement so far away from central Greece, the opinion of the group of Epaminondas and Pelopidas prevailed and Thebes agreed to enter into alliance with the Peloponnesians. The Elean loan of ten talents for the support of an army from central Greece to invade the Peloponnesus tipped the scales, and late in 370 such an army set out from Boeotia.[20]

The Theban commanders also led, in addition to their own troops, a mixed force of Phocians, Locrians, Euboeans, Acarnanians, Malians, and Heracleots.[21] The adherence of these peoples makes it plain that, after Leuctra, Thebes must have been successful in winning away the peoples of central Greece from their Spartan alliance, either by force or by persuasion. Phocis and Locris both appear in Diodorus' list of military districts drawn up by the Spartans to supply troops to "Sparta and its allies" in 378.[22] Euboea belonged to the Second Athenian League, as did Acarnania, and the presence of Euboean and Acarnanian troops with Epaminondas' army may signal their desertion of Athens.[23] In any case, it is clear that significant diplomatic activity had occurred since Leuctra, and no less than a diplomatic revolution had taken place in the Greek world. Sparta's system of military alliances had all but disappeared; of the ten districts established in 378, six were gone: the two furnished by the Arcadians (except for Orchomenus and a few others), and those of Elis, Acarnania, Phocis/Locris, and Olynthus and the allies in Thrace.[24] Only the troops supplied by the Lacedaemonians themselves and those from Achaea, Corinth and Megara, Sicyon and Phlius,

---

[19]See Cloché, *La politique étrangère,* pp. 97–99, for Athens' motives at this juncture.
[20]Diod. 15.62.3–4; cf. Xen. 6.5.22–23. See Buckler, *Theban Hegemony,* pp. 70–73.
[21]Xen. 6.5.23. See Buckler, *Theban Hegemony,* p. 74.
[22]Diod. 15.31.1–2.
[23]Cargill, *SAL,* p. 165, considers their presence as defection from the league. "The spate of rebellions, successful or unsuccessful, which afflicted the Athenian League in the next few years can be attributed mostly to the aggressiveness of Thebes, under the assertive leadership of Epaminondas and Pelopidas. Joining the Theban invasion of the Peloponnesos in 370 were (among others) Athenian League members from Euboea and Akarnania." Buckler's view, in *Theban Hegemony,* p. 74, is merely that "the Boiotian troops . . . formed the heart of a grand army that included contingents from Phokis, Lokris, Euboia, and other places in central and northern Greece."

[24]Olynthus is not mentioned as having deserted Sparta, or as taking part in the invasion of the Peloponnesus, but the Chalcidians, whose name appears on the Aristoteles Decree, ll. 101–2, are generally taken as those from Thrace; cf. Cargill, *SAL,* p. 42, in which older literature is cited.

and a handful of Arcadians could now be rallied. Thus, the Spartan defeat at Leuctra had precipitated wholesale rebellion from the Spartan system, prompted no doubt by the calculation that Sparta was too weak to prevent this, and based on longstanding resentments toward the Spartans for their treatment of their subject-allies.

Most of Arcadia had been forged into a new federal state, under the leadership of the Mantineians, and a new federal capital would soon be built in southwest Arcadia, to be named Megalopolis.[25] The Thebans had been inordinately successful not only in establishing their freedom and in reconstituting the Boeotian Confederacy under their hegemony, but also in extending their influence over neighboring peoples in central Greece. Athens remained neutral thus far, holding to the principles of the peace that it had sponsored in 371. The situation looked bleak indeed for the Spartans.

Not long after Agesilaus had smugly retired to Sparta after his invasion and ravaging of Arcadia, the army, led by the Boeotarchs but commanded by Epaminondas and Pelopidas, arrived in the Peloponnesus. Even though the Spartan army had already withdrawn, and Arcadia was no longer threatened, they were persuaded to march on to Mantineia, where a conference of war was held. The allies decided to launch an invasion of Laconia itself.[26] This decision was taken toward the last part of the year, and many of the Boeotarchs were reluctant to proceed for fear of failing to surrender their office as the law required. The Boeotian constitution provided that the Boeotarchs lay down their powers at the end of the civil year under pain of prosecution. But the campaign had begun late in the year, much later than was usual in Greek warfare, and Epaminondas argued persuasively that if they returned to Boeotia without accomplishing anything, they were just as likely to face public outcry and recrimination for that. He argued that the law had not foreseen the possibility of command running out while the Boeotarchs were still in the field, and it was inconceivable that the Boeotians would fail to understand the military imperative of continuing with the campaign, even if in technical violation of the law. His arguments prevailed, and the invasion went forth.[27]

[25]Paus. 8.27.2–9; Diodorus (15.72.4) puts the founding in 368, just after the so-called Tearless Victory, which Archidamus won, whereas Pausanias suggests 371/70 (at 8.27.8). See Larsen, *Greek Federal States,* pp. 185–86, for discussion; he argues persuasively that the initial idea, at least, of establishing Megalopolis fits best to 370, after Agesilaus' withdrawal and before Epaminondas' arrival.

[26]Xen. 6.5.22–23; Diod. 15.62.4–5; Plut. *Ages.* 31.1–2.

[27]Plut. *Pelop.* 24.1–2. The dilemma of Epaminondas foreshadowed that of the Roman general Publilius Philo, whose command ran out in the course of a siege of Naples; but

Because the combined allied armies numbered upwards of fifty thousand, more than twice the size of the typical Greek army—at the Nemea, for example, neither side had more than about twenty-four thousand, and at Coroneia the armies were probably a bit smaller—the allies assumed that they would easily crush any Spartan resistance and perhaps utterly destroy the Spartans.[28] Indeed, Epaminondas had urged his troops at Leuctra to do exactly that: to crush the Spartans and thus to break the opposition of the enemy entirely. But the very thing that gave Epaminondas his advantage, namely, his overwhelming numerical superiority, presented him with other difficulties: those of supply and of movement. Therefore, he determined to divide his forces into four columns and to strike into Laconia by different routes, where they would link up again.[29]

Because the passes into Laconia were narrow, Epaminondas could not bring his numbers to bear in forcing those passes, and he risked little in dividing his armies. The Argives were to invade from the east, through the Thyreatis, while the Eleans were to move into Laconia from the northwest, along the route from Sparta to Olympia. Epaminondas himself would take the Thebans south from Tegea via Sellasia, while the Arcadians would march southwest from Tegea, via Caryae, into Laconia. Intelligence was at hand from numerous perioeci and some of the inhabitants of Caryae, who promised to assist the invaders and gave assurances that there would be extensive uprisings among helots and perioeci.[30] Encouraged by these signs, Epaminondas launched his invasions, and met with little significant resistance. The Spartan Ischolaus, holding Caryae with a garrison of exiles, was easily pinned by the Arcadian forces and overcome, and the Argives swept away the defenders of the pass over Mount Parnon from Thyreatis. The Eleans managed to bypass the defenders at Leuctron without engaging them at all, and they moved on Sellasia from the south, while the Thebans attacked from the north. Caught between the two armies, the

---

the Romans met the situation by improvising and extending his command through a grant of *imperium pro consule,* which set a fateful precedent for the future. See T. Liv. 8.23.

[28]Plutarch, in *Ages.* 31.1, states that Epaminondas had no fewer than forty thousand hoplites, plus numerous lightly armed and unarmed troops, whereas in *Pelop.* 24.2 he speaks of seventy thousand; Diodorus (15.62.5) puts the number at seventy thousand, which Wesseling has emended to fifty thousand. Xenophon does not give a number for the invading force. Buckler, *Theban Hegemony,* pp. 74–75, does not estimate the totals.

[29]On this strategy and the invasion routes, see the excellent treatment of Buckler, *Theban Hegemony,* pp. 77–81.

[30]Xen. 6.5.24–25; Diod. 15.63.4.

defenders of Sellasia were easily defeated, and the way now lay open to Sparta in the Eurotas Valley.[31]

Epaminondas led his forces down from Sellasia into the broad and fertile valley of the Eurotas, from which the city of Sparta could be seen, framed against the massive craggy shape of Mount Taygetus. Proceeding southward, along the river's left bank, the invaders met no resistance. They pillaged and burned as they marched, and the sight of smoke in the valley caused panic among the women of Sparta, who had never seen such a sight. Agesilaus, who commanded the defense, determined not to meet the enemy in frontal combat, no doubt a very wise decision in the circumstances, but rather to dispose his forces in such a way as to defend the unwalled city of Sparta itself. He distributed his troops at various points in the city, where they would have the advantage in any close fighting in the narrow streets, and where the numerical superiority of Epaminondas would be negated. He also stationed some contingents at strategic crossing points on the Eurotas.

When Epaminondas realized that he was not going to be able to lure the Spartans into a traditional hoplite encounter, he made one or two attempts to cross the Eurotas, but the river was swollen with winter rains, and the opposing forces guarding the fords made the effort fruitless. Instead, Epaminondas contented himself with a march southward, pillaging and burning all that he found in the plain, whether wealthy farmsteads or small villages. Eventually, he made his way to the coast, capturing Helos, but probably not the Spartan port of Gytheion, which had been fortified after a previous Athenian attack upon it. As time passed and the enemy still refused to engage and fight, allowing instead the devastation of its lands, Epaminondas and his allies determined to withdraw from Laconia and to wreak havoc where it would do permanent damage: in Messenia.[32]

It is not possible to know if Epaminondas had conceived the idea of the liberation of Messenia before his invasion of the Peloponnesus, but certainly he had decided to act on this plan before he retired from the charred and devastated valley of the Eurotas. Accompanied now by large numbers of helots and perioeci who had deserted Sparta in its hour of need, Epaminondas marched back into Arcadia and then southwest-

---

[31]Xen. 6.5.26–27; Diod. 15.64.1–6. For discussion of the invasion routes, see Buckler, *Theban Hegemony*, pp. 78–82, with plates.

[32]Xen. 6.5.27–28, 30–32; Diod. 15.65.1–5; Plut. *Ages.* 31.3–4, 32.1–3, and 8, *Pelop.* 24.2–4. See Buckler, *Theban Hegemony*, p. 86. Plutarch relates that, according to Theopompus, Agesilaus sent Phrykis with ten talents to hasten the withdrawal.

ward into an undefended Messenia.[33] This area had been the possession of Sparta for some 350 years, and the farms of many of the Spartiates were located there, worked for them by their helots. Messenia was absolutely vital to the economic and social well-being of Sparta, as it had evolved throughout the archaic and classical periods. If it were to be lost, the blow to Spartan prestige, not to mention the economy, would be severe.[34]

Epaminondas seems to have had little difficulty in taking Messenia, where he presumably proclaimed the independence of the unfree inhabitants and the birth of a new polis. To create a polis where one had never existed, however (the Messenians had first been conquered in the late eighth century before the institutions of the polis had fully emerged), presented certain difficulties. Epaminondas chose as the site of the new capital the legendary Mount Ithome, which had been the scene of fierce resistance to Sparta in the past, most recently following the earthquake of 464, when the Spartans proved incapable of ejecting the Messenian helots from their fortified position there.[35] He supervised the foundation of a city, girdled with thick walls of fine ashlar masonry, whose remains are impressive even today. To populate the new polis, he added to the newly liberated indigenous population such of the rebellious helots and perioeci from Laconia as wished to join, and he recalled from their various places of exile—in Libya, Naupactus, Messana, and elsewhere in Sicily and the west—those former Messenian helots who had been expelled from Messenia in the past.[36] When his work was done, Epaminondas left behind a permanent memorial to his invasion: a strongly fortified city, populated by a diverse collection of immigrants who shared one overriding concern—a determination to remain independent—and a hatred of Sparta. The devastation of Laconia paled in comparison with this accomplishment.

During the invasion itself, Agesilaus had to contend with several troubling episodes of disaffection among the Spartans. Let us first examine the role of the helots in the defense of Sparta in 370. When Epaminondas marched to the borders of Laconia, panic gripped Sparta. King Agesilaus was entrusted with the defense of the city, and his was not an easy task. The Spartan army itself, badly mauled in the previous

[33]Diod. 15.66.1, 67.1; Plut. *Pelop.* 24.5. See Buckler, *Theban Hegemony,* pp. 86–87.
[34]On the economic advantages of Messenia, see Cartledge, *Sparta,* pp. 115–18; and Michell, *Sparta,* pp. 5–6 and 10ff.
[35]Cf. Thuc. 1.101ff.
[36]Diod. 15.66.1; Paus. 4.26.5–8, 27.5–9.

year at Leuctra, was no match alone for the invaders. Some of Sparta's allies from the Peloponnesus were expected to help, but they had not yet arrived, and many of the perioeci had gone over to the enemy. In these desperate straits, the authorities issued a proclamation inviting the helots to volunteer for service in return for grants of freedom, and Xenophon tells us that six thousand did so and were armed by the state. If we can believe him (Diodorus says that only one thousand helots volunteered), we must be as astonished at their numbers, as were the Spartans.[37]

It is indeed surprising to learn that so many helots were willing to risk their lives fighting on behalf of their masters in hopes of freedom; the traditional view would suggest rather that these same helots would have been ready to turn on their masters and to join the enemy at such a critical juncture. Many of the perioeci, indeed, had done exactly that, and some of the helots joined Epaminondas' forces, as both Xenophon and Plutarch tell us.[38] After the Spartans had equipped them from the public armories, they were made very uneasy by the sight of the large number of helots under arms, and the Spartans began to have second thoughts about the wisdom of their action. But when some faithful Peloponnesian allies and mercenary troops arrived to stiffen the resistance, the panic over the armed helots subsided.[39] What Xenophon fails to mention, but Plutarch reports,[40] is that danger threatened from quite another quarter entirely.

In this hour of peril, with Epaminondas and his army on the other side of the Eurotas and poised to attempt to cross the stream, Agesilaus learned of two separate plots involving Spartans. He dealt with each in turn, employing guile and force to eliminate the threat.[41] In the first instance, some two hundred Spartans had occupied a fortified place within Sparta called the Issorium, near the Temple of Artemis. They are described as having long been disaffected and mutinous, although the

---

[37]Xen. 6.5.28–9; Diod. 15.65.6.

[38]The passage in Xenophon, 7.2.2, which relates that "many of the perioeci had revolted, together with all of the helots, and nearly all of the allies," is obviously exaggerated and clearly contradicts 6.5.28–29. I accept the latter passage as correct in essentials and consider the former to be an inaccurate generalization, the product of carelessness, which does not vitiate the report of the recruitment of six thousand helots. See also Plut. *Ages.* 32.7.

[39]Xen. 6.5.29.

[40]Plut. *Ages.* 32.3–7.

[41]See E. David, "Revolutionary Agitation in Sparta after Leuctra," *Athenaeum*, n.s. 68 (1980):299–308.

reasons for their attitude are not given. Fearing the spread of an insurrection, Agesilaus chose not to attack them, but to trick them into a false
sense of security. He approached them alone, saying that they had
misunderstood his orders and that some of them were to go here, and
others there; in this way he dissolved the group, who responded to his
commands, thinking that their plot had been undiscovered. Agesilaus
then occupied the Issorium with other, loyal troops, arrested fifteen of
the conspirators, presumably the ringleaders, and had them summarily
executed at night.

As for the second incident, this involved an even larger number of
Spartans who had gathered together in a house to conspire. Once again,
judging that a trial in the circumstances was impractical, Agesilaus
conferred with the ephors, arrested the men, and put them to death
without trial. What is important to note is that both of these plots are
said to have been formed by Spartans, not helots or perioeci, and those
arrested and executed in summary fashion were citizens; Plutarch remarks that up to that time no Spartan had ever been put to death in this
way.[42] No reliable details are provided about the aims of these conspirators, but we may guess that they had in mind some redistribution of
wealth and power within the Spartan ruling class, if not the entire
overthrow of the government.

We learn that many of the perioeci and many of the helots were in
revolt against Sparta, and we may well assume that these were largely,
but not exclusively, the Messenian helots and perioeci in that area; the
further campaign of Epaminondas which resulted in the liberation of
Messenia incorporated them into the new polis. Furthermore, two
relatively small groups of Spartan citizens plotted rebellion of some
sort, but were foiled before they succeeded. And, finally, six thousand
helots volunteered to serve as soldiers for Sparta in return for their
future freedom; that is, in exchange for the status of neodamodeis.
Clearly it would be both inaccurate and misleading to assume that the
Thucydidean proposition regarding the helots as the principal threat to
Sparta could apply to this situation.[43] Although some helots did indeed
seize the opportunity to rebel, with success, from Spartan control,
others did not. Moreover, the state was threatened by other social
elements, both among the Spartans themselves and among the perioeci.
It is a pity that we do not hear about the hypomeiones in this context; it

[42]Plut. *Ages.* 32.6.
[43]Thuc. 4.80: "The policy of the Lacedaemonians was governed at all times by the
necessity of taking precautions against the helots." On this topic, see Talbert, "Role of
the Helots," 22–40.

would be very instructive indeed to know how they responded to this crisis, and whether it had anything to do with the issues that were involved in Cinadon's conspiracy.

Xenophon's silence on this question, and indeed on the Spartan plots that Plutarch reports, is not difficult to explain. Xenophon's history is full of omissions, most notably at this point the entire campaign of Epaminondas which liberated Messenia![44] If he could ignore so momentous a military and political event, how much easier to pass over in silence the evidence of deep and serious political and social disaffection within the Spartan polity itself, if his informants even told him of this. A final point to seize is that Agesilaus seems to have been completely in control at Sparta, both in directing the defense and in dealing with these plots. It is Plutarch who tells us that all agree (and here he is speaking of those who wrote on this matter) that Agesilaus saved Sparta at this point, but also that he could not restore his city's power and reputation.[45] In this he was correct.

Devoid of all but a relative handful of allies from within the Peloponnesus, the Spartans decided to turn to Athens for aid after the withdrawal of the enemy from Laconia. An embassy was sent to Athens, in company with representatives of their allies, especially the Corinthians and Phliasians, and an appeal made for military assistance. The Athenians must have been alarmed at the bold stroke of the Thebans in extending their influence into the Peloponnesus, and they had no wish to see Sparta destroyed forever. Without a counterweight in the south, Athens might well find itself threatened by its powerful neighbor along an uncomfortably long border. In fact, it was probably at this time that the Athenians put into commission the system of border defense so well described by J. Ober.[46] They voted to send help to Sparta and immediately dispatched Iphicrates with a force to Corinth.[47] By this time, Epaminondas had completed his work in Messenia, and his campaign had already lasted four months. Many of his Argive and Elean allies were beginning to melt away to their homes, his supplies were running short, and his Boeotian troops wanted to return home. Thus he prepared to march through Arcadia to regain Boeotia via the isthmus.[48] Xenophon criticizes Iphicrates for failing to hold the pass east of Cor-

---

[44]For a discusssion of the numerous omissions in Xenophon, see Cawkwell's "Introduction" to the Penguin translation of the *Hellenica,* pp. 33–38.

[45]Plut. *Ages.* 33.1–2.

[46]Ober, *Fortress Attica,* pp. 111–207, at 191–207 esp.

[47]Xen. 6.5.33–49.

[48]Xen. 6.5.50.

inth, but unfairly so, for his purpose was probably primarily to speed Epaminondas on his way rather than to attempt battle with him.[49] In any case, by early spring the Theban invaders had departed, and Sparta could begin to survey the effects of the invasion. Without exaggeration, the results could be called appalling for them.

First, the Spartan alliance system had almost completely collapsed. Of the ten military divisions organized in 378, only four remained more or less intact. The three districts composed of Achaea, of Corinth and Megara, and of Sicyon and Phlius, as far as we can tell, remained loyal to Sparta. In addition, a few Arcadian communities were still inclined to follow Sparta's lead, but it was questionable whether they could withstand pressure from the Arcadian federation to join that now-powerful state. Next, as for the district represented by the Lacedaemonians themselves, the loss of Messenia and the rebellion of numerous perioeci no doubt meant that the forces available from this quarter were far fewer than they had been less than a decade earlier. Thus, the manpower reserves available to Sparta in the pursuit of any future goals were severely limited, as the state would learn. The existence of an independent Messene, moreover, represented a thorn in Sparta's side, because it would act as a magnet for any future rebellious helots or perioeci from Laconia. The Spartans would stolidly refuse to recognize Messenian independence down to the time of Philip and Alexander, and beyond, despite almost universal recognition of Messene as a polis elsewhere in Greece, and even in Persia.[50] This fact underscored a third aspect of their situation in and after 369: their growing isolation, politically and diplomatically. Whatever its shortsightedness in other areas, the government of Agesilaus recognized the need to combat this deficiency, and it sent another embassy to Athens in an attempt to combat its isolation.[51]

After the return of Epaminondas to Thebes, where he and Pelopidas had to face charges of illegally overstaying their term of command, Sparta sought a formal alliance with Athens. Its intent here was to formalize the ad hoc assistance rendered at the height of the invasion.[52]

---

[49]Xen. 6.5.51–52.

[50]See Isocrates' speech *Archidamus*, which purportedly was written for Agesilaus' son. The setting is the early 360s, and Archidamus is made to argue vigorously against acceptance of Messenian independence, representing control of Messenia as the birthright of the Spartans. For discussion, see C. D. Hamilton, "The Early Career of Archidamus," *EMC/CV* 26, n.s. 1 (1982):5–20, at 10–11 esp.

[51]Xen. 7.1.1. See D. J. Mosley, "Pharax and the Spartan Embassy to Athens in 370/69," *Historia* 12 (1963):247–50.

[52]According to Xen. 7.1.1, this embassy occurred "in the following year" and there-

Among other things, the two principal parties negotiated agreement on Athens' right to claim Amphipolis, and Sparta's to Messenia. On this occasion, the same Phliasian envoy, Procles, who had spoken so eloquently on Sparta's behalf in the winter, urged the acceptance of an alliance "on equal terms." This was interpreted to mean that the Athenians would command on the sea, while the Lacedaemonians held the command of land forces—in effect, a recognition of the respective hegemony of the two powers. But an Athenian, Cephisodorus, challenged the wisdom of such an arrangement, quite correctly pointing out that the Spartans would for the most part send helots and perioeci as sailors, so that Athens would command non-free elements, whereas the Spartans would be in charge of Athenian citizen troops in any land operations. The upshot of the matter was that the two powers agreed to rotate the command in all operations, each holding it for five days at a time.[53] The entire discussion indicates that the Athenians and Spartans were still thinking in terms of dividing the hegemony of the Greek world between them, as Isocrates, for example, had urged in 380,[54] and thus excluding Thebes from such a role. But this was not only a shortsighted but also an unrealistic view; while Athens might still aspire to naval hegemony, Sparta's days as hegemon in Greece were already at an end. In any case, when the terms of the alliance had been set, the Athenians sent off an army to Corinth to join the Spartans and their remaining allies in order to prevent the expected second Theban invasion of the Peloponnesus.[55] This was not long in occurring.

The Invasion of Summer 369

In summer 369, the Arcadians and their Peloponnesian allies sent to Thebes, requesting that another army be sent to their aid. The Boeotian assembly responded positively to this request, and appointed Epaminondas, as Boeotarch, to lead the invasion.[56] Epaminondas, as well as

fore in spring 369, in all likelihood; cf. G. E. Underhill, *A Commentary with Introduction and Appendix on the "Hellenica" of Xenophon* (Oxford, 1900), p. xciv. But see also Wiseman, "Epaminondas," 177–99, on chronological problems in the 360s. Wiseman argues, 192–95 and 197, that Epaminondas' second invasion of the Peloponnesus was in 368, rather than in 369. I favor the 369 date.

[53]Xen. 7.1.2–14; Diod. 15.67.1.
[54]Isoc. 4.129ff.; see the discussion in Hamilton, "Isocrates," 95–97.
[55]Xen. 7.1.15; Diod. 15.68.1.
[56]Diod. 15.68.1. See Buckler, *Theban Hegemony,* pp. 93–102.

his fellow Boeotarchs on the board of 370, had been brought to trial upon their return from the invasion of winter 370/69. They had all clearly violated the law which demanded that the Boeotarchs surrender their authority at the end of their term of office to the successive college of officials, but Epaminondas argued persuasively that expediency had demanded the continuation of their campaign into 369. When he said that he would willingly die as the law required, but that he wanted his accomplishments engraved on his tombstone as his, not Boeotia's, the jury dismissed the charges.[57] Thus, once again in command of his national army, Epaminondas led a force of some seven thousand infantry and six hundred cavalry toward the isthmus. His intention was to strike at Sparta's remaining allies within the Peloponnesus—the Corinthians, Sicyonians, Epidaurians, and others who had aided it in the previous year and still remained loyal—in an effort to reduce the power of Sparta's alliance still further. There was little point in invading Laconia again, for the land had not yet recovered from the ravaging of the previous winter, and Messene was not threatened.[58] The Arcadians had already demonstrated Sparta's vulnerability by attacking Pellana in northwest Laconia, which they captured by force, slaying a garrison of three hundred Lacedaemonians.[59] Epaminondas' objective was to harass and attack Sparta's allies whose lands stretched like a security belt across the northern Peloponnesus, from Epidaurus, Halieis, and Troizene in the northeast, through Corinthian and Phliasian territory near the isthmus, to Sicyon and Pellene along the Corinthian Gulf west of Corinth. Epaminondas hoped to pressure them so much that some of them, if not all, would desert Sparta's cause, thus further weakening and isolating Sparta.

Epaminondas encountered resistance from the Spartans, Athenians, and various loyal Peloponnesian contingents in the vicinity of Corinth, but he was able to force his way into the Peloponnesus. In anticipation of the Theban invasion, and the necessity of Epaminondas to link up his forces with those of his Arcadian allies south of the isthmus, the Spartans and their allies had determined to hold the passes at the isthmus. An Athenian force under Chabrias arrived in time to hold the main road past Corinth to Argos, while a force commanded by a Spartan polemarch held the eastern pass over Mount Oneion. In addition, the line

[57]Plut. *Pelop.* 25.1–2; Paus. 9.14.7. See Buckler, *Theban Hegemony,* pp. 138–43 and 304 n.55, on the trial, as well as J. Buckler, "Plutarch on the Trials of Pelopidas and Epameinondas (369 B.C.)," *CP* 73 (1978):36–42.

[58]Xen. 7.1.18; Diod. 15.69.1.

[59]Diod. 15.67.2.

from Corinth's port on the Saronic Gulf, Cenchreae, to its other port on the Corinthian Gulf, Lechaion, was fortified with palisades and ditches, which were quickly constructed by the large force of some twenty thousand gathered there.[60] Epaminondas first reconnoitered the situation, and then he determined to assault the pass over Oneion held by the Spartans and Pellenians. He managed to surprise the Spartan-led garrison at the changing of the watch, and the polemarch drew his force back, in disorder, to a nearby defensible height. Epaminondas considered the advisability of a frontal assault on the position and decided against it. He reasoned that the cost was not worth the effort, and he struck a truce that allowed the Spartan force to depart and the Thebans to cross the pass to join their Arcadian allies at Nemea.[61] From there they marched on Sicyon and Pellene. The former was attacked and surrendered after a short time; Epaminondas garrisoned the city but made no changes in its government. Then Pellene was approached, but that city apparently capitulated without any resistance and was made secure for the Thebans and Arcadians. Thus bases had been established on the southern shore of the Corinthian Gulf, which could serve for the transport of troops from central Greece to the Peloponnesus, if need be. And, of course, Sparta had been deprived of two more allied cities.[62]

Next Epaminondas countermarched eastward to Epidauria, where he failed to take any of the well-garrisoned cities but did extensively ravage their territories. Finally, he turned back again toward Corinth, the key point in holding the isthmus, and he succeeded in reaching the city wall by a quick march over the saddle between the Acrocorinth and its western spur, the hill called Penteskouphi. An encounter occurred near the Phliasian gate in the western portion of the Corinthian city walls, but the Athenian Chabrias not only managed to beat off the Theban attack, but also inflicted a defeat upon the Thebans, who recovered their dead under truce.[63]

At this juncture, help arrived unexpectedly for the Spartans in the form of twenty triremes sent by Dionysius I of Syracuse. The Celts, Iberians, and horsemen were a welcome addition to the forces in Corinth, and they played a small role thereafter.[64] Epaminondas made no further attempt on the virtually impregnable walls of Corinth, but

---

[60]Xen. 7.1.15; Diod. 15.68.2–3.

[61]Xen. 7.1.15–17; Diod. 15.68.4–5.

[62]Xen. 7.1.18, cf. 2.11; Diod. 15.69.1; Polyaenus 5.16.3; Paus. 6.3.3. See Buckler, *Theban Hegemony*, pp. 93–104.

[63]Xen. 7.1.18–19; Diod. 15.69.1–4.

[64]Xen. 7.1.20–22; Diod. 15.70.1.

contented himself with ravaging the rich fields west of the city, along the coastal plain. This activity prompted only desultory cavalry action from the troops of Dionysius. When they scored some minor victories over his pillagers, Epaminondas dismissed his Peloponnesian allies and led his Boeotian troops home via the isthmus. His campaign was certainly less dramatic and less fruitful than that of the previous year, but it did produce results. Several of the allies of Sparta had been won (or forced) away from its alliance; others had suffered serious devastation of their lands, while the Spartans did nothing to protect them. In the future, only Corinth and Phlius remained actively engaged in the war on the side of Sparta, and even their enthusiasm was waning. The showing of the polemarch who had been defeated at the pass, and then retired under truce to save his remaining troops, reflected poorly on the Spartans and their military reputation. As the campaigning season drew to a close, Sparta's remaining Peloponnesian allies began to give thought to a diplomatic solution to the conflict. An opportunity to exercise such a solution was offered during the ensuing winter of 369/68.

The Diplomacy of Philiscus at Delphi

In spring 368, Philiscus of Abydus arrived in Greece to negotiate an end to the fighting.[65] He had been sent by the satrap Ariobarzanes and the Great King, Artaxerxes, who were anxious to bring an end to warfare in Greece in order to be able to recruit Greek mercenaries for service again in the Persian Empire. Artaxerxes was still anxious to reclaim his rebellious province of Egypt, and there were signs already of widespread rebellions, which would soon occur and would constitute what has been called the "Great Satraps' Revolt."[66] Peace in Greece, to produce a fertile recruiting ground for mercenaries, was highly desirable in Persia. Acting on his instructions, Philiscus convened a congress of Greeks at Delphi. The selection of such a neutral site is indicative of the judgment that neither Sparta nor Athens was any longer powerful enough to provide a suitable location for a major diplomatic conference. Xenophon mentions only the Thebans, their allies, and the Lacedaemonians among those gathered at Delphi, but Diodorus' account implies that others were there as well, and it is quite likely that the Athenians

[65]Xen. 7.1.27, cf. 5.1.28; Diod. 15.70.2.
[66]See A. T. Olmstead, *History of the Persian Empire* (Chicago, 1948), pp. 411–14; and J. M. Cook, *The Persian Empire* (New York, 1983), pp. 220–22, on Persia and the "Great Satraps' Revolt."

took part in the proceedings. In any case, the conference achieved nothing, because the Thebans refused to surrender their claims over Boeotia, nor would they agree that Messene should be subject once again to Sparta.[67] Indeed, viewed objectively, the situation was such as to give the Thebans no reason whatsoever to make concessions. They were still very powerful, with strong allies in the Peloponnesus, and Sparta appeared to have its back to the wall. There were no incentives for the Thebans to undo their accomplishments, and even the veiled hint of Persian intervention on behalf of Sparta had no effect. As a result, Philiscus departed unsuccessful, but not before he had recruited and paid a picked mercenary force of two thousand to serve with the Spartans.[68]

Although Philiscus had failed in his principal mission, to make peace in Greece, his intervention had given heart to the Spartans. The mercenary force that he had supplied stiffened their military strength, and the arrival soon after of a second force sent by Dionysius of Syracuse added another important contingent to their army. Thus, they debated whether to send the newly arrived force to Thessaly, to oppose Theban activities there, or to Laconia. Although the Athenians pushed for sending the Syracusan force to Thessaly, the Spartans prevailed, and they were shipped around the Peloponnesus to Gytheion. In command of a considerable force of allies, mercenaries, and Lacedaemonian citizen troops, Archidamus took the field and launched an invasion of Arcadia.[69] The situation had been reversed from the pattern of the two previous years, in which the Spartans had been on the defensive against invasions. One of the principal reasons for Archidamus' success in invading Arcadia was that the Thebans declined to come to the aid of their southern allies in 368. Internal politics in Boeotia, as well as more pressing concerns in Thessaly, explain this decision, which was to have an important effect on events in Arcadia.[70] In the meantime, Archidamus did not waste any time in carrying out his plans for a retaliatory invasion of his northern neighbors. He struck swiftly at the garrison in Caryae, which he caught by surprise and executed to a man, and then he marched over the border into Arcadia proper. After ravaging the land of

[67]See Xenophon, 7.1.27, for Messenia; and Diodorus, 15.70.2, on Boeotia. Ryder, Appendix V, "Philiscus' Peace Proposals," in *Koine Eirene,* pp. 134–35, treats this topic.
[68]Xen. 7.1.27; Diod. 15.70.2; see Buckler, *Theban Hegemony,* pp. 102–4.
[69]Xen. 7.1.28.
[70]Epaminondas faced his second trial and was deposed from the office of Boeotarch; cf. Diod. 15.72.1–2; Plut. *Pelop.* 28.1. See also Buckler, "Plutarch on the Trials," 36–42; and idem, *Theban Hegemony,* pp. 105ff.

the Parrhasians, he retired to a defensible position in the hills near Melea when a mixed force of Arcadians and Argives mustered to support the Parrhasians. At this point, the commander of the Syracusan force indicated that the time allotted for his campaigning had run out and that he had to withdraw his troops. As he was retiring toward Laconia, a Messenian force attacked his troops. He sent to Archidamus for aid. The prince responded immediately, and he joined the Syracusans, but then the combined force found itself blocked in its march to Sparta by the Argives and Arcadians.[71] Archidamus prepared to give battle, drew up his phalanx, and engaged the enemy. The Arcadians fled almost at the first stroke of battle, and Archidamus won a signal victory, killing numbers of the fleeing enemy and losing not a single man himself. The news of this Tearless Victory heartened the Spartans greatly, for it was the first real victory they had enjoyed since before the Battle of Leuctra. Archidamus set up a trophy and sent a herald to announce the news at Sparta. Upon hearing it, the authorities, beginning with Agesilaus and including the ephors and the members of the Gerousia, all wept tears of joy.[72]

Xenophon mentions that the Eleans and the Thebans were almost as pleased at the news of the Arcadian defeat as the Spartans, for they were becoming exasperated with Arcadian presumption. The Eleans had originally refused the Peace of Athens in 371 in the hopes of recovering their border territory of Triphylia, but the Triphylians claimed to be Arcadians and applied to join the new Arcadian federation. Lycomedes and the other Arcadian leaders received the Triphylians into the union, and this caused a rift between Elis and Arcadia.[73] And the Thebans were growing resentful of a series of campaigns in the Peloponnesus which were costly to them but seemed to bring advantage only to the Arcadians. Thus, the stage was set for a falling out among the allies who had wrought such havoc on Sparta between 370 and 368. The Spartans quickly attempted to exploit this situation to their own advantage. Buoyed no doubt by the encouragement of Philiscus, and their military success in 368, they decided to send envoys to Persia to seek Persian intervention once again in Greek affairs. But they had not counted on the skillful diplomacy of Pelopidas, who managed to turn a conference in Persia in 367 to his advantage.

[71]Xen. 7.1.28–29.
[72]Xen. 7.1.30–32; Diod. 15.72.3; Plut. Ages. 33.3–5.
[73]Xen. 7.1.32, cf. 23–26.

The Peace Negotiations of 367

It is clear from Xenophon's account, and corroborated by that of Plutarch,[74] that the Lacedaemonians took the initiative for the negotiations in Susa. The Spartan Euthycles was already at the Persian court when the Thebans proposed to send their own envoys to counteract the diplomacy of their foes. Pelopidas was chosen as ambassador from Thebes, and, when the Thebans invited their Peloponnesian allies to accompany them, the Eleans sent Archidamus, the Arcadians sent Antiochus, and the Argives sent an envoy who is unnamed. The Athenians, hearing the news, sent Timagoras and Leon. From the outset, Pelopidas enjoyed a great advantage over the other diplomats. He could argue that his state had, alone of all the Greeks, fought on the Persian side at Plataea—a dubious point, perhaps, from the patriotic viewpoint, but diplomatically useful in the circumstances—and that Thebes had taken no part in warfare against Persia since, which, manifestly, neither Athens nor Sparta could claim. His exploits at Leuctra had already been noised abroad, and the man who had blockaded Agesilaus between Eurotas and Taygetus deserved praise for thus cowing the commander who had threatened the Persian control of western Asia Minor in the 390s.[75] Furthermore, Artaxerxes believed Pelopidas' proposals to be simpler than the Athenians' and more acceptable than the Spartans'. Although these terms are not detailed, we may surmise that they included recognition for recent Athenian expansion into the Aegean area and Spartan claims to reassert their authority within the Peloponnesus, including the reduction of Messene as a *sine qua non* for peace.

Artaxerxes rightly saw no particular reason to approve of such requests, which would have overturned the status quo in Greece, coming as they did from states that had often been hostile to Persia in the past. Instead, Artaxerxes granted Pelopidas' request to issue a rescript reasserting the autonomy of all poleis, including the right of Messene to exist, and requiring the beaching of the Athenian fleet—a veiled reference to Athenian maritime expansion, both within and outside of the Second Athenian League. The terms also seem to have included recognition of Arcadia's right to Triphylia and granting to Amphipolis the status of friend and ally of the Great King.[76] The Athenian envoy Leon

---

[74]Xen. 7.1.33; cf. Plut. *Pelop.* 30.1.

[75]Xen. 7.1.33–35; Plut. *Pelop.* 30.1–2.

[76]Xen. 7.1.35–37; Plut. *Pelop.* 30.3–5; see Ryder, *Koine Eirene*, pp. 80–82, and Appendix VI, p. 136, for discussion of the terms and citations of other sources.

objected to such terms, and Artaxerxes made a concession, instructing the Athenians, if they knew of more just proposals, to put them to him.[77] At the time, however, nothing came of this offer on his part. The Athenians then returned to Greece with the other ambassadors, whereupon Leon charged his colleague with accepting bribes and conspiring with Pelopidas. Timagoras, therefore, was condemned to death.[78]

At a later date, the Thebans invited representatives from the states to come to Thebes to hear what the Great King had decreed. Ambassadors did come, but when they were asked to swear oaths to accept the Great King's dictates, they refused, saying that their instructions had only been to listen to the Great King's word, and not to swear to accept it. If the Thebans wished to have the states take oaths, they could send to the individual cities, as had been done after the Peace of Athens in 371. Lycomedes and the envoys from Arcadia left Thebes in a huff, asserting that it was not even proper for the conference to have taken place in a city that was not the seat of war. Their abrupt departure adumbrated future dissention between Arcadia and Thebes. Of course, the Athenians would have nothing to do with these terms, and, at Sparta, Agesilaus himself appears to have opposed the peace.[79]

Faced with no other alternative, the Thebans sent ambassadors to the various cities, believing that each would be compelled to sign the agreement in this fashion. But the Corinthians, who were first pressed to take the oath, replied that they had no wish to share an oath with the Great King, and other cities followed the Corinthian lead. Thus, in the end, the attempt of Thebes to gain hegemony in Greece with the support of the Great King failed, although the agreement reaffirmed a basic principle long ago accepted in Greek interstate diplomacy, the autonomy of all cities, great and small.[80] And Messene failed to receive formal recognition of its right to exist. Agesilaus in particular had opposed this, although of course none of the erstwhile allies of Thebes would have refused to resist any Spartan attempt to reduce Messene by

[77]Xen. 7.1.37.

[78]Xen. 7.1.38; Plut. *Artax.* 22.5–6; *Pelop.* 30.6–7. See D. J. Mosley, "Leon and Timagoras: Co-envoys for Four Years?" *GRBS* 9 (1968):157–60.

[79]Plut. *Ages.* 34.2. Plutarch also remarks on the suicide of Antalcidas (*Artax.* 22.4), following a diplomatic reversal at Persian hands, and some scholars have dated this to 367. Buckler, however, has argued against such an interpretation in "Plutarch and the Fate of Antalkidas," *GRBS* 18 (1977):139–45, in which he suggests that the suicide of Antalcidas is better located after the Common Peace of 362/1, which followed the Second Battle of Mantineia. The problem seems intractable, but I am inclined to place the mission of Antalcidas to Persia and his suicide in 367/6. See the Epilogue.

[80]Xen. 7.1.39–40; see Ryder, *Koine Eirene,* p. 81.

force. But such an action was no longer within Sparta's power. The impassioned speech attributed to the young Spartan prince, Archidamus, and written by Isocrates, if it belongs to this period, was unsuccessful.

In spring 367, Epaminondas invaded the Peloponnesus again, managing to bypass the troops guarding the pass at Mount Oneion and entering Achaea, his objective. This area had remained faithful to Sparta, one of the few allies in the Peloponnesus to do so, and Epaminondas wished to change all that. He established control, but did not leave garrisons or change governments there. After his return to Boeotia, appeals from the democratic factions in Achaea resulted in the dispatch of Theban harmosts and garrisons, and the exile of aristocratic elements from the cities. These exiles then banded together and managed to regain control of their cities, despite the Theban garrisons, and then became even more committed to the Spartans. Thus, Boeotian policy in Achaea was a failure.[81]

Toward the end of 367, the situation in Greece remained unstable, with neither Thebes, Athens, nor Sparta in a clear position of dominance. Within the Peloponnesus, matters were even more complicated, for the Eleans and the Arcadians had fallen out over Triphylia, and there was growing evidence of Arcadian disaffection toward Thebes.

The Events of 366 and Their Sequel

Following the failure of the Thebans to organize a peace in Greece to their liking, a period of frenetic and chaotic activity ensued. Within the Peloponnesus, Elis and Arcadia fell out, while Arcadia itself began to be split into factions. Athens began more energetic efforts to extend its control over areas that it had held in the fifth century, and whose loss it had always bitterly felt, specifically, the city of Amphipolis and the Thracian Chersonesus. The Thebans were preoccupied with events in the north, in Thessaly and Macedon, and they failed to exert satisfactory leadership within the Peloponnesus. The Spartans cast about for assistance, and they resorted to sending their now-aged king, Agesilaus, to Asia Minor to assist the satrap Ariobarzanes as a mercenary general; the state needed all the money it could raise to hire mercenary soldiers to help in the ongoing struggle against Arcadia.[82]

[81]Xen. 7.1.41–43.
[82]Xenophon (*Ages.* 2.25–27) says that Agesilaus went to Asia Minor as an envoy, not

The Athenians elected Timotheus general again for 366/5, for the first time since he had been deposed and brought to trial in 373. His return to active service coincided with a period of intense naval activity in the northeastern Aegean. First Timotheus went to the aid of Ariobarzanes, who had favored the Spartans and Athenians at the time of Philiscus' mission to Greece. But he had been given explicit instructions not to do anything that was against the interests of the Great King. Thus, he seems to have broken off his contact with Ariobarzanes in order to put Samos under siege. A Persian garrison apparently held that island in contravention of the autonomy provisions of the peace.[83] In any case, Timotheus maintained the siege for some ten months, until he took the island, probably in midsummer 365. Shortly thereafter, an Athenian cleruchy was dispatched to the island. Although not in technical violation of the provisions of the Aristoteles Decree, this action was certainly a violation of the spirit of that document, and Athens' remaining allies began to suspect its motives.[84] Following this action, in all probability, Timotheus then operated in the area of the Chersonesus, where he received from Ariobarzanes not money for his services, as did Agesilaus, but rather control of two towns, Sestus and Crithote.[85]

While these events were transpiring, matters in Greece had developed apace. In early 366, the Thebans had seized control of Oropus in northeastern Boeotia. Oropus had been in and out of Athenian control for a long time, and was important as a loading port for grain sent over from Euboea. When the Athenians marched out and sent for their allies in the Peloponnesus to assist in retaking Oropus, they were met with a cool response: none of the allies came.[86] Thus, they had to leave Oropus under Theban control. As a result, the influence of Callistratus, who had been the principal architect of Athenian foreign policy since the early 370s, was severely curtailed. He was brought to trial and, although acquitted, nonetheless lost his political influence for the next few years.[87] Iphicrates now was sent out to recover Amphipolis, which

---

as a mercenary. Nonetheless, in the course of his adventures there, which Xenophon mentions only very briefly, Mausolus and others seem to have rewarded him amply. We need not doubt that his mission was a mercenary one, as was his subsequent service in Egypt.

[83]Nepos *Tim.* 1.3; Dem. 9.16; 19.137; Isoc. 15.111. On Timotheus' activities in these years, see L. Kallet, "Iphikrates, Timotheos, and Athens, 371–360 B.C.," *GRBS* 24 (1983):239–52.

[84]Isoc. 15.111. See Cargill *SAL*, pp. 148–49, on the Samian cleruchy.

[85]Nepos *Tim.* 1.3.

[86]Xen. 7.4.1.

[87]See B. R. Sealey, "Callistratus of Aphidna and His Contemporaries," *Historia* 5

had been recognized as belonging of right to the Athenians by the assembled Greeks, the Great King of Persia, and King Amyntas of Macedon at the Peace Conference in Sparta in 371.[88]

For the next several years, the Athenians operated in the area and, although they failed to recapture Amphipolis, they did take Pydna and other places along the coast of the Thermaic Gulf. As a further indication of the shift in Athenian foreign policy, Athens made an alliance with Arcadia, engineered by Lycomedes. This meant that it was allied with Arcadia, which was at war with Sparta, also its ally; a complicated situation indeed, but the result no doubt of Athenian perceptions that the Spartans were little interested in helping them, but rather in whatever help they could get from Athens in the south.[89]

The Athenians, fearing loss of control of Corinth and the possibility of Theban seizure of that city, decided to take the city themselves by a coup. This policy had been debated in open assembly in Athens, and the decision was not slow to reach the Corinthians. In turn, the Corinthians relieved the Athenian garrison, which was on duty in Corinth, and they refused to admit the fleet that Chabrias brought to Cenchreae in his abortive attempt to seize control of the city. This rather perfidious act of the Athenians, however, determined the Corinthians to make one more effort to seek safety through a treaty.[90] They sent to Thebes to seek to negotiate a peace. When the Thebans said that they would entertain proposals, the Corinthians sought and received permission to ask others to join with them, including the Spartans. Surprisingly, the Spartans indicated that they could not defend the interests of the Corinthians and the others, and gave their permission to them to make a separate peace with Thebes, although they would continue to fight to recover Messenia. This would have been in 366, and it must have occurred while Agesilaus was still out of Sparta serving as a mercenary with Ariobarzanes; he would never have permitted the few remaining allies of Sparta to defect in such a fashion, and especially to make peace with his inveterate enemy, Thebes.[91]

Thus the Corinthians, along with other envoys from the smaller

(1956):178–203; reprinted in his *Essays in Greek Politics* (New York, n.d.), pp. 133–63, at 149.

[88]Dem. 19.253; Aesch. 2.32–33.

[89]Xen. 7.4.2.

[90]Xen. 7.4.4–5.

[91]Xen. 7.4.6–9, *Ages.* 2.26–27. Isocrates' speech *Archidamus,* in which the prince is made to argue vigorously against the surrender of Messenia, is probably to be dated to this occasion. See n. 50 above.

Peloponnesian states still allied with Sparta, returned to Thebes. There the Thebans tried to convince them not only to make peace, but also to conclude an alliance with them, but the Corinthians refused, saying that to exchange one alliance for another was merely to change sides in the war, and not to achieve peace. The Thebans admired their courage, and granted a peace to the Corinthians, the Phliasians, and such others as had come with them, apparently including the Argives. Although Argos and Phlius continued to dispute some border territory between them, the settlement otherwise went into effect.[92] Thus, the results of the separate peace of 366 between Corinth, Phlius and others, and Thebes included the further decline of Sparta's Peloponnesian alliance. The district that had included Sicyon and Phlius was now gone; Sicyon had been lost to Thebes in the course of Epaminondas' second invasion of 369, and now Phlius no longer aided Sparta. As for that formed by Corinth and Megara, Corinth was also now unattached, and Megara is not mentioned as sending troops to assist Sparta at this period. In fact, the only one of the original ten military districts that Sparta had organized in 378 left to it to call upon for troops was that of Laconia itself, and perhaps a few Arcadian towns that had resisted the pressure to join the new Arcadian League and remained loyal to Sparta. To be sure, there were groups of exiles, from Tegea, Boeotia, Sicyon, and Achaea who still would fight for Sparta, but the Peloponnesian League itself was at an end. The news of the defection of Corinth and Phlius must have been bitter indeed for Agesilaus, when it reached him, in all probability, in Asia Minor.[93]

In 365 Epaminondas rather surprisingly proposed that the Thebans build and launch a fleet, apparently to contest control of the seas with Athens. Even more surprisingly, the Boeotian assembly accepted the proposal, and in 364 a fleet of a hundred ships was launched. Although it carried out some activity during that year, the entire project seems soon

[92]Xen. 7.4.10–11; Diod. 15.75.3. For the earlier history of affairs in Phlius, which Xenophon praises for its loyalty to Sparta throughout this period, see 7.2.1–12. No doubt Xenophon means to suggest that this loyalty was the result of Agesilaus' intervention in Phliasian affairs in the 380s, but the fact is that Phlius now left the Spartan cause and remained neutral for the next several years. See W. E. Thompson, "Chares at Phlius," *Philologus* 127 (1983):303–5, on an incident in Phlius' history in this period.

[93]Diod. 15.76.3. The nature of the conference that took place in Thebes in 366/5 has been much discussed. Cawkwell considers it to have been a Common Peace, arguing that Athens and Persia took part, whereas Ryder believes that it was not properly a Common Peace. See T. T. B. Ryder, "The Supposed Common Peace of 366/5 B.C.," *CQ*, n.s. 7 (1957):199–205; and G. L. Cawkwell, "The Common Peace of 366/5 B.C.," *CQ*, n.s. 11 (1961):80–86. I favor Ryder's view.

to have been abandoned, and little more is heard of the Theban fleet after 364.[94] Pelopidas met his death in Thessaly in 364, and with his passing one of the two great statesmen who had shaped Thebes' dominance of Greece in the 370s and 360s was lost.[95] But Thebes went on to expand its power. Thebes savagely destroyed Orchomenus, its age-old rival, in 364, to the horror of many of its contemporaries. This destruction was now added to that of Plataea in 373, and of Thespiae in the late 370s. The price of opposing Theban ambition in Boeotia was clear: annihilation.[96]

Meanwhile, in the Peloponnesus, strife between the Arcadian communities broke out. The immediate cause was the sacred shrine of Olympia. In their dispute with Elis over control of the cities of Triphylia, which had been admitted to the Arcadian federation, the Arcadians had invaded Elean territory and actually seized control of Olympia in 364. They then turned the shrine over to the control of the Pisatans, who had an ancient claim to preside over the games. Fighting back and forth went on between the Eleans and Arcadians for some time, and, in the course of it, the Arcadians began to make use of the extensive treasures of the shrine to pay their picked troops, the five thousand *eparitoi*.[97] The Mantineians objected to this misuse of sacred funds, and before long a rift had developed within the Arcadian League. By the end of 363, the situation had become quite fluid again, with the Eleans once more turning to Sparta for aid against the Arcadians, and the Arcadians themselves split into factions, with Mantineia favoring Elis and Sparta, and Tegea the Thebans. The stage was being set for the final invasion of the Peloponnesus by Epaminondas in the next year, 362. By then new coalitions had developed, and Sparta found itself able to count on aid from Athens, Elis, and Mantineia, as well as a few remaining members of its alliance, in opposition to the Thebans, Phocians, Locrians, Euboeans, and the bulk of the Arcadians, still aided by Argos, and Messene. Thus practically all the states of mainland Greece were involved in the great confrontation that was the Second Battle of Mantineia. Even King Agesilaus, back from service abroad, was able to play a role in the second defense of Sparta.

[94]Diod. 15.78.4–79.2. See Buckler, *Theban Hegemony*, pp. 160–75.
[95]Diod. 15.80.1–81.4; Plut. *Pelop.* 32.
[96]Diod. 15.79.3–6; cf. Isoc. 6.27 (Orchomenus is not mentioned there, but Plataea and Thespiae are); Paus. 9.14.2–4; Dem. 20.109; Plut. *Comp. Pelop. et Marcel.* 1.1.
[97]Xen. 7.4.13–32; Diod, 15.77.1–4, 78.2–3. See W. E. Thompson, "Arcadian Factionalism in the 360's," *Historia* 32 (1983):149–60, for discussion.

In Arcadia, the situation developed as follows. The Arcadian leaders were using the treasures of Olympia for the conduct of the war against Elis, and especially for the support of the special group known as the eparitoi. The Mantineians began to object to this illegal use of the sacred monies, and they voted to pay their share of the support monies due from their own revenues in Mantineia. The leaders[98] of the Arcadian League said that the Mantineians were doing harm to the league by so acting, and they summoned their rulers to come before the federal authorities. The Mantineian leaders refused to do so, and they were accordingly condemned *in absentia*. The eparitoi were then sent to Mantineia to arrest them. The Mantineians shut their gates and refused to give up their magistrates. This act caused other Arcadians to rethink the actions of the federal leaders, and a motion was passed in the Arcadian assembly known as the Ten Thousand to cease using the sacred monies. As a result, the eparitoi began to disintegrate, with those who required monetary support to continue quickly melting away, while others, who had no need of such money, joined in their place, in order to control the force. Clearly, the eparitoi were turning into an aristocratic, elite force, rather than the democratic army it had been.

At this point, the Arcadian leaders who had handled the sacred monies began to realize that they would be held responsible for their actions, and so they sent to Thebes, requesting intervention to prevent the Arcadians from going over again to Sparta. Whether the aristocratic elements within Arcadia would have gone so far in their fear and suspicion of the democrats is unclear, but the argument received credence in Thebes, and they now prepared to take the field for a fourth invasion of the Peloponnesus. But now, "those who had the best interests of the Peloponnesus at heart" (whatever Xenophon means by that) persuaded the general assembly of the Arcadians to send another embassy to Thebes, telling them not to come unless specifically summoned. They also negotiated with the Eleans to give back control of Olympia to them, and on these terms a truce was arranged. Thus, it seemed that the situation within Arcadia could be resolved without further fighting, although there was still tension between the aristocratic elements and the democrats in Mantineia.[99]

[98]Why doesn't Xenophon identify them by name? Surely he could have ascertained this information. Another Xenophontic mystery.

[99]Xen. 7.4.33–35; Diod. 15.82.1–2 has the Arcadian situation reversed, with Mantineia using the sacred monies. See Roy, "Arcadia and Boeotia," 584–88, for further discussion of this situation.

In Tegea, the situation deteriorated. All had taken oaths to uphold the settlement, including the Theban governors who chanced to be there in command of three hundred Boeotians. But while the bulk of the Arcadians, still in Tegea, made merry and celebrated, the Theban and those Arcadian leaders who were fearful about their accounts closed the city gates and, with the help of the Boeotians and their partisans among the eparitoi, proceeded to arrest the aristocrats. But the coup seems to have been rather a fiasco, with the jails unable to hold all of those arrested; most of the Mantineians, who were in any case the primary intended victims, managed to escape to their own city. There they raised a hue and cry, summoning the rest of the Arcadians to prepare to arm and to hold the passes. The Mantineians then sent to Tegea, demanding the release of all the Mantineians held, and forbidding the retention or execution of anyone without trial. They would give surety for any subsequently brought to trial. At a loss, the Theban governor released all those imprisoned. In his defense, he claimed that he had been deceived, having been told that the Spartans were in arms on the borders and that some Arcadians were planning to betray Arcadia. Although he was acquitted on the spot, he was nonetheless denounced at Thebes for misconduct. There Epaminondas argued that the governor had done nothing wrong, but rather that the Arcadians had acted wrongly in making peace with Elis without the consent of the Thebans, their allies. He said, therefore, that the Thebans would appear in Arcadia to wage war in company with those who agreed with them.[100]

When Epaminondas' speech had been reported to them, the Mantineians and some other Arcadians, as well as the Eleans and Achaeans, concerned that the Theban objective was to reduce the Peloponnesus to subjection, took measures for their security. They sent envoys to Athens, seeking aid, and to Lacedaemon. As for the question of leadership (a sticky issue in the Atheno-Spartan alliance of 369), it was agreed that each people would hold it in its own territory.[101]

The Battle of Mantineia

Epaminondas meanwhile was gathering his forces for the march to the Peloponnesus. He mustered all of the Boeotians, the Euboeans, and many Thessalians, but the Phocians refused to come, saying that their

[100]Xen. 7.4.36–40.
[101]Xen. 7.5.1–3; Diod. 15.82.4.

obligation was only to assist the Thebans when attacked.[102] Now
Epaminondas assembled his forces at Nemea, where he hoped to inter-
cept the Athenians in their advance by land from Athens. But the
Athenians learned of his plan and sent their infantry by sea, to land at
Gytheion, and to proceed to Arcadia through Laconia. When Epaminondas realized this, he marched on to Tegea, where his allies gathered.
There were, in addition to those from central Greece, Tegeans and other
Arcadians, Messenians, and Argives.[103] While Epaminondas was delay-
ing at Nemea, the enemy were gathering at Mantineia: Eleans, Achaeans, the remaining Arcadians, and Lacedaemonians and Athenians who
finally arrived via the sea and Laconia.[104] Epaminondas now marched
on to Tegea, where he encamped within the town walls (for which
Xenophon praises him in one of the few passages of the *Hellenica*
devoted to Epaminondas).[105]

As Epaminondas realized that no cities were coming over to him, that
is, that there were no disaffections among the enemy, and that time was
passing, he decided to risk a quick march to Sparta in a second invasion
of Laconia, while the principal forces were away. He learned that his
enemy, in a strong position at Mantineia, had sent for Agesilaus and the
Lacedaemonians to aid them and that Agesilaus was already at Pellana
on his outward march. Fortunately for Agesilaus, he discovered that
Epaminondas was descending on Sparta by a forced march, and he was
able to warn the defenders of the city and to turn his own forces back.
He arrived in time to direct the defense of Sparta, still unwalled.[106] This
time he took vigorous measures, stationing his men throughout the city
in positions of natural strength, from which they could minimize their
numerical inferiority. His son, Archidamus, was to play an important
role in the defense, leading a small group of one hundred men against
the advancing Thebans at one point, and driving them back with heavy
losses. Later, he set up a trophy to commemorate this minor victory.
The Spartan defenders were few, for their cavalry, their mercenaries,
and three of the twelve *lochoi* (companies) were away in Arcadia and

---

[102]Xenophon does not mention the Locrians, but Diodorus speaks of them as being at
the battle. Incidentally, the Achaeans mentioned by Diodorus (15.84.4) as present with
Epaminondas must be from Achaea Phthiotis in Thessaly, for the Peloponnesian
Achaeans were present on the side of the Spartan-Mantineian-Athenian alliance; cf.
Diod. 15.85.2 and Xen. 7.5.18.

[103]Xen. 7.5.4–7.

[104]Xen. 7.5.7.

[105]Xen. 7.5.8–9.

[106]Xen. 7.5.9–10; Plut. *Ages.* 34.3–4.

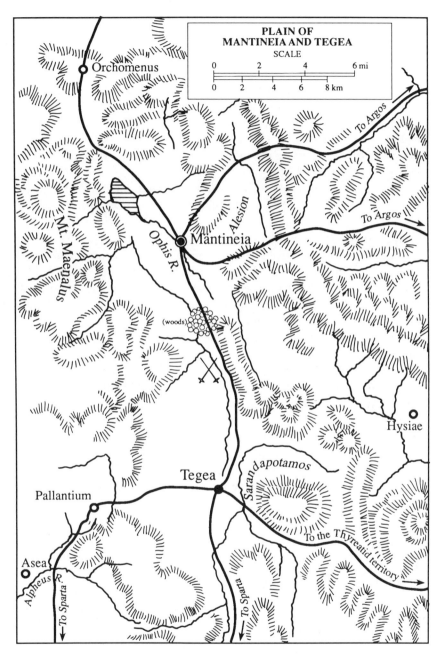

The Second Battle of Mantineia

unable to return in time.[107] Fighting developed both in the suburbs and within the city itself, for Epaminondas easily crossed the Eurotas, but the Spartans fought fiercely and drove back their attackers. Epaminondas now expected that the Arcadians would come to the aid of the Spartans, and their other elements would also soon return, and he had no heart for a fight against this combined force, especially after his recent defeat. Consequently, he beat a retreat to Tegea. There he rested his hoplites, but sent his cavalry on to Mantineia to attack the citizens who were then harvesting the fields, in the expectation that they would be largely undefended.[108]

There ensued a minor cavalry action near Mantineia, involving the Theban horse and the Athenians, who had come via Corinth, where they had been involved in a skirmish. Note that the Corinthians, as well as Megarians and Phliasians, are not mentioned as taking any part in the fighting; they were probably remaining neutral in keeping with their Peace of Thebes of 366.[109] In any case, the Athenians went out to protect the Mantineian harvesters and, although they sustained no small losses themselves, carried the engagement, erecting a trophy and handing back the enemy dead under truce. The engagement seems not to have had any particular impact on the confrontation, aside from spurring on both sides to engage their main forces. By now, Epaminondas had sustained two minor, but embarrassing, defeats: in the attack upon Sparta, which he had led in person, and in the cavalry fight at Mantineia, where his Theban and Thessalian force had been bested. Because the time was close at hand when he would have to return to Boeotia, Epaminondas decided to risk a major engagement of his entire army.[110] Thus the stage was set for the Battle of Mantineia itself.

Plutarch says that the battle occurred a few days after the attack upon Sparta.[111] When Epaminondas withdrew to Tegea, so did the allies to

---

[107]Xen. 7.5.10, cf. 4.20.

[108]Xen. 7.5.11–14; Plut. *Ages.* 34.4–8; Diod. 15.82.5–83.5; Polyb. 9.8.

[109]Xen. 7.5.15–17; on Megara, cf. Isoc. 8.118, and see R. P. Legon, *Megara: The Political History of a Greek City State to 336 B.C.* (Ithaca, N.Y., 1981), pp. 263–79, on Megara's role in this period. But the Megarians may have contested the passing of the Athenian horse, although certainly not the large army of Epaminondas on its march south earlier in the summer. Xenophon describes the cavalry encounter with some interest, and in some detail, possibly because it may have been this encounter in which his son Gryllus was killed as a horseman for the Spartans. Paus. 1.3.4 and 8.9.8–10; Diog. Laert. 2.54–5. See Anderson, *Xenophon*, pp. 193–94.

[110]Xen. 7.5.18. It is not clear whether the government had put a time limit on his expedition, or his allies had indicated that they would soon be departing.

[111]Plut. *Ages.* 35.1. Modern studies of the battle include Anderson, *Military Theory,*

Mantineia, in expectation of a battle. As a result, the confrontation took place in the plain between the two cities. The Theban force was commanded by Epaminondas, and it included the Boeotians, Thessalians, Euboeans, Argives, Messenians, Tegeates, and other Arcadians; that is, Megalopolitans, Aseans, Pallantians, and a few others.[112] The commander of the allied force is not named, although Diodorus says that there were several famous commanders in this battle and that their forces included the Lacedaemonians, Athenians, Eleans, Mantineians, and Achaeans. According to Diodorus, the Theban army numbered more than thirty thousand hoplites and not less than three thousand horse, while the allies had twenty thousand hoplites and two thousand horse; the only contingent whose specific size is given is the Athenian, with six thousand.[113] Xenophon provides few particulars on the order of battle, but Diodorus gives a very detailed description. In his account, the Thebans held their own left wing, supported by the Arcadians; their right was given to the Argives; and the center was held by Euboeans, Locrians, Sicyonians, Messenians, Malians, Aenianians, Thessalians, and other allies. This account agrees, so far as it can be determined, with that of Xenophon, who implies that the Thebans held their left wing.[114] In the opposite line, the Mantineians and other Arcadians held the right wing, supported by the Lacedaemonians next, and then the Eleans and Achaeans; the weaker forces were in the center (although it is difficult to ascertain who these were); and the Athenians held their left wing. Xenophon once again corroborates the presence of the Athenians on their left, but gives no other specifics on the dispositions of this army.[115]

Xenophon tells us that Epaminondas led his army out into the plain, toward the mountains west of Tegea, and, when he had reached their foot, he drew up his phalanx in battle order. Thus, having led the army, he would have been on its left flank when he wheeled the columns right into battle order. He then began to move successive companies to the wing where he was stationed, thus strengthening the mass formation on the left.[116] This tactic is reminiscent of Leuctra, where Epaminondas

---

pp. 221–24; and Buckler, *Theban Hegemony,* pp. 206–19. Lazenby, *Spartan Army,* p. 168, contains a mere mention.

[112]Xen. 7.5.4–5; Diodorus (15.85.2) gives essentially the same list, although he does not name the Euboeans or Messenians and in the order of battle he gives the Locrians, Malians, and Aenianians.

[113]Diod. 15.84.4, cf. 2.

[114]Diod. 15.85.2; cf. Xen. 7.5.21–22.

[115]Xen. 7.5.24.

[116]Xen. 7.5.22–23.

again had deepened his left wing to a depth of fifty shields in order to provide a massed array that would sweep its opposition before it. Xenophon mentions that the Athenians were faced by a combined force of horse and hoplites opposite them, on some low hills. Xenophon says nothing more about the dispositions before the actual battle.[117] In contrast, Diodorus gives a much more circumstantial account of the order of battle and the tactical dispositions. After describing the order of battle, he tells us that both sides disposed cavalry on each wing. Diodorus then describes a cavalry engagement which is not mentioned by Xenophon. Basically, the Theban cavalry on their left had the better of those opposed to them, and this gave the hoplites encouragement for the main engagement.[118]

Xenophon says, quite simply, that the attack of Epaminondas carried all before him, and that the enemy were in flight when he was himself struck down and carried, mortally wounded, from the field to the camp.[119] As a result, his troops failed to exploit their victory or to pursue the enemy. On the right wing, the footmen and peltasts followed up on the victory of their cavalry, but, as they pushed forward, most were slain by the Athenians. Thus, both sides claimed victory; both erected trophies; and both received back their dead under truce. The battle was a stalemate.[120]

Diodorus says that the Thebans attacked the Lacedaemonians and that this attack led to fierce fighting; there is not the precipitate flight mentioned by Xenophon, although eventually the Thebans drove off the Lacedaemonians. But then Epaminondas was mortally wounded by a spear. He says that, on the Theban right, the Euboeans were defeated by the Athenians, who seized the heights and claimed both the victory and the bodies of their slain enemies.[121] With the Theban victory over the Lacedaemonians, but the mortal wounding of Epaminondas, and the Athenian victory over their opponents, both sides claimed victory.

[117]Xen. 7.5.24.

[118]Diod. 15.85.2–8.

[119]Xen. 7.5.24–25. Agesilaus is nowhere attested as being in command of the Spartan forces at Mantineia, but scholars generally assume that he commanded there. See Buckler, *Theban Hegemony*: "The full Spartan contingent was still led by Agesilaus, the real commander of these forces, although Xenophon in deference to the old king mercifully omits all mention of him" (p. 216).

[120]Xen. 7.5.25–26.

[121]But how did the Euboeans get to the right wing, for Diodorus gave their position in the order of battle as holding the center, and apparently on the left of the center? This point is quite unclear.

Thus, the two accounts agree in major particulars, especially on the fact that the battle was a stalemate.[122] Plutarch's account in the *Agesilaus* merely discusses the wounding of Epaminondas and gives no details on troop dispositions or movements.

Before they retired from the field, the two armies concluded a truce, and both sides recovered their dead under truce. As Xenophon records, nothing substantial had been changed by the battle; neither side was any better off after the battle than before, either in territory, or city, or rule. Indecision and chaos descended upon Greece. Diodorus reports that after the battle the cities decided to make peace, and they did so upon the now-familiar terms of granting autonomy for all poleis. But the Spartans held out, refusing to recognize the independence of Messene, and as a result, they alone were excluded from the peace. Apparently the independence of the cities of Boeotia was a dead letter, or at least not an issue on which anyone now wished to insist.[123] If there were any real winners, we might conclude that the Thebans had had the better of things. But the loss of Epaminondas proved irrecoverable.

Xenophon closed his *Hellenica* with the account of the Battle of Mantineia. As so often elsewhere in his work, he refrained from any overall assessment of the significance of the battle, contenting himself with the remark that "there was even more confusion and disorder in Greece after than before the battle" and with the wish, if such it is, that "the events after these will perhaps be the concern of another writer."[124] In a real sense, Mantineia is a fitting point to conclude our study, although we should not miss the opportunity to assess its significance. Neither side had truly won, but this meant, for Sparta particularly, defeat of great proportions. Its hegemony was gone forever; the Peloponnesian League was no more; and its territory had shrunk to Laconia itself. But Agesilaus lived for another few years, into his eighties, and he would have one final adventure in a last, futile attempt to empower his state to reclaim its former position, before his death. This story is the subject of the Epilogue.

[122]Diod. 15.86.1–87.6; Xen. 7.5.26.
[123]Xen. 7.5.26–27; Diod. 15.89.1–2.
[124]Xen. 7.5.27.

The Final Years

Sparta's position after the Battle of Mantineia was even worse than it had been before. Exhausted by some fifteen years of war, the various Greek states decided once again to make peace. As the sources show, this was to be a Common Peace, and there is some evidence that the Great King of Persia had a hand in it.[1] There was to be an end to hostilities, with each state keeping the territories it then possessed, disbandment of armed forces, and the recognition of the principle of autonomy for all poleis. Sparta refused to recognize the existence of Messene, and as a result it was excluded from the peace. But unlike previous situations, Sparta was now virtually without allies in Greece. So long as other differences were either resolved or under adjudication, no state was prepared to aid Sparta in what would prove to be an abortive effort to recover Messenia. Left to their own devices, the Spartans had to seek other means to pursue their objective of reconquering Messenia.

Slim though it is, the evidence suggests that Agesilaus and his partisans were still dominant in Sparta. If Agesilaus had commanded at Mantineia, and therefore bore some of the blame for the poor showing of the Lacedaemonians on that occasion, there is no hint of criticism for this in the sources. Instead he is chastised in particular for failing to heal his state's wounds and for continuing to stir up trouble over Messenia.[2]

---

[1]Diod. 15.89.1; Plut. *Ages.* 35.3–4; Polyb. 4.33.8–9. See Ryder, Appendix 8, in *Koine Eirene,* pp. 140–44, and Tod, *GHI,* no. 145, 2:138–41.
[2]Plut. *Ages.* 35.3–4.

What Plutarch fails to recognize in this criticism is the contemporary perception that possession of Messenia was utterly essential to the integrity of the Lacedaemonian state; the land and its inhabitants had been held in subjection for 350 years, and the Spartans viewed its permanent loss as untenable.[3] Because the political situation had changed frequently over the last dozen years, perhaps the Spartans can be forgiven for what may appear as a shortsighted attitude. From their perspective, however, the recovery of Messenia was a *sine qua non* for a return to normalcy within the Peloponnesus. They reasoned that without Messenia their dominance of the region was at an end, and the Peloponnesian League could not be reconstituted. Unfortunately for them, the Spartans' narrow focus on the recovery of Messenia, and their refusal to enter into a peace that recognized its right to exist, put them *hors de combat* to any effective degree in Peloponnesian politics for the next several decades.[4] With the loss of their allies as sources of reinforcement, the Spartans were necessarily led to seek other means of augmenting their resources. They resorted to a policy often enough employed by the Athenians in this period, but one that seems rather pathetic in the case of Sparta: the hiring out of their best general, King Agesilaus, as a mercenary commander to the rebel king of Egypt, Tachos, for his planned invasion of Persian territory.

Xenophon makes every effort to put the best light on the Egyptian service of Agesilaus, providing several motives for his undertaking this assignment. Xenophon claims that the king was delighted when a summons came from Tachos to serve under him, for Agesilaus felt that he could thus repay the Egyptian for good offices to Sparta, set free the Greeks of Asia Minor once again, and pay back the Great King for his former hostility and for demanding that, while an ally of Sparta, they should surrender their claim to Messene. Quite clearly, Xenophon here tries to exonerate his hero from charges of demeaning himself by accepting mercenary service. The reasons he alleges for the act are at least slightly suspect.[5] For one thing, the good offices of Tachos to Sparta are not otherwise known. The reference to the liberation of the Greeks of Asia Minor, taken by some scholars as further proof of

[3]See Isoc. 6 (*Archid.*) 11–13, 16–32, and 70–79, for arguments to this effect. The dramatic date seems to be about 367/6, but the ideas presented and their justification surely fit the end of the 360s.
[4]See C. D. Hamilton, "Philip II and Archidamus," in *Philip II*, pp. 61–83, for detailed discussion of the reign of Archidamus, Agesilaus' son and successor, in this period.
[5]Xen. *Ages.* 2.28–9.

Agesilaus' continued panhellenic policy, is almost gratuitous. There was little chance that mercenary service to the Egyptian king would result in the liberation of the Greek cities, unless as a by-product of contributing to the success of the so-called Great Satraps' Revolt. But Agesilaus could hardly have convinced anyone that he actually hoped to liberate the Greeks through this course of action, and we must ask whether this was not the invention of Xenophon in response to some critic of Agesilaus' last campaign (as suggested by Plutarch's account). Finally, the reference to the king as "saying that he was now an ally" is at least rather puzzling. As far as we can judge, Sparta had been at war, at least indirectly, with the king since his sponsorship of the Peace of Pelopidas in 367. Agesilaus had campaigned on behalf of Ariobarzanes for an indefinite period of time starting in 366. If the Great King took part in the Peace of 362, following Mantineia, and supported the independence of Messene, as Xenophon says, then he could hardly be regarded as an ally by the Spartans. Buckler, however, places the occasion of diplomatic negotiations which led to the suicide of a disappointed Antalcidas at roughly this time.[6] But this scenario makes Antalcidas' mission to Susa coincide with Agesilaus' activity in Egypt. This is very difficult to accept, for it is not easy to see how the Spartans could hope to persuade the Great King to any beneficent course of action toward Sparta while their king was in service to a monarch regarded as a rebel by the Persian, and who was moreover planning an attack on Persian territory in Phoenicia at that very time. It seems best to accept the opinion of a majority of scholars who link the story of Antalcidas' last mission and suicide to the negotiations in Susa in 367.[7]

On the invitation of the Egyptian king, Agesilaus was sent out by formal decision of the Spartan state. He was accompanied by thirty councillors, as he had been in 396. With the money supplied by Tachos, he was able to recruit one thousand troops, which he took with him by ship to Egypt. These are much more likely to have been mercenaries than citizen troops, which Diodorus seems to imply.[8] When he arrived in Egypt, Agesilaus became the object of widespread attention, but he disappointed practically everyone because of his modest demeanor and ordinary dress; indeed, he almost became an object of derision. There were, no doubt, other, more cogent reasons for Tachos' decision to restrict him to the command of the Greek mercenaries, rather than to give him the overall command of the operations that he desired and had

[6]J. Buckler, "Plutarch and the Fate of Antalkidas," *GRBS* 18 (1977):139–45.
[7]Plut. *Artax.* 22.4; cf. Ryder, *Koine Eirene*, p. 81.
[8]Diod. 15.92.2.

expected. Tachos retained overall command himself, while delegating to Chabrias command of the fleet. Unlike Agesilaus, the latter had come as a private commander, and not in Athens' service. The date of Agesilaus' arrival in Egypt cannot be determined precisely, except that it was manifestly after the Peace Conference that followed Mantineia. I place his arrival sometime in the sailing season; that is, spring or summer 361. This would agree with the archon date given by Diodorus (Molon = 362/1), and, more importantly, with the information furnished by Xenophon and Plutarch about the king's age. Xenophon says that he was "about eighty" when he went out, and Plutarch records that he was eighty-four at the time of his death when returning from Egypt.[9]

After a period of preparation, Tachos launched his invasion of Phoenicia. This may have occurred in 360. While the army was conducting operations in Phoenicia and Syria, a revolt against the authority of Tachos took place in Egypt. Nameless in the sources, the rebel nominated his son Nektanebo, then in command of the Egyptian forces in Syria, to succeed as king. In the ensuing struggle, the support of Agesilaus, or rather of the mercenaries whom he commanded, proved the decisive factor. Agesilaus pretended to seek direction from Sparta, although he secretly sent asking the authorities there to order him to support Nektanebo. Both rivals also sent envoys to Sparta seeking support.[10] Clearly, these negotiations would have required some time, and in the end Agesilaus swung his support to the upstart, Nektanebo. Tachos fled to Artaxerxes, from whom he received pardon and mercy. But in the meanwhile, Agesilaus and Nektanebo returned to Egypt to secure control there. A third pretender arose, also nameless, in the city of Mendes. As a result of the faint-heartedness of Nektanebo, Agesilaus' army was besieged in a delta town. The enemy began to encircle the town with a wall and a ditch, and Agesilaus showed his tactical skill by waiting until the ditch was almost complete before launching an attack upon the numerically superior enemy. Because fighting could only be conducted within a rather narrow area, delimited by the ends of the ditch, Agesilaus easily overcame his opponents and sent them into flight.[11]

Agesilaus seems to have followed up this encounter some short time later with another attack upon the enemy, in which once again he

[9]Xen. *Ages.* 2.28; Plut. *Ages.* 40.2. See Hamilton, "Etude chronologique," 281–96. On the history of this period in Egypt, see F. K. Kienitz, *Die politische Geschichte Aegyptens vom 7. bis zum 4. Jahrhundert vor der Zeitwende* (Berlin, 1953), pp. 92–99.
[10]Plut. *Ages.* 37.1–6; Diod. 15.92.3–5; cf. Xen. *Ages.* 2.30–31.
[11]Plut. *Ages.* 38.1–39.4; Diod. 15.93.2–5.

proved his tactical skill. This time, he managed to bottle up his enemy on a piece of land surrounded by canals, so that the only way out was along the spit of land which Agesilaus held with his mercenaries. Again, the superior ability of the Greeks enabled them to defeat their Egyptian foes.[12] After this, Nektanebo tried to persuade Agesilaus to remain in his service, but the king was eager to return to Greece with the money he had received to bolster Sparta's war against Messene. He set off accordingly, even though it was still winter, with 230 talents of silver. On the homeward voyage, Agesilaus fell ill and died at a place on the coast of Libya known as the Harbor of Menelaus. His body was preserved in melted wax, for they had no honey, and transported back to Sparta for burial.[13] Thus ended a long life and an extraordinary career.[14]

With the passing of Agesilaus, Sparta ended its last period of greatness on the international scene in Greece.[15] Indeed, Sparta had lost its position as a major power in the years immediately following the Battle of Leuctra. Sparta's failure was not primarily a military one, nor even the result of demographic changes, important as these were, but rather a political one. Since the King's Peace, when Sparta was largely under the influence of Agesilaus and his policies, the state had followed a foreign policy that ever more alienated its subjects and allies. Once the myth of the invincibility of the Spartan army had been dispelled at Leuctra, Sparta was unable to devise new policies to stem the tide of disaffection from its league. And here again Agesilaus must be made to bear a major portion of the responsibility, because he was virtually unopposed within Sparta in this period. The Spartans seemed capable only of reaction to the initiatives of others from 370 on. Their one attempt to seize the diplomatic initiative, in 367, had resulted in disaster when Pelopidas

---

[12]Plut. *Ages*. 39.5.

[13]Plut. *Ages*. 40; Nepos, *Ages*. 8.7; Diod. 15.93.6; cf. Xen. *Ages*. 2.31.

[14]See M. A. Flower, "Agesilaus of Sparta and the Origins of the Ruler Cult," *CQ*, n.s. 38 (1988):123–34, for a discussion of the tradition found in Plutarch (*Mor*. 210D) that Agesilaus had received, and rejected, an offer of divine honors, probably from the Samians, around 394. He had also forbidden the making of any images or pictures of himself (Plut. *Ages*. 2.2). Thus, his reputation would be based on the record of his deeds and his words, not as a god but as a hero, as he hoped. His accomplishments were filtered, first by Xenophon, and later by Plutarch, according to their own purposes and objectives in writing about the king.

[15]For recent treatment of Sparta after the 360s, see L. J. Piper, *Spartan Twilight* (New Rochelle, N.Y., 1986); and P. Cartledge and A. Spawforth, *Hellenistic and Roman Sparta: A Tale of Two Cities* (New York, 1989). Cartledge and Spawforth argue, in particular, that Sparta played a role of some importance in the Hellenistic world, but it is undeniable that the shadow of Macedon lay over Greece from the reign of Philip II until the coming of Rome.

persuaded the Great King to support his interpretation of the peace. And with the loss of the manpower of its allies, coupled with the disastrous decline in native Spartiate population and the refusal of the authorities to consider any measures that might have enlarged the franchise and the pool of homoioi, Sparta was no longer able to play the role of a great power. Its decline was swift, and it followed not so much from its military defeat at Leuctra as from the counterproductive foreign policy of repression and intervention which it had followed consistently from 386 on. To this extent, Agesilaus must shoulder the burden for the failure of the Spartan Hegemony.

Selected Bibliography

Abbadi, M. A. H. El. "The Greek Attitude toward the King's Peace of 386 B.C." *Bulletin de la Société Royale d'Archéologie d' Alexandrie* 43 (1979):17–41.

Accame, Silvio. *L'imperialismo Ateniese all'inizio del secolo IV a.C.: La crisi della polis.* rev. ed. Naples, 1966.

———. *La Lega Ateniese del sec. IV a.C.* Rome, 1941.

———. *Ricerche intorno alla guerra Corinzia.* Naples, 1951.

Adams, W. L., and E. N. Borza, eds. *Philip II, Alexander the Great, and the Macedonian Heritage.* Washington, D.C., 1982.

Adcock, F. E. *The Greek and Macedonian Art of War.* Berkeley and Los Angeles, 1957.

———, and D. J. Mosley. *Diplomacy in Ancient Greece.* New York, 1975.

Africa, T. W. "Homosexuals in Greek History." *Journal of Psychohistory* 9 (1982): 401–20.

Amit, M. *Great and Small Poleis.* Brussels, 1973.

Anderson, J. K. "The Battle of Sardis in 395 B.C." *California Studies in Classical Antiquity* 7 (1974):27–53.

———. *Military Theory and Practice in the Age of Xenophon.* Berkeley and Los Angeles, 1970.

———. *Xenophon.* New York, 1974.

Andrewes, A. "The Government of Classical Sparta." In *Ancient Society and Institutions,* edited by E. Badian, pp. 1–20. Oxford, 1966.

———. "Spartan Imperialism?" In *Imperialism in the Ancient World,* edited by P. D. A. Garnsey and C. R. Whittaker, pp. 91–102 with 302–6. Cambridge, 1976.

———. "Two Notes on Lysander." *Phoenix* 25 (1971):206–26.

Asheri, D. "Laws of Inheritance, Distribution of Land and Political Constitutions in Ancient Greece." *Historia* 12 (1963):1–21.

Aucello, E. "La genesi della Pace di Antalcida." *Helikon* 5 (1965):340–80.

Barber, G. L. *The Historian Ephorus.* Cambridge, 1935.

Barrow, R. H. *Plutarch and His Times*. London, 1967.

Bartoletti, V., ed. *Hellenika Oxyrhynchia*. Leipzig, 1959.

Beister, H. "Ein thebanisches Tropaion bereits vor Beginn der Schlacht bei Leuktra: Zur Interpretationen von IG VII 2462 und Paus. 4.32.5 f." *Chiron* 3 (1973):65–84.

Beloch, K. J. *Die attische Politik seit Perikles*. Leipzig, 1884.

———. *Griechische Geschichte*. 2d ed. 4 vols. in 8. Strassburg, Berlin, and Leipzig, 1912–27.

Bengtson, H. *Griechische Geschichte*. 5th ed. Munich, 1977.

———. *Griechische Staatsmänner des 5. und 4. Jahrhunderts v. Chr.* Munich, 1983.

———. *Die Staatsverträge des Altertums. II: Die Verträge der griechisch-römischen Welt von 700 bis 338 v. Chr.* Munich and Berlin, 1962 (2d ed. 1975).

Best, J.G.P. *Thracian Peltasts and Their Influence on Greek Warfare*. Groningen, 1969.

Bloch, H. "Studies in Historical Literature of the Fourth Century B.C." In *Athenian Studies*, pp. 303–76. Cambridge, Mass., 1940.

Bockisch, G. "Harmostai," *Klio* 46 (1965):129–239.

Bommelaer, J.-F. *Lysandre de Sparte: Histoire et Traditions*. Paris, 1981.

Boring, T. A. *Literacy in Ancient Sparta*. Leiden, 1979.

Borza, E. N. "The Natural Resources of Early Macedonia." In *Philip II, Alexander the Great, and the Macedonian Heritage*, edited by W. L. Adams and E. N. Borza, pp. 1–20. Washington, D.C., 1982.

Breitenbach, H. R. "Hellenika Oxyrhynchia," *RE* Supp. 12 (1970):cols. 383–426.

———. "Xenophon," *RE* 9A (1967):cols. 1569–2052.

Brenk, F. E. *In Mist Apparelled: Religious Themes in Plutarch's "Moralia" and "Lives."* Leiden, 1977.

Bringmann, K. "Xenophons Hellenika und Agesilaos: Zu ihrer Entstehungsweise und Datierung." *Gymnasium* 78 (1971):224–41.

Brown, T. S. *The Greek Historians*. Lexington, Mass., 1973.

Bruce, I. A. F. "Athenian Embassies in the Early Fourth Century." *Historia* 15 (1966):272–81.

———. "Athenian Foreign Policy in 396–395 B.C." *Classical Journal* 58 (1963):289–95.

———. *An Historical Commentary on the "Hellenica Oxyrhynchia."* Cambridge, 1967.

———. "Internal Politics and the Outbreak of the Corinthian War." *Emerita* 28 (1960):75–86.

Buckler, J. "The Alleged Achaian Arbitration after Leuktra." *Symbolae Osloenses* 53 (1978):85–96.

———. "The Alleged Theban-Spartan Alliance of 386 B.C." *Eranos* 78 (1980):179–85.

———. "Dating the Peace of 375/4." *Greek, Roman, and Byzantine Studies* 12 (1971):353–61.

———. "Plutarch and the Fate of Antalkidas." *Greek, Roman, and Byzantine Studies* 18 (1977):139–45.

———. "Plutarch on Leuktra." *Symbolae Osloenses* 55 (1980):75–93.

———. "Plutarch on the Trials of Pelopidas and Epameinondas (369 B.C.)." *Classical Philology* 73 (1978):36–42.

———. "The Re-establishment of the Boiotarchia (378 B.C.)." *American Journal of Ancient History* 4 (1979):50–64.

———. "A Second Look at the Monument of Chabrias." *Hesperia* 41 (1972):466–74.
———. *The Theban Hegemony, 371–362 B.C.* Cambridge, Mass., 1980.
———. "The Thespians at Leuktra." *Wiener Studien*, n.s. 11 (1977):76–79.
———. "Xenophon's Speeches and the Theban Hegemony." *Athenaeum*, n.s. 60 (1982):180–204.
Burnett, A. P. "Thebes and the Expansion of the Second Athenian Confederacy: IG II²40 and IG II²43." *Historia* 11 (1962):1–17.
Bury, J. B., S. A. Cook, and F. E. Adcock. *The Cambridge Ancient History*. Vols. 5 and 6. Cambridge, 1927.
———, and R. Meiggs. *A History of Greece*. London, 1975.
Busolt, G. "Der neue Historiker und Xenophon." *Hermes* 43 (1908):255–85.
———, and H. Swoboda. *Griechische Staatskunde*. 2 vols. Munich, 1920–26.
Cargill, J. *The Second Athenian League: Empire or Free Alliance?* Berkeley and Los Angeles, 1981.
Carlier, P. "La royauté Grecque." Thèse de Doctorat d'Etat. University of Paris, 1982.
———. "La vie politique à Sparte sous le règne de Cléomene Iᵉʳ: Essai d' interpretation." *Ktema* 2 (1977):65–84.
Cartledge, P. *Agesilaos and the Crisis of Sparta*. Baltimore, 1987.
———. "Literacy in the Spartan Oligarchy." *Journal of Hellenic Studies* 98 (1978):25–37.
———. "The Politics of Spartan Pederasty." *Proceedings of the Cambridge Philological Society*, n.s. 30 (1981):17–36.
———. "Seismicity and Spartan Society." *Liverpool Classical Monthly* 1 (1976):25–28.
———. *Sparta and Lakonia: A Regional History c. 1300–362 B.C.* Boston, 1979.
———. "Spartan Wives: Liberation or Licence?" *Classical Quarterly*, n.s. 31 (1981):84–105.
———. "Toward the Spartan Revolution." *Arethusa* 8 (1975):59–84.
———, and J. Spawforth. *Hellenistic and Roman Sparta: A Tale of Two Cities*. New York, 1989.
Cavaignac, E. "Les dekarchies de Lysandre." *Revue des Etudes Historiques* 90 (1924):285–316.
———. "L'histoire Grecque de Theopompe." *Revue des Etudes Grecques* 25 (1912):129–57.
———. "La population du Péloponnèse aux Vᵉ et IVᵉ siècles." *Klio* 12 (1912):261–80.
Cawkwell, G. L. "Agesilaus and Sparta." *Classical Quarterly*, n.s. 26 (1976):62–84.
———. "The Common Peace of 366/5 B.C." *Classical Quarterly*, n.s. 11 (1961):80–86.
———. "The Decline of Sparta." *Classical Quarterly*, n.s. 33 (1983):385–400.
———. "Epaminondas and Thebes." *Classical Quarterly*, n.s. 22 (1972):254–78.
———. "The Foundation of the Second Athenian Confederacy." *Classical Quarterly*, n.s. 23 (1973):47–60.
———. "The Imperialism of Thrasybulus." *Classical Quarterly*, n.s. 26 (1976):270–77.
———. "Introduction," in *Xenophon: A History of My Times*. Trans. R. Warner, Harmondsworth, Eng., 1979.
———. "Introduction," in *Xenophon: The Persian Expedition*. Trans. R. Warner,

Harmondsworth, Eng., 1972.
——. "The King's Peace." *Classical Quarterly,* n.s. 31 (1981):69–83.
——. "Notes on the Peace of 375/4." *Historia* 12 (1963):84–95.
——. "The Power of Persia." *Arepo* 1 (1968):1–5.
Chambers, J. "On Messenian and Lakonian Helots in the Fifth Century B.C." *Historian* 40 (1978):271–85.
Christien, J. "La loi d' Epitadeus: Un aspect de l'histoire economique et sociale à Sparte." *Revue du Droit Français et Etranger* 52 (1974):197–221.
Clausewitz, C. von. *On War,* ed. and trans. M. Howard and P. Paget. Princeton, 1976.
Cloché, P. "Aristote et les institutions de Sparte." *Les Etudes Classiques* 11 (1942): 289–313.
——. "Les conflits politiques et sociaux à Athènes pendant la guerre Corinthienne (395–387 avant J.-C.)." *Revue des Etudes Anciennes* 21 (1919):157–92.
——. "La Gréce et l'Egypte de 405/4 à 342/1 avant J.-C." *Revue Egyptologique,* n.s. 1 (1919–20):82–127.
——. "Les 'Helléniques' de Xenophon (livres III–VII) et Lacédémone." *Revue des Etudes Anciennes* 46 (1944):12–46.
——. "Isocrate et la politique Lacédémonienne." *Revue des Etudes Anciennes* 35 (1933):129–45.
——. "Notes sur la politique Athénienne au début du IVᵉ siècle et pendant la guerre du Péloponnèse." *Revue des Etudes Anciennes* 43 (1941):16–32.
——. "La politique de l'Athénien Callistratos (391–361 avant J.-C.)." *Revue des Etudes Anciennes* 25 (1923):5–32.
——. *La politique étrangère d'Athènes de 404 à 338 a.C.* Paris, 1934.
——. "La politique Thébaine de 404 à 396 av. J.-C." *Revue des Etudes Grècques* 31 (1918):315–43.
——. "Sur le rôle des rois de Sparte." *Les Etudes Classiques* 17 (1949):113–38, 343–81.
——. *Thébes de Béotie.* Namur, 1952.
Colin, Gaston. *Xenophon Historien, d'après le livre II des Helléniques (Hiver 406/5 à 401/0).* Annales de l'Est, mem. 2. Paris, 1933.
Cook, J. M. *The Persian Empire.* London, 1983.
Cook, M. "Ancient Political Factions: Boeotia 404–395." *Transactions of the American Philological Association* 118 (1988):57–85.
Cornelius, F. "Die Schlacht bei Sardes." *Klio* 26 (1932):29–31.
David, E. "The Conspiracy of Cinadon." *Athenaeum,* n.s. 57 (1979):239–59.
——. "The Influx of Money into Sparta at the End of the Fifth Century B.C." *Scripta Classica Israelitica* 5 (1979/80):30–45.
——. "The Pamphlet of Pausanias." *La Parola del Passato* 34 (1979):94–116.
——. "Revolutionary Agitation in Sparta after Leuctra." *Athenaeum,* n.s. 58 (1980): 299–308.
——. *Sparta between Empire and Revolution, 404–243 B.C.: Internal Problems and Their Impact in Contemporary Greek Consciousness.* New York, 1981.
Day, J. *The Glory of Athens.* Chicago, 1980.
Delebecque, E. *Essai sur la vie de Xenophon.* Paris, 1957.

De Sanctis, G. "Nuovi studi sulle 'Elleniche' di Oxyrhynchus." *Atti della Reale Accademia delle Scienze di Torino: Scienze Morali* 66 (1930–31):158–94.

DeVoto, J. G. "Agesilaos, Antalcidas, and the Failed Peace of 392/1 B.C." *Classical Philology* 81 (1986):191–202.

———. "Agesilaos II and the Politics of Sparta, 404–377 B.C.," Ph.D. diss., Loyola University of Chicago, 1982.

Dorjahn, A. P. "On Pausanias' Battle with Thrasybulus." *Classical Journal* 20 (1925): 368–69.

Dover, K. J. *Greek Homosexuality.* Cambridge, Mass., 1978.

Drews, R. "Diodorus and His Sources." *American Journal of Philology* 83 (1962):382–92.

———. "Ephorus and History Written *kata genos.*" *American Journal of Philology* 84 (1963):244–55.

Ducat, J. "Le mépris des hilotes." *Annales* (ESC) 29 (1974):1451–64.

Dugas, Ch. "La campagne d'Agésilas en Asie Mineure (395): Xenophon et l'anonyme d'Oxyrhynchos." *Bulletin de Correspondance Hellénique* 34 (1910):58–95.

Ehrenberg, V. *From Solon to Socrates.* London, 1968.

———. *The Greek State.* 2d ed. London, 1969.

———. *Polis und Imperium. Beiträge zur alten geschichte,* edited by K. F. Stroheker and A. J. Graham. Zurich and Stuttgart, 1965.

———. "Sparta." *RE* 3A (1929):cols. 1373–1453.

Ellis, W. M. *Alcibiades.* New York, 1989.

Engels, D. *Alexander the Great and the Logistics of the Macedonian Army.* Berkeley and Los Angeles, 1978.

Erikson, E. *Young Man Luther.* New York, 1958.

Fabricius, E. "Die Befreiung Thebens." *Rheinisches Museum für Philologie* 48 (1893): 448–71.

Ferrill, A. *The Origins of War: From the Stone Age to Alexander the Great.* New York, 1985.

Figueira, T. J. "Mess Contributions and Subsistence at Sparta." *Transactions of the American Philological Association* 114 (1984):87–109.

———. "Population Patterns in Late Archaic and Classical Sparta." *Transactions of the American Philological Association* 116 (1986):165–213.

Finley, M. I. *Ancient Slavery and Modern Ideology.* London, 1980.

———. *Economy and Society in Ancient Greece,* edited by B. D. Shaw and R. P. Saller. London, 1981.

———. *The Use and Abuse of History.* New York, 1975.

Flower, M. A. "Agesilaus of Sparta and the Origins of the Ruler Cult." *Classical Quarterly,* n.s. 38 (1988):123–34.

Forrest, W. G. *A History of Sparta c. 950–192 B.C.* London, 1980 (reprint, with new "Preface," of 1969 original).

———. "Legislation in Sparta." *Phoenix* 21 (1967):11–19.

Frazer, J. G. *Pausanias' Description of Greece.* 5 vols. London, 1913.

Fritz, K. von. "The Historian Theopompos." *American Historical Review* 46 (1941): 761–85.

Frost, F. "Plutarch and Clio." In *Panhellenica: Essays in Ancient History and Histo-*

264 Selected Bibliography

riography in Honor of Truesdell S. Brown, edited by S. M. Burstein and L. Okin, pp. 155–70. Lawrence, Kans., 1980.

Funke, P. *Homonoia und Arche. Athen und die griechische Staatenwelt vom Ende des Peloponnesischen Krieges bis zum Königsfrieden (404/3–387/6 v.Chr.).* Wiesbaden, 1980.

Garlan, Y. *La guerre dans l'antiquité.* Paris, 1972.

Garnsey, P. D. A. and C. R. Whittaker, eds., *Imperialism in the Ancient World.* Cambridge, 1978.

Gilbert, G. *The Constitutional Antiquities of Sparta and Athens (Greek Constitutional Antiquities I).* 2d ed. London, 1895.

Gill, C. "The Character-Personality Distinction." In *Characterization and Individuality in Greek Literature,* edited by C. Pelling, pp. 1–31. Oxford, 1990.

Glotz, G. "Le conseil fédéral des Béotiens." *Bulletin de Correspondance Hellénique* 32 (1908):271–78.

———, and R. Cohen. *Histoire Grecque, III.* Paris, 1941.

Goligher, W. A. "The New Greek Historical Fragment Attributed to Theopompus or Cratippus." *English Historical Review* 23 (1908):277–83.

Gomme, A. W. *The Population of Athens in the Fifth and Fourth Centuries B.C.* Oxford, 1933.

Gonzalez, J. P. "La politica Tebana de 379 a 371 A.C." *Studia Zamorensia* 7 (1986): 383–409.

———. "El surgimiento de una facción democratica Tebana (382–379 A.C.)." *Faventia* 8 (1986):69–83.

Graefe, F. "Die Operationen des Antialkidas im Hellespont." *Klio* 28 (1935):262–70.

Grant, J. R. "A Note on the Tone of Greek Diplomacy." *Classical Quarterly,* n.s. 15 (1965):261–66.

Gray, V. J. *The Character of Xenophon's "Hellenica."* London, 1989.

———. "Dialogue in Xenophon's Hellenica." *Classical Quarterly,* n.s. 31 (1981):321–34.

———. "Two Different Approaches to the Battle of Sardis in 395 B.C.: Xenophon *Hellenica* 3.4.20–24 and *Hellenica Oxyrhynchia* 11 (6).4–6." *California Studies in Classical Antiquity* 12 (1979):183–200.

———. "The Years 375 to 371 B.C.: A Case Study in the Reliability of Diodorus Siculus and Xenophon." *Classical Quarterly,* n.s. 30 (1980):306–26.

Greenidge, A. H. J. *A Handbook of Greek Constitutional History.* London, 1902.

Grenfell, B. P., and A. S. Hunt, eds. *The Oxyrhychus Papyri Part V,* nos. 840–844. London, 1908.

Griffith, G. T. *Mercenaries of the Hellenistic World.* Cambridge, 1935 (reprint, Chicago, 1975.)

———. "The Union of Corinth and Argos." *Historia* 1 (1950):236–56.

Grote, G. *History of Greece.* 10 vols. London, 1888.

Gschnitzer, Fritz. *Abhangige Orte im griechischen Altertum.* Munich, 1958.

Habicht, C. *Gottmenschentum und Griechische Städte.* 2d ed. Munich, 1971.

———. *Pausanias' Guide to Ancient Greece.* Berkeley and Los Angeles, 1985.

Hack, H. M. "Thebes and the Spartan Hegemony, 386–382 B.C." *American Journal of Philology* 99 (1978):210–27.

Halliwell, S. "Traditional Conceptions of Character." In *Characterization and Individuality in Greek Literature,* edited by C. Pelling, pp. 42–56. Oxford, 1990.

Hamilton, C. D. "Agesilaus and the Failure of Spartan Hegemony." *Ancient World* 5 (1982):67–78.

———. "Amyntas III and Agesilaus: Macedon and Sparta in the Fourth Century." *Ancient Macedonia* 4 (1986):239–45.

———. "Diodorus on the Establishment of the Second Athenian League." *Ancient History Bulletin* 3 (1989):93–102.

———. "The Early Career of Archidamus." *Echos du Monde Classique/Classical Views* 26, n.s. 1 (1982):5–20.

———. "Etude chronologique sur le règne d'Agésilas." *Ktema* 7 (1982):281–96.

———. "The Generalship of King Agesilaus of Sparta." *Ancient World* 8 (1983):119–27.

———. "Isocrates, IG ii² 43, Greek Propaganda and Imperialism." *Traditio* 36 (1980):83–109.

———. "On the Perils of Extraordinary Honors: The Cases of Lysander and Conon." *Ancient World* 2 (1979):87–90.

———. "Philip II and Archidamus." In *Philip II, Alexander the Great, and the Macedonian Heritage,* edited by W. L. Adams and E. N. Borza, pp. 61–83. Washington, D.C., 1982.

———. "The Politics of Revolution in Corinth, 395–386 B.C." *Historia* 21 (1972):21–37.

———. "Politische Bewegungen und Tendenzen vom Frieden des Nikias bis zum Wiederbeginn des Krieges." In *Hellenische Poleis,* 3 vols., edited by E. Ch. Welskopf, vol. 1, pp. 5–24. Berlin, 1973.

———. "Problems of Alliance and Hegemony in Fourth Century Greece Reconsidered." *Echos du Monde Classique/Classical Views* 26, n.s. 1 (1982):297–318.

———. "Spartan Politics and Policy, 405–401 B.C." *American Journal of Philology* 91 (1970):294–314.

———. *Sparta's Bitter Victories: Politics and Diplomacy in the Corinthian War.* Ithaca, N.Y., 1979.

Hammond, M. "A Famous Exemplum of Spartan Toughness." *Classical Journal* 75 (1979–80):97–109.

Hammond, N. G. L. *A History of Greece to 322 B.C.* 3d ed. Oxford, 1986.

———. "The Main Road from Boeotia to the Peloponnese through the Northern Megarid." *Annual of the British School at Athens* 49 (1954):103–22.

———, and H. H. Scullard, eds. *The Oxford Classical Dictionary.* 2d ed. Oxford, 1971.

Hampl, F. *Die griechischen Staatsverträge des 4. Jahrhunderts v. Christi.* Leipzig, 1938.

Hanson, V. D. "Epameinondas, the Battle of Leuktra (371 B.C.), and the 'Revolution' in Greek Battle Tactics." *Classical Antiquity* 7 (1988):190–207.

———. *Warfare and Agriculture in Classical Greece.* Pisa, 1983.

———. *The Western Way of War.* New York, 1989.

Hardy, W. G. "The *Hellenica Oxyhynchia* and the Devastation of Attica." *Classical Philology* 21 (1926):346–55.

Harrison, E. "A Problem in the Corinthian War." *Classical Quarterly* 7 (1913):132.

Hatzfeld, J. *Alcibiade,* 2d ed. Paris, 1951.

——. "Notes sur la composition des 'Helléniques.' " *Revue de Philologie, de Littéra-* (1933):387–409.

——. "Notes sur la chronologie des 'Helléniques.' " *Revue de Philologie, de Littérature et d'Histoire Anciennes,* 3d ser., 4 (1930):113–27, 209–26.

Henry, W. P. *Greek Historical Writing.* Chicago, 1967.

Hertzberg, G. F. *Das Leben des Königs Agesilaos II von Sparta.* Halle, 1856.

Higgins, W. E. *Xenophon the Athenian: The Problem of the Individual and the Society of the Polis.* Albany, N.Y., 1977.

Hirsch, S. *The Friendship of the Barbarians.* Hanover, N.H., 1985.

Hodkinson, S. J. "Inheritance, Marriage and Demography: Perspectives upon the Success and Decline of Classical Sparta." In *Classical Sparta: Techniques behind Her Success,* edited by A. Powell, pp. 79–121. Norman, Okla., 1989.

——. "Land Tenure and Inheritance in Classical Sparta." *Classical Quarterly,* n.s. 36 (1986):378–406.

——. "Social Order and the Conflict of Values in Classical Sparta." *Chiron* 13 (1983):239–81.

Holladay, A. J. "Hoplites and Heresies." *Journal of Hellenic Studies* 102 (1982):94–103.

——. "Spartan Austerity." *Classical Quarterly,* n.s. 27 (1977):111–26.

Hooker, J. T. *The Ancient Spartans.* London, 1980.

How, W. W. and J. Wells. *A Commentary on Herodotus.* 2 vols. Oxford, 1912 (reprint, 1967).

Jacoby, F. *Abhandlung en zur griechischen Geschichtschreibung.* Leiden, 1956.

——. *Die Fragmente der Griechischen Historiker.* 3 vols. in 15. Berlin and Leiden, 1924–69.

——. *Griechische Historiker.* Stuttgart, 1956.

Jaeger, W. *Paideia: The Ideals of Greek Culture.* 2d ed., 3 vols. New York, 1945.

Jeanmaire, H. "La kryptie Lacédémonienne." *Revue des Etudes Grecques* 26 (1913): 121–50.

Jones, A. H. M. *Athenian Democracy.* Oxford, 1957.

Jones, C. P. *Plutarch and Rome.* Oxford, 1971.

Judeich, W. "Antalkidas." *RE* 1 (1894):cols. 234–46.

——. "Artaxerxes." (2) *RE* 2 (1896):cols. 1314–18.

——. "Athen und Theben vom Königsfrieden bis zur Schlacht bei Leuktra." *Rheinisches Museum für Philologie* 76 (1927):171–97.

——. *Kleinasiatische Studien: Untersuchungen zur griechisch-persischen Geschichte des IV Jahrhunderts v. Chr.* Marburg, 1892.

——. "Theopomps Hellenica." *Rheinisches Museum für Philologie* 66 (1911):94–139.

Kagan, D. *The Archidamian War.* Ithaca, N.Y., 1974.

——. "Argive Politics and Policy after the Peace of Nicias." *Classical Philology* 57 (1962):209–18.

——. "Corinthian Diplomacy after the Peace of Nicias." *American Journal of Philology* 81 (1960):291–310.

——. "Corinthian Politics and the Revolution of 392 B.C." *Historia* 11 (1962):447–57.

——. "The Economic Origins of the Corinthian War." *La Parola del Passato* 16 (1961):321–41.

——. *The Fall of the Athenian Empire*. Ithaca, N.Y., 1987.

——. *The Outbreak of the Peloponnesian War*. Ithaca, N.Y., 1969.

——. *The Peace of Nicias and the Sicilian Expedition*. Ithaca, N.Y., 1981.

Kahrstedt, U. *Forschungen zur Geschichte des ausgehenden fünften und des vierten Jahrhunderts*. Berlin, 1910.

——. *Griechisches Staatsrecht, I: Sparta und seine Symmachie*. Göttingen, 1922.

——. "Iphikrates." *RE* 9 (1916):cols. 2019–21.

——. "Lysandros." *RE* 13 (1927):cols. 2503–6.

Kallet, L. "Iphikrates, Timotheus, and Athens, 371–360 B.C." *Greek, Roman, and Byzantine Studies* 24 (1983):239–52.

Kallet-Marx, R. M. "Athens, Thebes, and the Foundation of the Second Athenian League." *Classical Antiquity* 4 (1985):127–51.

Kelly, D. H. "Agesilaus' Strategy in Asia Minor, 396–395 B.C." *Liverpool Classical Monthly* 3 (1978):97–98.

——. "Policy-making in the Spartan Assembly." *Antichthon* 14 (1981):47–61.

Kienitz, F. K. *Die politische Geschichte Aegyptens vom 7. bis zum 4. Jahrhundert vor der Zeitwende*. Berlin, 1953.

Kirchner, J. *Prosopographia Attica*. 2 vols. Berlin, 1901.

Kornemann, E. "Zur Geschichte der antiken Herrscherkulte." *Klio* 1 (1901):51–146.

Krentz, P. *The Thirty at Athens*. Ithaca, N.Y., 1982.

Kromayer, J., and G. Veith. *Antike Schlachtfelder*. 4 vols. Berlin, 1903–31.

Lanzillotta, E., ed. *Problemi di Storia e Cultura Spartana*. Rome, 1984.

Larsen, J. A. O. "The Constitution of the Peloponnesian League." *Classical Philology* 28 (1933):256–76, and 29 (1934):1–19.

——. *Greek Federal States*. Oxford, 1968.

——. "Perioikoi." *RE* 19 (1937):cols. 816–33.

——. *Representative Government in Greek and Roman History*. Berkeley and Los Angeles, 1955.

Lauffer, S. "Die Diodordublette XV 38 = 50 über die Friedenschlusse zu Sparta 374 und 371 v. Chr." *Historia* 8 (1959):315–48.

Lawrence, A. W. *Greek Aims in Fortification*. Oxford, 1979.

Lazenby, J. F. *The Spartan Army*. Chicago, 1985.

Legon, R. P. *Megara: The Political History of a Greek City State to 336 B.C.* Ithaca, N.Y., 1981.

——. "Phliasian Politics and Policy in the Early Fourth Century B.C." *Historia* 16 (1967):324–37.

Lenschau, Th. "Pharnabazus." *RE* 19 (1938):cols. 1842–48.

——. "Die Sendung des Timokrates und der Ausbruch des Korinthischen Krieges." *Phil. Wochenschrift* 53 (1933):1325–28.

Levi, M. A. "Le fonti per la Pace di Antalcida." *Acme* 8 (1955):105–11.

Levy, E. *Athènes devant la défaite de 404: Histoire d'une crise idéologique*. Paris, 1976.

——. "Les trois traités entre Sparte et le roi." *Bulletin de Correspondance Hellénique* 107 (1983):221–41.

Lewis, D. M. *Sparta and Persia.* Leiden, 1977.

Lins, H. *Kritische Betrachtung der Feldzüge des Agesilaus in Kleinasien.* Halle, 1914.

Littman, R. J. "The Loves of Alcibiades." *Transactions of the American Philological Association* 101 (1970):263–79.

——. "A New Date for Leotychidas." *Phoenix* 23 (1969):269–77.

Lotze, D. *Lysander und der Peloponnesische Krieg. Abhandlung der Sachsischen Akademie der Wissenschaften zu Leipzig, Phil.-hist. Klasse,* 57. Berlin, 1964.

——. "Mothakes." *Historia* 11 (1962):427–35.

Luppino Manes, E. "Tradizione e innovazione: Una costante della *Basileia* di Agesilao." *Miscellanea Greca e Romana* 12 (1987):45–65.

Luria, S. "Zum politischen Kampf in Sparta gegen Ende des fünften Jahrhunderts." *Klio* 20 (1926), 404–20.

MacDonald, A. G. "A Note on the Raid of Sphodrias." *Historia* 21 (1972):38–44.

MacDowell, D. M. *Spartan Law.* Edinburgh, 1986.

MacGregor, M. F. *The Athenians and Their Empire.* Vancouver, 1988.

McKay, K. L. "The Oxyrhynchus Historian and the Outbreak of the 'Corinthian War.'" *Classical Review,* n.s. 3 (1953):6–7.

MacLaren, M. "On the Composition of Xenophon's Hellenica." *American Journal of Philology* 55 (1934):121–39, 249–62.

Marrou, H.-I. *Histoire de l'éducation dans l'antiquité.* 6th ed. Paris, 1965.

Marshall, F. S. *The Second Athenian Confederacy.* Cambridge, 1905.

Martin, V. "Sur une interpretation nouvelle de la 'Paix du Roi.'" *Museum Helveticum* 6 (1949):127–39.

——. "Le traitement de l'histoire diplomatique dans la tradition littéraire du IVme siècle avant J.-C." *Museum Helveticum* 1 (1944):13–30.

——. *La vie internationale dans la Grèce des cités (VIe–IVe s. av. J.-C.).* Paris, 1940.

Mazlish, B., ed. *Psychoanalysis and History.* New York, 1971.

Meiggs, R. L. *The Athenian Empire.* Oxford, 1972.

——, and D. Lewis. *A Selection of Greek Historical Inscriptions.* Oxford, 1969.

Meloni, Piero. "Tiribazo satrapo di Sardi." *Athenaeum,* n.s. 28 (1950):292–339.

Meyer, E. *Forschungen zur alten Geschichte.* 2 vols. Halle, 1892–99.

——. *Geschichte des Altertums.* 5 vols. Stuttgart and Berlin, 1913–31.

——. *Theopomps Hellenika.* Halle, 1909.

Michell, H. *Sparta.* Cambridge, 1952.

Michler, M. "Die Krankheit des Agesilaos in Megara." *Sudhoffs Archiv für Geschichte der Medizin* 47 (1963):179–83.

Missiou-Ladi, A. "Coercive Diplomacy in Greek Interstate Relations." *Classical Quarterly,* n.s. 37 (1987):336–45.

Momigliano, A. "Androzione e le 'Elleniche' di Ossirinco." *Atti della R. Accademia delle Scienze di Torino: Classe di Sc. Morali* 66 (1930–31):29–49.

——. *The Development of Greek Biography.* Cambridge, Mass., 1971.

——. "La *Koine Eirene* dal 386 al 338." *Rivista di Filologia e di Istruzione Classica* 12 (1934): 482–514.

——. "Persian Empire and Greek Freedom." In *The Idea of Freedom: Essays in Honour of Isaiah Berlin,* edited by A. Ryan, pp. 39–51. Oxford, 1979.
Mosley, D. J. "The Athenian Embassy to Sparta in 371 B.C." *Proceedings of the Cambridge Philological Society,* n.s. 8 (1962):41–46.
——. "Diplomacy and Disunion in Ancient Greece." *Phoenix* 25 (1971):319–30.
——. "Diplomacy by Conference: Almost a Spartan Contribution to Diplomacy?" *Emerita* 39 (1971):187–93.
——. "Diplomacy in Classical Greece." *Ancient Society* 3 (1972):1–16.
——. *Envoys and Diplomacy in Ancient Greece.* Wiesbaden, 1973.
——. "Euthycles: One or Two Spartan Envoys?" *Classical Review,* n.s. 22 (1972): 167–69.
——. "Leon and Timagoras: Co-envoys for Four Years?" *Greek, Roman, and Byzantine Studies* 9 (1968):157–60.
——. "Pharax and the Spartan Embassy to Athens in 370/69." *Historia* 12 (1963): 247–50.
——. "Spartan Kings and Proxeny." *Athenaeum,* n.s. 49 (1971):433–35.
——. "Theban Diplomacy in 371 B.C." *Revue des Etudes Grecques* 85 (1972):312–18.
Mosse, Claude. *La fin de la démocratie Athénienne.* Paris, 1962.
——. "Le rôle politique des armées dans le monde Grec à l'époque classique." In *Problèmes de la guerre en Grèce ancienne,* edited by J. P. Vernant, pp. 221–29. Paris, 1968.
Munn, M. H. "Agesilaos' Boiotian Campaigns and the Theban Stockade of 378–377 B.C." *Classical Antiquity* 6 (1987):106–38.
Munro, J. A. R. "The End of the Peloponnesian War." *Classical Quarterly* 31 (1937):32–38.
——. "Theramenes against Lysander." *Classical Quarterly* 32 (1938):18–26.
Murray, G. "Reactions to the Peloponnesian War." *Journal of Hellenic Studies* 64 (1944):1–9.
Niese, B. "Agesilaos." (4) *RE* 1 (1894):cols. 796–804.
——. "Agis." (2) *RE* 1 (1894):cols. 817–19.
Nolte, F. *Die historisch-politischen Voraussetzungen des Königsfriedens.* Bamberg, 1923.
Ober, J. *Fortress Attica: Defense of the Athenian Land Frontier, 404–322 B.C.* Leiden, 1985.
Oliva, P. *Sparta and Her Social Problems.* Amsterdam and Prague, 1971.
Ollier, F. *Le mirage Spartiate: Etude sur l'idéalisation de Sparte dans l'antiquité Grècque. I. De l'origine jusqu'aux cyniques; II. Du début de l'école cynique jusqu'à la fin de la cité.* Paris, 1933–43 (reprint in one vol., New York, 1973).
——, ed. *Xenophon: La république des Lacédémoniens* (Annales de l'Université de Lyon, n.s. 2, fasc. 47). Lyon and Paris, 1934.
Olmstead, A. T. *History of the Persian Empire.* Chicago, 1948.
Ostwald, M. P. *Autonomia: Its Genesis and Early History.* Chico, Calif., 1982.
Pareti, Luigi. "Elementi formatori e dissolventi dell'egemonia Spartana in Grecia." *Atti della R. Accademia della Scienze di Torino* 47 (1911–12):108–26.
——. *Ricerche sulla potenza marittima degli Spartani e sulla cronologia dei Navarchi. Memorie della R. Accademia delle Scienze di Torino: Cl. di sc. Morali,* ser. 2, 59 (1909):71–160.

Parke, H. W. "The Deposing of Spartan Kings." *Classical Quarterly* 39 (1945):106–12.

———. "The Development of the Second Spartan Empire (405–371 B.C.)." *Journal of Hellenic Studies* 50 (1930):37–79.

———. *Greek Mercenary Soldiers from the Earliest Times to the Battle of Ipsus.* Oxford, 1933.

———. *The Oracles of Zeus.* Cambridge, Mass., 1967.

———. "The Tithe of Apollo and the Harmost at Decelea, 412–404 B.C." *Journal of Hellenic Studies* 52 (1932):42–46.

———, and D. E. W. Wormell. *The Delphic Oracle.* 2 vols. Oxford, 1956.

Pauly, A., G. Wissowa, W. Kroll, and others, eds. *Real-Encyclopädie der classischen Altertumswissenschaft.* 34 vols. Stuttgart, 1894–1972.

Pelling, C. "Childhood and Personality in Greek Biography." In *Characterization and Individuality in Greek Literature,* edited by C. Pelling, pp. 213–44. Oxford, 1990.

Perlman, S. "Athenian Democracy and the Revival of Imperialistic Expansion at the Beginning of the Fourth Century B.C." *Classical Philology* 63 (1968):257–67.

———. "The Causes and Outbreak of the Corinthian War." *Classical Quarterly,* n.s. 14 (1964):64–111.

———. "Panhellenism, the Polis and Imperialism." *Historia* 25 (1976):1–30.

———. "Political Leadership in Athens in the Fourth Century B.C." *La Parola del Passato* 22 (1967):161–76.

———. "The Politicians of the Athenian Democracy of the Fourth Century B.C." *Athenaeum* 41 (1963):327–55.

———. "The Ten Thousand: A Chapter in the Military, Social, and Economic History of the Fourth Century." *Rivista Storica dell'Antichità* 6–7 (1976–77):241–84.

Piper, L. J. *Spartan Twilight.* New Rochelle, N.Y., 1986.

Pomper, P. *The Structure of Mind in History.* New York, 1985.

Poralla, P. *Prosopographie der Lakedaimonier bis auf die Zeit Alexander des Grossen.* Breslau, 1913.

Powell, A., ed. *Classical Sparta: Techniques behind Her Success.* Norman, Okla., 1989.

Prentice, W. K. "The Character of Lysander." *American Journal of Archaeology* 38 (1934):37–42.

Pritchett, W. K. *The Greek State at War.* 4 vols. Berkeley and Los Angeles, 1971–85.

———. *Studies in Ancient Greek Topography.* 2 vols. Berkeley and Los Angeles, 1965–69.

Rahe, P. A. "Lysander and the Spartan Settlement, 407–403 B.C." Ph.D. diss., Yale University, 1977.

———. "The Selection of Ephors at Sparta." *Historia* 29 (1980):385–401.

Rahn, P. J. "The Date of Xenophon's Exile." In *Classical Contributions: Studies in Honour of M. F. MacGregor,* edited by G. S. Shrimpton and D. J. McCargar, pp. 103–19. Locust Valley, N.Y., 1981.

Rawson, E. *The Spartan Tradition in European Thought.* Oxford, 1969.

Rhodes, P. J. "The Selection of Ephors at Sparta." *Historia* 30 (1981):498–502.

Rice, D. G. "Agesilaus, Agesipolis, and Spartan Politics, 386–379 B.C." *Historia* 23 (1974):164–82.

———. "Why Sparta Failed." Ph.D. diss., Yale University, 1971.
———. "Xenophon, Diodorus and the Years 379/78 B.C.: Reconstruction and Reappraisal." *Yale Classical Studies* 24 (1975):95–130.
Rios Fernandez, M. "Los silencios de Jenofonte en el *Agesilao* de Plutarco." *Habis* 15 (1984):41–70.
Robert, L. "Diodore, XIV, 84, 3." *Revue de Philologie* 8 (1934):43–48.
Roos, A. "The Peace of Sparta of 374 B.C." *Mnemosyne*, n.s. 2 (1949):265–85.
Roy, J. "Arcadia and Boeotia in Peloponnesian Affairs, 370–362 B.C." *Historia* 20 (1971):569–99.
———. "Diodorus Siculus XV.40—the Peloponnesian Revolutions of 374 B.C." *Klio* 55 (1973):135–39.
Russell, D. A. "On Reading Plutarch's 'Lives.'" *Greece and Rome*, n.s. 13 (1966): 139–54.
———. *Plutarch*. London, 1973.
Ryder, T. T. B. "Athenian Foreign Policy and the Peace-conference at Sparta in 371 B.C." *Classical Quarterly*, n.s. 13 (1963):237–41.
———. *Koine Eirene: General Peace and Local Independence in Ancient Greece*. Oxford, 1965.
———. "Spartan Relations with Persia after the King's Peace: A Strange Story in Diodorus 15.9." *Classical Quarterly*, n.s. 13 (1963):105–9.
———. "The Supposed Common Peace of 366/5 B.C." *Classical Quarterly*, n.s. 7 (1957):199–205.
Ste. Croix, G. E. M. de. *The Origins of the Peloponnesian War*. Ithaca, N.Y., 1972.
Sansone, D. "Lysander and Dionysius (Plut. *Lys.* 2)." *Classical Philology* 76 (1981): 202–6 (with addendum by R. Renehan, 206–7).
Schaefer, H. "Pausanias." (25) *RE* 18.2 (1949):cols. 2578–84.
———. *Probleme der alten Geschichte*. Göttingen, 1963.
———. "Tiribazos." *RE* 6A (1937):cols. 1431–37.
———. "Tissaphernes." *RE* Suppl. 7 (1940): cols. 1579–99.
Schäme, R. *Die Amtsantritt der spartanischen Nauarchen und der Anfang des korinthischen Krieges*. Leipzig, 1915.
Schober, F. "Thebai (Boiotien) Geschichte." *RE* 5A (1934): cols. 1452–92.
Schwahn, W. "Thrasybulos." (3) *RE* 6A (1937):cols. 568–76.
Schwartz, E. *Griechische Geschichtschreiber*. Leipzig, 1959.
———. "Quellenuntersuchungen zur griechischen Geschichte." *Rheinisches Museum für Philologie* 44 (1889):161–93.
Seager, R. "Agesilaus in Asia: Propaganda and Objectives." *Liverpool Classical Monthly* 2 (1977):183–84.
———. "The King's Peace and the Balance of Power in Greece, 386–62 B.C." *Athenaeum*, n.s. 52 (1974):36–63.
———. "Thrasybulus, Conon and Athenian Imperialism, 396–386 B.C." *Journal of Hellenic Studies* 87 (1967):95–115.
———, and C. J. Tuplin. "The Freedom of the Greeks of Asia." *Journal of Hellenic Studies* 100 (1980):141–57.
Sealey, B. R. "Callistratos of Aphidna and His Contemporaries." *Historia* 5 (1956): 178–203.

272   Selected Bibliography

——. *A History of the Greek City-States ca. 700–338 B.C.* Berkeley and Los Angeles, 1977.

——. "*IG* II², 1609, and the Transformation of the Second Athenian Sea-League." *Phoenix* 11 (1957):95–111.

Seltman, C. *Greek Coins.* 2d ed. London, 1955.

Shrimpton, G. S. "The Theban Supremacy in Fourth-Century Literature." *Phoenix* 25 (1971):310–18.

Sinclair, R. K. "Diodorus Siculus and the Writing of History." *Proceedings of the African Classical Association* 6 (1963):36–45.

——. "The King's Peace and the Employment of Military and Naval Forces 387–378." *Chiron* 8 (1978):29–54.

Smith, R. E. "Lysander and the Spartan Empire." *Classical Philology* 43 (1948):145–56.

——. "The Opposition to Agesilaus' Foreign Policy, 394–371 B.C." *Historia* 2 (1953–54):274–88.

Smits, J. *Plutarchus' Leven van Lysander: Inleiding, Tekst, Commentaar.* Amsterdam and Paris, 1939.

Sordi, M. "La pace di Atene del 371/0." *Rivista di Filologia e di Istruzione Classica* 79 (1951):34–64.

Stadter, P. A. *Plutarch's Historical Methods: An Analysis of the "Mulierum Virtutes."* Cambridge, Mass., 1965.

Starr, C. G. "Greeks and Persians in the Fourth Century B.C. I. A Study of Cultural Contacts before Alexander." *Iranica Antiqua* 11 (1975):39–99.

——. "Greeks and Persians in the Fourth Century B.C. II. The Meeting of Two Cultures." *Iranica Antiqua* 12 (1977):49–115.

——. *Political Intelligence in Classical Greece.* Leiden, 1974.

Stern, E. von. *Geschichte der spartanischen und thebanischen Hegemonie vom Königsfrieden bis zur Schlacht bei Mantineia.* Dorpat, 1884.

Strauss, B. *Athens after the Peloponnesian War: Class, Faction, and Policy, 403–386 B.C.* London, 1986.

Swoboda, H. "Konon." *RE* 11 (1922):cols. 1319–34.

——. "Studien zur Verfassung Boiotiens." *Klio* 10 (1910):915–34.

Talbert, R. J. A. *Plutarch on Sparta.* London, 1988.

——. "The Role of the Helots in the Class Struggle at Sparta." *Historia* 38 (1989):22–40.

Thomas, C. G. "On the Role of the Spartan Kings." *Historia* 24 (1975):257–70.

——. "The Spartan Diarchy in Comparative Perspective." *La Parola del Passato* 38 (1983):81–104.

Thompson, W. E. "Arcadian Factionalism in the 360's." *Historia* 32 (1983):149–60.

——. "Chares at Phlius." *Philologus* 127 (1983):303–5.

——. "Observations on Spartan Politics." *Rivista Storica dell'Antichita* 3 (1973):47–58.

——. "The Politics of Phlius." *Eranos* 68 (1970):224–30.

Tod, M. N. *A Selection of Greek Historical Inscriptions,* 2 vols. Oxford, 1946–48.

Toepffer, J. "Androkleidas." *RE* 1 (1894):col. 2147.

Toynbee, A. J. *Some Problems in Greek History.* Oxford, 1969.

Treves, Piero. "Introduzione alla storia della Guerra Corinzia." *Athenaeum*, n.s. 16 (1938):65–84, 164–93.

———. "Note su la Guerra Corinzia." *Rivista di Filologia e di Istruzione Classica*, n.s. 15 (1937):113–40, 278–83.

———. "The Problem of a History of Messenia." *Journal of Hellenic Studies* 64 (1944): 102–6.

Tuplin, C. J. "The Athenian Embassy to Sparta 372/1." *Liverpool Classical Monthly* 2 (1977):51–56.

———. "The Date of the Union of Corinth and Argos." *Classical Quarterly*, n.s. 32 (1982):75–83.

———. "The Leuctra Campaign: Some Outstanding Problems." *Klio* 69 (1987):72–107.

———. "Pausanias and Plutarch's *Epaminondas*." *Classical Quarterly*, n.s. 34 (1984): 346–58.

———. "Timotheus and Corcyra: Problems in Greek History, 375–373 B.C." *Athenaeum*, n.s. 62 (1984):537–68.

———. "Xenophon: A Didactic Historian?" *Proceedings of the Classical Association* 74 (1977):26–27.

Underhill, G. E. "Athens and the Peace of Antalcides." *Classical Review* 10 (1896): 19–21.

———. "The Chronology of the Corinthian War." *Journal of Philology* 22 (1894):129–43.

———. "The Chronology of the Elean War." *Classical Review* 7 (1893):156–58.

———. *A Commentary with Introduction and Appendix on the "Hellenica" of Xenophon*. Oxford, 1900.

Usher, S. *The Historians of Greece and Rome*. London, 1969.

Vannier, F. *Le IVᵉ siècle Grec*. 2d ed. Paris, 1967.

Vernant, J. P. *Problèmes de la guerre en Grèce ancienne*. Paris and The Hague, 1968.

Walker, E. M. "Cratippus or Theopompus?" *Klio* 8 (1908):356–71.

———. *Hellenica Oxyrhynchia*. Oxford, 1913.

Wardman, A. *Plutarch's Lives*. Berkeley and Los Angeles, 1974.

———. "Plutarch's Methods in the 'Lives.'" *Classical Quarterly*, n.s. 21 (1971):254–61.

Welskopf, E. Ch., ed. *Hellenische Poleis: Krise-Wandlung-Wirkung*. 3 vols. Berlin, 1974.

West, A. B. *The History of the Chalcidic League*. Madison, Wis., 1918 (reprint, New York, 1973).

Westlake, H. D. *Essays on the Greek Historians and Greek History*. New York, 1969.

———. "Reelection to the Ephorate?" *Greek, Roman, and Byzantine Studies* 17 (1976): 343–52.

———. "The Sources for the Spartan Debacle at Haliartus." *Phoenix* 39 (1985):119–33.

———. "Spartan Intervention in Asia, 400–397 B.C." *Historia* 35 (1986):405–26.

———. *Thessaly in the Fourth Century B.C.* London, 1935.

———. "Xenophon and Epaminondas." *Greek, Roman, and Byzantine Studies* 17 (1975):23–40.

Wickersham, J., and G. Verbrugghe. *Greek Historical Documents: The Fourth Century B.C.* Toronto, 1973.

Wilcken, U. "Uber Enstehung und Zweck des Königsfriedens," pp. 3–20. *Abhandlung der Preussischen Akademie: Phil.-hist. Klasse,* no. 15. Berlin, 1941.

Wiseman, J. "Epaminondas and the Theban Invasions." *Klio* 51 (1969):177–99.

Wolman, B., ed. *The Psychoanalytic Interpretation of History.* New York, 1971.

Zeilhofer, G. *Sparta, Delphoi und die Amphiktyonen im 5. Jahrhundert vor Christus.* Erlangen, 1959.

Zierke, E. *Agesilaos. Beiträge zum Lebensbild und zur Politik des Spartanerkönigs.* Ph.D. diss. Frankfurt am Main, 1936.

Zunkel, G. *Untersuchungen zur griechischen Geschichte der Jahre 395–386.* Weimar, 1911.

Index

Library of Congress Cataloging-in-Publication Data

Hamilton, Charles D. (Charles Daniel), 1940–
  Agesilaus and the failure of Spartan hegemony / Charles D. Hamilton.
    p. cm.
  Includes bibliographical references and index.
  ISBN 0-8014-2540-9 (cloth: alk. paper)
  1. Agesilaus II, King of Sparta. 2. Sparta (Ancient city)—History. 3. Greece—
History—Spartan and Theban Supremacies, 404–362 B.C. 4. Sparta (Ancient city)—
Kings and rulers—Biography. I. Title.
DF232.A33H36 1991
938'.906'092—dc20   90-55738
[B]